Telethons

Telethons

SPECTACLE, DISABILITY, AND THE BUSINESS OF CHARITY

Paul K. Longmore

Edited by Catherine Kudlick

OXFORD

UNIVERSITY PRESS

Oxford University Press is a department of the University of Oxford. It furthers
the University's objective of excellence in research, scholarship, and education
by publishing worldwide. Oxford is a registered trade mark of Oxford University
Press in the UK and in certain other countries

Published in the United States of America by Oxford University Press
198 Madison Avenue, New York, NY 10016, United States of America

Cataloging-in-Publication data is on file at the Library of Congress

ISBN 978-0-19-026207-5

1 3 5 7 9 8 6 4 2
Printed by Sheridan, USA

{ CONTENTS }

{ ABBREVIATIONS }

ACCD	American Coalition of Citizens with Disabilities
ADA	Americans with Disabilities Act
ADAPT	American Disabled for Attendant Programs Today (previously American Disabled for Accessible Public Transit)
AHCA	American Health Care Association
ALS	Amyotrophic Lateral Sclerosis
AP	Associated Press
CSE	Citizens for a Sound Economy
DIA	Disabled in Action
DMD	Duchenne Muscular Dystrophy
DRC	Disability Rights Center
EEOC	Equal Employment Opportunity Commission
IL	Independent Living
MDA	Muscular Dystrophy Association
MS Society	National Multiple Sclerosis Society
NFIP	National Foundation for Infantile Paralysis
PAS	Personal Assistance Services
SMA	Spinal Muscular Atrophy
TCI	Tele-Communications Inc.
UCP	United Cerebral Palsy Associations
VR	Vocational Rehabilitation

{ EDITOR'S NOTE }

How unfortunate that Paul Longmore did not live long enough to savor the Muscular Dystrophy Association's (MDA) May 1, 2015 announcement that it was pulling the plug on its yearly televised Labor Day Telethon. The veritable media institution that filled living rooms for over half a century had already lost its luster even as Longmore grappled with the pages that follow. Yet as readers will discover, the yearly programs and the phenomenon in general offered front-row seats to something much bigger than a kitschy parade of prominent celebrities and handicapped (*sic*) children. Quintessentially American, telethons brought together medical research, promises of a cure, compassion, corporate greed, media sensationalism, changing ideas of embodiment, disability rights, and much more. As a scholar, activist, and astute cultural observer, Longmore was in a unique position to appreciate the ironies and possibilities that came from blending so many fundamental themes together within a distinctive program that both reflected and shaped twentieth-century America. From the cogent analysis and down-to-earth erudition that permeate this book, readers will have a pretty good idea of what Longmore might have said to mark the end of an era. His study makes it clear that the programs continue to influence today's world. Not only will his insights apply to MDA's plan to shift its fundraising efforts online, but they also urge us to understand history's continuities at a time when rapid change is considered a given. Put another way: this provocative, deeply researched book has implications well beyond Telethons.

Completing the book of another has required a touchingly large team effort. Since Paul Longmore died before he could write his own acknowledgments, thanks must be limited to people who helped me in the process. I wish to thank Ellen Longmore Brown, Eugene Chelberg, Anne Cohen, Robert A. Corrigan, Rosemarie Garland-Thomson, Trevor Getz, and Barbara Loomis for contributing in their own generous and supportive way to this publication. Paul Longmore's research assistants Jessica Blake and Stephanie Springer provided fact-checking and manuscript clean-up in the early phase. Lauri Umansky shared the most difficult parts of turning the manuscript into manageable text that rang true to what Paul would have wanted. Douglas Baynton, Anne Finger, Carol Gill, Kim Nielsen, Susan Schweik, and Sandra Sufian read drafts and discussed thorny editorial issues. Brendan O'Neill rose to the occasion by being an editor in the long-lost sense of the job, offering detailed feedback on every page. Invariably, as happens with a posthumous publication, there are errors that might have escaped the team and inadvertently found their way into the manuscript despite, or perhaps because of our best intentions. Rather than assume full responsibility for such flaws, I trust Paul to smile as I blame him for all that is wrong. But this means he gets full credit for all that is right in what readers will soon discover to be a tour de force.

Paul Longmore's awareness of his public relationship to telethons might be traced back fifty years to a story his older sister Ellen told at his memorial service in October 2010: "On one occasion, he and some others of us were at a Bob's Big Boy restaurant and as we were paying the bill, he leaned over the counter and wrapped his arm around the March of Dimes container sitting there and said to the teenage waitress, 'Should I take the money now or should I just wait for them to send it to me?'"

Before Longmore (1946–2010) unexpectedly passed away, he had drafted much of this manuscript, which he considered to be his crowning academic achievement. Over the years, he worked out an argument about how popular culture shaped attitudes toward people with disabilities, a link that might seem obvious now, but one that he played a leading role in introducing through various presentations and publications. For him, the telethons symbolized the convergence of experiences and historical forces that lay at the root of what he saw as most Americans' only encounter with disabled people, which left a lasting impression on them. Employing his skills as a historian and his powers of observation as an activist and social critic, he wanted to question prevailing reactions of pity that feed so seamlessly into stereotyping and stigma. By showing readers how the yearly spectacles were, in fact, the product of larger economic, political, and social forces of which most people remained unaware, he hoped to clear the way for more complex and realistic portrayals of a group that today makes up nearly 20 percent of the US population. He knew he was fighting an uphill battle, since these ideas are so pervasive that challenging cherished and seemingly uncontroversial notions such as "generosity" and "good intentions" provokes defensiveness and sometimes even hostility. But he persevered, believing with a certain grudging optimism that rigorous scholarship could begin to change hearts and minds.

The result: a meditation on big business, American government, popular culture, US Cold War values, and "activism" both narrowly and broadly defined. At the center are people with disabilities who, thanks to a particular kind of historical-cultural marginalizing, turn out to be the ideal tools to promote corporate interests, privatize health care and class divisions that somehow always seem to be ignored. Yet at the same time, maybe for the same reasons, people with disabilities end up being insightful critics who expose inherent problems in the system for everyone.

Longmore had begun studying telethons during the 1980s, but took time to launch his teaching career as a historian at San Francisco State

University and turn his PhD dissertation into a book, *The Invention of George Washington* (1998), and to publish his numerous pieces on academics and advocacy in his collection *Why I Burned My Book and Other Essays on Disability* (2003). He also hosted (with Professor Rosemarie Garland-Thomson) the first National Endowment for the Humanities Summer Institute for University and College Teachers on the theme of disability studies in the humanities in 2000 and coedited with Professor Lauri Umansky the pathbreaking collection *The New Disability History: American Perspectives* (2001). Somewhere in the midst of all this academic work that launched and profoundly shaped an entire field of scholarship, he carried on his formal and informal advocacy on behalf of people with disabilities through numerous speaking engagements and countless hours offering advice to students and colleagues from around the world. Somewhere, too, he found time to watch old movies, go to jazz concerts, read daily newspapers cover to cover, make the rounds of SF State, darting across campus in his motorized chair searching out everyone, be it the university president, his history department colleagues, or his coterie of adoring students to gossip, to debate, to flirt, to influence.

And somewhere, somehow Longmore produced enough of this book that a team of colleagues and friends could complete it for publication. At the time of his death, he left a full draft of the book's original fourteen chapters, some parts more polished than others. Most contained either a basic argument or strands of text that pointed in a certain direction, which we have tried to elaborate. Most chapters also contained a number of random entries either in the text or in footnotes—excerpts of scholarly articles and notes from numerous telethons that he'd hoped to incorporate. We tried to balance his legendary love of examples with the need to provide a streamlined argument that remained true to what we understood to be the intent of the book. In many cases, we placed his observations and fragments into endnotes, which helps explain their unusual detail and length.

We tried where possible to add information regarding specific dates and transitions, although it appeared from his notes that he was still working out the overall periodization. The book concludes provocatively, more than definitively. We don't know how he would have described today's greatly diminished telethons or the impact of the Affordable Care Act or social media sensations such as the ALS "Ice Bucket Challenge" that enlisted celebrities in charitable efforts. Rather than try to fill in the details of his roughly hewn challenges pieced together from fragments, we decided it best to leave them as he did his various communities and those who loved him: too soon, yet with much to ponder and exciting work to do.

Catherine Kudlick

Professor of History and Director

Paul K. Longmore Institute on Disability, San Francisco State University

{ INTRODUCTION }

The telethon is a distinctively American invention. In the second half of the twentieth century, these protracted programs combining entertainment with charity solicitation became a unique television genre and influential cultural institution. It seemed as though every concern and cause mounted a telethon. There were telethons for orphanages and Toys for Tots, for sickle cell anemia and burn injuries and mental health,[1] for victims of an earthquake in Guatemala, hurricanes in Mississippi and Puerto Rico, and floods in the northeastern and midwestern United States.[2] There was Live Aid for Ethiopian famine relief and Farm Aid to help indebted American farmers and Comic Relief to assist homeless people. Telecasts by St. Jude's Hospital, Variety Clubs International, and the Children's Miracle Network sought support for children's hospitals. In the early 1970s, the Democratic Party tried telethons to pay off its campaign debts,[3] and all through the 1980s, 1990s, and beyond, the United Negro College Fund telethon promoted higher education for African American young people.[4] Lots of local telethons sought to raise money for sports teams, schools, and the arts, including a five-hour "Dodgerthon" in 1958 to support a ballot initiative to build a stadium that, it was argued, would persuade the Dodgers baseball team to stay in Los Angeles.[5]

In the ultimate nod to their pervasiveness and cherished place in American popular culture, telethons were lampooned throughout the era. In 1967 comedian Steve Allen satirized them in a classic sketch, "The Prickly Heat Telethon." In 2009 *MADtv* ended its fourteen-year run with a telethon parody. Real telethons were mocked, too. A newspaper writer snickered that a 1966 Ulster County, New York, telethon solicited for the Community Chest by using "professional, amateur and imaginary talent."[6]

Mocked and not always successful telethons demonstrated TV's unique capacity to reach enormous audiences.[7] One of the first, a fourteen-and-a-half hour broadcast in 1952 hosted by entertainers Bob Hope and Bing Crosby and carried simultaneously on both the CBS and NBC networks, raised money to send the US team to the Olympic Games in Helsinki, Finland. That show was seen as a test of the young medium's power against its chief competitor, the motion picture theater.[8] From the beginning of commercial TV, telethons were a communications and cultural phenomenon.

The telethons that epitomized the genre, those that became the pattern for all such programs, captured the greatest attention, and provoked the strongest reactions, were produced by national disability-related charities: the United

Cerebral Palsy Associations (UCP), the Arthritis Foundation, the March of Dimes, the National Easter Seals Society, and the Muscular Dystrophy Association (MDA). These shows generated extensive and surprisingly heated public discussion. Perhaps that was because they were not only mechanisms to raise money for medical treatments and research, but also a means to work through a number of intertwined social, cultural, political, and, at root, moral dilemmas. Most obvious were issues of health and welfare. Equally important were the cultural meaning and social and political function of charity, disease, and disability.

In the late twentieth century, nearly everyone who talked about telethons—whether they were defenders or critics, including most disability rights activists—focused on the MDA Telethon and its host, comedian Jerry Lewis. That was not surprising. In the intensely competitive arena of televised charity solicitation, the MDA's became the most successful and praised of the programs, as well as the most scorned. In 1989 National Public Radio's Scott Simon described it as "the largest, single-day, private fundraising effort in the world, an extravaganza of entertainment, and fundraising sensation."[9] In 1984 an executive with A.C. Nielsen, the television ratings service, asked a reporter to "name two telethons," specifying "one of them can't be Muscular Dystrophy." Speaking for himself, he said, "I can't think of another telethon."[10] From the late 1960s on, MDA's show set the pace among telethons and Jerry Lewis became the very measure of the charity telecast pitchman. Perhaps his persona and the impact of the MDA program were the reasons public discussion of telethons largely became a debate about Lewis's tactics and style, his motives and motivations.[11]

But this is not a book about Jerry Lewis, just as it is not a comprehensive history of disability-related telethons or the charities that produced them. Rather, it uses these cultural phenomena to explore the historical roots of a distinctive social, economic, and political system that emerged in the United States during the second half of the twentieth century. By looking beyond an individual man or even a single industry, we gain greater insight into matters of health and welfare, the peculiar ways that private corporations and public charity worked in tandem and how each changed as a result, how such popular media extravaganzas drew on existing perceptions of disease and disability as well as gender roles and notions of kinship and family, even as they perpetuated new ideas and possibilities. This broader approach to telethons allows us to see them as inherently political, be it the desire of American businesses to repair a tarnished image or the drive of disability rights activists to promote new views of people with disabilities. As much as Americans lauded, laughed at, or condemned these media solicitations, by understanding telethons to be self-contained cultural entities, they failed to appreciate them as a pedagogic public space that shaped popular perceptions as much as they did economic and political opportunities.[12] As the following pages reveal, disability and disabled people occupied a historical stage far greater than the one accorded them on the yearly ritualistic television broadcasts.[13]

People with disabilities have largely been excluded from these wide-ranging discussions of US history because of what has come to be known as the "medical model." This dominant paradigm defines *disability* as the physical and psychological experience of biological defect deriving from one of a series of illnesses or injuries located within the bodies of "afflicted" individuals. Medical practitioners have largely seen cure, or at least correction of functioning, as the only possible way to bring about the social integration of people with disabilities. This a-historical approach not only medicalizes disability, it also makes individual and private what is in fundamental ways a social and political problem with far-reaching public implications. The book builds on an alternative view rooted in a minority consciousness that began to emerge in the United States with the disability rights movement in the late 1960s. Two decades later, it became common for scholars to refer to a "minority" or "social model" of disability. According to this paradigm, the historic and cultural devaluation of physically different persons has produced socioeconomic discrimination against them. It follows that a variety of people with disabilities, despite considerable differences in etiology, have historically confronted a common set of stigmatizing cultural values and social hazards.[14] Analyzing telethons from this wider perspective allows us to understand seemingly familiar aspects of US history in challenging new ways.

Given the issues this book takes up, it seems both appropriate and necessary to explain my own background and qualification regarding this particular study.[15] I come to it as both a professional historian and a person with a disability. As a scholar, I have focused on two areas: early American history, particularly the transformative moment that began the American Revolution, and the modern history of disability. In both fields, I have explored how cultural values, social and political ideologies, and social processes shaped individual and collective identities and how revolutions in ideas and institutions redefined those identities.[16] While I have studied "revolutions" as a historian, I have also actively participated in the present-day disability rights revolution. I see these roles as reciprocal and critically interacting and consider the study of history as an aid to social analysis and reconstruction.[17]

I have lived most of my life with a major physical disability. At the age of 7, I contracted polio. I spent most of my first year with the disease living in an iron lung—a device that allowed me to continue breathing despite the paralysis of my respiratory muscles—and was gradually weaned from it. At the age of 11, I underwent a number of surgeries to straighten my spine, spending another year confined to the hospital and then to my bed at home. The operations saved my life, but an unintended consequence was that in my teenage years my spine began to bow forward to an extreme degree. As a result, it became necessary for me to use a ventilator at night. As the years went by, I relied on my ventilators more and more and now use them most of the time. When I contracted polio, I was at first paralyzed from the neck down. Gradually, I regained the use of my respiratory muscles and my legs but not my arms. For many years, I walked fairly easily and even strenuously. But in middle age as my legs began to weaken, I chose to switch to driving a power wheelchair. During all of the decades since I got polio, I have had the use of my right hand, but not the left, and neither arm. For that reason, I have always needed considerable assistance with the basic tasks of daily living.

Fortunately for me, I came of age at a time when a new generation of people with disabilities demanded the right to live in their own homes, go to school, and go to work. Because of the accomplishments of the independent living movement, a contingent of the larger disability rights movement, I have been able to live my entire adult life in my own household and pursue advanced education and a career as a scholar and university teacher.

During elementary school, I was placed in special education classes for several grades. Then when I entered junior high, I was "mainstreamed." This was before that term came into currency to describe the educational integration of children with disabilities. After that, I pursued the rest of my secondary, college, and graduate education in integrated settings. But that meant also that I had little contact with other students with disabilities, since few enjoyed the same educational opportunities. Along the way, a number of key mentors supported my aspiration to become a university professor, while other teachers discouraged my dream, at times expressing demoralizing prejudice about people with disabilities. Two of my graduate school professors rejected my application for a fellowship, because, they said, "No one will ever hire you." For years, I struggled to get my career going. One historian told me that though I impressed his colleagues, they rejected me for a tenure-track position because "they don't think you could do the job." Meanwhile, I battled government policies that undermined the efforts of people with disabilities to get jobs and work productively. Finally, a Mellon Postdoctoral Fellowship at Stanford University in the early 1990s helped me prove that I could indeed do the work expected of a professor of history. That, in turn, aided me in securing my current position. As I write in 2010, I am about to begin my nineteenth year as a professor of history at San Francisco State University,[18] one of the leading public urban universities in the United States and an institution that includes people with disabilities in its commitment to "equity, social justice, and diversity."

One day while I was teaching at Stanford University, I attended a colloquium to discuss a chapter of a doctoral dissertation on US social welfare policies in the 1960s. As I listened to the discussion, it struck me that none of the faculty or graduate students knew what it was like "to be on welfare." So I asked, "Has anyone here but me ever been on welfare?" No one else had. I told the assembled scholars, "It's not like what you think." I explain all of this to make clear that when I talk about people with disabilities and especially people with major physical disabilities, I do not come at their experience in some abstract academic way. I know it firsthand.

Furthermore, I have long believed that the social, cultural, and political experience of disability can form the basis of a useful, indeed searching, examination of history in general and modern cultures in particular. The social marginalization of disabled people is not just a matter of deprivation and disadvantage. It can also provide us with the critical distance essential to a realistic analysis of our societies. I take it as the task of disabled intellectuals to formulate those sorts of disability-based analyses and to facilitate the clarification of values grounded in the historical experience of people with disabilities, distinctive values that can provide an alternative to culturally dominant values.

To those ends, this book offers a critical inspection of American culture and society from a disabled perspective. By that I mean, in part, that my own experience as a person with a disability, my positioning in the world—a location that is at once existential, sociological, and political—has profoundly influenced and, I believe, aided my understanding of the social phenomena I seek to explain. In addition, my viewpoint on these matters is informed by the minority-group analysis that underpins the US disability rights movement. When I speak of a disabled perspective, I mean that a critical social theory grounded in disability experiences offers a lens through which to scrutinize culture and society. Rather than a pathological condition that constitutes a limiting and distorting state of being, disability can serve as an illuminating mode of critical analysis. Therefore, just as I use the term "disabled" to denote not just a physiological condition but a cultural and political situation, I use the deliberately jarring double negative "nondisabled" to recenter the discussion.

In addition, I move beyond what is called "people first" language. I use "people with disabilities" and "disabled people" interchangeably. The requirement of "people first" phrasings is monotonous, sometimes leads to ludicrous linguistic barbarisms such as "people with blindness," and ultimately fails in its laudable but ineffectual effort to combat stigma. Adopting the usage of many of my historical subjects, leading disability rights activists, I use the adjective "disabled" as a descriptor comparable to "black," "gay," or "Irish"—that is to say, it is simultaneously a designation of social experience, status, and identity and, for some people, a declaration of self and collective affirmation.

At the same time, I do not intend to propagate the opinions of disability rights advocates credulously or dogmatically. Instead, I will critically examine disability rights activists and disability studies scholars' views of telethons and, more important, their understandings of disability.

In that regard, I would begin by pointing out that many of the historical actors with disabilities who are central subjects of this study did not carefully distinguish among the physiological and sociological, the medical and political elements of disability experience. In contrast, telethon presenters and disability rights activists', as well as scholars studying disability from various theoretical perspectives, have often tried to differentiate "illness" or "impairment" from "disability" (and/or "handicap"). Those components may seem separable under analysis, but in historical experience they were bound together in intricate and inextricable ways that varied according to the kaleidoscope of contexts within which people with disabilities lived. As a result, many people with disabilities had complex views of their situations and selves. Some saw themselves as ruined physically and socially. Others considered their disabilities as simply variations along a spectrum of human differences; for them, disability was difference rather than defect. Still others freely declared that they dealt with significant medical needs and major issues of physical functioning but they also—and this point is historically most transformative and significant—viewed disability as difference. They demanded attention to socially constructed restrictions and oppressions—namely, prejudice and discrimination; accessibility and the right to accommodations. Moreover, challenging the dominant ideology that pathologized people with disabilities, growing numbers asserted alternative values grounded in the experience of disability and affirmed positive disability-based identities. This was not some inspirationalist triumph over adversity, but a mature and realistic view of themselves as "people with disabilities." Their definitions of their identities did not fit the framings of charity fundraisers or many disability rights activists, let alone the abstract theories of many scholars. Stereotypes and dogmas of all kinds have too often buried the complicated lived experience of disability under layers of ideological imposition. As a result, people with disabilities have effectively been made to disappear. Enforced invisibility is a major theme of this study.

All of this also indicates that disability is not a homogeneous category. There is no single disability experience or identity; there are multiple experiences and more than one identity. The people with disabilities discussed in this book had varying experiences and perspectives. But this does not mean that these were incommensurable. One task of disability historians is to develop the painstaking comparative historical analysis that will reconstruct both the differences and commonalities across disability categories and constituencies, experiences, and identities.

For all of these historical reasons, this study uses the one word "disability" to encompass all aspects of disabled people's experience. In every instance, the context will make apparent which of those elements, physical or social, medical or political, is most salient at that moment. And for these reasons, I also conclude that a minority-group analysis most accurately and comprehensively explains disability in all of its dimensions.

In the end, I expect that thorough and thoughtful study of these multilayered cultural rituals called telethons can help us to rethink the sociocultural meaning of disability and the social roles and identities available to people with disabilities. At the same time, I believe such an analysis can offer a new perspective on the workings of American culture and society as a whole.

Telethons

Charity Professionals

AMBIVALENT GENEROSITY AND THE NEW
BUSINESS OF PHILANTHROPY

The telethon was invented just after World War II by private health charities as a tool to tap into the emerging mass medium of broadcast television. "Telethon" is a portmanteau word combining "television" and "marathon." The first "television marathon" aired in April 1949 on behalf of the Damon Runyon Cancer Fund. Transmitted by the National Broadcasting Company (NBC) to twelve cities in the eastern United States and hosted by TV's first major star, comedian Milton Berle, it was a broadcast sensation. Berle MCed three more Runyon Fund shows, each longer than the one before and carried by even more NBC affiliates. The fourth, which ran in whole or in part in forty-seven TV markets, was the first "coast to coast" telethon.[1] Then in February 1953, NBC announced it would no longer broadcast telethons because of its affiliates' complaints that "the disruption of schedules, rebates for canceled programs and incidental costs for carrying the charity shows far outweighed the benefits derived."[2] Declaring that the novelty of telethons had worn off, commentators predicted their imminent demise.[3]

But, in fact, they flourished. Their success was due in significant part to five disability-related charities. The National Society for Crippled Children and Adults—it would rename itself the National Easter Seals Society in 1979—had been at work for three decades before the advent of TV, while the National Foundation for Infantile Paralysis (NFIP)'s "March of Dimes" campaign had been in existence since the late 1930s. Three more agencies emerged at the dawn of the television age: the Arthritis Foundation in 1948, the United Cerebral Palsy (UCP) Associations in 1949, and the Muscular Dystrophy Association (MDA) in 1950.[4]

Leaders of these charities played a major role in developing the telethon as both a classic TV format and a major mode of late-twentieth-century American charitable solicitation. In 1950 UCP presented a two-and-a-half

hour benefit show on NBC with the popular comedian Milton Berle as host.[5]
That same year, when the average television broadcast aired no longer than
thirty minutes, UCP produced the first multihour disability-related fundraising show, *Celebrity Parade*, a fifteen-hour broadcast in Chicago.[6] In 1951
UCP Telethons aired in Cincinnati, Philadelphia, San Francisco, and New
York,[7] followed by programs in many other local TV markets. UCP's strategy reflected its decentralized organization. Rather than mounting a national
broadcast, local telethons raised funds for local UCP programs.[8] Many of
these shows brought in national TV stars as hosts. Dennis James, one of early
television's most popular game show hosts and credited with a great many
"firsts" in broadcast TV, including first announcer to do a television commercial, became the UCP Telethons' principal and perennial MC.[9] From the
1950s into the 1980s, the March of Dimes—which after the virtual eradication of polio in the United States in the late 1950s switched its focus to congenital physical disabilities—produced numerous local telethons, as did some
chapters of the Crippled Children's Society.[10] Meanwhile, the first Arthritis
Foundation Telethon aired in New York City in November 1953. Featuring
more than 300 stars from all branches of entertainment and sports, it demonstrated the enormous interest in this still-new broadcast phenomenon.[11] From
the advent of disability-related telethons in 1950 until the end of the 1960s,
most Americans who saw any of these benefit shows probably watched a UCP
or March of Dimes Telethon. And they probably thought of Dennis James
rather than Jerry Lewis as the quintessential telethon MC.

Then late in the 1960s, Lewis and MDA introduced a new format that, during the 1970s, changed the way all disability-related telethons were done. The
first MDA Telethon appears to have been produced by its Washington, DC,
chapter in 1952 as a fourteen-and-a-half hour show that aired at Christmas
time.[12] Meanwhile, in 1953 the comedy team of Dean Martin and Jerry Lewis
made plans for a multihour MDA Telethon on their home network, NBC.
Blocked by NBC's new policy against airing telethons, they turned to ABC.
And so it was that on Thanksgiving eve 1953, Martin and Lewis headlined a
two-hour, late-night MDA benefit show carried by ABC's television and radio
networks.[13] In 1955 comedian George Jessel MCed a seventeen-hour MDA
fundraiser locally in New York City.[14] A year later, Martin and Lewis took
over that show.[15] For almost a decade after that, Lewis, now a solo performer
following his breakup with Martin, MCed a sporadic series of MDA benefit
shows in New York City, some running seventeen hours, others as short as
one or two. Some of the shorter programs were videotaped for distribution to
stations around the country, while some MDA chapters outside of New York
produced their own local and statewide telethons.[16]

Perhaps Lewis and MDA's greatest contribution to the telethon phenomenon was how they transformed it for the national arena while allowing it to
maintain a distinct local character. In 1966 and 1967, MDA abandoned the

Thanksgiving tradition, and presented the first Jerry Lewis Labor Day tele-thons, nineteen-hour telecasts to New York City and the surrounding region. Two years later, they expanded the programming to twenty cities, all in the eastern United States. Then in 1970, MDA mounted a truly national telethon, linking sixty-five cities. By the end of the decade, the program reached a peak of 213 stations. As important as the number of stations affiliating with this two-day temporary network was the telethon's new format. In each hour it alternated between a lengthy national segment and a shorter local one. That structure drew on a national telecast's power to attract not only big-name entertainers and sports celebrities but also major corporate sponsors. At the same time, it retained a local show's ability to connect with individuals, small businesses, and service organizations in local communities.[17]

During the 1970s and early 1980s, the other disability-related charities switched from separate local telethons to the new national format. In the following decades, four major disability-related telethons aired nationally at various times during the year. The charities claimed to reach an enormous audience. UCP did not give out estimates of the number of viewers, but in 1993 one of its hosts declared that at various times some 22 million house-holds tuned in. In the mid-1990s, the Arthritis Foundation Telethon reckoned that it reached 35 to 40 million viewers. During its peak years in the late 1960s and 1970s, the Easter Seals Telethon was broadcast to an audience it estimated at 60 million. And the MDA Telethon, at its zenith, counted its audience as 100 million viewers. According to the charities' own estimates, their collec-tive audience numbered around a quarter of a billion people in the United States and Canada.[18]

But by the early 1990s, the telethons were, in fact, in decline. As early as 1987, Fox Broadcasting decided to stop carrying the MDA show on its owned-and-operated stations, which included the two biggest markets, New York and Los Angeles. Local stations started to shed the UCP program, too. On the 1995 telecast, Dennis James announced that UCP had lost Buffalo, Providence, and eighteen other markets in just the last year. By 1996 the UCP Telethon was down to seventy-seven stations.[19]

The decline of telethons resulted, in part, from changes in the television business during the 1980s and 1990s. In the early years of broadcast TV, the telethons had no competitors for the overnight hours because most stations went off the air in the early morning hours.[20] Local TV outlets not only could afford to donate the time, that contribution counted toward the Federal Communications Commission (FCC) mandate that they provide community service programming. Deregulation by the Reagan-era FCC virtually elimi-nated that requirement. Stations also began to charge the charities. This usually entailed the cost of transmitting the shows plus a fee for preempting regular pro-gramming. Although the charities paid at reduced rates, the price could exceed a quarter of a million dollars an hour. In addition, a growing number of local stations were unwilling to hand over large blocks of time to telethons when they could profit from those slots with programming that drew bigger audiences. Meanwhile, the proliferation of telethons for various causes, as well as the expanding viewing options on both broadcast and cable TV, reduced the disability-related shows' drawing power. Ratings reports indicated that viewers were turning away. In 1987 UCP Fundraising Director Norman H. Kimball admitted, "We used to peak at an 8 or a 10 share; now we're at 4 or 5."[21] On the other hand, if some cable channels were stealing viewers from the telethons, others helped extend the fundraising telecasts' lives. Also, in the mid- and late 1990s, Easter Seals tried to transform its program into something less like a traditional telethon. Nevertheless, as the twentieth century ended, the Easter Seals and UCP Telethons, along with the Arthritis Foundation show, disappeared as national telecasts. Only the MDA program remained, but its audience dropped by more than a third.[22]

Philanthropy and Mixed Emotions

Throughout the second half of the twentieth century, these telethons and the charities that produced them exemplified American patterns of voluntary giving and civic volunteerism. Yet mixed public attitudes reflected characteristically American ambivalence about giving and receiving assistance. Meanwhile, new ideas concerning people with disabilities clashed with older ones to raise questions about what it meant to give and to receive charity. These complex forces made telethons anything but clear-cut occasions for participating in a time-honored American tradition.

To telethon supporters, charity toward those who were ill or disabled was self-evidently necessary and praiseworthy. Fellow Americans, fellow human beings, were suffering. They needed help. Volunteers and donors responded, not just out of duty, but from a heartfelt impulse to care for the "afflicted" and "less fortunate." The givers were hailed as exemplifying some of the finest traits of the American character: neighborliness, generosity, altruism. They were lauded for their public spiritedness, volunteerism, and community service. In the supporters' view and in historical fact, involvement with telethons, whether through volunteering or donating, was one major expression of culturewide patterns of charitable activity and civic engagement.

Americans took enormous pride in what they considered their national predisposition toward benevolence of all kinds. They celebrated their commitment to voluntary charitable donation and community service as a collective virtue. Commemorating the 100th anniversary of the United Way in 1986, President Ronald Reagan exulted: "Since earliest times, we Americans have joined together to help each other and to strengthen our communities. Our deep-rooted spirit of caring, of neighbor helping neighbor, has become an American trademark—and an American way of life. Over the years, our generous and inventive people have created an ingenious network of voluntary organizations to give help where help is needed." One did not have to be a Republican to agree with Mr. Reagan. In 1997 his Democratic successor Bill Clinton hosted a national summit on volunteerism attended by activists from across the political spectrum. "Citizen service," proclaimed President Clinton, "belongs to no party, no ideology. It is an American idea, which every American should embrace."[23]

The jubilation over American benevolence was perennial. In 1966 Arnaud C. Marts, former president of Bucknell University, published *The Generosity of Americans: Its Source, Its Achievements*, a tome celebrating American philanthropic volunteerism. He proclaimed that this sort of collective open-handedness had been developed in the United States and nowhere else in the history of the world.[24] If Dr. Marts failed to appreciate that other societies had devised other means of providing for social needs, he was certainly correct that Americans had fashioned their own distinctive mode. Five years prior to this paean to American liberality, Richard Carter's 1961 *The Gentle Legions*, more temperately than Dr. Marts and perhaps more effectively than any other advocate, made the arguments for voluntarism (everything that is voluntary) and volunteerism (the spirit of contributing). Carter specifically focused on the national health charities. What critics condemned as needlessly competitive, chaotic, and costly, he extolled as free and voluntary and democratic. He—and indeed every proponent of this system—applauded voluntary charitable donation and service as "the American way."[25]

Carter did more than simply glory in that American way: He championed it as a living tradition. So did the national health agencies he supported, as did virtually every American cause that depended on freely given monetary contributions and volunteer labor. Reflecting that imperative, UCP Telethon host Dennis James honored active and practical American benevolence by reciting, year after year, an "Ode to Volunteers":

> Many will be shocked to find
> When the Day of Judgment nears—
> That there's a special place in Heaven
> Set aside for volunteers,
> Furnished with big recliners,
> Satin couches and footstools—
> Where there's no committee chair,
> No group leaders for carpools.
> Telephone lists will be outlawed,
> But a finger snap will bring
> Cool drinks and gourmet dinners,
> And rare treats fit for a king.

You ask, who will serve the privileged few
And work for all they're worth?
Why, those who reaped the benefits
And not once volunteered on earth.[26]

If the poem's warning of future rewards and punishments was perhaps tongue-in-cheek, its moral warning was serious. Maintaining the American tradition of voluntary charitable contribution and volunteer service required occasional admonition.

In 1967 the nationally syndicated columnist Erma Bombeck delivered one such chiding in a piece entitled "Without Volunteers, A Lost Civilization." She told readers of her dream—really, it was a nightmare—"that every volunteer in this country, disillusioned with the lack of compassion, had set sail for another country." As a result, health agencies, social agencies, and cultural institutions had all closed down. "The blind listened for a voice that never came. The infirm were imprisoned by wheels on a chair that never moved. ... All the social agencies had closed their doors, unable to implement their programs of scouting, recreation, drug control. ... The health agencies had a sign in the window, 'Cures for cancer, muscular dystrophy, birth defects, multiple sclerosis, emphysema, sickle cell anemia, kidney disorders, heart diseases, etc., have been cancelled due to lack of interest.'"[27]

The sermonizing, like the celebration, indicated that charity donations and philanthropic good works not only served an important function in American society, they were central to many Americans' understanding of their nation's culture, character, and self-image. Yet even while those Americans gloried in their collective dedication to charity and service and enjoined one another to fulfill that mission, many also responded to these putative national commitments with uneasiness, complaint, and even resistance.[28]

In 1960 Robert H. Bremner, the first scholar to examine comprehensively the history of American charitable giving, began his study by noting the self-glorification and implicitly questioning it. "Ever since the seventeenth century, when Cotton Mather announced that Boston's helpfulness and readiness to every good work were well and favorably known in Heaven, Americans have regarded themselves as an unusually philanthropic people. In the twentieth century, celebration of American philanthropy has reached such heights that one can scarcely read a newspaper or magazine without being reminded, in editorials or advertisements, that the United States is the country with a heart, that giving is the great American game, and that philanthropy ranks as one of the leading industries of the age. Americans seem never to tire of saying, or of hearing, that they are generous to a fault—the most compassionate, open-handed people the world has ever known."[29]

Bremner's critical tone was startling. He more than implied that Americans' panegyrics to their own generosity were excessive. Also surprising, he linked this boasting to an underlying ambivalence about both the giving and receiving of charity. "The word philanthropy and the ideas it carries with it arouse mixed emotions in American breasts," he said. Americans sometimes deemed "the philanthropic streak in the national character . . . more a genial failing than an asset or virtue." Many also fretted "lest their countrymen's generosity be abused." More sternly, they often questioned benefactors' motives, criticized "foolish or hypocritical philanthropists," and condemned "unwise giving." "But on a deeper level," said Bremner, "there is something about philanthropy that seems to go against the democratic grain. We may be willing to help others, but we are not humble enough to appreciate the efforts of those who would bend down to help us. 'Don't try to uplift me,' we say. 'I can lift myself.'"[30]

Bremner spoke of American philanthropy in general. Richard Carter's *The Gentle Legions*, mentioned earlier, specifically addressed criticisms of voluntary health agencies and their fundraising campaigns. He noted that articles in leading magazines and newspapers, along with editorials in scores of periodicals, "subjected the national health philanthropies to astonishingly rigorous and occasionally bitter analysis." Critics complained that as the proliferating number of charities competed aggressively, they pestered potential donors without letup. Some agencies, it was argued, pressed their causes far out of proportion to the social impact of the diseases they sought to eradicate. Many allegedly made themselves self-perpetuating while spending far too much of contributors' money on administration rather than medical research or client services. Some campaigns were accused of shamelessly manipulating prospective donors' emotions in order to extract their money. But the most far-reaching criticism argued that the public as a whole, rather than just the fraction who voluntarily donated, should pay for public health needs through tax-funded programs.[31]

Like Bremner, Carter had partly attributed criticism of the national voluntary health agencies to Americans' aversion to charity. "Perhaps the discomfort arises," he speculated, "because many of us have been educated to understand charity as a tradition whereby the indulgent mighty confer alms on the undignified and somehow suspect lowly. During the Depression, newspapers kept this painful attitude alive by publishing maudlin articles in praise of families that were found in desperate straits but were 'too proud' to accept the indignity of charitable help. Small wonder that, in giving alms or any gift that seems related to alms, sensitive Americans regret that there is not some 'better' way of meeting social need."[32] To counter this attitude, Carter contended that modern fundraising had changed. "The point is, no matter how many disabled children parade across my television screen during the voluntary health agencies' marathon appeal for charitable support, and no matter how heavy grows the lump in my throat as I sign the check, my gift is far different from the old-fashioned kind that red-blooded Americans

were 'too proud' to accept." Noting that "my gift nourishes science, not handicapped children," Carter explained that "for the first time in all the centuries
that have elapsed since the days of early Christianity, we find the interests of
giver and recipient inextricably merged."[33]

A generation after Carter, Bremner, and Bombeck, sociologist Robert
Wuthnow documented the persistence of these cultural patterns. His 1991
study *Acts of Compassion: Caring for Others and Helping Ourselves* reported
that community service still operated extensively, much of it "within the
context of a voluntary association," and voluntary organizations still exerted
enormous influence over what Americans considered compassionate behavior. Yet Erma Bombeck's accusation that too few Americans were willing to
serve also continued. Public opinion surveys from the late 1970s into the early
1990s repeatedly recorded that many people thought their fellow Americans
had become more self-centered, and they saw this selfishness as "a large problem." They themselves were caring and "concerned about helping the needy,"
they said, but most other people were not. Registering the findings of his own
national survey, Wuthnow announced that volunteers who acted to help the
needy were seen as exceptional, unusual, "deviant in a positive sense," but
deviating from the social norm nonetheless. Moreover, his data also suggested the endurance of negative attitudes toward recipients of charity. In
his survey, 4 out of 5 respondents agreed with the statement "I can do anything I want to, if I just try hard enough," while a majority (54 percent) shared
the belief that "people generally bring suffering on themselves." Wuthnow
interpreted these views as reflecting two widely shared American cultural
assumptions: Success lay within the grasp of individuals who applied themselves diligently; failure—and one might add, many forms of suffering—came
about through individual fault. American culture and the US economy, he
said, authorized the competitive pursuit of self-interest, success, and material comfort. These values, widespread and well-institutionalized, operated in
tension and even conflict with the imperative to practice benevolence.[34]

Wuthnow's study, Carter's apologia, and Bombeck's scolding provide a
framework for situating people with disabilities and telethons as ambivalent
examples of late-twentieth-century American charity. All three indicated
that disabled people were perennially seen as objects of charity rather than
bestowers of benevolence. Some of the national disability-related charities
that Carter had defended in 1961 were already producing telethons and other
broadcast solicitations that would become contested during the decades that
followed. However, it seemed that for many Americans the vaunted marking
off of traditional charity from modern donation was a distinction without a
difference. For them, the old dichotomy held sway. Something about charity
in any form went "against the democratic grain." Faultfinders often disap-
proved of what they considered the tastelessness of televised charity fundraising. Some mocked the telethons' crass showmanship, panning them as

a combination variety show and infomercial, patriotic pageant and revival tent meeting, sideshow and pep rally. Others snickered at their sentimental excesses. One TV critic called them "institutionalized kitsch."[35]

Though defenders of telethons usually derided the detractors with phrases such as "snooty arbiters of good taste," they sometimes agreed that the programs were indeed vulgar. But, they claimed, the crassness was necessary because it worked. *The Encyclopedia of Bad Taste* sums it up: "How agonizing it is to see people parade their afflictions in order to solicit money, but the mendicancy works. . . . Who can see the afflicted . . . and not feel the urge to help?"[36]

Likewise, some of the critics ended up agreeing with the defenders that the desirable results justified the disagreeable means. For years, syndicated columnist Bob Greene had been critical of the way Jerry Lewis conducted his telethon but at last came to understand "that he is, indeed, doing a good thing, and doing it in the only way that will work." Greene declared in 1981, "Regardless of what you think of Lewis' tactics and style, the one undisputed fact is that, for a few days at the end of each summer, he manages to make millions of people think about others less fortunate than themselves. You may be appalled at how he does it. . . . But you can't stop thinking about what he wants you to think about. . . ."[37]

Greene's defense of Lewis and the MDA telethon seemed to be responding to a *New York Times* opinion piece printed a few days earlier by Evan Kemp Jr., a man with a neuromuscular condition who was a Republican and a disability rights attorney. Kemp, whose parents had helped found the MDA, charged that the telethon's "pity approach to fund-raising" bolstered social prejudice against people with disabilities. He accused it of dealing in stereotypes that only served to hinder their independence and alienate them from the rest of society. In addition, claimed Kemp, the telethon reinforced "the public's tendency to equate handicap with total 'hopelessness,'" thereby intensifying "the awkward embarrassment" of interpersonal interactions, as well as strengthening public fears and buttressing social barriers. Kemp called on the telethon to instead depict the countless examples of independent disabled people who worked, raised families, and actively participated in community life. This new message, he concluded, would "be a service to the disabled and to the country."[38]

Evan Kemp's and Bob Greene's opinion columns reflected a shift in the debate about, not just telethons, but illness, disability, and charity. Greene restated common long-reigning beliefs, while Kemp expressed a new perspective, a political critique growing out of the disability rights movement. Greene thought in terms of sick people, "less fortunate," needing care. Kemp spoke for a new generation of people with disabilities who, devalued and discriminated against, demanded justice and opportunity. Pragmatic about tactics, Greene called for compassion and charity. Politically activist, Kemp demanded social respect and civil rights. Each man represented a distinct American tradition of voluntary community action; each stood in a different sector of civil society. Greene advocated charity to fight disease and care for those who were sick or disabled. Kemp agitated for social and political reforms to correct injustice. Contrary to Greene, Kemp claimed that the traditional telethon mold and message was not "the only way" for US society to address the situation of Americans with disabilities.

The Business of Charity

In the first half of the twentieth century, charity became a business, and the business of charity reflected America's business culture. Its modes of operation copied corporate values and imperatives. Professionalized charity involved continuous planning for periodic fundraising that typically focused on a major annual thrust. It devised "scientific" methods, harnessed modern mass media, and adopted the techniques of high-pressure publicity. Its institutional organization and the substance of its appeals reflected a historic shift away from religious sponsorship and motivation for charity to a secular base and basis, though it retained quasi-religious rhetoric and symbolism. It also democratized giving. No longer relying mainly on a social elite's sense of noblesse oblige, it mobilized mass publics and sought to instill in them the habit of giving. In reaching the public through the mass media, charity fundraising reflected and reinforced the interpersonal disconnectedness of modern life as it widened the social distance between givers and receivers. But by motivating large numbers of donors to make myriad small contributions, it proved successful, generating enormous, indeed unprecedented, amounts of money.[39]

To touch potential donors, professional fundraisers forged innovative techniques. Some were as small as a postage stamp, others as extravagant as a parade. In 1903 a Danish postal official came up with the idea of a postal sticker to raise money for tuberculosis research and treatment. Campaigners in many countries soon began to sell such stickers; the National Tuberculosis Association in the United States turned them into a lucrative tool. Beginning in 1907, they sold Christmas Seals through an intensive publicity effort that also disseminated its message. In 1934 the National Society for Crippled Children borrowed the technique to issue its first so-called Easter Seal. If postal stickers were small, mass publicity made them pervasive. At the opposite end of the scale, early-twentieth-century fundraisers staged spectacles such as parades that foreshadowed other forms of showmanship which came later: the Warm Springs Foundation's "President's Birthday Balls" to raise money for polio in the 1930s, Las Vegas–style entertainment on telethons in the 1970s, 5 and 10K runs in the 1990s. Drawing on solicitations strategies from the 1910s that offered campaign clocks, telethon tote boards used a different mechanism to convey the same message: Time is running out for us to reach our goal. Despite having generated considerable complaints over the years, such high-pressure tactics became the hallmark of professional American charity fundraising.[40]

More than any other organizations, the Warm Springs Foundation and the subsequent allied NFIP forged in the 1930s the methods that became the standard fundraising tools of disability-related charities. The Foundation organized President's Birthday Balls to pay tribute to Franklin Delano Roosevelt, "a man who overcame a great affliction to rise to the highest position." Tens of thousands of people across the United States attended some 6000 of these "Paralysis Dances" in 1934 alone. In May of that same year, a ceremony at the White House introduced two gimmicks that became commonplace. Publicist Carl Byoir, who spearheaded the Birthday Balls, handed President Roosevelt an oversized parchment check, a yard long and 18 inches wide, in the amount of $1,003,030.08. Sporting his trademark grin, FDR bet Byoir "a good tie that you can't top this figure next year." Twelve months later, Byoir, of course, won the wager. Oversized checks and, more important, topping last year's total would be standard devices on telethons. With the 1935 and 1936 Birthday Balls, Byoir ushered in corporate sponsorship. First, he convinced both Western Union and Postal Telegraph to allow individuals to send the president birthday greetings, with the 25-cent fee going to the Warm Springs Foundation. The following year, the organizers solicited companies to buy space in the fundraising *Bulletin* and the annual *Birthday Magazine*. In that way, the campaign sold the idea of institutional advertising at a charity event as a form of corporate public relations. By 1937 the polio crusade also hosted many ancillary fundraising events, everything "from checker tournaments to box suppers to the now standard gala pageant in the Waldorf-Astoria where as always Mrs. Sara Delano Roosevelt was the honored guest." In later years, the March of Dimes collected coins in canisters, sent volunteers door-to-door, staged fashion shows, and held bowling tournaments. All of these techniques became stock elements of disability-related and other charity fundraising.[41]

Applying high-pressure public-relations techniques as never before, the polio campaign made innovative use of the mass media. Planners of both the Birthday Balls and the March of Dimes filled the nation's newspapers with stories and photos. They enlisted radio celebrities to publicize the efforts. And they targeted moviegoers by persuading studios such as Warner Brothers and Walt Disney to produce special charity appeals for theater owners to screen. When the health and disability charities launched their telethons in the postwar era, the polio crusade's creative exploitation of modern mass communications was carried into a new medium.[42]

In mobilizing the popular media, the inventors of modern solicitation devised a central role for show business celebrities. Early-twentieth-century strategists had presented wealthy and prestigious contributors as ethical exemplars for smaller donors. But as motion pictures, radio, and, later, television reached deeper into ordinary Americans' lives, popular entertainers became more familiar and emulated than many of the traditional elites. In 1934 the Birthday Balls organizers recruited gossip reporter Walter Winchell and other radio personalities to publicize the dances, while two years later, planners of the Washington Birthday Ball brought movie stars from Hollywood to the nation's capital to lend their glamour to that event. Comedian Eddie Cantor and top radio performers made pitches for what Cantor dubbed the "March of Dimes" in 1938. From the beginning, telethons deployed radio, motion picture, and television luminaries and marketed celebrity entertainers as moral exhorters and role models.[43]

The stars also helped the charities tap into the American status system and power structure. In the last decades of the twentieth century, as a later chapter will show, the charity professionals who designed the telethons introduced yet another high-status character: the corporate executive as community moral leader. By hobnobbing with the stars, business chiefs gained a measure of moral credibility and public respect. Use of these exalted solicitors and donors pointed to the interlocking character of America's cultural, business, social, and political elites. Presentation of them as moral leaders did more than draw dollars. It reinforced the legitimacy of the existing system of status and power, all under a cloak of moral respectability.

Disability in Public

Among the most notable changes to which they contributed, charity professionals helped make disease and disability topics of public discussion and people with disabilities a public presence. The extent and significance of that shift become apparent when we remember that in the period from just after the Civil War to World War I, many jurisdictions across the United States adopted or seriously considered statutes that barred people with visible disabilities from public places. The Columbus, Ohio, ordinance of 1894 was virtually identical to most other such laws: "Whoever being in any way diseased, maimed, mutilated or deformed, so as to be an unsightly or disgusting object, shall expose himself or herself to public view upon any street, sidewalk, or in any public place for the purpose of soliciting alms or exciting sympathy, interest or curiosity shall upon conviction thereof be fined not exceeding twenty dollars, or be imprisoned not more than ten days, or both." Many statutes permitted magistrates to waive the fine and jail time if they committed the violator to an almshouse or hospital.

These laws aimed at much more than regulating disabled beggars or looking after destitute people with disabilities. And, contrary to later disability rights activists who thought the ordinances stigmatized disabled people as "ugly," the statutes, which did not use that word, were not merely registering aesthetic distaste. Instead, they undertook to cleanse public space of people deemed, in the words of Chicago's aldermen, "unsightly and unseemly." Unseemliness entailed an accusation of indecency. Disgust expressed both moral revulsion and social contempt. The attribution of unsightliness declared that some things, some people, must be kept hidden. This regulatory campaign, backed by progressives and conservatives alike, reflected imperatives that also spurred the eugenics and euthanasia crusade to keep the "unfit" from reproducing their kind or even existing. Not only disabled beggars but also anyone with a visible disability threatened the community with disorder.[44]

Throughout this earlier era, some disabled individuals fought back against these segregationist ordinances. One of them was Arthur Franklin Fuller, who made his living traveling the country peddling his self-published books. Several were memoirs of his life with a major physical disability. In 1907, running afoul of Brooklyn's unsightly beggar ordinance, he was warned to leave the city.[45] A generation later in the mid-1930s, the members of New York City's militant League of the Physically Handicapped defied the bias that had incited those laws. Protesting job discrimination by government agencies and private industry, they marched in sidewalk picket lines and engaged in acts of civil disobedience. Their public demonstrations required them to battle not only persisting prejudice but also their own internalization of it as shame.[46] During those same years, the life and political career of Franklin D. Roosevelt also challenged the bigotry that people with visible disabilities had no rightful place in the public sphere. FDR rarely spoke of his condition publicly and kept his wheelchair hidden, but—contrary to subsequent activists' mythologizing and historians' erroneous explanations—he occasionally talked openly about his disability, and on many occasions, he walked in public while visibly wearing leg braces and overtly using crutches or a cane.[47] The polio crusade of the early and mid-1930s also called attention to his experience. Building on FDR as a role model, in the 1940s and 1950s, the March of Dimes spotlighted other individuals striving to "overcome" postpolio disabilities. To be sure, they were pictured as subjects of sympathy and charity, but given the earlier campaign to ban disabled people from appearing in public for just such purposes, this imagery signaled an important shift. Although the March of Dimes sidestepped the problem of discrimination, it did help make the experience of disability a topic of public discussion. And it designed a way for people with physical disabilities to participate in the public realm, not just as objects of charity but as people who through rehabilitation—not cure—could become contributing members of the community and economy.[48]

Meanwhile, American Cancer Society staffers tried to overturn the cultural taboo against publicly mentioning the disease, a move that would help bring discussions of previously "unseemly" topics into the open. Newspaper obituaries had always avoided listing cancer as a cause of death, while patients and their families kept their condition secret for fear of social stigma. Then in 1945, Cancer Society publicists persuaded radio executives to drop policies prohibiting on-air talk about cancer. Well-known personalities such as Bob Hope, along with "Fibber McGee and Mollie," now began to address their audiences about the disease.[49]

Also in the mid- and late 1940s, parents of children with cerebral palsy set up local advocacy groups and ultimately a national association. Two founders of Cerebral Palsy of New York were entertainment executive Leonard Goldenson and his wife Isabelle, whose daughter Cookie had cerebral palsy. Along with New York City philanthropists Jack and Ethel Hausman, also parents of a child with cerebral palsy, they not only raised funds for families without their own abundant financial resources, but also sought to educate those families and the public about the widely misunderstood condition. In this era, doctors often told parents that they should institutionalize their afflicted children, forget about them, and try to have "normal" children. The UCP campaign did more than promote medical and rehabilitative treatments. It aimed to dispel superstitious folklore about "spastics" and end abusive institutionalization.[50]

Whether the charities focused on cancer, cerebral palsy, or polio, they worked against ancient false beliefs about disease and disability. By speaking of these common human experiences in public in the postwar era, they implicitly fought the shame enforced by cultural silence. Conditions long stigmatized, experiences long made shameful, were less and less hidden. People shunned to the shadows increasingly came out into the open.

Yet, as we shall see, these fundraising messages created new limits of their own to public discourse about disease and disability. Year after year at the opening of the MDA Telethon, Jerry Lewis implicitly spoke for all health-charity fundraisers when he announced some variation on the phrase: "We will inform you. We will give you the facts." Rather than provide basic information, telethons tended to focus on ideas about disease and disability in ways designed to both increase the social visibility of particular medical conditions and promote specific charity crusades. Telethon MCs and celebrity guests, of course, were not the main authors of the messages they conveyed. A good deal of the time hosts and stars read from cue cards or teleprompters. To be sure, some of them—especially Lewis and UCP's Dennis James—ad libbed. But even when MCs and celebrities departed from the script, they for the most part stayed on message. In addition, telethons presented individual clients and their families in scripted filmed profiles and live interviews that were hardly impromptu. The producers carefully thought out what hosts would ask, just as in editing the vignettes they methodically selected from what the interviewees said about their lives and needs. In the end, most of the telecasts' content—MCs' and guest stars' appeals, the filmed segments and on-stage interviews, and the presentations of donations, too—were stage-managed by the professionals who ran the disability-related charities.[51]

Elaborating on his observation about the social negotiations that made some medical conditions more visible than others, historian Charles Rosenberg wrote, "We see and fear what we have been prepared to see." Charity professionals sought to prepare the public to see particular diseases and disabilities as major health problems that urgently demanded attention. They instructed prospective donors, not only *what* to fear, but *how* to fear. They became skilled at molding and wielding tools that elicited donations. They learned what methods worked, what images stirred, what appeals moved, what hopes and fears, concerns and anxieties, motivated their fellow Americans. In the latter half of the twentieth century, they developed the telethon as one of the most visible instruments of their efforts.[52]

Neither Public nor Private

TELETHONS IN THE US HEALTH
AND WELFARE SYSTEM

As with all modern charity fundraising, the professionals who produced the telethons depicted their agencies as operating within an independent non-profit sector. But, in fact, the charities were part of the hybrid, public–private US system of providing and paying for health care, social services, and medical research. Here more than anywhere, the charity tradition and medical-model thinking of disability solely as an individual pathology needing a cure framed the needs of people with disabilities, even as they limited disabled people's access to health insurance and health care. In response, the disability rights movement's sociopolitical analysis critiqued the system's pervasive discrimination against disabled people.

Fundraising Chaos

Modeled on modern business methods, professional charity fundraising emphasized organization and efficiency, while at the same time it exemplified and upheld the disorderliness and disparities of market competition. For decades reformers called for financial accountability, while the health charities resisted. The agencies fought government regulation and even balked at voluntary private oversight. As a result, charities had no standardized system of financial reporting. With objective information hard to come by, prospective donors had difficulty comparing various charities' operational efficiency.[1] Critics condemned the high proportion of donations spent on the fundraising itself. The 1938 March of Dimes campaign provoked controversy that became common regarding charity solicitation. The drive yielded an impressive $1.8 million. But critics complained that 42 percent of donations went to promotional expenses. Two decades later, a reform advocate charged that between 1938 and 1958 NFIP spent twice as much on fundraising as on medical research.[2]

From their beginning, telethons attracted the same criticism. In 1954 the Los Angeles City Social Service Commission reported that various local telethons had passed on to their "nominal beneficiaries . . . as little as 23 percent of the funds contributed." The commission could not ban telethons, but it did announce that it would no longer sanction them. The Multiple Sclerosis Society of Southern California and the United Cerebral Palsy Association of Los Angeles County protested. According to the *New York Times*, the head of the former charity "called the city's step a 'police state' action," while the president of the latter condemned it as "an abridgment of free expression and action." They called on the mayor and City Council to overrule the commission.[3] Meanwhile, other observers questioned the effectiveness of telethons in drawing donations. Reviewing a broadcast for New York City's Lighthouse for the Blind in 1953, *New York Times* television critic Jack Gould complained: "If past experience with these marathon benefits is a gauge, perhaps $50,000 will be received in actual cash. Somehow that seems a pitifully small return on sixteen and a half hours of effort. . . . [T]he telethon has become a dubious device for raising funds. There never have been clear-cut figures of the final receipts of telethons, though in some cases the difference between the pledges and real totals is understood to be little short of shocking."[4]

In the late twentieth century, the consumer movement's growing clout led to closer questioning and greater scrutiny of charity fundraising. Cynicism about real corruption in some agencies provoked false accusations that Jerry Lewis and other celebrities got paid to do the MDA Telethon.[5] More important were complaints that charities spent too much on fundraising and administration as compared to program services. By the 1980s, advisory bodies, such as the National Charities Information Bureau (NCIB) and the Council of Better Business Bureaus' Philanthropic Advisory Service (CBBBPAS), offered prospective donors some guidance. But not everyone accepted the pronouncements of even those watchdogs. In 1989 a *Newsweek* columnist noted that the NCIB recommended that at least 60 percent of total expenses go to the cause itself, while the CBBBPAS suggested 50 percent of total income. "Both figures seem low to me," he said skeptically. More than that, these monitors' differing standards reflected the continuing lack of uniform measures of accountability. As a result, in 1984 the CBBBPAS listed MDA as meeting its standards, while NCIB announced that the charity fell short of its criteria. NCIB said MDA not only spent too high a percentage of contributions on fundraising but also masked some of that expenditure under "public health education." MDA answered that it and NCIB disagreed about material MDA considered "educational but also designed to bring in donations." Those clashing opinions once more pointed to the absence of consistent and uniform accountability.[6]

In response to mounting consumer watchfulness, some telethons began to report on monitors' evaluations of their agencies. In 1991 a local Easter Seals host announced that for the eleventh consecutive year the National Health Council had named the Society the nationwide leader among voluntary, nonprofit health-care organizations in the proportion of spending devoted directly to client services. On the 1993 MDA Telethon, cohost Casey Kasem trumpeted that the *Chronicle of Philanthropy* had awarded a similar title to MDA, ranking it first among large health agencies in percentage of income allocated to program services. Meanwhile, he reported, *Money Magazine* had listed MDA as one of the top ten "best-managed" charities. "Eighty-three cents of each dollar you pledged last year went directly to help MDA clients," he assured viewers. The accounting got a little confusing when at another point Kasem explained that 17 percent of MDA's spending went to fundraising and 6.9 percent to administration. That left just over 76 cents out of every dollar for program services and medical research, not 83 cents. Still, even that lower figure was better than the proportions the charity watchdogs recommended. In the end though, both MDA's and Easter Seals' declarations about outside evaluations again called attention to the lack of clear and consistent standards for charity spending and reporting.[7]

If would-be givers had a hard time getting reliable information about how charities spent the money, the proliferation of agencies, especially disease- and disability-related ones, added to their bewilderment about where to donate. In 1958 *Harper's Magazine* declared, "No one knows just how many different groups are soliciting funds across the country for how many different diseases." A single locality illustrated the national problem. "In a spot check of Chatham County, Georgia, the Savannah *Morning Herald* tallied up nineteen organizations passing the hat for the blind; seven for disabled veterans; six for the crippled; four for mental illness; five for cancer; two each for muscular dystrophy, polio, leprosy, brain injury, and alcoholism; and one apiece of heart disease, retarded children, cerebral palsy, deafness, tuberculosis, multiple sclerosis, arthritis, myasthenia gravis, nephrosis, facial disfigurement, tropical diseases, diabetes, epilepsy, allergic diseases, hemophilia, and paraplegia."[8] During the postwar era, agencies such as these multiplied across America.[9] In 1951 *Advertising Age* complained: "It does not seem to be too much to ask all the people who are worried about the ravages of one particular disease or condition to the exclusion of all others, to get together and worry a little about the sum total of human health, and the sum total of the public's ability to stand the strain of an increasingly expanding number of drives. There are just too many diseases for each to have its own special organization, complete with radio hitchhikes, sponsored ads, expensive brochures, pledge cards, team captains and collection envelopes."[10] A Stamford, Connecticut, businessman sighed, "We are punch drunk trying to keep up with all these appeals."

As late as the 1980s some commentators warned that constant wheedling for worthy causes of all kinds—many of them disability-related—would sooner or later backfire.[11]

For many Americans, disability- and disease-related campaigns epitomized what seemed wrong with charitable solicitation: Professional fundraisers ceaselessly squeezed prospective donors' sympathies as they plucked at their pocketbooks. It was all just too much. Americans such as these didn't question the worthiness of most causes. They didn't doubt the need for medical research and treatment and other services and money to pay for those things. They, too, saw the recipients as afflicted and less fortunate. They only complained about the methods and extent of solicitation.[12]

To deal with the baffling profusion of charities, reformers before and after World War II proposed federated fundraising, a plan to unify and systematize private financial support for the whole spectrum of health, welfare, cultural, and other projects. By replacing competition with cooperation, "united funds" would reduce solicitation and administrative costs, increase the total amount available for all programs, and serve more people. A unified and cooperative system, argued reformers, would be more efficient and economical than the wasteful free-for-all among jockeying agencies.[13]

The competition and overlap among multiplying charities troubled at least one disabled man who claimed to speak for other people with disabilities. Addressing the New York State Association for Crippled Children in 1948, Harold A. Littledale—former assistant to the *New York Times*' managing editor and a wheelchair rider as a result of a 1941 plane crash—declared that people with disabilities wanted public health agencies to work together. "The disabled need medical care, physical therapy, vocational guidance and instruction and the cooperation of employers in getting a job," he said. He criticized the piecemeal arrangement in which agencies rigidly limited their activities to a specialty. Because of this situation, he charged that jealousies arose "between groups, and resulting duplication [wasted] money and time. "What then do the disabled want?" he asked. "They want cooperation, not rivalry, among agencies. They want consolidation of effort. They want unity of plan. They want singleness of purpose."[14]

Critics also condemned charity professionals' influence. They complained that money went, not to the areas of greatest need, but disproportionately to campaigns with the most skillful fundraisers, the shrewdest publicists, the most popular spokespersons, the greatest "heart appeal." Most notable, in the 1930s the charisma of a celebrated figure, FDR, and the image of children "crippled" by polio, drew lopsided notice to a disease that affected relatively few Americans. One critic pointed out that the polio epidemics involved only 30,000 to 35,000 cases in any one year. Likewise, in 1958 more donated funds addressed the needs of the 150,000 Americans lumped under the rubric muscular dystrophy than served the 16 million identified as having mental disorders. Already in the late 1950s, the star power of a national celebrity, Jerry Lewis, along with the emotional impact of the poster children who would come to be called his "kids," garnered public attention for one particular health need far greater than its incidence and social impact would have forecast.[15]

Almost from the beginning, and well into the 1990s, disability-related charities fought against growing criticism that they drew attention and funds to a narrow range of medical conditions. They used a variety of strategies to counter perceptions that their efforts had only a limited impact on society. For example, the March of Dimes publicized the growing extent and increasing severity of polio epidemics. By the postwar era, it was no longer simply *infantile* paralysis but a disease contracted by increasing numbers of teenagers and young adults, thus broadening the number of people potentially touched by the disease.[16] Other disability-related charities challenged assertions of narrowness by vastly expanding their clienteles. In 1958, 150,000 Americans were identified as having muscular dystrophy; three decades later, MDA's Telethon announced that more than 8 million had one of the forty neuromuscular conditions that it now handled.[17] In the mid-1990s, UCP said that some 700,000 children and adults in the United States had cerebral palsy, a catchall term for a wide range of conditions with varying effects on motor functioning. In addition, UCP noted, while most of its clients acquired their disabilities just before or after birth, others incurred brain injuries through strokes and accidents later in life. The National Easter Seals Society cast its net even more widely to encompass virtually every kind of disability experienced by upwards of 35 million people. To be sure, as telethon hosts explained, the agency served only about a million each year, 600,000 of them children.[18] But a million clients was not a small number, and Easter Seals was one of the largest providers of rehabilitation services in the United States, not to mention that its clientele also overlapped the other charities by including people with cerebral palsy, muscular dystrophy, and arthritis.[19] The Arthritis Foundation claimed the largest numbers of all, addressing more than 100 connective-tissue diseases affecting some 37 million people, 1 out of 7 Americans.[20]

To be sure, these charities played an important role in drawing attention to medical conditions that had received little organized attention prior to World War II. With the growing success of American medicine and the expanding role of popular media, the postwar era marked a significant change. Rather than focusing narrowly on a few relatively low-incidence diseases, the telethon-producing charities eventually aided a couple of million Americans. Given the structuring of the US health-care and health insurance system, those individuals probably would have missed out on essential treatments and services without the charities to champion their situations. The voluntary health agencies drew attention to and mobilized resources on behalf of public health needs that, in the absence of universal, comprehensive national health insurance, might have been neglected. No one could gainsay that these organizations offered vital assistance to many people.

But it was the charities' effectiveness at fundraising that drew the most compelling criticisms. For in the end, even if they benefited more people with a wider range of conditions than critics recognized, the fact remained that dollars were not distributed according to the statistical frequency of any particular medical condition, or its economic impact, or its severity or lethality. Funds were apportioned in line with agencies' proficiency in organizing and publicizing their particular causes. Money went to the conditions charity professionals made, in medical historian Charles Rosenberg's word, more "visible."[21] Reformers protested that fundraisers' success perpetuated the unevenness and unfairness of the US health-care system, the maldistribution of monies, the discrepancies in services. If one observer of modern American charity fundraising somewhat complacently described such disparity as "inevitable in a system of voluntarism," another charged that "crusades are built on pity and terror, not statistics," while a third scorned the voluntary health charities as "the emotional and disorderly field of benevolence."[22]

In the immediate postwar period, the health charities effectively exerted their public influence to resist regulation and reorganization. The four largest agencies—the American Cancer Society, the American Heart Association, the National Tuberculosis Association, and the NFIP—spearheaded the opposition. They refused to join local united funds and fought the formation of a national federated health fund. They asserted that the separate drives drew attention to particular medical needs that otherwise would have been neglected, conducted necessary public education campaigns about their specific programs, and mobilized volunteers to generate both private and public funding. The charities' executives ominously pictured a consolidated effort as a "national welfare trust" that would enforce "compulsory federated giving." Basil O'Connor, longtime leader of the powerful NFIP, for years battled what he called "the Super Fund" idea. In 1961 he warned that a proposed National Commission on Voluntary Health Agencies would wreck "one of the most cherished privileges of democracy by inflicting on volunteers a government by vigilante."[23]

O'Connor's argument did more than defend the multiplication of charities, the cacophony of solicitations, and the lack of uniform standards for charitable spending and accounting. He proclaimed modern American charity's core ideology and mythology. As we saw in the previous chapter, charity fundraising tapped into a deeply embedded American cultural tradition that honored volunteers. Acting out of a sense of neighborly compassion and civic duty, these unpaid private individuals solicited their fellow citizens on behalf of "the unfortunate." Both the solicitors and the donors gave their time, money, and energy voluntarily; the former did not plead at state instigation; the latter did not pay under compulsory government taxation. All assumedly made uncoerced choices as free moral agents. They allegedly operated as independent Americans.[24]

But even while this ideology and mythology reaffirmed long-held American values, they helped to obscure the realities of modern American solicitations. Charity drive organizers continued to rely on and celebrate volunteers when, in fact, professional fundraising specialists and public-relations experts designed and managed those campaigns. Professionals more and more displaced amateurs from the key roles, or rather, superseded and supervised them. In addition, though the charities lauded the principle of voluntarism, the fundraisers' high-pressure public-relations tactics, along with corporations' pressing employees to give, rendered many individual donors' decisions something less than uncoerced. Contributions constituted payment of a *social* tax.[25]

In seeking to fulfill a public void, the private charities nonetheless raised questions about efficiency, coverage, and ultimate responsibility within the quickly evolving landscape of how to make mass appeals. The charities argued that Americans should contribute because "this" disease or disability could happen to them or to someone they loved and then they would need the charities' assistance. Critics replied that if "this" could happen to anyone, then everyone should pay for it and the funding of medical care, equipment, and research should not be left to voluntary private donation.[26] The development of a health and welfare system that visibly and emphatically incorporated charitable solicitation had little to do with the necessities of funding. Telethons were not created because, as syndicated columnist Bob Greene and many other Americans thought, they were "the only way" to pay for medical research and services.[27] Nor were they the most efficient, being as one research study put it "among the least effective ways of getting donations," less effective than "even a stranger soliciting door-to-door."[28] The charity fundraising components of the US health and welfare system were, in fact, the outcome of a process of social and political "negotiations" in which the private health charities had a powerful voice. Their influence contributed to the construction of a distinctly American arrangement of providing for health and welfare needs. Professional celebrity-centered fundraising on telethons is more comprehensible when viewed in relation to two other segments of that system: private and public health insurance.

Telethons as Disability Insurance

A specific set of late-twentieth-century health insurance problems revealed one way in which "disability" was constructed as a social condition and role. People with major disabilities were more likely than either nondisabled people or people with minor disabilities to depend on government insurance through Medicare and Medicaid. At the same time, those with minor disabilities were the most likely of the three groups to have no insurance at all; more than one in three was uninsured. Ranked among the working poor, their incomes and financial resources were high enough to disqualify them for government aid but too meager to pay for their health care and disability-related living expenses.

People with any kind of disability, major or minor, were less likely than nondisabled people to have private health insurance for several reasons. For one thing, they faced widespread discrimination by insurers. Sometimes companies denied them any insurance at all. At other times, insurers granted limited coverage but also often made disabled people pay at exorbitant rates, well above what they charged nondisabled customers. In addition, insurers might drop coverage if they decided that a medical condition had become too costly. Meanwhile, some employers refused to hire prospective employees with disabilities, fearing that they might file workers' compensation claims. Other companies sometimes fired disabled employees to save on health-care costs. Because of this situation, from the 1970s on, activists targeted insurance discrimination as a major disability rights issue.[29]

In his memoir, *Moving Violations: War Zones, Wheelchairs, and Declarations of Independence*, the broadcast journalist and writer John Hockenberry cataloged the pecking order of disabilities produced by disparate insurance coverage. Injured in a 1976 car accident, he, along with his fellow patients in a rehabilitation hospital, came face-to-face with the system's "bizarre priorities and patterns of care." The kinds of treatment and amount of services individuals received were pegged to the type of insurance they carried and even, strange as it seems, to the circumstances under which they became sick or disabled. Because they belonged to a pool of all licensed drivers, people injured in car accidents could expect almost complete medical coverage, including wheelchairs provided for the rest of their lives. Next came folks injured in public places such as playgrounds or swimming pools. They usually benefited from a facility's insurance policy and might get a financial settlement if they sued. For those injured on the job, workers' compensation coverage was less than for auto accidents, but fairly complete, though purchase of wheelchairs proved more problematic. In considerably worse shape were people with degenerative conditions who often ran through their insurance quickly, leaving them little or nothing for physical therapy. Recipients of what Hockenberry described as "a kind of medical rationing," they could get "less than state-of-the-art wheelchairs and accessories" paid for by charities, but if a wheelchair "broke down, the Easter Seals donors did not have the resources simply to replace it." At the very bottom were people with "rare degenerative diseases that no one had ever heard of. They had no insurance, no treatment, and the most expensive care." This appalling situation was epitomized by one boy in particular: "A six-year-old covered with oozing bandages roamed our halls in a little electric cart. ... Little Roger's disease had no treatment, its rarity meant that it was not considered by insurance companies, and it had little chance of finding its own telethon." The boy was permanently confined to the hospital "because no one could afford to pay" for him to live at home.[30]

The extraordinary variations in insurance coverage for health-care treatments, medical rehabilitation, and technological devices endured by "Little Roger," John Hockenberry, and countless other Americans resulted from the hybrid, public–private, health and welfare system. One function of the telethon-producing charities was to fill in some of the gaps for individuals fortunate enough to acquire a medical condition that attracted vigorous media representation.

The ironic experience of one California woman illustrated the problems with a system that, because it relied in part on celebrity-generated fundraising, paid for research and treatment for some medical conditions while neglecting others. For a quarter of a century, Karen Brown energetically raised money for MDA, bringing in some $3 million. Then in 1998, she was diagnosed with systemic sclerosis, the most severe and progressive form of scleroderma, a connective-tissue disease that hardens and scars the skin and attacks the internal organs. In a cruel twist of fate, scleroderma, a largely ignored disease, forced Brown to give up her volunteer work on behalf of a high-profile one, muscular dystrophy. MDA supported research and treatments for neuromuscular conditions, not connective-tissue diseases, so the clinics and research it supported could not help her. Her husband hoped someone would "put as much energy into fighting scleroderma as his wife has put into fighting muscular dystrophy."[31]

The irony went even further. The Associated Press (AP) reported in 1991 that scleroderma was "more prevalent than muscular dystrophy and AIDS." Some 300,000 Americans had the disease. Despite those numbers and its severity and deadliness, people with scleroderma did not get the public attention directed toward individuals with those other conditions. There were several obvious explanations. For one thing, unlike AIDS in the 1990s or polio two and three generations earlier, scleroderma was not contagious. But none of the neuromuscular conditions MDA addressed were communicable either, and people with those diseases got plenty of notice. So there had to be other reasons for the neglect of people with scleroderma. Surely, an additional factor was that women were three times more likely than men to develop the disease, with the typical woman affected being middle-aged. But if demographics helped shape recognition of diseases and disabilities as important public health problems demanding action, organized publicity was even more important. "[N]o famous comedian holds telethons for" scleroderma, reported AP. "That's what we need: a celebrity spokesman," said the president of the Scleroderma Society. "We need a Jerry Lewis." In the US health-care system, where "public" meant celebrity rather than universality, the lack of a star making a disease publicly visible on a telethon could lead to fatal neglect.[32]

Jerry Lewis himself implicitly acknowledged this dangerous shortcoming of the system. In the summer of 1987, the March of Dimes announced it would stop producing its telethon. "What about the birth defects children?" worried Lewis. "Where does that leave them? I just hope the management that has decided not to do a telethon for the March of Dimes has another source to raise money for the kids." If celebrity-dependent charitable solicitation disappeared, what would replace it? In Lewis's mind, it would have to be some other means of drawing private donations. He could not imagine another way.[33]

Filling the Gaps

Limiting assumptions such as Lewis's grew out of an ideology and mythology of American individualism, both in approaches to charity and in how most thought about disabled people. These views lauded voluntarism and the supposed superiority of charity fundraising in and through the private sector. But in historical fact, that putatively independent sector's efforts were inseparable from the system of private insurance as well as political decision making and public policy formation. The interlocking functions of the public and private sectors of the US health and welfare system became more obvious in the 1990s. The critical situation of federal and state government budgets, along with the inroads made by managed care, prompted the disability charities to fashion a new argument for donation. They announced that they played an even more necessary role than previously. They declared that they filled the gaps left by cutbacks in government funding and under managed care. And they accomplished this, they assured prospective donors, without inflicting the stigma of welfare or charity. By offering a supposedly nongovernmental—which was also to say a supposedly nonpolitical—solution to the limited funding and coverage of health care, the charities implicitly redirected public attention away from the inequities of the system as a whole. But in fact, the structuring of health insurance and health care forced adults with disabilities and the parents of children with disabilities to scrounge for aid wherever they could find it. A charity tradition and medical approach focused on problem individual bodies thus helped to depoliticize disability issues by diverting attention from larger economic and social concerns that shaped the lives and prospects for disabled people.

One segment of the 1992 Easter Seals San Francisco Bay Area Telethon offers a striking example. Explaining that previously the charity supplemented the services her daughter Hallie received at one of California's regional centers for people with developmental disabilities, a mother lamented that reductions in government funding of those centers and other community services now forced her family to rely on Easter Seals alone. "If it weren't for Easter Seals," she reported that her daughter wouldn't be getting the therapy she needed. "Easter Seals isn't a supplement anymore," she explained, "it's an absolute necessity."[34]

Over the next few years, hosts hammered home the same message: Private giving was more necessary than ever because of cuts in publicly funded programs. "If the services that Easter Seals provides were to disappear just overnight," warned one MC in San Francisco, "millions of Americans nationwide would be left with absolutely nowhere to turn for assistance. ... This isn't money that comes from the federal government or anything else. It has to come from you. But it fulfills a lot of the services that the federal government would otherwise serve with tax money and so on."[35] Meanwhile, the head of Chicago Easter Seals reported that since the 1994 congressional elections, Washington had moved to put more responsibility for social services back on local communities. As a result, Easter Seals expected demand for its programs to double in the next five years. In another segment, an Illinois state senator talked about the scramble for a piece of the public pie. "Well, I think it's important for the general public to understand there's a lot of competition for the tax dollars these days," he said. "And so it is extremely, extremely important for the private sector to respond to the Easter Seals program."[36]

If curtailments in government funding deprived people of needed services, so too did cutbacks in private insurance coverage under the managed-care system. A young mother on the Easter Seals telecast talked about the therapy her little daughter received from the charity. The family could not have afforded it out of their private insurance, she explained.[37] The limitations of health insurance coverage had an impact on middle- and working-class families of all ethnic groups. On MDA's San Jose segment, another mother related that her family's insurance did not include clinic visits for her son and daughter, both of whom had neuromuscular disabilities. MDA paid for those examinations and the equipment they used.[38] A doctor told the Bay Area Easter Seals audience about an experimental aphasia support group. The trouble was that insurance would now pay for only a limited period of therapy, even though people still had difficulty speaking. One woman who belonged to the support group summed things up: "If the insurance is out, you're out, more or less." If it weren't for Easter Seals, she would have no place to go for continuing therapy, she said.[39]

These pleas for assistance avoided politicizing the issues. The telethon hosts, the Illinois state senator, and—most poignantly and therefore probably most effectively—the woman with aphasia and the moms of disabled children, all asked viewers to fill in the gaps from cuts in government funding and limited coverage under managed care; none of them urged the audience to lobby elected officials to restore the cuts. Nor did they call for government regulation to ensure patients' rights under managed care. Instead, they proposed private charity solutions to political and policy problems. In making their case, the telethons again implicitly bolstered the preference for private-sector voluntary initiatives. Contradicting the agencies' own mobilization of their clients as political constituents who lobbied the federal and state governments to fund research and services related to particular medical conditions, the telethons' messages reflected the American charity tradition, in effect, by removing disease and disability from the realm of politics and government.

As part of this appeal, the agencies stressed that they offered neither welfare nor charity. They depicted their programs as a form of group insurance. Contributions became a type of insurance premium; receiving services as a payout on the insurance policy. They borrowed this framing from the March of Dimes campaigns of the 1950s. Back then a March of Dimes chapter chairman declared: "It's not charity, it is a trust fund, established by you and you to take care of you when you need it." Another officer claimed: "There's no charity involved. It's direct monetary aid, without numerous forms to fill out and taking the pauper's oath and that sort of thing." A volunteer believed that the most important feature "in the long run" was "the factor of getting together and assisting without the stigma of charity."[40] The approach of the NFIP reversed the usual pattern of social welfare. Local NFIP chapters actively sought out families in which a member had contracted polio. They asked "only the most brief and general questions" about a "family's financial position." They said nothing about repayment of financial aid. Sociologist Fred Davis's pathbreaking study of such families corroborated that the NFIP's "sizable and virtually unconditional aid" protected them from "what might otherwise have proved a crushing financial burden." And while many parents of children who contracted polio "voluntarily promised" to repay the assistance, a few viewed it as "a form of insurance payment, [a] return on their contributions over the years. . . ."[41]

The NFIP's financial aid policies and the reactions of American families to them had controversial political and cultural implications. Davis interviewed a number of doctors who treated polio patients. They "expressed strong resentment against the Foundation for what they regarded as overindulgent policies toward polio families. They felt that such subsidies not only were an ominous precursor of socialized medicine but also engendered lax and unappreciative attitudes in the families toward the medical care and treatment that the child received."[42] In the doctors' opinion, recipients of charity should show gratitude. They must not take access to health care for granted as though it were some sort of social right. The conflicts among the NFIP's practices, the physicians' perspective, and the attitudes of the families highlighted disparities and tensions in the US system of health insurance and health care.

The telethon-producing charities did not have the NFIP's financial resources; they could not cover all the costs bearing down on their clients. And so their messages and policies never raised the specter of socialized medicine or challenged traditional notions of giving and receiving charity. They merely borrowed from the March of Dimes the fundraising gimmick that donation was a form of purchasing insurance. A Bay Area Easter Seals MC declared: "You know, supporting Easter Seals is just like buying an insurance policy for yourself or a friend or a family member. Think of it that way. We never know when accident or stroke will pay an unwelcome visit to someone we love."[43] UCP national host Dennis James assured potential contributors that medical research was "more and more and more . . . cutting down on the causes of cerebral palsy at birth. ... That's the kind of insurance policy you're buying right now."[44]

Calling such services "insurance" was a way to de-stigmatize them. The approach assured the mostly middle-class clients that they remained a safe distance from stooping to welfare, that they weren't like the disreputable, lazy poor seeking a free government ride. Easter Seals repeatedly declared that it helped people "regardless of their ability to pay." A host of Chicago's local Easter Seals telethon underscored this message with an anecdote about a father who went to his local branch to get therapy for his disabled child. He worried that the first question would be, "How are you going to pay for this?" He had no idea how. To his surprise, the staff person instead asked, "How can we help?"[45] This wasn't charity or welfare. MDA announced over and over that it imposed no "means test."

The agencies could help without subjecting clients to a demeaning bureaucratic ordeal, telethon hosts reminded viewers, because contributors shouldered their civic duty. After interviewing the mother of a little girl with cerebral palsy, Dennis James exhorted: "What would she do? Do you think she could handle this alone? There's no way. It's not a family thing. It's a nation thing. We all have to get behind it. No one family can afford having a child with cerebral palsy."[46] Because the typical American family could not be expected to handle the financial burdens of a major disability alone, it became a collective obligation, "a nation thing."

Yet it was also definitely not a "government thing." Telethons implicitly and sometimes explicitly declared that this collective national obligation was best fulfilled through private voluntary efforts. MDA is not "government-oriented," Jerry Lewis told his audience in 1993. "This is one of my great prides. We've never been subsidized by the government. We have done this ourselves, between you and me. And we have been terrific. I cannot see going to the government and asking for a wheelchair for a child and then seeing a requisition written by some employee that will then process it over a nine- or ten-month period. We are in fact capable of getting a wheelchair to a child within forty-eight hours. It makes a big difference. You have helped us do that. We're terribly independent."[47]

In many respects then, organizations fundraised on the telethons by implicitly and sometimes explicitly promising to replace government. As Lewis noted, bureaucrats could take months to authorize—or disapprove—a wheelchair or other needed equipment. And as Dennis James observed, most American families could not afford the high cost of living with a major medical condition. Services and equipment were expensive, with the costs continually rising. Two mothers informed the Bay Area MDA audience about those expenses. One explained that her growing young daughter needed new leg braces every year, but a pair cost about a thousand dollars. The other said her daughter's shoe insert last month cost $700, while her son's electric wheelchair cost $8000.[48] One of MDA's Denver hosts asked viewers: "Can you imagine somebody in dire needs [*sic*] that didn't have the money to purchase a wheelchair? . . . The financial burden of it is monumental. You couldn't even think about what would happen if you had to pay for that suddenly out of your own pocket." The Bay Area boy who needed the power wheelchair also had to have two operations. MDA paid for those surgeries. "MDA is there," said the Denver MC.[49] For many American families who had a member with a neuromuscular disability or cerebral palsy or one of the other conditions supported by a charity, that agency's assistance was absolutely essential.[50] Viewed through the lens of the telethons, turning to the government simply wasn't an option.

But, in fact, neither MDA nor the other charities could "be there" to pay the full price of all the equipment and services many people with significant disabilities needed. The costs were too high, the agencies' resources too limited. The power wheelchair driven by the Bay Area boy cost $8000; MDA kicked in $5000. Certainly, one cannot fault MDA or the other organizations for their incapacity to cover the entire expense of such devices. Even partial payment was vital to these families. "It's been wonderful to have [MDA] assist us financially," announced the mother of the girl who needed new leg braces. The mother of the boy who needed the power wheelchair summed up the sort of aid charities could provide. "The Muscular Dystrophy Association helps to pay for all of that," she said. But the charities could not pay for everything. And, as John Hockenberry pointed out, if a device like an electric wheelchair broke down, the donating agency might "not have the resources simply to replace it."[51]

And when economic times turned tough, organizations like the MDA found it even harder to stand in for public assistance. An article in the *Atlanta Constitution* in early January 2010 announced that the MDA was eliminating grants because of declining private donations and investment losses. The article told the story of Joey Feltner, 27 and his mother, Kathy Bray, of Carrollton, who "unhappily discovered the program cut after his manual wheelchair was stolen." Upon calling MDA's Atlanta office, which had provided previous grants of up to $2000 for wheelchairs, Bray was informed that "the program no longer existed because of budget cuts." According to the article, MDA had run "multi-million dollar deficits since 2007," losses that only increased in subsequent years. For the first time in decades, American charitable giving had declined by 5 percent, while the demand for assistance rose. Meanwhile, the article reported, despite the fact that MDA had been forced to cut its highly visible $6 million wheelchair program and $4 million from its $47 million medical research budget, it had substantially increased the salary and benefits of its CEO Gerald Weinberg from $313,215 to $409,063 in 2008. "Our CEO's compensation is appropriate for what he does and has done for over four decades [with the MDA]," a spokesman for the organization said. "He helps create magic for MDA every day, every year." For Feltner and his mother, the magic now meant having to remain at home until a suitable replacement could be found. Promising not to give up, the Atlanta office of MDA offered "to try to find a used chair or to try to piece one together out of donated parts," which after three attempts proved unworkable. "We are very sad to hear her frustration and empathize with that," MDA's Georgia Executive Director Amy Alvarez said. "Whether the family is willing to take what we can offer is up to them." Meanwhile, Medicaid's $372 maximum for a wheelchair provided barely a fifth of the cost of a suitable replacement, an impossible burden on Bray, a cosmetologist.[52]

MDA did not impose a means test, but it did have an eligibility and payment policy. It would "assist with payment only for those services authorized in its program that are not covered by private or public insurance plans or other community resources." It would also assist "with the purchase and reasonable repair of wheelchairs or leg braces" if a local MDA clinic physician medically prescribed that equipment. "In addition to utilizing whatever medical insurance may be applicable, the person for whom the equipment has been prescribed or that person's family may be asked to assist with its purchase through personal resources." MDA annually established "the maximum allowable assistance" toward the purchase or repair of wheelchairs and leg braces.[53] Easter Seals announced a similar policy. "Easter Seals receives funding from a variety of sources, including private insurers, government agencies and fee-for-service. To make our services accessible to as many people as possible Easter Seals also relies on public contributions." The need for donations highlighted the limitations of private charities. "Public contributions," explained Easter Seals, "help cover the difference between actual program costs and what our clients can afford."[54]

While Jerry Lewis felt proud that MDA itself was "terribly independent" and never "subsidized by the government," it was unlikely that many of MDA's clients, and many people who sought help from other charities, enjoyed the luxury of that sort of independence. They and their families needed to forage for financial help. The San Jose boy had to have an electric wheelchair that cost $8000. In good economic times, MDA would pay more than 60 percent of that price, but where would the other $3000 come from? Individuals and families often had to juggle combinations of charity assistance, private insurance, and out-of-pocket spending. Many found it necessary to qualify for government assistance such as Medicaid, which meant that they had to impoverish themselves. Sometimes married adults who acquired major disabilities had to divorce in order to become eligible for the needed financial aid. Sometimes parents split up in order to get government benefits for their children. Too often, marriages and families foundered on the financial burdens and resulting emotional stresses inflicted by these arrangements.

The disparities of the US system forced disabled people and their families into these demeaning, rending situations. The confusing, contradictory, inadequate, and inefficient hybrid public–private system of health insurance, health-care delivery, social welfare, and charity fundraising made living with a significant chronic disease or disability in late-twentieth-century America an expensive and complicated proposition. Moreover, the complex web of different public and private agencies made it easy for individuals and organizations to pass the buck, or in the words of columnist Steve Blow of the *Dallas Morning News*, "We all just figure that there's someone else out there who stands ready to fix every problem."[55]

The Hidden Politics of Telethons

WHERE VOLUNTEERISM, GOVERNMENT, AND BUSINESS MEET

The telethon-producing charities played an important role in setting American agendas related to morals, attitudes, and policies regarding health and welfare.[1] Contrasting the United States to Western Europe and Canada, they proclaimed private charity and voluntary private giving as "the American way" that met, and even did a better job of meeting, average Americans' health-care needs.[2] At the same time, they lobbied for government funding of medical research, treatments, and rehabilitation.[3] In both modes, they participated in a related political process, the ongoing debate over the proper mix of private and public means of addressing social needs. In addition, they made their telecasts available to corporate sponsors to propagate corporate agendas in an allegedly neutral, commercial-free environment. Even though the nonprofit sector did not in the late twentieth century—or at any time in American history—have the material resources to cope with all of those needs, public opinion polls suggested that many Americans believed the myth, a myth that helped disguise and detract from the political decisions and policy choices that structured the US health-care system and corporate self-interest.[4] This chapter explores telethons as underappreciated fronts in these cultural and political contests.

The major turning point in the debate between voluntary private giving and public government support came with the unprecedented crisis of the Great Depression. The massive social and economic dislocation called into question claims about private health and welfare philanthropy and forcibly brought the issue into the political arena. A growing number of Americans complained that private charity furnished uneven and inadequate services. They came to believe that the government must take the lead in meeting the vast need. In response, the New Deal and subsequent political administrations greatly expanded the federal government's role in ensuring the general welfare.[5]

Yet the emergence and growth of an American welfare state did not settle the debate over public versus private approaches. The efforts of Franklin

D. Roosevelt regarding health and social welfare, as with so much else in his character and career, manifested the contradictions in Americans' thinking. He launched both the New Deal and the NFIP; that is, the emerging, modern American welfare state and the most innovative and influential instance of modern American, health-related, private charity fundraising.[6] That pattern continued in the post–World War II era. Even as the public sector expanded enormously, the "voluntary" sector, with increasing backing from the corporate realm, proliferated too.

During the postwar decades, critics repeatedly challenged the national health charities' claims that they effectively met the demand for medical research and care. In his 1958 book *Before We Sleep*, Hank Bloomgarden elaborated a charge made again and again. "The voluntary agencies have failed down the line to admit to themselves that their own resources would not do to support a proper offensive employing every possible line of attack. . . . They have always assumed (or found it more profitable so to believe) the conditions were not ripe for anything but the tin-cup approach to disease." The agencies, claimed Bloomgarden, used public relations to make it appear that private charity fundraising was the right and sensible way to fund medical research and treatment. He called for more federal spending. He especially wanted more for medical research to find cures.[7] In fact, the health charities did lobby for increased federal spending on medical research and health care, though of course it was research and treatments specifically for their particular constituencies. Yet, masking their lobbying efforts, they continued to characterize their efforts as emanating from an independent voluntary sector.[8]

In the latter half of the twentieth century, the three sectors—voluntary, government, and business, which had always interpenetrated more than many Americans acknowledged—became even more intertwined. Some of the telethon-producing charities illustrated this pattern. All of them relied heavily on corporate contributions. Easter Seals and UCP also depended on federal government contracts.[9] Although the MDA proudly proclaimed that it never took government money, many of the clinics it supported counted on federal grants. Meanwhile, as explained in chapter 2, clients of all the charities often had to hunt for multiple sources of financial assistance, including government aid. Despite the material and political fact of the three sectors' close involvement with one another, public discourse generally persisted in dichotomizing health and welfare issues in terms of state versus private approaches.

Compassionate Conservatism

Political electioneering was another sort of agenda setting. George W. Bush's 2000 presidential campaign promoted a conservative perspective on both health and welfare issues and the disputed values underlying them. In important ways, his agenda complemented those of the telethons. At a South Carolina campaign stop, Bush took a question from Christine Green, a legally blind biology major at Coastal Carolina University. She needed a $400 micro-scope eyepiece, a diopter, in order to take the last required class and finish her degree. But neither she nor the school could afford to pay for it, she said. Her question wasn't about herself, though. She was using her situation to illus-trate a larger problem. She wanted to know what Bush as president would do for people with disabilities. It was politically significant that neither she nor he seemed aware that both the 1973 Rehabilitation Act's Section 504 and the Americans with Disabilities Act of 1990 required the school to provide this sort of equipment as a reasonable accommodation. Her question concerned public policy, but Bush sought to remove the problem from the overtly politi-cal realm by framing her situation as a matter of individual need that could and should be dealt with through private charity.

Shifting into the role of a charity fundraising MC who often called on prospective donors to help pay for technological devices, Bush declared, "I bet somebody will help you get a diopter. I bet somebody right here in this audience may stand up and help you get it. You know something, do I hear a bidder?" "In an instant," reported AP, "Buck Limehouse, a Republican can-didate for Congress from Charleston, said he would pay for the piece. As the audience applauded, Limehouse and Green embraced in the center of the uni-versity's gymnasium." But afterward, Green said "she had mixed emotions" about Bush's response. "I'm very appreciative that he got the money for me, but I'm not the only disabled person in the world." She complained that he hadn't answered her larger question.

In fact, Bush *had* given her an answer. His handling of her question illustrated one perspective in the ongoing debate about how to provide for Americans' health and welfare. He called it "compassionate conservatism," a new label on an old approach, which held that the government should help people under certain circumstances and in limited ways. To fill the gaps that would remain, he spoke of " 'rallying the armies of compassion,' private groups and people who help the less fortunate." The phrase put the issue in terms of charity and worthiness to receive charity, rather than claimable social rights.

The president's approach also removed disability from the realm of politics and policy making. Green had meant to use her dilemma to illustrate the larger situation of many Americans with disabilities. She wanted to elicit can-didate Bush's policy position on disability accommodations. She was fram-ing disability as a political issue. He instead individualized and privatized it, taking disability out of the political and policy arena. A college student with a vision disability needed a diopter. A lone benefactor could buy it for her. That maneuver reduced the matter to a personal need that private char-ity could meet. It depoliticized disability needs by mustering a conventional fundraising ritual. His shrewd gesture conjured a familiar mechanism of the

American charity tradition. The parallels with the telethons illustrated the political nature of supposedly apolitical benevolence.[10]

The controversy over public versus private means continued because it involved more than competition between opposing political factions and programs. It grew out of flawed thinking about the structuring of the American welfare state and its relationship to civil society and a capitalist market economy.[11] At the same time, both the ongoing debate and the failure of ideology reflected fundamental contradictions in values. From the 1930s on, many Americans simultaneously affirmed individuals' duty to give voluntarily and to volunteer, and expected government to address basic social needs. Their thinking was shaped by a constellation of shared and, at times, competing values: Individuals were responsible for their own welfare and it was also the responsibility of the community to undergird its members. Many were also divided, not just in the public arena but in their own minds, about how much to expect of, how much power to give to, the state on the one hand, and how much they could and should rely on private voluntary efforts on the other. Their values expressed contending ideals and imperatives regarding the relationship between the public and the private, the state and civil society, communal responsibility and individual need, collective compulsory solutions and private voluntary initiatives, without ultimately reconciling any of these.[12] The disability charities and their fundraising activities also reflected these contradictions and complications.

Corporate Agendas

In addition to lobbying and extolling the virtues of private volunteerism over government welfare, telethon charities played a political role by offering a platform for corporate sponsors to press agendas of their own. Appearing on the yearly telethons, private companies bolstered the belief that government charity was less desirable, less efficient, even less American than examples of individual generosity, including that of corporations. Such ideas dovetailed with those behind the telethons at the same time that they nourished corporate images and underscored medicalized notions about disabled people. The snowmobile industry and the corporate nursing home system—each deeply implicated in issues of health, welfare, and disability—reveal the inner workings of this mutually beneficial relationship.

During the late 1960s and early 1970s, snowmobiling exploded in popularity. Arctic Enterprises, the largest snowmobile manufacturer, increased sales a hundred-fold from 1966 to 1972. Arctic competed with sixty other makers. By 1974 some 2.5 million of these machines roared around the United States. The companies also sold accessories such as saddlebags, clothing, tow sleds, and trailers. Hundreds of thousands of Americans joined snowmobile clubs and subscribed to the growing number of snowmobile magazines. Snowmobile "ranches" sprouted up near eastern and midwestern cities, in the mountain West, and at ski resorts everywhere. Snowmobiling became a billion-dollar-a-year business. Promoters talked about the appeal of nature's serenity, but snowmobilers admitted that what really enticed them was the excitement of speed, power, and noise.[13]

Those were the very features of snowmobiling that critics deplored. They complained that the machines emitted foul odors and polluted the country-side with noise, while ravaging the rural landscape and its wildlife.[14] Others pointed out the dangers to the people who rode them. In the 1971–1972 sea-son, 164 snowmobilers were killed and 428 seriously injured. In 1974 inju-ries sent some 19,000 riders to emergency rooms. The American Academy of Pediatrics' committee on recreation and sports warned that snowmobil-ing posed serious health risks for children. Other studies reported that the vehicles' extremely high noise levels caused severe hearing loss.[15] The chorus of complaints compelled government action. The Nixon and Carter admin-istrations, the National Transportation Safety Board, Congress, the State of New York, and other government entities considered regulating and restrict-ing snowmobiles.[16]

This negative publicity hurt the industry. So did the mid-1970s energy cri-sis, which prompted calls to reduce nonessential gas consumption by raising taxes on gas-guzzling vehicles such as snowmobiles. Sales in 1974 fell almost a third from the 1972 peak. By 1977 they were down by half. While 107 manu-facturers built snowmobiles in 1971, by 1977 the number had dwindled to only seven.[17]

To protect the industry's interests, its publicists planted favorable canned articles as news stories in snow country newspapers. Industry lobbyists suc-cessfully blocked regulatory legislation in various state governments and Congress. A torrent of letters, phone calls, and telegrams, some of them "vitu-perative and threatening," excoriated the Carter administration's plan to curb off-road vehicles from many public lands. Said one government official, "They are all screaming and yelling that their American rights are being violated."[18]

Lobbying to protect one's rights against regulation was one thing. But how might one refute a negative public image of selfishness and even down-right destructiveness? One way was through highly publicized acts of char-ity toward children with "special needs." In the mid-1970s, snowmobile associations organized rides at Easter Seals fundraising events. Later on, the National Snowmobile Foundation became an Easter Seals corporate spon-sor, a relationship that continues to this day. Snowmobilers "opened their hearts and wallets." They sent children with disabilities to Easter Seals camps in snow country. The Colorado Snowmobile Association started holding an annual Easter Seals Ride, one year for children with disabilities, the next for adults. These were special charity events, not integrated regular Association activities. And while disabled adults sometimes participated, the telethon featured nondisabled adult snowmobilers giving rides to Easter Seals child clients, handing them trophies, offering them "a day none of them will ever forget." "Snowmobilers across the country care about children and adults with disabilities and special needs served by Easter Seals," declared the charity's website. "This caring couldn't be more visible than through the efforts of snowmobilers. . . ."[19]

Easter Seals offered public relations aid to a business burdened by a negative public image. Drawing attention away from damage to the environment and some snowmobilers' bodies, the industry could show itself helping to rehabilitate physically disabled children and adults. It could present itself as philanthropically cheering up "special needs" kids. The charity link complemented the industry's political lobbying. Both propagated the snowmobile agenda.

If snowmobiling faced public criticism, the nursing home industry had an even bigger PR problem. The industry constantly drew bad press for subjecting large numbers of disabled adults of all ages to the abuses that historically have been inflicted on institutionalized disabled people.[20] It also needed to shape public opinion in order to safeguard its huge financial stake in federal government funding. The Arthritis Foundation Telethon gave it a platform to promote its agenda.

Beverly Enterprises' 1,052 facilities and 100,000 inmates in 1988 made its nationwide nursing home chain the largest in the United States. But a *Los Angeles Times* investigation found appalling conditions in some of Beverly's California facilities. In its Mountain View center, staff let ants swarm over residents' bodies. The creatures even crawled into one woman's open tracheotomy. In some homes, workers allowed decubitis ulcers—bed sores—to develop on inmates' backsides. These were not simply unsightly blemishes; if left untended, they could develop into gangrene, sometimes resulting in the amputation of a limb if not death. State health "inspectors reported that some patients were so neglected that their bedsores had blackened and consumed flesh down to the bone." In other instances, investigators charged staff with repeatedly leaving patients in urine-soaked beds, raping residents, and incorrectly dispensing medication. In a few cases, the neglect caused death.[21]

Beverly Enterprises' nursing homes in other states were also charged with mistreating patients. Missouri, Texas, and Oregon officials found major violations. In Missouri in 1991, Beverly agreed "to send in special teams of trained workers to detect and resolve problems at homes it operated." The state Department of Aging's deputy director believed that by 1995 conditions had improved. In 1993 Oregon regulators verified that negligence caused six deaths in Beverly-operated facilities. The company paid more than $1 million to settle patient-care violations. Soon after, it sold all of its Oregon nursing homes. The state's deputy long-term care ombudsman said "he was glad to see that the company had ended its operations in the state." Beverly was a huge corporate chain, but it typified problems throughout the for-profit nursing home industry.[22]

Approximately 7 out of 10 nursing homes belonged to for-profit companies. The director of California Advocates for Nursing Home Reform charged, "Because of their quest for profits these corporate chains often don't provide good care." Their biggest cost was labor: 7 out of 10 workers were "low-skilled, poorly paid nurse's aides." They got relatively little training but were required to care for more patients than they could properly serve. In 1987 Beverly raised its employees' wages across the board by about 50 cents an hour. President David R. Banks claimed his company could not afford additional raises. But in 1988 it took in over $2 billion in revenues, while a survey put its three top-ranking officers among California's one hundred highest paid executives, with Banks standing twenty-first on that list. In 1986 Banks collected $1.3 million in salary, bonuses, and long-term compensation such as stock options.[23]

With all of this bad press, the for-profit home-care industry turned to the Arthritis Foundation. Nursing home companies held fundraisers; then they trumpeted their good deeds on the Arthritis Telethon. On the 1991 show, a Beverly Enterprises representative offered his corporation's brochure on what to look for in selecting a nursing home for a loved one. Beverly also promoted a nursing home sweepstakes, an annual competition to see which of its units could raise the most money for the Foundation. The program also gave industry representatives a chance to tout the high quality of care they provided. Under themes such as "Pride in Caring," industry representatives affirmed their belief that America's elderly deserved the best long-term care.[24] A New York Health Facilities Association spokesman even invited everyone to visit a home during National Nursing Home Week for 1990 so they could see the outstanding job nursing homes were doing.[25]

The home-care industry was especially eager to promote these images in the face of mounting criticism from disabled activists. ADAPT, a disability organization founded in 1982 that contained many members who had been held in institutions, challenged both the nursing home corporations and federal funding priorities for "long-term care."[26] Of the $2 billion in revenue that Beverly Enterprises received in 1988, two-thirds had come from public funds. The industry as a whole drew revenues that year of over $43 billion, with Medicaid and Medicare putting in nearly half of the total. But the federal government spent only $3.4 billion on personal assistance services (PAS) that enabled disabled adults to live in their own homes.[27] By 1992 it was paying the nursing home industry $23 billion; by 1999 $39 billion.[28] The institutional bias of both public and private funding, protested ADAPT, locked up disabled people, "with little chance of getting out. We have few choices because the dollars flow to the institutions—not to where we want to live."[29]

The political struggles over institutionalization versus independent living (and even the contest over the impact of snowmobiling) were part of the larger ongoing debate over how Americans should address issues of health and welfare. During the second half of the twentieth century, the telethons played an unrecognized role in those discussions and controversies. However, several of the charities, at least some of the time, promoted disabled Americans' civil rights, as a later chapter will show.

Preserving the Corporate Status Quo

Corporations beyond sports and health care also saw great benefits in telethons. Eager to preserve their privileged, influential place within the American political and economic system, they used the television programs and other forms of charity fundraising to deflect attention away from their support for unpopular practices, policies, or causes. Throughout the twentieth century, businesses donated to community chests and individual charities to forestall government intervention in the private sector by demonstrating that the latter could handle social needs. Some executives saw corporate philanthropy as an antidote to creeping socialism.[30] Corporate contributions to the disability-related agencies continued this tradition of using charity to shape public perceptions of businesses somehow being apolitical both within the workplace and beyond. Such giving ultimately suggested the basic benevolence of the US economic system; not only did it help stave off discontent among employees by creating a common culture of giving, but it also promoted a caring public image that masked cutthroat competition.

Corporate sponsors talked a lot about "helping." For example, on the 1993 Easter Seals telecast, the director of marketing services for Sterling Health proclaimed: "This marks the eleventh year that Sterling Health has participated in the Easter Seals coupon program. ... And once again we're giving our viewers the opportunity to join us in that effort." "Now, what can they do to help?" inquired Pat Boone. "Well, Pat," answered the marketing director, "by redeeming the Sterling Health coupons delivered in tomorrow's Easter Seals newspaper insert, they'll be helping themselves to savings on fine products, like Phillips Milk of Magnesia, Midol, and our new line of Bayer Select Pain Relievers, and at the same time help us build our 1993 donation." "Now these are great products that we all use," the enthusiastic Boone exhorted viewers, "and this is a great great plan. So folks, please help yourself to the savings and help Easter Seals by clipping and redeeming the Sterling Health coupons wherever you are."

The corporate and telethon uses of the word "help" were varied and slippery. Consumers were invited to help themselves to savings, that is, to advance their own economic interests. The pursuit of financial advantage,

whether individual or corporate, was simultaneously represented as help to
people with disabilities. Most pertinent to the present point, consumers were
urged to help companies build their pledges.

This obfuscating terminology clouded the fact that these donations came,
not from the corporations themselves, but from their customers and employees. Unlike other telethon hosts, Jerry Lewis tried to distinguish corporate
contributions from individual donations. The checks business executives
handed to him should not be confused with the mounting figure on the electronic tote board, he would insist. The latter reflected individuals' phoned-
in pledges, the former were corporate sponsors' contributions. But Lewis's
determined contrast was a distinction without a difference, for only a small
fraction of corporate donations involved company funds. Consumers and
workers were paying for the pledges for which the corporations took credit
on the air.

Corporations generated these donations in four ways. One major fundraising strategy—which the next chapter will examine fully—used product
promotions to stimulate greater sales. Corporations donated a portion of the
bigger profits. Then they claimed much of the credit for what their customers
had, in effect, given.

A second tool was in-store coin canisters. Here again, the donated funds
came from customers and even employees who dropped their change into
these containers. Circle K, Taco Bell, and Payless Drug Stores all collected
coins for UCP. Payless gathered spare change for the Arthritis Foundation,
too. Citgo retailers, 7-11 convenience stores, and stores participating in the
"Aisles of Smiles" promotion picked up small donations for MDA. A Taco Bell
rep on the UCP show presented a check for $100,000. "You know," he said,
"this contribution was made possible by our very successful in-store canister program. I'd especially like to thank our customers for their generous
contributions. Without their support, our donation would not be possible."[31]
Companies got positive PR for merely handing over coins that had come out
of customers' pockets.[32]

Telethon corporate sponsors' third method of building donations encouraged employees to contribute out of their paychecks. Small worker-authorized
deductions went into company funds that allocation committees distributed
to charities. Business had originated this tactic as early as the 1920s. Workers
often resented that employers pressured them to "give through a payroll
deduction plan which in the eyes of many employees amount[ed] to a compulsory tax," while the company took credit for the employees' deductions.[33]
On the telethons, corporate spokespersons continued this long-established
practice.

Some corporate supporters generated customer contributions by a fourth
method, company-sponsored fundraising events. Kroger's and Von's gro-
cery stores and A&W restaurants held hop-a-thons and walk-a-thons and

bowl-a-thons to raise money for the Arthritis Foundation. Circle K had casino nights, golf tournaments, family picnics, and bowl-a-thons for UCP. MDA corporate sponsors KinderCare Learning Centers and Brunswick Recreation Centers, respectively, put on hop-a-thons and bowl-a-thons. For Easter Seals, Friendly's Restaurants' employees organized raffles, bake sales, and bowl-a-thons.[34] As always, corporate officers handed over checks from the proceeds as though they were their company's gift. Year after year, Safeway executive and Easter Seals National Board Member Bob Bradford pulled large mock checks out of small toy Safeway trucks to announce the amounts each of the corporation's divisions generated. On one telecast, a San Francisco Safeway employee presented funds from a wine tasting and an A&W root-beer float sale and made the typical transfer of credit. "Our customers helped us out in raising this money," he said.[35]

Promoting fundraising among their employees served the interests of corporate sponsors in other ways. A leading expert on cause-related marketing recommended it as, more than a stratagem to boost sales, an opportunity to manage human resources, which was to say, workers, more effectively. It could motivate employees, build their morale, and generate pride in the company, she explained. Research showed that these feelings were directly correlated to workers' sense of loyalty and the company's ability to retain them.[36] Business executives presenting donations on telethons recognized this advantage. On the MDA Telethon, Citgo Oil President Ron Hall explained: "Our people have fun doing it. It's a morale builder. It's a team-building exercise."[37] By urging their employees to volunteer for a charity, corporate sponsors believed they might help convince workers that the companies truly cared about people.

Encouraging workers to volunteer for the health charities could also divert attention from the way US companies were cutting back on insuring employees and their families. During the last quarter of the twentieth century, many corporations reduced their costs by shifting a larger share of health insurance costs to workers. Some eliminated employees' and employee dependents' health insurance altogether. In the decades following World War II, nearly two-thirds of American families covered by health insurance obtained it through employment. Many workers received it directly from their employers, while family members not employed outside the home often secured it indirectly through a wage-earning spouse or parent. Employer-sponsored insurance "served as the foundation for the U.S. health insurance system," explained a study for the Commonwealth Fund by the National Center for Health Policy. The report called it "the linchpin of the nation's health insurance system." But during the 1980s and early 1990s, the proportion of Americans covered by such insurance declined markedly. These cuts hit low- and modest-wage workers in blue-collar and service jobs hardest.[38] And even when employers still provided health insurance, the vast majority began to require employees to contribute a percentage.[39]

US law did not require employers to pay any share of the cost of health insurance. And employers and insurance companies often found ways to refuse coverage for those with chronic or preexisting conditions. These restrictions left blue-collar and middle-class families with few options. If a member acquired a serious medical condition or disability, the family could turn to private charities, including those that raised funds through telethons. Or they could sink into poverty—often through divorce and breakup of the family—and the sick or disabled family member would become eligible for federal Medicaid. Either way, employers were off the hook for covering financially undesirable insureds. During the quarter-century from the mid-1970s to the end of the 1990s, as the coverage provided to working- and middle-class American families by employment-based health insurance steadily declined, corporate cause-related marketing, including telethon sponsorship, soared.

In the late twentieth century, Americans complained about the rising price of health insurance and the inadequacy of coverage. They wanted the system reformed, but they were bombarded with political messages asserting that a government-run program would cost blue-collar and middle-class taxpayers too much. Meanwhile, the private charity system, which the telethons promoted and protected, enabled large corporations to appear to be helping middle- and working-class families with sick or disabled members, while disguising that the financial aid, the donations, had come out of the purses and wallets of those same sorts of families. The volunteerism and private philanthropy favored by big business helped hide the true costs of the US health insurance system.[40]

Providing for their needs through private charities and business philanthropy allegedly demonstrated the beneficence and equitability of the US economic system, especially in health and welfare. Telethon images of compassionate caring bolstered the agenda-setting argument that the American way of meeting such needs was mainly nongovernmental and voluntary. The rhetoric of individual and corporate charity depoliticized fundamentally political choices as the structural inequalities and systems that perpetuated them were made invisible by seemingly spontaneous acts of generosity.

"They've Got a Good Thing with Us and We've Got a Good Thing with Them"

TELETHONS AND CAUSE-RELATED MARKETING

In 1983 American Express made a deal with the Statue of Liberty-Ellis Island Foundation. For every transaction using its credit cards during a three-month period, it would donate a penny to restoring those historical monuments; for each new card enrollment, it would give a dollar. The arrangement yielded the Foundation $17 million, while boosting American Express credit card transactions by almost a third and increasing approved card applications by 15 percent. The company had experimented earlier with links to local philanthropies. This highly publicized scheme was its first national project. In the following years, more and more businesses used charitable giving in behalf of merchandising. They called this innovation in the American charity tradition "cause-related marketing."[1]

Marketing specialists, business journalists, and fundraising professionals commonly credit the American Express campaign with inventing this strategy, but they overlook the earlier pioneering role of disability-related charities.[2] The Muscular Dystrophy Association led the way. From its very beginning in the early 1950s, the MDA Telethon enlisted support from businesses such as Seven-Up and McDonald's, a technique perfected over the next decades.[3] With a guarantee of product exclusivity, and a prize of $100,000 in donations, corporate contributors could be seen on network television surrounded by talent that could not possibly be bought for that relatively small amount.[4] Year after year, large companies made telethon-linked sales a top marketing priority. For example, in 1976 McDonald's promotion was called "large fries for small fries." That same year, 7-Eleven convenience stores and its parent company, the Southland Corporation, became an MDA national corporate sponsor. On TV commercials all that summer and then on the telethon, Jerry Lewis sang a jingle that linked their sales to donations. The lyrics implored:

> Can I have your love? . . .
> And could you arrange
> to let me have the change
> for my kids?

Lewis performed this sort of advertising service for MDA's other corporate sponsors, too. He did radio spots for Hickory Farm's beef sticks. He posed with that year's poster child on 7 Up billboards. In 1976 Schick Safety Razors signed on as a major MDA corporate sponsor. Addressing its regional, divisional, and district managers on film, Lewis declared, "Together we can do a job for these kids and at the same time you can get the extra sales opportunities that make corporate sense." Schick's marketing campaign featured not only TV spots and print ads displaying Lewis and the MDA poster child, but also coupons, product samples, and the sponsorship of marathon fundraising dances in college gyms.[5] The larger the donations the corporate sponsors delivered, the more camera time they got on the telethon.[6] "We see definite marketing benefits from participation in the telethon for Schlitz," wrote the company's vice president for marketing.[7]

Professional surveys of American viewing habits suggested that this was corporate money well spent. Nielsen survey ratings indicated that over 60 million TV households, over 80 percent of all US homes, were tuned into the telethon for at least fifteen minutes. From a marketer's point of view, the cost efficiency is impressive. When the tax benefits are considered, corporate participation in the telethon becomes even more attractive. A study for UCP showed that 1 out of 4 viewers was able to identify the UCP Telethon's major sponsors or contributors.[8]

Research into marketing practices indicates that corporations were well aware of these benefits. Responding to a questionnaire in the mid-1980s, more than half of the fifty corporations supporting recent telethons indicated they had spent more in promotional support of their participation than they donated. A significant proportion cited the telethon's Nielsen rating as a factor in their decision to participate and many categorized the telethon donation as a promotion expense. Almost three-quarters of respondents agreed that the national charity telethon was an effective marketing tool, and the telethon played an important role in their own promotion programs.[9]

During the late 1970s and early 1980s, other corporations tapped into telethon-related marketing. Merchandisers began to distribute massive numbers of discount coupons linked to the UCP and Easter Seals shows. According to *Advertising Age*, the companies aimed to take advantage of the "do-good charity overlay."[10] In 1980 alone, Easter Seals corporate sponsors donated

$3 million.[11] One public relations specialist explained that the telecasts supplied "full network exposure" and "cooperative merchandising packages."[12]

Corporations would increasingly invest money in telethons because they offered "corporate image enhancement with a bottom line value."[13] That phrase captured both sides of the advantageous partnership of corporations with the charities, succinctly stating the twin objectives of cause-related marketing. It was just the sort of public relations scheme US corporations needed to counter growing public cynicism about them.

Good Corporate Citizens and Family Men

The public relations problems faced by the snowmobile and nursing home industries discussed in the previous chapter were part of a much larger trend. Beginning in the 1970s, public confidence in US business and business leaders plummeted. Average Americans grew suspicious of, then cynical about, executives and the powerful corporations they ran. This shift in public opinion was partly spurred by the growing militancy and impact of the consumer and environmental movements. A newly invigorated consumer campaign left behind the more moderate approach of earlier decades. Spearheaded by such outspoken advocates as Ralph Nader, it accused large corporations of routinely putting profits ahead of safety. Meanwhile, environmentalists charged many of those same companies with ravaging the natural environment and injuring public health. Lending support to this activism, a younger generation of investigative reporters, energized by the powerful impact of the news media in covering both the civil rights movement and the Vietnam War in the 1950s and 1960s, produced "critical and rigorous exposés of corporate wrongdoing. The cumulative effect was a considerable public relations crisis for big business."[14] While a 1969 Louis Harris poll found 58 percent of respondents trustful of major companies, just five years later the percentage had dropped in half to 29 percent. In 1976 and again in 1981, the proportion of "Americans with 'a great deal of confidence' in people running major companies" was a dismal 16 percent.[15]

Some corporate leaders grew alarmed at the public's cynicism. It was "not just an unpleasant fact," one of them warned colleagues in 1974. It was dangerous because it threatened the free enterprise system itself. To correct what one marketing expert called the "huge communications problem" of big business, executives began "speaking out, trying to convince audiences that business is not all bad." Some companies joined in "community affairs, conducting intern programs to acquaint young people with the business world, and undertaking public relations campaigns intended to build or revive confidence in industrial management." Some corporations tried to help solve social problems and spent money on cleaning up the environment.[16] During the 1970s, business interests launched a powerful multidimensional counter-offensive that included grassroots lobbying, the creation of corporate political action committees that raised and distributed campaign funds, the establishment of trade associations and public affairs offices, the reinvigoration of the Chamber of Commerce, the formation of corporate foundations, the launching of think tanks and research institutes, and the funding of professorships committed to "free enterprise" at American universities.[17] "What is under way now," announced *U.S. News and & World Report* in 1978, "is a concerted drive to improve [the companies'] image and to convince the public that business is not as bad as it is sometimes painted."[18]

Charitable giving offered one means of repairing corporate America's reputation. Big business philanthropy had already skyrocketed during the quarter century following World War II. Executives and their public relations advisors talked much of serving the public interest and playing the role of good corporate citizen. They backed publicity and educational campaigns promoting the free enterprise system as the American way. They were partly motivated by fear that what they saw as creeping socialism threatened free enterprise. But a historian of charity fundraising writing in the mid-1960s concluded that they mostly desired "to build that loosely defined asset 'good will' and thus maintain an environment favorable to the profit-making enterprise." The "corporations seldom hide their philanthropic light under a bushel," he said, "and it is no accident that their contributions committees usually include the director of public relations."[19] But even as this highly publicized beneficence burgeoned, business lent only limited support to the national health charities. Corporate PR and marketing planners had yet to tap the enormous potential of those fundraising drives.[20]

Then in the 1970s as public opinion turned against corporations and disability-related telethons went national, public relations strategists hit on cause-related marketing to help refurbish corporations' and corporate executives' images. This development was part of a larger, long-term, late-twentieth-century transformation in corporate decision making about charitable giving. In earlier years, presidents of privately owned companies might make choices themselves based on personal concerns or in response to local pressures. But more and more, larger corporations established screening processes that carefully took into account public relations and marketing.[21]

Mobilizing the rhetoric of business philanthropy, executives on telethons described this strategy as good corporate citizenship. The president of PayLess Drugstores might have been speaking for all business leaders on all telethons when he told the UCP audience: "Being a responsible corporate citizen is very important to us at PayLess Drugstores. . . . Our company mission statement . . . states that we are committed to being partners with our customers in the life of their communities. . . . Our store personnel [work] together with local UCP staff and volunteers to generate funds and programs and support for people with cerebral palsy" so that they "can become full participants in their communities."[22] Amway Corporation Chairman Jay Van Andel ended an Easter Seals pitch: "Amway distributors are good citizens. They're neighbors who are concerned with their community's needs." "Amway," concluded the narrator, "we're your neighbors and your friends."[23] An Anheuser-Busch commercial linked to the MDA Telethon declared that corporation "glad to be your neighbor, proud to be your friend."[24] Telethons allowed big business to take credit for helping those socially invalidated by disability become fully legitimate citizens. At the same time, this community service revalidated the public identities of the companies as responsible contributors to the well-being of American families and communities.[25]

Corporate donations also enabled executives to serve as personal models of responsible citizenship for average Americans. Business patriarchs exhorted ordinary folks to follow their lead. "During this telethon," said Hearst Corporation President and CEO Frank Bennack, "my colleagues from each of the Hearst operating groups . . . have made pledges to United Cerebral Palsy totaling $400,000. Now we're asking for your donation."[26] Citgo Oil President Ron Hall reported, "I'm asked frequently by people, 'Why does [sic] Citgo, its employees, and its customers get so deeply involved in MDA?' And that's kind of an odd question. ... But in the final analysis, really, what it is, it's just the right thing to do." He believed that the people watching would help Jerry Lewis go $1 above last year because they too knew it was the right thing to do.[27] Amway President Rich De Vos and Chairman Van Andel played the role of moral preceptors for Easter Seals. "It's the collective effort of all of us that brings about a positive change of benefit to people," preached Van Andel. "It takes more than what large corporations could do. Everyone's help is needed." "And this is the kind of cause that needs to be on the heart of everyone," opined De Vos.[28] Telethons enabled corporate executives, like Van Andel and De Vos, Hall and Bennack, to present themselves as practitioners of good corporate citizenship and don the mantle of community moral leadership.[29]

Telethon-based cause-related marketing also helped combat public cynicism about business leaders by making the corporate elites seem more human. The charity shows gave them positive visibility as friendly figures. Individual CEOs and vice presidents became featured performers on the telethons—not household names, but familiar faces. Joshing with Jerry Lewis on Labor Day or with Pat Boone on the Easter Seals telecast, they showed that they were, after all, regular guys. Lewis would talk about the times he spent with them, at their headquarters, conventions, and "pump-up meetings." Over the years, they cultivated the image of their relationships as personal friendships rather than business associations. Accepting the final $1 million check from Citgo President Hall, Lewis said, "Thank you, Ron," hugged him, and assured, "I'll be with you in October."[30] During a UCP Telethon, Frank Hickingbotham, the founder of TCBY [The Country's Best Yogurt] Enterprises, stood next to

Santa Claus and looked down at a girl with cerebral palsy.[31] The bonhomie was in one way an anointing. The celebrity hosts transmitted some of their own public good will to the business chieftains. Their ritual task was to confirm the executives' humanity. Lewis enlightened his 1976 audience about that fact. "You often hear people wondering . . . if corporation executives are really human up there in their ivory towers," he said. "Well, I've gotten to know these people, and lemme tell you—these *big corporation executives* are nothing but marshmallow pussycats. Pushovers."[32]

Telethons were especially useful in recasting public perceptions because cynicism about business leaders ran deeper among women than men, while women—mothers and grandmothers—were a disproportionate share of telethon audiences and donors.[33] The shows invented a powerful family icon: a disabled child dependent on the strength, compassion, and generosity of a male business executive. Rarely were these corporate patriarchs shown meeting adults with disabilities who might have been or become their employees or colleagues. Instead, telethons displayed poster children alongside corporate bosses who played the role of surrogate fathers.[34]

The image of a disabled child cared for by a business patriarch promoted the idea that executives and their companies upheld family values. Each charity reinforced that message by gathering around a corporate family. "The partnership that's been formed with TCBY and UCP is more than a partnership," said the director of UCP of Central Arkansas. "It's an expansion of a family."[35] Electronics manufacturer JVC felt "proud to be a member of the MDA family," announced its executive vice president, while American Airlines' vice president of marketing planning said that his company took pride in belonging to the Easter Seals "family of sponsors."[36] UCP host Dennis James summed it up: "You know, over the years it's been my pleasure to introduce the presidents of some of America's leading corporations. They've all been part of the UCP corporate family. Now you might think that the words 'corporate' and 'family' contradict each other, but from our experience, nothing could be further from the truth. The corporations you've seen on this show represent the best in family values America has to offer."[37]

Not only did the corporations belong to telethon "families," they were "families" themselves. Eugene Freedman, head of Enesco Corporation, a maker of gifts and home decor, appeared annually on the Easter Seals show as patriarch of "the Enesco family." He declared their pride in supporting Easter Seals because Enesco based itself on the "values of family and home."[38] The MDA Telethon featured representatives of "the Anheuser-Busch family," "the Harley-Davidson family," and other corporate "families." Miller Brewing, one of UCP's biggest corporate sponsors, was able to deliver its 1993 contribution through "the combined commitment and dedication of the entire Miller family," which embraced "distributors, store managers, bartenders, and consumers." As families, members of telethon families, upholders of family values, these businesses sought to dispel their image as huge, impersonal, profit-driven corporations.

The icon of the disabled child dependent on a male business executive's paternal benevolence refuted the public's negative impression of corporations and corporate heads. "We're here to help your kids," the executives would assure Jerry Lewis. Unacknowledged were the ways in which "Jerry's" and the other telethons' "kids"—most of whom lacked even the basic health insurance enjoyed by the telethons' sponsors and guests—*helped* the bosses salvage their moral standing in the public mind. Disabled children provided occasions for businessmen to show that everyone had been wrong about them. Not greedy and grasping, they were "pushovers," "marshmallow pussycats," benign patriarchs. Like the transformed Scrooge, they became "second fathers" to Tiny Tim's siblings.[39] And, as we shall see, they helped with a company's bottom line.

Bring in the Green

Cause-related marketing did more than humanize business leaders and boost their moral stock. Even while telethons enabled executives to present themselves as caring people and their companies as responsible corporate citizens, it offered them strategies to boost profits. That was the other function—indeed, the main function—of cause-related marketing. It was strategic philanthropy, explained a guidebook on how to use the technique. "It happens to have a philanthropic result, but its primary purpose is *sales*."[40] As Sue Adkins, who published a book on the phenomenon in 1999, puts it, "Whatever Cause Related Marketing is, it is certainly not philanthropy nor is it altruism."[41]

On local telethon segments, most sponsors were small businesses. The shows shined special spotlights on them as well as individuals who gave in the few-hundred-dollar range. MDA called these donors "Star Patrons." Easter Seals put their names on "Angel Boards." The Arthritis Telethon recognized them through "VIP Salutes." Their names were affixed to gold or silver stars or angels or some other graphic image, then read on the air.[42] Promoting Easter Seals' "Angel Board" as a form of advertising, an LA host advised, "If I owned a business in this area, I would call in a $200 or more pledge right now. Get my name up here. Think of the advertising. You wear a white hat in the community because people know that you are helping Easter Seals ... $200 or more, we put your name up here. It stays up here eighteen hours. Think of all the publicity that your company will get."[43] Local small businesses saw the advantage. In 1991 the Easter Seals LA Angel Board bore the names of a flower shop, an office products firm, and two catering services, while MDA's 1992 Star Patron program in Los Angeles publicized a towing company, a print shop, a real estate broker, a moving and storage company, and a psychic.[44]

Telethon-based cause-related marketing could boost small businesses, but big companies benefited more. Charity professionals and corporate sponsors devised shrewd methods for showing that people with disabilities, especially children, could generate sales. Spokespersons for some of America's major companies—supermarket and convenience stores, pharmaceutical houses and brewing companies—plugged everything from root beer to laundry bleach to breakfast cereal to pain-relief ointment to laxatives to alcoholic beverages. Sometimes they promoted them while making their on-air pledges; other times they exploited tie-ins with stores and businesses.

Sales promotions tied to telethons proved an especially effective marketing tactic. To move charity-linked products, stores set up displays associating consumer goods with particular causes. The Arthritis Foundation arranged with two supermarket chains, Von's in California and Tom Thumb in Texas, to have special displays of products whose makers agreed to contribute to that charity.[45] MDA originated this promotional scheme in 1987 under the name "Aisles of Smiles." On the telethon's local segments, a list of participating stores scrolled on the left side of TV screens while designated products ran on the right. Each time customers bought one of the products, the manufacturer would contribute a percentage of the profit. MDA-connected displays showed Jerry Lewis holding each year's national poster child. He also appeared with that youngster on Aisles of Smiles TV commercials. In both media, he pleaded with shoppers to "help my kids" by buying the products he was plugging.[46]

The cable TV industry came up with a promotion called "Cable Cares about Jerry's Kids." Participating companies offered free installations or upgrades to anyone donating $5 to MDA. In the mid-1990s, Tele-Communications Inc. (TCI), the nation's largest cable company, became the most visible promoter—and beneficiary—of this scheme. Typical of cause-related marketing, TCI urged viewers to benefit themselves, too: "You'll get great entertainment. You'll be helping MDA."[47] "SAVE $30.00 ON CABLE TV INSTALLATION!" trumpeted a large newspaper ad. "Get Cable and Help Fight Muscular Dystrophy." The ad showed MDA's national poster child draped over Jerry Lewis's shoulders.[48]

All of the telethons also collaborated with manufacturers on coupon redemption programs. For instance, each year on the Sunday of the Easter Seals show, freestanding inserts in newspapers offered discount coupons on consumer products. In 1989 and 1990, a Lever Foods Division spokesman explained that his company would make a donation for every coupon redeemed. In 1991 Clorox tied in donations to coupon-related sales of Pine-Sol,

Tilex, Formula 409, and Soft Scrub. In 1995 the Sunday supplement contained coupons for Glade Air Freshener that would "help" the manufacturer donate $100,000 to Easter Seals. The inserts had photos of Pat Boone with the Easter Seals national child.[49]

Discount coupons, Aisles of Smiles, and other product tie-ins boosted sales. The companies drew their donations out of the additional revenue. Rather than contributing to the charities themselves, they took credit for money generated by consumer purchases. Moreover, they gave just a portion of that money. Passing on to the charities part of the increased profits, corporations pocketed the rest. That was how cause-related marketing worked. It offered what might be called "corporate image enhancement with a bottom line value."

And to top it off, the donations paid for airtime that was, in essence, another kind of commercial.[50] Some advertisers used the broadcasts to promote new products: Clorox linked the sales campaign for its "New Lemon Fresh Clorox Bleach" to the 1989 Easter Seals Telethon. A "Special Easter Seals Edition" freestanding newspaper insert included a discount coupon. A Clorox executive presented a check for $50,000, a contribution that bought commercial time to plug the company's product. Similarly, a Kellogg's vice president beat the drum for a new cereal,[51] while on the 1990 Arthritis Telethon, CIBA Consumer promoted coupons for its new pain relief ointment Eucalyptamint and returned with a hefty donation the following year "because our involvement with the Arthritis Foundation last year was a major reason behind the success of one of our new products."[52]

Ostensibly noncommercial shows, telethons understood and relied on savvy advertising practices linked to television as an increasingly influential medium. Programs were structured in a standard TV format: Entertainment tried to hold audiences long enough to expose them to advertising. Commercial telecasters' business was selling audiences to sponsors. They designed programs to attract certain types of viewers, to pull in preferred demographic groups. Programmers could then persuade advertisers to buy commercial time during the shows. For example, drug companies were major buyers of the Arthritis Foundation Telethon's advertising time, courting the niche demographic of seniors. Among other products, they peddled analgesics to the 37 million Americans with arthritis, many of whom were elderly. Corporate sponsors Ciba-Geigy and G.D. Searle, Pfizer, Smith Kline Beecham, and Upjohn, along with Lederle Laboratories and Wyeth-Ayerst, made the Arthritis Foundation program the telethon of the pharmaceutical giants. Many of these firms, along with more than 20,000 food and drug retailers, also participated in the annual Arthritis Foundation Telethon–connected "Help Is in Your Grasp" promotion.[53] It was an elder counterpart to MDA's "kids"-based "Aisles of Smiles."

The Arthritis Telethon's niche audience appealed to other corporate sponsors, including makers of some high-priced products such as Pacific Marquis hydrotherapy spas. In April and May of 1990, its dealers donated $100 from the proceeds of every sale to the Arthritis Foundation. A spokesman urged telethon viewers to visit a local dealer and pick up a brochure on the benefits of warm-water exercise, where, no doubt, a salesperson would try to sell them on contributing to the Arthritis Foundation by buying a spa. To demonstrate his company's support of the Foundation's work, he presented an initial check for $50,000, the cost of about fifteen spas. The telethon also welcomed the president of the National Pool and Spa Institute, an organization designed to promote and protect the industry. Its programs to inform consumers and educate industry members about the importance of warm-water exercise were, as he explained, strategies to boost sales. "The spa industry wins," he said, "because we are able to reach an expanded market. The person with arthritis wins because they are able to experience the benefits of warm-water therapy. And the Arthritis Foundation wins because it gets money for needed research." Then he presented a check for $96,000. Cohost Larry Van Nuys credited this donation to the 12,000 spa-business conventioneers he had met at the annual gathering in Houston. The $96,000 from 12,000 attendees averaged out to $8 apiece. The cheapest no-frills spa sold for around $3,500, $100 of which went to charity.[54]

Even alcoholic beverage makers got into the act. Using identical methods, competitors Miller Brewing and Anheuser-Busch raised funds for UCP and MDA, respectively. Each enlisted stores and taverns to sell paper emblems to customers. Miller peddled Christmas wreaths. Anheuser-Busch hawked St. Patrick's Day "Shamrocks for MDA." Customers signed their names on these paper tokens; the tavern or store posted them in a prominent place. Miller also sold "Big Bucks," paper deer antlers and noses that Miller imbibers wore to pose for snapshots that were then mounted in the places of business. A portion of the proceeds went to UCP or MDA in the names of Miller or Anheuser-Busch as well as their distributors, retailers, and customers, but the money came from the customers.[55]

In ads to consumers, the brewers touted telethon-related promotions as supporting medical research and treatment that would give children with disabilities socially valid identities. Budweiser TV spots run in the weeks before the MDA show urged consumers to buy Bud and "help Jerry's Kids just be kids." Meanwhile, Anheuser-Busch and Miller ads in beverage-industry periodicals told retailers that telethon-linked marketing would swell their sales. Miller counseled tavern keepers and store owners, "The Miller Advantage, Profit From It." An Anheuser-Busch trade magazine ad trumpeted the financial gain retailers would reap from the "Shamrocks" scheme: "BRING IN THE GREEN WITH AMERICA'S #1 FAMILY OF BEERS, America's Fastest Growing Brand Family."[56]

"A Cynical and Perverted Perspective"

Nonprofit charities engaging in cause-related marketing had to tread carefully. While offering their corporate sponsors means to boost sales, they needed to safeguard their own credibility with the public. The 1994 Arthritis Foundation telecast's end-credits posted a disclaimer: "The appearances or verbal mentions of companies supporting the Arthritis Foundation Telethon in no way imply product endorsement by the Arthritis Foundation." But the following year, the organization tried a new marketing ploy that did endorse a product, a strategic decision that embroiled it in controversy. It licensed its name to McNeil Consumer Products to market Arthritis Foundation Pain Reliever. It expected the plan to yield more than $1 million a year in royalties. *Advertising Age* said the arrangement was "the buzz" among health charities. The head of the Foundation called it "the prototype for future relationships between not-for-profit organizations and corporate America." Although experts on marketing and nonprofits warned that the organization might be jeopardizing its reputation, its president/CEO declared: "The not-for-profits who will thrive in the future are the ones who are innovative and take risks . . . and corporate America is waiting to help." But the risk-taking backfired. Critics charged the charity with compromising "its ability to provide objective advice on all forms of pain relief." They also called the ads misleading for implying that the analgesics were new and that the Foundation had helped develop them. When eighteen state governments threatened to sue McNeil, the company dropped the Arthritis Foundation–linked product line. But the Foundation remained open to other possible endorsements of products that would bring it corporate donations.[57]

The disconnect between cause-related marketing and a charitable message became especially apparent in 1993 when the Marin Institute for the Prevention of Alcohol and Other Drug Problems investigated the relationship between disability-related charities and the alcohol industry.[58] It also examined alcohol as a cause of impairment, along with alcohol abuse by people with disabilities. And it sought disability rights leaders' views about these matters. The nonprofit reported that alcohol consumption was a cause of congenital disabilities such as cerebral palsy, mental retardation, and fetal alcohol syndrome and a major cause of spinal cord and head injuries. Corroborating these findings, the Rehabilitation Institute of Chicago said that half of the 100,000 spinal cord injuries sustained annually in the United States occurred in alcohol-related incidents.[59]

The 1993 UCP Telethon acknowledged the link between alcohol use and cerebral palsy. Actresses Stephanie Hodge and Connie Sellecca talked about how to prevent congenital impairments. "We know many precautions an expectant mother can take to help prevent CP," explained Hodge, "such as staying away from alcohol, drugs and cigarettes." Sellecca, a new mother her-self, gave the same advice more pointedly to soon-to-be mothers: "If you're pregnant, don't smoke, don't drink alcohol, and refrain from all recreational drugs." Yet just minutes after Hodge delivered UCP's admonition, a Miller executive dispensed its contribution. Miller, a subsidiary of the tobacco-products giant Phillip Morris and a UCP corporate sponsor for eleven years, had handed UCP some $8 million collected from beer drinkers.[60]

Disability rights leaders interviewed by the Marin Institute felt more con-cerned about another alcohol-related problem. The incidence of alcohol and drug abuse was, by all accounts, significantly higher among people with dis-abilities than in the general population. The Resource Center on Substance Abuse Prevention and Disability estimated that between 15 and 30 percent of disabled people abused alcohol or other drugs, as compared to about 1 out of 10 nondisabled people.[61] And probably more than half of individuals with spinal cord or head injuries mishandled those substances. Disabled people were at greater risk for substance abuse, reported the Resource Center, because they often used alcohol and drugs as medications for chronic pain or to deal with "increased family life stress, fewer social supports, excess free time, and lack of access to appropriate substance abuse prevention resources." In addition, they endured higher rates of unemployment, poverty, and welfare dependency because of job discrimination and inaccessibility. Government policies also took away Medicaid health insurance if disabled adults earned even small incomes. Given this array of hazards, most of them socially constructed rather than inherent in a disability, alcohol and drug abuse among disabled people was predictable. Despite its extent, there was not enough research on this problem and too few counselors trained to deal with it. Both disability-focused organizations and substance abuse agencies commonly failed to provide appropriate services, while the latter were also often physically inaccessible.[62]

While most chose to ignore it, this situation disturbed at least one charity. Responding to the link between alcohol consumption and developmental dis-abilities, in 1991 Special Olympics International founders Eunice and Sargent Shriver compelled Special Olympics of Texas to end its relationship with Miller Brewing, a connection that had brought in a million dollars a year. But other charities refused to forego alcohol industry contributions even though they made up no more than 4 percent of total donations. "They need every cent, they say, to find a cure or treat the disease or offer support to families," reported the Marin Institute.[63]

Furthermore, charity executives told Marin investigators that "they never heard of alcohol being a problem among people with disabilities."[64] Advocates scorned this admission as showing just how out of touch the charities were with disabled people's real problems. They condemned the link between the agencies and the beverage makers. Dr. Carol J. Gill of the University of Illinois, Chicago, said: "As a psychologist who has treated patients with disabilities,

I have seen a tremendous amount of alcohol and other drug abuse. To me, the alcohol companies are showing how enlightened and wonderful they are by donating to the charities to make up for the damage their product does. There is no way a health organization can accept profits from that industry without it being a real conflict of interest." Edward V. Roberts, an international disability rights leader and president of the World Institute on Disability in Oakland, California, agreed. "That these health charities would join with an industry that causes such problems among people with disabilities is morally wrong." He called the connection "unconscionable." "It might hurt [UCP and MDA] to refuse the money," he said, "but it wouldn't be the end of them."[65]

Charity professionals have tended to deny the possibility that their agencies have fostered alcohol abuse by people with disabilities. The National Multiple Sclerosis Society's public affairs director argued: "Taking money from an alcohol company isn't as if we're advocating abuse of any kind. Nor are we encouraging our constituency to drink."[66] UCP's executive director said that "because constituents [had] failed to bring alcohol problems to the attention of the affiliates, he [was] unaware of the problem."[67] But it was clear that alcohol abuse *was* a serious problem among people with disabilities. How would the charities address it? The MS Society's public affairs director replied inadequately that "as long as alcohol and tobacco are legal . . . the only effective way to prevention is to build self-esteem." UCP's chief responded even more feebly that his organization dealt with "the frustration that may cause over-consumption . . . by advocating for removal of architectural barriers."[68]

The charities and the manufacturers claimed they were not endorsing greater alcohol use. UCP's executive director did not think his organization was "encouraging the public to consume alcohol by the nature of our relationship with Miller Brewing." He admitted, though, that it probably helped "create for Miller a more positive image in the minds of the public." He said he opposed "point-of-sale advertising that link[ed] increased consumption and sales to increased donations to his charity." But in fact, displays in retail stores were integral to Miller's UCP-related promotions. One poster proclaimed: "A donation to United Cerebral Palsy will be made for every case of Miller brands purchased." Miller's "director of industry affairs" claimed that her company did not interpret its UCP case commitment program as persuading people to buy more alcohol. Likewise, Anheuser-Busch's vice president for consumer awareness and education maintained that "Shamrockin' for MDA" did not promote increased consumption, just the choice of Budweiser by beer shoppers.[69] The Marin Institute reported that "alcohol companies say that only the most cynical observer would accuse them of legitimizing their product through charities or encouraging consumption through their charity-related ads and promotions," with the Anheuser-Busch vice president calling the disabled activists' criticisms a "cynical and perverted perspective."[70]

The activists especially castigated the use of disabled children in charity-related alcohol ads, yet MDA's director of public affairs defended the practice. "More than 40 percent of those we serve are children," he said. "We do not use children. We present our constituency." He overlooked the fact that 6 out of 10 of those constituents were adults. Anthony Tusler, president of the Institute on Alcohol, Drugs and Disability, responded: "Children should never be used in advertisements by alcohol companies. It's illegal for them to drink and I believe the industry is hoping the imagery of the innocent child extends to the product, which is far from innocent in my community."[71]

Tusler and disabled sociologist Irving Kenneth Zola of Brandeis University summed up the general criticism: "The alcohol industry's attempt to deny its role in either producing disabling conditions or in compounding the harm to people with disabilities is unconscionable," adding: "It is hypocritical to claim to help people with disabilities while at the same time promoting a product that causes so many problems."[72]

In condemning the disability charities–alcohol industry alliance, activists also challenged nondisabled control of the decision making and discourse that defined the identities, issues, and needs of disabled persons. "Many of the problems outlined would be solved if people with disabilities were included in decisions about their own destiny," contended Zola and Tusler. "It is unfortunate," added Tusler, "that we cannot copyright our images and identities and license them to whom we choose."[73]

Fair Weather Friends

Cause-related marketing involved more than maudlin commercial exploitation. In deploying sentimentalized images of disabled children as part of a sales strategy, the corporations and the telethon-producing agencies redefined the meaning of marketing, consumption, and charity. They transformed product promotion from a profit-seeking stratagem into a philanthropic act. They conflated a corporation's merchandise and its very identity with charitable giving. As one executive noted, the scheme "positions the company as a caring corporation that's directly involved in the community." At the same time, this device boosted public awareness of the business and consumer recognition of its brands, which in turn increased sales.[74] Research bore out that cause-related marketing enhanced companies' images, differentiated theirs from competitors' products, encouraged consumers to switch brands, and fostered consumer loyalty. "The strength of [cause-related marketing] over more traditional forms of marketing," explained one expert, "is that it can provide the emotional as well as the rational engagement of the consumer. It engages the consumer's heart as well as their mind, and thereby has the potential to build a much stronger and enduring relationship."[75] "In each case," suggested another observer, "an element of altruism appears to be wrapped inside an advantage to the business."[76] In fact, the arrangement was just the other way around. Cause-related marketers used an altruistic wrapping to disguise an advantage-seeking business maneuver.[77]

Such an approach also exposed a perennial problem in the American system of private charity fundraising. It made support for particular social needs dependent on an agency's success in gaining public visibility. In this case, visibility referred to the marketability of the link between a cause and a company's products. Marketability also meant that corporate sponsors would support a charity only as long as the connection offered a competitive edge. Once the sales value of the charity tie-in disappeared, a company's sponsorship stopped. Corporate altruism was contingent on commercial advantage.[78]

Furthermore, whether the emotions evoked were cloying sentimentality or genuine human empathy, those feelings were made into marketing tools. Philanthropy itself was sold as a commodity. Compassion and charitable giving were melded with, indeed they were made indistinguishable from, eating breakfast cereal, buying video cassette players, or drinking beer. A McDonald's public relations executive put it plainly, "People don't mind feeling good about corporations. And where the product and the price choice are similar, people will be influenced by . . . the image of the company."[79] Here, ambivalence about charity and ambivalence about unsavory profit motives could cancel one another out to produce what appeared to be pure generosity without corporations having to make sacrifices.

It was understandable then that "some corporate sponsors got a little nervous" about rumors in the late 1980s and early 1990s that the telethons were on their way out. The *Los Angeles Times* reported in 1992 that "telethons need the largest possible audience, not only to attract pledges, but also to keep corporate sponsors happy. Beyond altruistic motives, corporate sponsors appreciate the exposure they get from making donations during telethons." "The telethon is more or less a thankyou [*sic*] vehicle [for business supporters] these days," reported a UCP of San Diego official.[80] That was a bit of an understatement. In fact, the companies pressed the charities to keep the shows going even though the shrinking audience meant their effectiveness in raising funds was on the wane. Former executives at two of the charities confidentially disclosed that their telethons lasted as long as they did only at the corporate sponsors' insistence.[81]

By the late 1990s, most of the disability telethons were passing from the American scene as mechanisms of cause-related marketing. Broadcasting costs had become prohibitive in many TV markets. The Arthritis Foundation, Easter Seals, and UCP Telethons all disappeared. But their demise did not mean the death of cause-related marketing. In October 2000 the keynote speaker at the Public Relations World Congress in Chicago restated the stratagem's benefits. Reynold Levy, professor at both the Harvard Business School and the Columbia School of Business, spoke on "This Business of Giving—and Taking." He made the obligatory nod to ethics and compassion: Corporate philanthropy was "the right thing to do." But then he got to the meat of the matter: It built brand loyalty, constituent support, and employee morale. "In short, corporate philanthropy can help win friends and influence people," he advised. "Contributing to nonprofits strengthens the donor as much as the donee. Philanthropy can be no less than a source of sustainable, competitive advantage."[82]

Having helped formulate those precepts, the disability charities did not forget them. With or without telethons, they offered their clients to corporate sponsors as cause-related marketing vehicles. Jerry Lewis noted the reciprocal advantages the corporations and the charities supplied each other. "They've got a good thing with us, and we've got a good thing with them."[83] "The sponsors," he asserted, "are here because they love what I'm doing for my kids. But the sponsors would also like you to know that they're human beings with feelings. And if you're going to buy their products, what the hell is wrong with that? That's good. It's good business."[84]

Telethon-based cause-related marketing propagated several interlocking images of people with disabilities. They were passive objects of charity. They were child recipients of patriarchal business benevolence. They were commodities that enhanced corporate images while boosting sales. As we shall see, for many people with disabilities, those images became part of their social identities. Ironically, these same images and roles were mobilized to reassure Americans, in general, that they had not forsaken their commitments to civic virtue and community.

Givers and Takers

CONSPICUOUS CONTRIBUTION AND A DISTINCTLY AMERICAN MORAL COMMUNITY

The president of one firefighters association laid down the ground rules for the MDA audience: "There are givers and there's takers in this world. Firefighters are givers. All those people who can hear me out there can be givers too."[1] This differentiation, which recurred on all telethons, was more than a ploy to prod donations. It drew an important moral boundary. It contrasted humane concern for one's neighbors with selfish preoccupation with one's private interests. It distinguished those who shouldered responsibility for the civic welfare from those who shirked those obligations. This marking off of givers and takers was a central symbolic task of telethons.

But as they drew that dichotomy, telethons ritualistically defined not just two, but three types of persons. There were not only givers and takers. It was necessary that there also be recipients of the giving, objects of the benevolence. Invention of the third category was indispensable to maintenance of the distinction between the first two. As with other framings, this one significantly shaped the social identities of people with disabilities.

As this chapter will show, in contriving that tripartite division, the disability-related charities modernized a Western charity tradition at least two millennia old. Its American version can be traced back to both hallowed religious sources and early modern US republican ideology. In the fashion of that tradition, telethons ritualistically used people with illnesses and disabilities to effect the spiritual redemption, moral restoration, and social elevation of their benefactors. At the same time, they attempted to resolve a number of ongoing dilemmas within American culture, predicaments that seemed particularly acute in the late twentieth century. One major task of these televised ceremonies was to restore a sense of American moral community.

Narcissism and Its Discontents

Beginning with the Revolution, the founding moment when they set into orbit the constellation of values that composed their cultural universe, Americans declared individuals' right to pursue their personal happiness, their private interests. The dynamic of individualism was one of the most powerful forces shaping their culture and society, for good and ill. It claimed for each citizen the twin rights to equality of opportunity and equality of esteem. Yet it also often seemed to many Americans to weaken the bonds of their community. From the beginning, they feared the centrifugal effects of that ethos. Their celebration of the value of the individual along with their liberation of individual potentialities simultaneously gave rein to privatistic and self-centered impulses. As American society emancipated its members to affirm the value and validity of their unique selves and advance their personal welfare, it also implicitly permitted them to ignore the public weal—and feel justified in doing so.[2]

In response to this social, political, and moral peril, many Americans throughout their nation's history warned themselves that their democratic experiment rested on the public virtue of the people at large. If citizens voluntarily put the common good above their private interests, free society would flourish. But if they set selfish concerns ahead of the general welfare, their society and polity would fail. The Revolution's ideology affirmed that all human beings had both an innate capacity for benevolence and a propensity toward benevolent action. The founding generation counted on those impulses to curb individuals' selfish tendencies and harmonize a community increasingly driven by capitalist competition. Benevolence was also foundational to their political and ethical thought. It and the closely related traits of sociability and reasonableness grounded the capacity for self-government in human nature. Within this ideology, individual acts of charity were at one and the same time practice in civic virtue and a warranty that Americans still possessed the moral traits necessary to their social, economic, and political order.[3] However, the matter was not settled: Those proofs of benevolence and public virtue continued to operate in tension with habits of self-centered individualism.[4]

A generation after the Revolution, the astute French visitor Alexis de Tocqueville saw a threat to American democracy in the individualism it brought forth. "There are more and more people," he reported, "who, though neither rich nor powerful enough to have much hold over others, have gained or kept enough wealth and enough understanding to look after their own needs. Such folk owe no man anything and hardly expect anything from anybody. They form the habit of thinking of themselves in isolation and imagine that their whole destiny is in their hands." These democratic individualists, he said, not only forgot both their ancestors and their descendants but also separated themselves from their contemporaries. "Each man is forever thrown back on himself alone, and there is danger that he may be shut up in the solitude of his own heart." To Tocqueville, self-isolation endangered the viability of free society by undermining individuals' capacity to function as other-regarding citizens. Meanwhile, the increasingly harsh commercial economy pitted individuals against one another in ferocious competition. The erosion of mutuality, warned Tocqueville, could render Americans powerless to oppose potentially despotic political forces. But, he announced, Americans had available a corrective to this antisocial absorption in private pursuits. It was the enlarging experience of involvement in America's rich array of civic associations, that is, charities.[5] Many Americans then and later endorsed this prescription. The antidote to selfish individualism, they believed, was civic-minded volunteerism and benevolence.

Yet even in the first half of the nineteenth century—the historical moment when Tocqueville and others prescribed this remedy—some critics charged that American voluntary benevolence had gone wrong. They condemned the forerunners of modern professional charities—national benevolent societies based in the Northeast that fought for issues like temperance reform, upright living, and other moral causes—as impersonal fundraising machines. They scorned organized mass charity that constituted a philanthropic equivalent to the emerging, ever-enlarging business corporations and mass, profession-alized political parties. All of these institutions, they lamented, displaced the personal connections essential to authentic community.[6]

In later historical moments when self-centered, rather than public-minded, individualism seemingly overtook their society, some Americans warned their fellow citizens—and themselves—of the imperative to practice public virtue. That sense of alarm became acute in the latter decades of the twentieth century as personal self-maximization seemed to become many Americans' credo. As noted in chapter 1, opinion surveys found that most Americans thought their society was in general selfish and becoming more so. Compassion, they felt, was the exception, not the rule.[7] Social critics charged that American culture trained individuals to aggrandize themselves in disregard of authentic attachments and at the expense of others. Some criticized capitalism for teaching that self-realization came through consumption. "Capitalism tells us that the meaningful life is the life that maximizes the self," wrote psychoanalyst Joel Kovel. "Whatever is 'me' has more, does more, achieves more; such is the good life, whether measured in terms of compact discs, muscles, orgasms, publicity, or cash."[8] Historian Christopher Lasch dissected a "culture of narcissism" whose members were disconnected from their past, disinterested in their posterity, and incapable of authentic development of their selves because they were incapacitated for genuine community.[9]

In *Habits of the Heart: Individualism and Commitment in American Life*, a study based on surveys and interviews conducted in the late 1970s and early 1980s, sociologist Robert N. Bellah and his associates described a society strangely different from "most societies in world history." In other societies, individuals found the meaning of their lives largely through relationships—to their parents and children, to local communities situated in particular geographical and cultural places, to a historical past and the historical future of their posterity. But in late-twentieth-century America, individuals were taught that they needed to break "free from family, community, and inherited ideas." They "must leave home, find their own way religiously and ideologically, support themselves, and find their own peer group." They were expected to fashion themselves, to become their own persons, "almost to give birth" to themselves. Some highly individuated Americans even found the relation between parents and children "anomalous . . . for the biologically normal dependence of children on adults is perceived as morally abnormal." At the same time, aging parents often dreaded any dependency on their adult children. Americans who saw themselves as self-made tended to overlook what they received from their parents and what they inherited from the past. Tocqueville's forecast "that Americans would come to forget their ancestors and their descendants" seemed to have come true. Unfortunately, observed Bellah and his associates, American culture did not offer "much guidance as to how to fill the contours of this autonomous, self-responsible self. . . ."[10]

Bellah's research team also discerned deep discontent with this way of life. Though many Americans had difficulty thinking positively about their own family ties, they often felt poignantly nostalgic for "the family." There was "tremendous nostalgia . . . for the idealized 'small town.'" All of this indicated that "however much Americans extol the autonomy and self-reliance of the individual, they do not imagine that a good life can be lived alone." Many tried to solve this problem by setting their private lives within "lifestyle enclaves." The trouble was that "whereas a community attempts to be an inclusive whole, celebrating the interdependence of public and private life and of the different callings of all, lifestyle is fundamentally segmental and celebrates the narcissism of similarity." Lifestyle enclaves took various forms. Suburbs were no longer communities in the same way that small towns once had been. Suburban tracts became residential enclaves in which individuals pursued private lifestyles in the company of other individuals who shared those choices. Even marriage became a type of enclave. These were perhaps the inevitable social forms of private life in a radically individualizing society, but they also seemed to be a way for people who felt disconnected to seek support.[11]

Bellah and his colleagues interpreted "the wish for a harmonious community" as in part "a wish to transform the roughness of utilitarian dealings in the marketplace, the courts, and government administration into neighborly conciliation." But this, too, was a form of nostalgia, "belied by the strong focus of American individualism on economic success." "The real arbiters of living" were "not the practices of the town meeting or the fellowship of the church," but "the rules of the competitive market." On another level, the community many Americans longed for reached beyond such narrow and homogeneous confines. They yearned to locate their activities and themselves in morally meaningful ways within a broader pluralistic American community. But they achieved this only rarely and with difficulty because of "the cultural hegemony of the managerial and therapeutic ethos" that shaped contemporary life. The corporate and bureaucratic managerial system operated beyond the ken or control of local communities. The therapeutic culture upheld a permissiveness that undercut the quest for a larger meaning to individual lives formed within a historically continuous community. Together, managerialism and therapeutics promoted radical individuation and segmented living.[12]

More fearful diagnoses and fiercer jeremiads about the decline of American community and the decadence of American culture emerged in the culture wars that raged from the late 1980s into the next century. Commentators conservative and liberal warned of the chaotic consequences of radical individualism. Harvard University sociologist Robert Putnam summed up many of these anxieties in his essay and subsequent book *Bowling Alone* (1995, 2000). League bowling as a team sport had given way to individual bowling. Putnam took this displacement as symptomatic of a general distancing of Americans from one another. Just as growing numbers of affluent Americans were separating themselves within gated enclaves, many people of all social ranks "were turning inward and looking out for themselves," all while working longer hours, often at several jobs just to make ends meet. Summarizing Putnam's analysis, historian James T. Patterson concluded that "the American people, renowned for their voluntarism, were becoming more fragmented, isolated, and detached from community concerns." Patterson confirmed that many of the major voluntary associations had become "largely top-down, professionally managed organizations that relied on foundations, mass mailings, and manipulation of the media to amass financial resources." It seemed that "grass-roots, face-to-face meetings of concerned and unpaid local people who devoted time and effort in order to promote better communities" were in danger of disappearing.[13]

Challenges to this trend arose in many quarters. They came, explained Bellah's research team, not only from those left out of contemporary prosperity, but even from some of its beneficiaries who criticized its moral defects. Some critics clung "to the last vestiges of the autonomous community and its ideal of the independent citizen." Others labored "to transform the whole society, and particularly its economy, so that a more effectively functioning democracy may emerge." In either case, their resistance expressed "not only the discontents of the present economic and social order, but the persistence of "biblical and republican cultural traditions."[14] Those legacies held fast the old ideals of civic-mindedness and benevolence.

Invoking modern versions of those traditions, the professionals who managed the disability charities tapped into the values of civic-mindedness and benevolence to motivate volunteers and donors. Rather than challenging the dominant economic and cultural system, they fashioned telethons as rituals that promised to renew American moral community without questioning the existing order. And they did so by using the tools of mass media and corporate advancement.

Restoring Public Virtue

On one level of cultural meaning, telethon donation was a collective rite designed to enable Americans to demonstrate to themselves that they still belonged to a moral community, that they were givers who fulfilled their obligations to their neighbors.[15] The display of charity on television was a communal response to the moral and social dangers of narcissism. Americans could use donation to reassure themselves of their individual and collective moral and social health. As with Ebenezer Scrooge, Dickens's symbol of rapacious nineteenth-century capitalism, aiding Tiny Tim, the embodiment of neglected human need, telethon poster children were made the means by which donors could prove that an egocentric and consumerist capitalist order had not corrupted them. The television ritual defined people with disabilities as dependent on the moral fitness of their benefactors. While takers repudiated their duty toward "the less fortunate," givers' compassion verified their moral standing by distinguishing them from both takers and those socially invalidated by disability. Telethons attested to the persistence of benevolence and public virtue through a ritualistic reversal of everyday reality. The ceremonial antidote to conspicuous consumption was conspicuous contribution.

The telethon ritual also proclaimed as an important fact that givers practiced their virtue voluntarily. This liturgy upheld the dogma that voluntarism, the decisions of individuals, freely and privately made, verified the reality of public virtue. Voluntarism reassured Americans of the viability of their democratic political order and the moral validity of their capitalist economic system. They defined these putatively free choices of each particular donor to give for the common good as more laudable than a collective decision to provide for that common good by taxing themselves. Western Europeans' communal commitments to comprehensive national social welfare systems implicitly seemed to many Americans not only politically undesirable but also morally suspect. Although those policies ensuring the well-being of the whole community were less expensive than the US private corporate system, many Americans scorned them as state intrusion. Always ambivalent about the role of the state, Americans expected their government "to promote the general welfare," but gauged the moral condition of their community by the volume of their individual donations to private charities. Private charitable donation and individual community volunteerism were the measures of American civic virtue.[16]

Participants in the telethon ritual, playing the role of moral leader, spelled out the message: charitable giving vindicated the moral superiority of American voluntarism and volunteerism. In 1994 Easter Seals cohost Robb Weller introduced someone who literally embodied American values, "the stunning young woman who will be representing the United States at the Miss Universe pageant . . . Miss U.S.A." Offering "some patriotic words about Easter Seals," Miss U.S.A. delivered this homily:

> Easter Seals typifies what America is all about: hard work, independence, and generosity. Generosity fills the heart of America, because when tragedy strikes, from Mississippi floods to California earthquakes, we Americans come together in the spirit of volunteerism, willing to give whatever we can to help our neighbors get back on their feet. But smaller tragedies happen everyday. An auto accident costs a young mother her ability to walk. A stroke paralyzes a middle-aged father of three. A stray gunshot causes a high-school senior to lose her sight. . . . Easter Seals does all it can to help turn tragedy into triumph. So please, reach into your hearts and feel that truly American spirit of generosity.[17]

Charity volunteers' generosity, which signified their independent moral agency, aimed to restore the independence of those whose competency as moral agents was compromised by tragedies, limitations resulting from natural catastrophes, or physical disabilities. The capacity to function as a true American depended on physical and economic autonomy. Givers acted to revalidate fellow Americans rendered socially illegitimate by disability.

Walter Anderson, publisher of widely distributed *Parade* magazine, speaking off the cuff, put the telethon lesson to the MDA audience. "Only this nation on this earth does volunteerism to this degree, that we care about one another. It's part of our uniqueness, that it matters, that we step forward. ... Also, if you want to feel patriotic, do it"—that is, pledge—"because a good American does that."[18] On the Arthritis Foundation's 1988 Telethon, radio personality Larry Van Nuys reinforced this jingoistic belief. "You won't see telethons in any other country," he claimed. "But America is unique in that way. Americans are wonderful and giving. ... I count on people coming through when it's really needed. ... If we haven't moved you during this telethon yet, maybe you're not going to be moved. I'd like to think that you're someone who will be moved if given the facts, and you've got 'em." This claim was false: Jerry Lewis launched his first telethon outside the United States in 1987.[19]

Organized charitable giving had long functioned to bolster patriotic Americanism.[20] It helped to renew or generate a sense of community among America's diverse ethnocultural and religious groups and socioeconomic classes.[21] In one sense, the glue that held Americans together was shared allegiance to what many regarded as a distinctive set of American values. The telethon ritual fortified that belief by marking off individuals who practiced those values from those who did not. It distinguished good, which was to say authentic, Americans from both bad ones and delegitimated ones, that is, takers and those invalidated by disability.

Telethons sometimes convoked themselves as nationalistic ceremonies by stirring viewers with patriotic anthems. In 1986 the short-lived March of Dimes Telethon kicked off with stage-performer Ben Vereen's "song and dance tribute" to the Statue of Liberty, filmed aboard a ship in New York Harbor.[22] On the 1990 MDA extravaganza, live on stage, the venerable pop singer Ray Charles trumpeted "America the Beautiful" while his young counterpart Michael Bolton, on tape at (perhaps predictably) a softball game, unfurled the "Star-Spangled Banner." The patriotic fervor became especially prominent during the Persian Gulf War. On the UCP's annual telecast in 1991, opera star Robert Merrill and the American Pilgrim Chorus offered a medley of patriotic songs that included "America the Beautiful" and "God Bless America." A few minutes afterward, that nationalistically named choir intoned, "This Is My Country." Several weeks later, the Easter Seals fundraiser featured pop singer Bobby Vinton declaring, "I'm Proud to Be an American."

Telethons not only incorporated features of a patriotic rally, they exhibited elements of a religious ceremony. Comparable to religious worship, they sought to mobilize spiritual power to achieve desired transformations of condition in a human community—to prevent threatening occurrences or reverse harmful ones. Telethons were rituals of redemption. Most obviously, they professed to ransom individuals invalidated by disability by not only rehabilitating them physically but also restoring them socially. Perhaps less apparent but just as important, they also redeemed takers, remaking them into socially and morally responsible givers.[23]

Telethon religiosity claimed to effect extraordinary transformations in the lives of the socially invalidated. A 7-Eleven store banner pleaded: "Make a Miracle for Jerry's Kids."[24] An Easter Seals host promised listeners that their pledges would "help produce miracles," and an Easter Seals announcer said of a little girl: "Taking her first steps with crutches is a small miracle."[25] "It is said that faith can move mountains," reminded a guest star reading UCP's teleprompter. "Well, we may not see mountains move on this show, but we will witness the power of faith. ... If the miracle of UCP is to continue, it needs your support. Please help people with CP keep the faith with a phone call and a pledge."[26]

Telethon rituals used prayerful songs to express the protective power of the charity-based faith. They appropriated traditional hymns: "Amazing Grace," "I Come to the Garden," "The Lord's Prayer." Jerry Lewis made the spiritually ersatz "You'll Never Walk Alone" an anthem for the annual MDA Telethons. Meanwhile, Pat Boone at the Easter Seals ceremony and actress Ann Jillian on the UCP show both sang the same pseudo-religious pop tune, "I Believe." These counterfeit hymns exemplified the secularized religiosity of late-twentieth-century American culture. The emptiness of their lyrics allowed listeners to fill them with whatever faith or source of hope the hearer brought to the song. They glibly reaffirmed Americans' insistence on happy endings. Their performance on the telethons comfortably reassured potential givers that those who kept faith with an American moral community would be preserved by some sort of unspecific providence, an amorphous higher power.

Religious rituals also often involve sacrifices. A priest conducts a ceremony of redemption that requires an actual or symbolic death. The orthodox version of telethon worship redeemed communicants through the ritualistic self-sacrifice of a priest who seemed ready to lay down his life for both the in-valid who needed physical and social healing and the socially valid who nonetheless stood condemned for their hardness of heart.

Thus, in an age of increasingly lax practice, only Jerry Lewis hewed to the pure and original faith. "You've seen other telethons where the host goes to sleep at midnight and comes back at ten in the morning refreshed," Lewis said scornfully in 1989. "That's not a telethon. You're supposed to be there and let your audience wonder whether you're gonna make it or not." "If I lose my throat in the twelfth hour," he vowed, "I'll go like a bastard for the next twelve. If it happens, it happens. If I get hurt—you know, what do we do if I get hurt in the fourth hour, if I fall into the pit? You can bet your ass that the show will go on, and I'll be there. I may be sitting. I may be in a cast, but nothing's gonna stop me from finishing it."[27] In December 1982 Lewis almost died of a heart attack. In fact, as he described it, he did die—and was resurrected. "I virtually died and they brought me back to life." His heart had stopped for five seconds.[28] Overlooking health and lifestyle factors that may have contributed to the heart attack, Lewis's rhetoric emphasized his sacrificial dedication to dying youngsters, some of whom, he was told, stayed alive only because of him and just long enough to bid him farewell.[29] "What probably put me in that hospital . . . was saying goodbye to those little giants," he asserted.[30] And if he did die, MDA should "Turn me into a theatrical martyr." The charity should "beg the people to give in his memory." It should proclaim: "Look at how much he gave; it probably killed him."[31]

But in the 1990s, as his health declined, Lewis did leave the stage frequently. No doubt like some of his disabled guests, he sensibly tried to conserve his energy for the important tasks in his life. He needed to rest, as did his aging announcer and sidekick Ed McMahon. So during the overnight hours, Lewis appeared on tape or substitute hosts filled in for him and McMahon. Still later, as Lewis became even more ill, increasingly bloated from medications, chronically in pain, unable to stand for long periods, audiences might indeed wonder if he was "going to make it."[32]

Thus, Lewis's physically grueling performance in earlier years was not simply mere showmanship. It was a form of religious ritual in which he was both high priest and symbolic sacrificial lamb. He mediated redemption through his own body. The host symbolically took on the suffering of the invalidated he would make whole while risking his life. In this ceremonial act, he stood in for nondisabled worshipers. By pledging donations, they partook of his vicarious sacrifice and thereby renewed their sense of moral wholeness, of benevolence and civic-mindedness. Through him, they purchased a sense of membership in a moral community many Americans feared was disintegrating.[33]

Other telethon MCs might not engage in marathon self-flagellation, but they did entreat viewers to join in the collective rite of expiation: Dennis James once admonished the UCP audience: "Sometimes we get to a point like this where I've got to be your conscience. I've been saying that now for forty-three years on this telethon. I've got to be your conscience."[34] Local hosts occasionally commanded phone answerers to stand until their phones rang. The hosts pressed watchers to call in so that the operators could sit down.[35] On one Easter Seals telethon, a local host harangued viewers like a tent-meeting preacher, exhorting them for several minutes at the top of her voice to call in pledges. Some of the operators whose phones were silent clapped in unison as one of the male hosts also began preaching. The two pled simultaneously: "We've got to do it! I know you can do it! I know we can do it! I believe!"[36]

The annual increase in telethon donations was taken as another sign of the maintenance of public virtue. Each year the MCs pressed viewers to help them top last year's total. "We have no goal," affirmed Dennis James on the UCP show. Then he announced their goal. "We want to make as much or more than we made last year." "No telethon has ever gone lower than the year before," he explained significantly. "That's our measure of success. So I know that you're not going to let us down."[37] Jerry Lewis agreed. He perennially declared his intention to get at least one dollar above the year before.

If the final total dropped, it would evidence a decline in benevolence and civic-mindedness. Americans were legendary scorekeepers. They rated everything they did with numerical records. They measured their achievements by the stats. MCs noted that many pledge-makers liked to phone in near the end of these protracted telecasts.[38] Telethon donation thus became a kind of competition, a sport, a game of reaching a new statistical high point. Were Americans more caring or less? More compassionate or more selfish? The figures flashing on the electronic tote boards would tell the tale of success or failure, of moral improvement or decline. Everyone was reassured when the telethons' final totals invariably rose above last year's pledges.

Like the rising donations numbers, the scripts guiding the hosts served to reassure viewers that Americans still loved one another, still sacrificed for "the less fortunate" and the common good. "The generosity we're seeing tonight again proves that Americans are loving caring people," affirmed John Ritter on the UCP rally. "Let's see how loving, how caring," urged cohost Henry Winkler. "Let's see the results." The two turned to the tote board.[39] "We are a marvelous country of terrific people," declared Jerry Lewis, pointing to *his* telethon's tote board. "Proof positive. People that care."[40] At the wrap-up of one UCP telethon, singer-actor Florence Henderson read: "You know, I never cease to marvel at the warmth and generosity of the American people. And these are not easy times financially. We all know that. Yet year after year Star-athon reinforces my faith, and I know all of us, all our faiths [*sic*], in the American spirit." Dennis James continued the thought: "I really believe that America's embarking, people, on a new era of giving something back to our country." This year, he added, the telethon would "go over the top."[41] The script read by UCP national cohost Nancy Dussault summed it up: "If we look at the headlines today, we are misled to believe that America is a nation of heartless, uncaring cynics. Nothing could be farther from the truth."[42]

The entertainment on the telethons reflected the desire to rebuild the American community. Critics snickered that the parade of veteran singers, standup comics, and novelty acts brought back not only the TV variety show but even vaudeville from the previous century. By the end of the telethon era, the performers served as a source of mockery mixed with nostalgia.[43] But the disdainful commentators usually failed to see that the resurrection of dated acts reflected the yearning of many viewers for the community they believed Americans once shared. These critics overlooked the correlation between the array of acts and the longing for a bygone America.

Washington Post television critic Tom Shales exemplified both the jibing and the longing. "The show itself," wrote Shales of one of the later MDA broadcasts, "was another triumphantly campy pageant—comics, magicians, cheerleaders, tap dancers, impressionists, Vegas-style singers in shiny tuxedos, even 'the Dancing Dads of Peoria, Ariz.' One could feel truly teleported in time, as if show business had been stopped and frozen in 1962. Out from the wings they came—all the performers, minor and major, who wait in the wings for what we used to consider 'entertainment' to make a comeback. And once a year, on Labor Day, it does. . . . Vaudeville rises from the grave, sparkling and glistening and shimmering in the light."[44]

In the end, Shales himself succumbed to that sentimental fantasy. As with so many derisive observers, his smirk gave way to a lump in his throat. "You could not be unmoved," he claimed. The dated but earnest

performances carried him—and, one presumes, many of those grandmothers and other viewers—back to an America they remembered as less
self-centered, less caustic, less disillusioned. "It doesn't matter that some,
even many, of the showbiz acts on the telethon are mediocre," he insisted,
"and it certainly doesn't matter that some seem to be from another time
(in many cases, a better time). What really matters," he concluded with
freshly burnished moralism, "is how hard they're trying to be good for
Jerry and his 'kids.'" His blasé condescension melted into wistfulness for
a less wised-up era. Small-timer or star, has-been or headliner, all of the
entertainers could serve as moral exemplars from the old days, from that
"better time."[45]

The United States has been called "a nation with the soul of a church."[46]
Telethons were ceremonies of America's civic religion. They were, of course,
overtly patriotic, employing music as well as appeals to what was unique
about the USA. As allegories of cleansing and renewal, they symbolized individual and collective turning away from the self-absorption many believed
had undermined or ruptured the national community. Though they ostensibly sought the physical and social repair of those invalidated by disability,
they were, at least as important, rituals of moral restoration for nondisabled
communicants. They offered donors a momentary sense of wholeness within
a moral community. In the midst of what many Americans believed had
become a materialistic atomized society, telethons projected brief annual
apparitions of that community.

Dignity Thieves

GREED, GENEROSITY, AND OBJECTS OF CHARITY

Telethon fundraisers tainted the civic-mindedness they claimed to renew by promoting the materialism and self-centeredness they promised to exorcise. Even while they called on viewers' sympathy, they appealed to their avarice and self-aggrandizement. That solicitation strategy subverted the vaunted restoration of moral community. Conspicuous contribution also ritually resolved American dilemmas about class and social status by modernizing and democratizing the Western tradition of almsgiving. For more than two millennia, publicized acts of charity effected benefactors' social exaltation as well as their spiritual and moral redemption. In the process, this beneficence marked people with disabilities as the natural objects of charity. That framing prescribed the social role of charity recipient as one of their primary personas. In the late twentieth century, disability rights activists resisted imposition of that identity.

Giving Is Receiving

The telethon-producing charities originally strove to ensure the altruistic motivation of givers. In 1977 an MDA executive instructed district and regional telethon coordinators: "There should be no offering of 'merchandise' in return for pledges or contributions. . . ."[1] But by the late 1980s, in order to draw donations, all of the telethons were offering bonuses and discounts, prizes and gifts. As we've seen in relation to telethons and the concept of cause-related marketing, corporate sponsors promoted consumer products through sales linked to the charities. They told customers that pursuing their personal economic advantage would help the "less fortunate." An Easter Seals newspaper insert urged consumers to join self-interest to condescension: "Save up to $8.00 and help us open doors for special people."[2] Hungry viewers could get discounts on food. Little Caesar's Pizza pushed Easter Seals–linked coupons. "This is a great way for customers to save money on their favorite foods and help out this great cause," declared a spokesman.[3] Consumers not in the mood for pizza could get a $5 Wienerschnitzel coupon book if they gave Easter Seals a dollar. A San Francisco telethon host coined a sales slogan: "Eat a corn dog, help Easter Seals."[4] Telethons not only enabled businesses to gain under the guise of "helping" people with disabilities, they offered individual consumer-contributors that advantage, too.

For those not enticed by coupons, telethons dispensed prizes, "gifts," and even the opportunity to turn shopping into a form of charity. Easter Seals annually announced the winners of its telethon sweepstakes.[5] In 1993 MDA tried out its own "Watch & Win Sweepstakes," whose booty included a limited-edition watch, a family trip to any United Airlines Hawaiian or international destination, a Harley-Davidson motorcycle, and a 3-carat diamond bracelet. Local telethon segments for every cause delivered most of the prizes such as cookbooks, home team sports caps, celebrity-autographed items, phone carrier discounts, show tickets, flower bouquets, and much more.[6] Younger philanthropists could profit, too, as MDA's "hop-a-thons" enabled nondis-abled schoolchildren to earn prizes while they hopped "for those who can't." Schools that sponsored such events were rewarded with items like playground equipment.[7] Fusing conspicuous contribution with conspicuous consump-tion, charities even tried to lure in possible donors through shopping. For a limited time in 1991, purchases at Target stores with American Express credit cards brought Easter Seals a donation from both companies. "You can get something you want," said a Target executive, "and help someone else get something they need."[8] Consumers who bought things for themselves could cast those acquisitions as help to people in need.

With so many offers, the telethon-producing agencies trained givers to regard people with disabilities not only as objects of their charity but also the means of their material enrichment. The use of incentives—tickets and trips, big-league caps and big-screen TVs, and prizes to nondisabled kids who hopped for kids who couldn't—exposed a selfish motive behind the boasted altruism. It betrayed giving as another means of getting. Just as corpora-tions, assisted by the charities, used cause-related marketing to redefine mer-chandising as a form of philanthropy, the charities and the companies sold potential donors on the idea that consuming those same products expressed compassion. They made conspicuous contribution interchangeable with con-spicuous consumption. But that belied the claim that charitable donation proved the persistence of benevolence and public virtue. It subverted the tele-thon ritual's efficacy in renewing American moral community.[9]

Even when the incentive was nonmaterial, the motive for giving pro-moted throughout the telethon era was often self-centered. Jesus Christ taught: "When you give alms, sound no trumpet before you, as the hypocrites do . . . that they may be praised by men. . . . But when you give alms, do not let your left hand know what your right hand is doing, so that your alms may be in secret; and your Father who sees in secret will reward you."[10] Later, Andy Warhol foretold: "In the future everyone will be famous for 15 minutes."[11] Rather than follow the commandment of the Israelite teacher, telethons fulfilled the forecast of the American prophet.

Every donor got a shot of celebrity. The national and local telecasts paraded check presenters from labor unions and fraternal orders, schools and sororities, small businesses and large corporations. On national segments, corporate executives with oversized checks in tow were a common sight. Usually, they presented their donations in several installments rather than one lump sum. This made the giving even more conspicuous. Corporate heads and union chiefs also introduced employees, distributors, retailers, and rank-and-file members from around the country who racked up the most pledges. Local hosts called to center stage representatives of companies, agencies, and service organizations who explained how they had raised the funds and then presented their checks. Local donors pledging moderate amounts were guaranteed recognition through MDA's "Star Patrons," Easter Seals' "Angel Boards," or the Arthritis Foundation Telethon's "VIP salutes" and "Special Donors Screens." While MDA's San Jose host explained the Star Patron program, silver and gold stars were superimposed on the screen. Above the dollar value of each star was the phrase "Your Name Here."[12]

Even the smallest contributors got a few seconds of fame. Callers heard their names and the amounts they pledged read on the air or saw them roll across the bottom or top of the screen. The National Arthritis Foundation, MDA, and UCP hosts read pledge makers' names, giving their hometowns and the sums promised.[13] MDA's San Jose affiliate ran a banner: "If You Pledge $25 or More, Your Name Will Be Read in the Next Local Segment!"[14] Easter Seals' Chicago telecast made the same guarantee.[15] "Would you call now? We will read your name as fast as we possibly can." Alluding to the prescient Andy Warhol, MDA's San Jose host pointed out: "We often talk about people having their own fifteen minutes of glory. You can have a moment of glory if you make that telephone call right now."[16] As the phones rang, local MCs, grabbing handfuls of pledge cards, reeled off names and numbers: "Allen Baumann from West Covina, $25. Mr. and Mrs. Gibbs from Reseda, $50. Joseph Withers in Long Beach, $40." And on and on.[17]

In twentieth-century America, elements of traditional elitist charity were democratized, making their spiritual and social rewards available to people of all ranks. Age-old Jewish and Christian admonitions to give anonymously gave way to publicized donations. Beginning in the 1920s and 1930s, a new brand of professional fundraiser converted private and individual almsgiving into the business of public and mass charity. "What the scriptures had commanded to be done in secret," said one observer, "would before long be celebrated in public and shouted from the rooftops by a different name: philanthropy."[18] "And the shouting would in time become shrill and incessant as it sought billions of dollars for welfare needs," commented a historian of modern fundraising. "In this profound change from charity to public philanthropy the skilled fund raiser and his high-pressure methods played a key role."[19] Giving was made "a matter of published performance . . . a virtual private tax with social penalties." Publicity, as carrot and stick, as personal incentive, social reward, and communal coercion, was central to fundraising.[20]

From their beginning, telethons drew criticism for inviting donors to advertise their generosity.[21] Some Americans, clinging to the traditional moral economy, objected. Among them were Jewish immigrants who found conspicuous contribution a dismaying practice in the new land. A 1923 editorial in Chicago's *Sunday Jewish Courier* took the city's Jewish community to task for having adopted American ideas of charity. Entitled "Too Much Charity—Too Little Tzdokoh," it reminded readers that "*Tzdokoh* means to give anonymously; charity is a matter of publicity. . . . One can live in a large Jewish community in Europe for twenty years, and not hear a word about charity and institutions, but one can live no more than three days in a Jewish community in America without hearing a great to-do about charitable affairs, drives, institutions, etc."[22] Conspicuous contribution became so integral to telethons that one gift took Easter Seals' LA hosts by surprise. A caller wanted to donate $10,000. He came over to the studio and wrote a check, but said he preferred to remain unnamed. He wanted to be identified only as "a gentleman from the Philippines." The MCs marveled at this act of anonymous generosity.[23]

In the late twentieth century, Americans publicized their giving with earnest and unflagging energy. The donation by the Filipino gentleman was unusual because one aspect of immigrants' acculturation taught them to authenticate their "American" identities by highly public charitable donation. On the broadcasts and at fundraising events throughout the year, many Americans not only put their charitable activities on display, they also endlessly congratulated themselves on their generosity as they sought public credit for it. They proclaimed themselves, noted historian Robert Bremner, the most generous people in the history of the world.[24]

Status Mobility

Telethons paraded donors across their stages and proclaimed their names on the air partly because those rituals touched on dilemmas of fundamental concern to Americans. "Beginning in the so-called Age of Jackson," said historian David Brion Davis, "white Americans of diverse backgrounds have anxiously tried to cast off any characteristics identifying them as members of a 'lower' class, that is, a class lower than the one with which they identify, precisely because they have believed in America as a land of opportunity—a land in which no fixed barriers prevent one from acquiring the skills, tastes, and demeanor, as shown in one's behavior as a consumer, that denote success."[25] Practicing conspicuous consumption to demonstrate their upward mobility, Americans obscured class restrictions. As a corollary, conspicuous contribution also marked class standing while masking class distinctions.

Charitable giving to aid the "less fortunate" camouflaged social class and economic disadvantage with tales of personal misfortune. This fictionalization occurred where Americans least recognized it: in the stories they told about those who were sick or disabled. Because disease and disability seemed self-evidently physiological facts rather than sociological constructions, the socioeconomic disadvantages burdening sick or disabled individuals were viewed as natural, indeed inevitable, social outcomes of biological states of being. But much of what Americans thought of as the natural results of illness or injury were artifacts of cultural values, social arrangements, and public policies.[26] For example, guaranteeing comprehensive health insurance and health care as a social right could have prevented much of the financial and emotional devastation visited on American families, especially those including people with disabilities. The private charity system was not only inadequate to meet those needs. It sustained myths of personal misfortune and of the insignificance of class for Americans' lives.

Charity donation also fortified class boundaries by visibly symbolizing status. In the nineteenth and early twentieth centuries, elites used benevolence, philanthropy, and reform partly to sharpen their differences from those below them.[27] Disability-related charities continued this practice. The successful registered their status by giving to help the invalidated. They gave the most conspicuously at black-tie banquets honoring their own. The second largest MDA fundraising event after the telethon itself was the annual Mary and Harry Zimmerman Dinner in Nashville, Tennessee, sponsored by the Zimmerman-founded Service Merchandise Company. Various celebrities were given the Harry Zimmerman Award as those banquets raised millions of dollars. Each year's telethon featured a video report on the dinner.[28] Likewise, on the evening before each UCP Telethon, a dinner was held for VIPs. Throughout the telethon, MC Dennis James referred to the wealthy and important personages who attended those parties, naming bankers, philanthropists, and other notables. High-status donors' conspicuous charity charted America's hierarchy.[29]

Telethons diagramed the class system in other ways. Though the shows' MCs said that even the smallest pledges mattered, the extra attention given to "heavy hitters," as a Chicago Easter Seals host described them, indicated that some donors mattered more than others.[30] Instead of answering calls from pledge makers, corporate executive VIPs showed off their clout by making calls to friends and colleagues, soliciting larger donations, then reading the names and amounts on the air. "Business and community leaders" in MDA "lock-ups" strutted their status by phoning acquaintances to raise the $2500 that would bail them out.[31] This focus on "heavy hitters" not only verified their individual status, it also bolstered the ruling elite in general.[32]

Meanwhile, continuing a practice begun in nineteenth- and early-twentieth-century American and European charitable solicitation,[33] the telethon system urged average folks to identify with big givers by buying smaller scraps of the same status. UCP's New York segment featured a "Labor Cares" panel of union officers who read the names of donating individuals, union locals, and companies. It was the blue-collar counterpart to celebrities and corporate executives reading out their wealthy friends' names. And if middle-class Americans couldn't afford black-tie banquets, some could attend dinner dances and silent auctions and wine-tasting parties. Small or big, all contributors were invited to place themselves on the validated side of a great social divide. Donations to aid people with disabilities helped obscure class lines.

Telethons also reinforced the class structure by profiling middle-class families as the focus of the charities' ministrations. The beneficiaries were seldom poor and never rich. During most of the telethon era, they were also overwhelmingly white. In later years, a growing proportion was African, Latino, or Asian American. But whatever their ethnicity, those families were middle class. That implicitly made them, as one local Easter Seals host put it, "very deserving."[34] As we saw in the earlier discussion of charity standing in for welfare, MDA's insistence that it provided its services without requiring a means test for families further effaced any associations with class standing. American charity long operated on the premise that middle-class families in crisis were morally and socially worthy of aid. Means tests and moral evaluations were for the poor who were inherently suspect.[35] MCs located telethon families in the social hierarchy by indicating to the vast middle-class audience, "They're just like your friends, your family, your neighbors." The telethon ritual aimed, in part, to rescue middle-class families from social invalidation.

Meanwhile, conspicuous contribution helped resolve dilemmas about social fluidity and status mobility. Americans invisibly braided the disavowed realities of social class with the much-vaunted fact of social fluidity. But that intertwining had problematic consequences because social mobility might be downward as well as upward. Through much of US history, it also produced a disorienting shapelessness. Hurtling geographical expansion, swift and ceaseless change, the relative newness of many institutions, and the ideology of individualism together generated not only an exhilarating sense of individual possibilities but also at times a terrifying lack of personal and social boundaries. While the fluidity of the social structure facilitated self-expression and individual advancement, it also left many adrift about who they were or what they should become. In 1959 the great novelist James Baldwin observed in an essay that Americans had fashioned a society "in which nothing is fixed and in which the individual must fight for his identity."[36] Liberated from rigid, traditional social hierarchies, many white Americans also felt dubiously emancipated from any clearly defined identity.

With every prospect seemingly available, no goal seemed sufficient. Many Americans found themselves drawn into an endless competition for status with no finish line, no resting place. As early as 1774, an observer noted that Americans were running "one continued race, in which everyone is endeavoring to distance all behind him, and to overtake or pass by, all before him; everyone flying from his Inferiors in Pursuit of his Superiors, who fly from him with equal Alacrity."[37] "People are not . . . terribly anxious to be equal," remarked Baldwin almost two centuries later, "but they love the idea of being superior. And this human truth has an especially grinding force here, where identity is almost impossible to achieve and people are perpetually attempting to find their feet on the shifting sands of status."[38] "There are no longer any universally accepted forms or standards," he pointed out in 1960, "and since all the roads to the achievement of an identity had vanished, the problem of status in American life became and it remains today acute. In a way, status became a kind of substitute for identity. . . ."[39] In their 1985 study *Habits of the Heart*, Robert N. Bellah and his colleagues reported that late in the twentieth century, even though the ambiguities of identity and status still troubled middle-class Americans, they continued to define success as upward status mobility and were perpetually calculating how to move up.[40]

With the success of American industrial capitalism, consumption became the most important yardstick of status, particularly in the decades after World War II. Monetary income and the material possessions and extra-occupational activities purchased by that income became primary measures of social standing. "Because money and the things money can buy is the universally accepted symbol here of status," said Baldwin, "we are often condemned as materialists. In fact, we are much closer to being metaphysical because nobody has ever expected from things the miracles that we expect."[41] With one another as audience, Americans earned and spent and consumed, endlessly striving to verify their inner worth and social validity.[42] The rise of new media like broadcast television afforded them unprecedented public opportunities to test and market these qualities for themselves and others.

Complementing conspicuous consumption, conspicuous contribution also verified one's social status. Like all charitable donation, telethon giving tried to counteract the morally and communally corrosive effects of consumerism. But charity organizations also made donation a consumable product guaranteed to boost the buyer's social and self-worth. The agencies manufactured "the less fortunate" as status-enhancing commodities. If conspicuous contribution ritualistically reversed the consequences of consumerism, it was also another form of conspicuous consumption that showcased social status.

Thus, by several means conspicuous contribution buttressed, even as it blurred, the realities of class. It disguised the social and political factors influencing allegedly natural misfortunes. It enabled the most privileged to display their superior status, thereby reinforcing their dominant position.[43] It encouraged middle-class Americans to disregard the disadvantages and dangers to them under the private charity and for-profit health-insurance and health-care system, prompting them instead to identify with those who would never need telethon charity. It verified individuals' upward social mobility and eligibility for equal membership in a democracy of free choices.

Altruism, Avarice, and the Gospel of Wealth

Conspicuous contribution symbolically reassured individual givers that they were not avaricious but altruistic, not materialistically self-centered but civic-minded. It demonstrated that they had escaped the taint of a culture of conspicuous consumption, that they retained the virtue necessary to maintain democratic community. "It shows you care," assured a local telethon host. "It shows you want to help other people." Another local MC suggested, "Let us read your name on the air so the rest of the world knows about it." Still another urged viewers to call because "you're going to feel really good about yourself."[44]

In making these appeals, telethons evidently reflected many Americans' motivations in performing "acts of compassion." In 1991 sociologist Robert Wuthnow reported that while people he surveyed asserted that human beings are innately compassionate, they admitted that they themselves were more often spurred by "utilitarian" impulses. Almost 2 out of 3 acknowledged that a major reason for them to be kind and caring was that it made them feel good about themselves. Nearly 8 out of 10 endorsed the idea that "If I help others, it is likely that someone will help me when I am in need." And so both reflecting and reinforcing those attitudes, fundraising professionals offered "the promise of good feelings" to volunteers and donors.[45]

Respected social commentators such as Wuthnow, Robert Bellah, and Daniel Bell interpreted this sort of self-gratification in the guise of altruism as not just contradictory but also symptomatic of a crisis in American values. Bellah suggested that because many Americans no longer grounded values such as interpersonal caring and social responsibility in higher-order principles or universalistic moral claims, they could justify them only by saying that doing good deeds made them feel good and, in particular, good about themselves. But, he pointed out, the rationale "what it does for me," in fact, undermined both regard for others and the moral reasoning behind it. Offering a similar analysis, Daniel Bell linked the preoccupation with pleasurable feelings to a collapse of confidence in absolutes and a consequent crisis of personal identity. Americans not only bought consumer goods to make themselves feel better, said Bell; they frantically sought intimacy in relationships by trying "to dissolve the boundaries" between themselves and others. Wuthnow suggested that the same desperate yearnings might lie behind Americans' "fleeting efforts to help strangers. We seek them out, offering to alleviate their burdens, but the underlying problem is how we feel about ourselves. We desperately want to be fulfilled, much more so than we desire to be of help."[46]

If the analyses of Wuthnow, Bell, and Bellah were correct, telethons may be viewed as manifestations of the late-twentieth-century cultural crisis that those ceremonies pledged to resolve. Telethon preceptors proclaimed that the ritual display of benevolence verified the moral health of individual givers and American society. And yet by promising "you're going to feel really good about yourself," they taught conspicuous contributors to equate narcissism with altruism, self-gratification with civic-mindedness. That contradiction indicated that telethons were as much a symptom of the American cultural predicament as an attempt to sort it out.

At the same time, conspicuous contribution in late-twentieth-century America was not an entirely new phenomenon in Western societies. Despite Christ's admonition to give in secret, social elites had a long history of publicly displaying their charity. Throughout twenty centuries of Western Christianity, charity enhanced the spiritual and moral security of those elites, as well as their social prestige and power. High-status donors used publicity to make their beneficence efficacious. The poor, who were often the objects of this benevolence, always included sick people and people with disabilities.[47]

In any era, charitable giving was vaunted as compensating for the contributor's sins. Boniface Ramsey, a historian of the early Christian church, describes patristic writings about almsgiving as "heavily donor-centered." They focused on the value of charity to the giver more than the recipient. It was "a classic means of atoning for sin," especially the sin of avarice. It could also help ensure the almsgiver a place in heaven. Charity was a negotiation with God, a bargain that put Christ in the donor's debt.[48] "God could have made all men rich," declared St. Eligius, "but He wanted there to be poor people in His world, that the rich might be able to redeem their sins." From the Middle Ages to the nineteenth century, almsgiving enabled both wealthy individuals and collective contributors such as guilds to set right their sins and open their way to heaven.[49]

Charitable giving was also used throughout Western history to rationalize the inequitable distribution of material resources. While early Christian theologians warned of the moral dangers of wealth, they did not disapprove of it per se. Rather, they condemned the rich man who failed to share his wealth with the poor through acts of charity. As a corollary, the proper use of material possessions, namely almsgiving, justified the possession of wealth by demonstrating that the rich man was fulfilling the purpose for which God had made him rich.[50] The Protestant Reformation elaborated on this symbolic function of charity. It offered prosperous persons occasions to exercise and demonstrate their stewardship of wealth. They thereby verified that they deserved the prosperity bestowed on them.[51] For the antebellum era's most conservative commentators, social inequality was a divinely ordained and permanent state in order to inspire industriousness and ambition, while offering opportunities "of doing good to others by acts of encouragement, beneficence and charity." Benevolent individuals, according to this view, must endeavor to ease the effects of poverty but should not attempt to erase inequality itself, lest they eliminate their own "means of moral improvement." Benevolence here served as a moral lesson, one whose importance rested with the donor rather than the recipient.[52] In Gilded Age America, robber baron philanthropists such as Andrew Carnegie propagated an updated version of the rationale of stewardship, which Carnegie called "The Gospel of Wealth."[53]

Conspicuous genteel charitable contribution always involved considerations of publicity and public recognition. In sixteenth-century German principalities, city magistrates passed out prints of themselves giving alms. In early modern and then modern Europe, elite benefactors competed with one another to gain reputations for generosity. In the nineteenth century, declining and increasingly superfluous European aristocracies displayed their charity to prove their continued usefulness to society. At the same time, the rising middle classes sought to compensate for their political powerlessness and claim the capacity and right to help shape civil society by visible involvement in charitable endeavors. The institutions that depended on all this beneficence quickly learned that publishing donors' names, publicly bestowing the honors and prestige sought by contributors, generated still more giving.[54]

Throughout this history of conspicuous contribution, charitable giving was always a matter of voluntary compassion rather than an obligation to promote social and economic justice. Although early Christian theologians implicitly viewed almsgiving as an aspect of justice, they saw it mainly as a spiritual exercise for the sake of the benefactor rather than a program to ameliorate social and economic inequities. Focusing intently on donors, their writings about charity depicted poor people as depersonalized abstractions. "There are," wrote Ramsey, "very few sympathetic depictions of the underprivileged, portraying them as human beings with particular needs and desires of their own, as persons in their own right." Instead, in sermons and essays entreating almsgiving, the poor exist "for the sake of the rich, to offer them opportunities for beneficence or to test them." "All this represents an attitude," remarked Ramsey, "that a later age will find somewhat unpalatable."[55] But in fact in any era, poor, sick, and disabled people were a means for the spiritual enlargement of their social betters. Depictions of them served a didactic purpose. Those images were used to stir the compassions of elites who could then display their beneficence without in any way challenging, let alone changing, social and economic arrangements.

This hallowed ordering of social relations prescribed reciprocal tasks for recipients of charity. The church fathers promised almsgivers the benefit of the prayers of the poor, assuring that they would plead their benefactors' cause on the day of judgment.[56] In the Middle Ages, as a condition of receiving alms, poor people were required to pray for donors' souls. This obeisance was summed up in the concept of "gratitude," a posture of both spiritual lowliness and social subordination.[57]

The radical differentiation of givers from receivers remained in force in some Americans' thinking about charity at the very end of the twentieth century. At a symposium on "the Ethics of Giving and Receiving," ethicist Leon R. Kass declared: "[L]ike them or not," most Great Society programs "sprang from a humane compassion for the less fortunate among us—the poor, the sick, and the needy; the ill-fed, the ill-housed, and the ill-educated; the deprived, the despised, and the disabled. Caring for the unfortunate has always been part of the mission of private charities, especially those connected to religious organizations." Christian love, he went on, "stands out for its capacity to love the naturally unlovable—not only the poor, the weak, the deformed, and the crazed, but even the wicked and vicious. ... [I]t is no accident that charity—both Christian and secular—has come to mean primarily benevolence and beneficence towards the lowliest among us, those who are unable to help themselves."[58] Kass's haughty dichotomization repeated the historic separation of the beneficent from "the unfortunate [and] naturally unlovable" as though they were two utterly different orders of being.

Invasions of Privacy and Public Display

The late-twentieth-century American charity system continued the tradition of defining people with disabilities as objects of benevolence rather than as autonomous subjects. With rare exceptions, those doing the giving on telethons were nondisabled. People with disabilities were the ones ceremonially defined and displayed as inevitable objects of charity. Telethons offered occasions for individuals to act upon genuinely compassionate regard for their fellow human beings, but this caring was inseparable from the restrictive and depersonalizing social identity imposed on disabled people.[59]

Little wonder then that the activist magazine *The Disability Rag* reported that disabled people often found their privacy invaded in public places by nondisabled individuals who treated them as though they were mendicants.

A wheelchair-riding disability rights activist was sitting "in front of a convenience store, talking with a friend with whom he'd just had a coffee break." A passerby "dropped a five-dollar bill into his almost-empty cup." The disabled man "was furiously angry, especially when the Good Samaritan disappeared before he could return the money and give the donor a heated lecture."[60] Mary-Lou Breslin, executive director of the Disability Rights Education and Defense Fund in Berkeley, California, was sitting on her power wheelchair at an airport waiting to board a flight. Wearing a "dressed-for-success businesswoman's outfit," she was drinking a cup of coffee. Just then, another woman, also in business attire, "plunked a quarter into the plastic cup Breslin held in her hand. The coin sent the coffee flying, staining Breslin's blouse, and the well-meaning woman, embarrassed, hurried on."[61] A deaf woman found that when she and her boyfriend, who was quadriplegic, were together in public, "gifts magically flow[ed] in their direction. Once they were walking and wheeling along a highway when a man pulled his car off the road, ran back to them and stuffed a wad of bills in their hands—$50 worth."[62]

These activists did not see such gestures as expressing compassion, let alone respect. In their view, the American charity system had given nondisabled people license to invade the privacy of disabled strangers, to press unwanted gifts on them, to ask the most obtrusive personal questions. Charity portrayals, they charged, taught many nondisabled people to think of people with disabilities as a form of public property. A bill stuffed into a pocket reiterated one-on-one the difference between givers and recipients propagated by the charities. Passersby who dropped coins in coffee cups restated the dichotomy declared by telethon donors who contrasted themselves with the "less fortunate."

Telethons buoyed the difference between the ostensibly autonomous and the allegedly incapacitated in another important way: They ceaselessly displayed people with disabilities as objects of charity. Normal people gave alms; invalids took them. They no longer squatted on street corners proffering tin cups, but they were beggars just the same. It was their role to receive these gifts gratefully. They existed to supply nondisabled people with an occasion to exercise charity and thereby reaffirm their own normality.

Disabled people were hopeless, helpless, and futureless—without nondisabled charity. They passively depended on nondisabled good will to have their needs met. Until the compassionate, the "normal," acted, they could only wait. "Right now there's a child waiting for your heart to open," said a local Easter Seals host in 1989, "a child in your home town . . . who needs therapy, encouragement, and a friend. So, please, will you be that friend?" Unless the "normal" expressed their compassion, children and adults with disabilities would not get treatment or cure. The disabled were portrayed repeatedly as powerless, incapable of realizing their dreams. "You know," said a local Easter Seals host, "it comes down to people with feelings, hopes, and dreams that won't be fulfilled unless we help. Your call and gift of $15 or $25 can help provide therapy, care, and equipment that is needed to provide indepen-dence."[63] Apparently, more than just independence was at stake: A donation could supply a real life.

Even when the normal did not pay for the privilege, they still had the invalidated available to contrast with themselves, as the disabled writer Ed Hooper found out one day. "Two respectable looking women walked past me in a shopping mall recently," he wrote to his peers in *The Disability Rag.* "They must have been discussing some problem in one or the other's life when I heard the taller woman say, 'See, Ellen, it could be worse.' Ellen, glancing toward me, nodded her head in agreement. She was talking about me. What on earth was I worse than, I wondered: Alcoholism? Drug abuse? Divorce? Rape? These women had learned, as have millions of others, that it's accept-able—even therapeutic—to take something that isn't theirs: due regard for their fellow human being."[64] Hooper called people like these two women "dignity thieves." In stealing social esteem from individuals with disabili-ties, they simply emulated, he said, "the big dignity thieves—the telethons—'pity-a-thons'—that systematically robbed disabled people in general."[65] Such individual acts of degradation were patterned after and legitimated by the collectively enacted telethon rituals that socially invalidated people with disabilities.

In order for givers to have regular occasions on which to ritually reas-sure themselves of their moral health and social validity, it was necessary to perpetuate the social and moral invalidation of people with disabilities. *Invalids* served an essential cultural function. They played a central, if pas-sive, role. Thus, telethon hosts repeatedly distinguished the crippled from the compassionate. Celebrities and donors ceaselessly contrasted themselves with the "less fortunate." Modern fundraising represented Americans with dis-abilities as perennial objects of charity in order to reassure putatively normal Americans of their own individual moral health, of the continued vibrancy of American moral community.

Like charity recipients throughout the centuries, those highlighted on telethons and other disabled people were instruments of both salvation and publicity. Conspicuous contributors could use them to magnify their moral standing and social status, while gratifying themselves emotionally and materially. People with disabilities were also vehicles to replenish belief in American moral community. They were made symbols and occasions, mech-anisms and means to others' redemption and elevation. But, like the recipi-ents of alms in any era, like the fictional Tiny Tim and the real-life Laura Bridgman, they were not persons in their own right. Their function was to ensure that modern almsgivers received the spiritual and social credit due them. Their duty was to display gratitude, to make their benefactors feel good about themselves. Thanks to prevailing emotional notions that frame disabled people in particular ways, the task proved depressingly easy to accomplish.

Suffering as Spectacle

PITY, PATHOS, AND IDEOLOGY

"If it's pity, we'll get some money," Jerry Lewis candidly admitted on *CBS Sunday Morning* in 2001.[1] In fact, to draw donations, the MDA and other telethons mobilized not just pity, but many kinds of pathos. They presented people with disabilities as poignant, sometimes tragic and hoping against hope, often heroic, ever striving and inspirational. They stirred sorrow, admiration, and sympathy.[2] Fundraisers taught potential donors not only what to feel but also how to feel. In doing so, they extended the American charity tradition, a tradition influenced by the Anglo-American culture of sensibility and sentimentality. They also presented American cultural framings of how individuals and the community should give sympathy and alms. Distinctions between deserving and undeserving recipients of charity promoted certain images of disabled people while maintaining socioeconomic hierarchies. Moreover, sentimentalism in tandem with the medical model of disability obfuscated disability's political dimensions.[3]

Commonly thought of as an individual and personal reaction rooted in pure feelings, sympathy is, in fact, largely formed by cultural values and social arrangements. In her study of late-twentieth-century American sympathy practices, sociologist Candace Clark notes that individuals typically deliver sympathy and acts of compassion in ways their culture and society consider socially and therefore morally appropriate. "These interior processes seem natural to us," says Clark, "but really they are socially channeled." Yet just as social "rules and logics help shape emotions," emotions, in turn, "help shape the social structure." Sympathy does not simply emerge spontaneously and, as it were, organically. It is formed by and helps to form cultural values, social ideologies, and institutional structures that provide relief and succor.[4]

A class of social actors Clark calls "sympathy entrepreneurs" promoted and brokered twentieth-century American cultural responses to suffering. Some were volunteers spurred by dedication to a need or cause. Others owned or worked for a business—for instance, greeting card companies—that profited by encouraging expressions of sympathy. Still others were motivated by concern about a plight but also made it their livelihood, namely charity professionals such as those who ran telethons. Stimulating public emotions, these "entrepreneurs" urged individuals to practice acts of kindness, such as sending sympathy cards, volunteering, or donating to an array of causes. Often they competed with one another to capture the public's imagination, manage their sentiments, and perhaps make money. Sympathy entrepreneurship played a key role in shaping late-twentieth-century American morals, charity practices, and even political thinking.[5]

The Roots of Appropriate Feeling

The sympathy practices they promoted had historical roots in eighteenth- and nineteenth-century Anglo-American cultures of sensibility and sentimentality. This long-term, bourgeois "civilizing process" was part of a broad reformation of manners that ultimately produced a modern consciousness of feelings: a heightened awareness of not only one's own emotions, but also those of other people and even animals with whom one learned to sympathize. Its ideal figure was the "man of feeling," whose heartfelt sympathy toward suffering was taken as evidence of his virtue.[6] Sensibility's requirements became dogmas not only in religion and philosophy but also aesthetics. Vaunted as more than individual self-cultivation and self-expression, sensibility was closely related to the notions of sociability and benevolence many Americans believed would guarantee the viability of their experiment in republican self-government, as well as humaneness in their emerging capitalist economic order. Sensibility offered a new vision of social relations and, with it, an energizing expectation that philanthropic effort and social reform could transform society. Though early modern thinking attributed greater sensibility to persons of higher social rank, its assumed origins in human nature and its potential for development through education implied the democratic possibility that it could be fostered in almost everyone and that virtually anyone could school him- or herself in it. This impulse helped give rise not only to medical treatment, rehabilitation, and education for people with various disabilities but also the civil rights and other advocacy movements of and for those same groups.[7]

The forces of sensitivity and sentimentality mobilized by telethons can be found in a robust eighteenth- and nineteenth-century Anglo-American cultural tradition that highlighted pain and suffering. Paintings, novels, and illustrations offered scenes of poverty, imprisonment, slavery, the aftermath of war, tormented animals, women in distress—all, in the words of historian Karen Halttunen, "aimed at arousing readers' spectatorial sympathy and thus enhancing (and demonstrating) their virtue." Such depictions of misery always sought to teach the feeling heart a correct response.[8]

During the Victorian period, this sentimentality expanded further into popular culture, epitomized by literature and theater that featured many characters woefully afflicted by various disabilities. Unlike "freak" show stages that displayed those with unusual physical traits to repudiate them, popular fiction and nonfiction presented blind, deaf, or physically disabled people that many Victorians in Britain and America would have encountered and even regularly related to in their neighborhoods or families. In these portrayals, disability commonly meant misery and grief and in some instances inspirational Christian stoicism. In some instances, they represented malevolence and villainy, but more often characters with disabilities were seen as needing and deserving compassion. These characters' typicality makes literary depictions of them and prescribed reactions to them historically significant.[9]

Victorian humanitarian reformers were the first modern sympathy entrepreneurs. Applying to real people with disabilities what literary scholar Martha Stoddard Holmes calls a "rhetoric of affliction," writers, educators, social reformers, journalists, and doctors habitually described them as "afflicted," "deprived," and "defective," regularly using melodramatic affect-laden language to evoke readers' sympathy in behalf of humanitarian causes. During the nineteenth century, sympathy practices became increasingly institutionalized and professionalized. Not taking for granted that their audiences would respond in appropriate ways, sympathy entrepreneurs assumed a didactic tone to instruct reader/spectators in the exercise of sympathy by providing suitable scenarios and role models.[10]

Tracing sentimentality's development in Victorian fiction and nonfiction, Stoddard Holmes calls it a "cultural shorthand" that prescribed how to respond to people with disabilities that persisted into the late twentieth century. In stories that were typically sentimental, sensational, and melodramatic, Victorian writers taught readers to react to characters with disabilities in intense but emotionally restricted ways. Mawkishness and bathos were central not only to literary and theatrical fiction but also all Victorian discourses of disability, including humanitarian reform propaganda. Stage plays triggered audiences' extravagant feelings with visual cues of bodily differences where exterior appearances signified characters' woeful interior states of being. During and long after the Victorian era, countless narratives conditioned readers and spectators to respond reflexively to people with disabilities. Stories of disability became familiar tales, says Stoddard Holmes, "of pitying or heart-warmed tears, inner triumph, mirror-smashing rages, suicide attempts, angst and abjection, saintly compassion, bitterness, troubled relationships, and courageous overcoming." Virtually always, those depictions connected disability with melodrama, which easily translated into the mass entertainment media of movies and television.[11]

The redemptive power of sympathy through spectatorship is perhaps most memorably portrayed in *A Christmas Carol* (1843), written by Charles Dickens, arguably the preeminent sympathy entrepreneur of the Victorian era. The physically disabled boy Tiny Tim is fully aware of his function as an instructive spectacle. When Bob Cratchit and Tiny Tim return from Christmas worship, Bob reports that the child said "he hoped the people saw him in church, because he was a cripple, and it might be pleasant for them to remember upon Christmas Day, who made lame beggars walk and blind men see." Peering in at the window of the Cratchits' cottage almost as though he is watching them on television, Scrooge is literally a spectator, not only of this conversation, but also of Tim's suffering and the family's plight, as well as their deep affectionate ties to one another. Dickens has Scrooge respond appropriately to the scene he witnesses. Literary scholar Mary Klages explains that for "the first time in his adult life," he feels "concern for the welfare of someone other than himself" and then determines to act to save Tiny Tim and relieve the family. Not only does Scrooge serve as a model of sympathy and benevolence for readers, the story provides them with a template of how to respond to sentimental scenarios.[12]

Entrepreneurial Weeping

In late-twentieth-century America, the sympathy entrepreneurs who produced the telethons modernized this sentimental spectatorship. Jerry Lewis concisely restated all of the traditional themes: "We're going to give the information that will touch your heart, possibly tap a nerve end here and there. It'll certainly wrench you, because these are human beings that you can certainly identify with. Our purpose here is to do that. In the interim, [we'll] try to entertain and keep you glued to that set."[13] Critics scorned Lewis for his tear-stained fundraising style, but he became the epitome of telethon sentimentality because he was the most effective sympathy entrepreneur on the air. Other telethon hosts aimed for the same impact but less skillfully. Dick Van Patten, an actor who built his career on sentimental domesticity, opened one Easter Seals show by announcing in a piteous voice that for the next eighteen hours, "We're going to be together and we're going to cry together. I just hope one moment will touch you and open your eyes and show you how much good you can do."[14] "The Easter Seals way of caring," said another host, "is . . . one heart reaching out in love to another heart in need of compassion."[15]

In this "reaching out," telethon sympathy entrepreneurs perpetuated the Anglo-American culture of sentimentality by deploying long-established rhetorical forms.[16] Seeking to realize the democratic implications of sensibility, they made their telethons a form of mass popular education in sentimental ethics by schooling millions of spectators. Following in the centuries-old sentimental tradition, they presented instructive scenarios of suffering and sympathy. They enacted dramas of affliction and then prescribed the "correct response" of "the feeling heart" by contrasting sympathetic and generous Americans with those who were hardhearted Scrooges. And as in Victorian sentimental literature, telethons presented people with disabilities, not as "freaks," but ordinary human beings who were struggling with affliction. Frequently employing the use of "we," telethon hosts underscored the fact that their guests were "just like your neighbors," "just like you and your family." Indeed, they could be you and your family. Viewers participated in these scenarios vicariously, "identifying with the emotions being portrayed."[17] Then some of them acted upon their virtuous sensibility by phoning in pledges of money.

Telethons unconsciously adapted narrative techniques, character, and plot devices used in sentimental literature and Victorian fiction, combining three standard sentimental devices: unmerited affliction through illness or accident, the suffering of innocent children, and emotional excess. For example, "Tiny Tim" was an implicit source of the central charity icon, the poster child. A March of Dimes publicist summed up the strategy of all the charities: "[T]here is an emotional appeal with a child with crutches and braces—that's going to bring the money in."[18] Tableaus featuring those children would soften hearts and open purses. During the 1980s, national UCP headquarters urged local affiliates' public relations officers to use "poignant pictures of children and adults."[19] Promoting Easter Seals summer camps, Dick Van Patten plaintively asked viewers: "Could you look into your heart and see if a child's smile is worth . . . $40? And a child with a disability, well, he'll have a memory to cherish forever." The Arthritis Foundation Telethon presented innocent suffering in the form of a little girl. Her mother explained tenderly and with a tinge of sadness: "She never asks much of anybody. She really doesn't, but she's always so concerned about other people. She's just an angel with very heavy wings." Easter Seals MC Mary Jane Popp was in tears after a filmed profile of one child. "Oh, folks, how can you resist a little girl like Laura? If that doesn't make it for you, then nothing will. I get choked up when I see something like that, because it's showing the hope you can give these kids. Please, I don't know what else to say," she sobbed. "Call, please."[20]

In sentimental literature, an innocent child's suffering was often matched by a devoted mother's self-sacrificing love. For Victorian sentimentalism that feminized the culture of sensibility, the home and the family formed the center of emotional affection and moral instruction; woman as mother was the source of that love and virtue. The sentimental plot was often a "story of salvation through motherly love."[21] Telethons presented a version of that story. They promulgated the view of disability as distorting family life, even ravaging it. Mothers labored heroically, self-sacrificingly, to save their children and families from disability's destructive impact. On one Arthritis Foundation

Telethon, for example, a mother named Denise talked about her daughter Linda. "I cry when I can't help her." Host Sarah Purcell amplified: "Tears are a part of Denise's life, but hope is an even bigger part. She has the hope that one day because of research, the tears will be gone. That hope is what gives her strength. Your pledge is what gives her that hope. . . . The longer you wait, the longer Denise and Linda have to wait."[22]

Many times telethons reduced disabled children's communication with their mothers to this sentimental phrase, to the point that it eclipsed other positive, less maudlin realities. For instance, the bright 10-year-old Elizabeth understood both English and Hungarian, and no doubt had much more to offer her mother and television viewers than "I love you."[23] Another host, this one on the Easter Seals Telethon, presented a boy with cerebral palsy who used an electronic communication board, asking viewers to help a child say "I love you" to his mother; she did not say that his device would enable him to develop his language skills and get an education, or that it would give him his own voice in the world.[24]

Love also figured prominently in an important purveyor of sentimentality on telethons: songs. One singer called on the Arthritis Foundation's audience to see the difficulties of people with arthritis "Through the Eyes of Love."[25] For Easter Seals, Ben Vereen invoked the Whitney Houston hit "The Greatest Love of All," and Lucie Arnaz, daughter of Lucille Ball and Desi Arnaz, professed, "I Still Believe in Love."[26] Clint Holmes, the Las Vegas mainstay, appealed to UCP viewers, "If We Only Have Love," while a singing group preached to an Easter Seals audience, "What the World Needs Now Is Love, Sweet Love."[27]

Songs relied on other emotions to kindle pathos, most notably pity and hope. On the MDA Telethon, for example, Maureen McGovern prayed, "There's Got to Be a Morning After," the theme song from a disaster movie about the sinking of a modern-day *Titanic*.[28] A UCP singer intoned, "God Bless the Child That's Got His Own."[29] On Easter Seals telecasts, Pat Boone lamented, "Nobody Knows the Trouble I've Seen" and "Look Down That Lonesome Road," while another singer affirmed, "I Believe the Sun Will Shine Again," and Phylicia Rashad declared, "I Made It Through the Rain."[30] Jerry Lewis always ended the MDA show with "You'll Never Walk Alone," sometimes weeping when he called on announcer Ed McMahon to read the final figure from the tote board. Such songs beseeched spectators to feel love for suffering fellow human beings who depend on their compassion.

Just as the culture of sympathy traditionally instructed readers through sentimental scenarios, telethons presented profiles that were, in effect, miniature dramas. They enacted each particular charity's sentimental framing of its clients' lives. Even when UCP portrayed people with cerebral palsy as striving to build meaningful lives, sentimentalism kept contradicting that message. Year after year, Dennis James recited "Heaven's Very Special Child," a saccharine poem about a council in heaven that urges God to carefully choose parents for a "very special" child who will have a disability. The poem "tells our whole story," announced James. On some telecasts, James recited it as many as three times, even including embellishments such as during the 1995 telethon when his cohosts hummed "Amazing Grace" in the background.

Arthritis Foundation Telethon dramas depicted innocent suffering, dependency and uncertainty, pain now and fear for the future. One showed boys in baseball uniforms at a batting cage. Then the camera pulled back as another boy turned around and in a doleful voice spoke the words the telethon-makers had given him. "Hi. My name's Steven and I'm ten years-old. Sometimes I close my eyes, and I pretend like I'm over there playing baseball with my friends. But then I remember that I can't play baseball or run or even walk without hurting," he said. The camera pulled back farther to show that Steven was wearing a splint on each hand and standing with a walker. "It's arthritis, you know," he said dejectedly. "I've had it for six years. My grandma tells me that she's gonna help stop arthritis. She's remembered the Arthritis Foundation in her will, whatever that means. She says that it'll help find a cure. Grandma says that she can't do it alone, but she knows others will care. So," pleaded Steven, "won't you help?" Then he suddenly put on a smile of surprise and hope. "Boy!" he exclaimed. "Imagine me playing baseball!" This was followed by a local host of the Arthritis Foundation's show saying, "Steven wants to play baseball. There are lots of things he wants to do. The only way he is going to be able to do it is with your help."[31] Without compassionate charity, she implied, not only would he be unable to play baseball, he would be pathetically incapacitated to do almost anything.

Though only a small percentage of MDA's clientele had terminal conditions, a great many of the dramas it presented told of deterioration and death that echoed Victorian sentimental literature.[32] Fathers and mothers, widows and adult children told agonizing tales of loss and grief. One father said that his baby daughter never had the strength to smile. But then one day as he was leaving her hospital room, she gave him a "huge smile." Only later did he realize that she was saying goodbye. She died the next morning. "We want a healthy family," he pleaded through his tears, "and we know with you people someday that we can." Story after heartbreaking story left loved ones, Jerry Lewis, the studio audience, and, one presumes, viewers at home weeping. Sometimes Lewis would comfort the spectators: "Don't be ashamed of those tears."[33]

Sentimentality, Moral Worthiness, and Capitalism

As sympathy entrepreneurs, telethons served as social and moral gatekeepers by setting forth criteria for judging both sympathizers' and recipients' moral worthiness. As they framed appropriate modes of responding, they addressed Americans' uneasiness about giving and receiving sympathy and charity. They also endeavored—usually without directly saying so—to reset moral perceptions of disease and disability. Telethon sentimentality aimed, in part, to counter ancient prejudices that inflicted stigma and shame on sick people and people with disabilities at the same time that the programs reinforced many of these same notions.

In her study *The Managed Heart: The Commercialization of Human Feeling*, sociologist Arlie Russell Hochschild found strong links between modern capitalism and sentimentality through what she called the proliferation of "feeling rules."[34] Arguing that acts of emotion management are not simply private acts, she showed how these rules represent "standards used in emotional conversation to determine what is rightly owed and owing in the currency of feeling." Through them, we tell what is due in each relation, each role.[35] "It does not take capitalism to turn feeling into a commodity or to turn our capacity for managing feeling into an instrument," Hochschild explains. "But capitalism has found a use for emotional management, and so it has organized it more efficiently and pushed it further. And perhaps it does take a capitalist sort of incentive system to connect emotional labor to competition and to go so far as to actually advertise a 'sincere' smile, train workers to produce such a smile, supervise their production of it, and then forge a link between this activity and corporate profit."[36]

Links among capitalism, sentimentality, and charity had existed since the eighteenth century.[37] Traditional Christian ideals of compassion became increasingly permeated with an emerging capitalist morality and cultural ethos. Certainly, it was no coincidence that the Enlightenment's premier theorist of political economy, Adam Smith, authored *The Wealth of Nations* (1776) as well as *The Theory of Moral Sentiments* (1759). "How selfish soever man may be supposed, there are evidently some principles in his nature, which interest him in the fortunes of others, and render their happiness necessary to him, though he derives nothing from it, except the pleasure of seeing it," Smith states. "Of this kind is pity or compassion, the emotion we feel for the misery of others, when we either see it, or are made to conceive it in a very lively manner."[38] Sensibility's reflection of early modern capitalist values foreshadowed aspects of conspicuous contribution discussed earlier. Yet the relationship between sensibility/sentimentality and capitalism was not simple. The former was not merely an ideological rationalization of the latter. Sentimentality was also available to express alarm at the brutalities of industrial capitalism, as in Dickens's stories about the poor in Victorian England. But overall, sentimentality protested capitalism's harshness without fundamentally challenging the emerging order.[39]

Integral to the script of bestowing sympathy was the need to make a formal distinction between deserving and undeserving recipients. Many people with disabilities—particularly children—played a complementary role. Like Tiny Tim, they were the quintessential recipients of sympathy and charity. This perception of children with disabilities and of childlike disabled adults simplified the problem of differentiating the deserving from the undeserving. At the same time, the prodigious efforts to formulate objective means of making that distinction reflected a deep-seated ambivalence—and even hostility—in American culture toward anyone who might seek sympathy and social aid, including people with disabilities.[40]

The logic of American sympathy reflected "the just world hypothesis," the belief that, for the most part, people "get what they deserve and deserve what they get." Sympathy was appropriate when bad luck happened to a worthy person but inappropriate if the person was unworthy.[41] In general, Americans seem to have determined worthiness and unworthiness according to three criteria. First of all, there was causation: How did this event happen to this person? What were its immediate and ultimate causes? Next came the issue of the person's response: Had the person dealt with his or her difficulty in morally laudable and socially acceptable ways? Finally, the issue of social traits was raised: Did the person's other characteristics unrelated to the plight show that he or she is socially worthy or unworthy?

People with disabilities were judged to be more—or less—legitimate recipients of public sympathy depending on their responsibility for their fate. Children were usually seen as innocent, seldom at fault. Adults were blamable if they had heedlessly put themselves at risk, for instance, by driving drunk, but blameless if they were struck by a car driven by a drunk driver.[42] As one executive of a disability-related organization explained, "Not all disabilities are alike. Some are more acceptable to the general public and easier to sell. People want to help children and those who were not responsible for their disability."[43]

These attitudes were shaped by persisting notions that illness and disability often were ultimately caused by sin, either specific acts of wrongdoing or, more broadly, a general pattern of wrong living. These were not archaic superstitions. Nor were they exclusively associated with religion. They appeared in many cultures, including modern secular ones. In America, these notions were also mediated by a social and economic system that ascribed individual success or failure to personal efforts more than cosmic fate or structural inequities. Individuals were assumed to have considerable control over their personal destinies.[44]

Telethon-producing charities tapped into and often reinforced characteristically widespread American assessments of moral culpability and social worthiness.[45] Yet, by presenting children and adults as blameless, they implicitly—and sometimes explicitly—opposed the age-old prejudices attributing illness and disability to wrongdoing or wrong living. They offered people with disabilities and their families several means of escape from that moral stigma.

One way to counter moral blame was to explain disease as a neutral biological process. Entertainment executive and UCP cofounder Leonard Goldenson, whose daughter had cerebral palsy, intended UCP's Telethons to educate other parents and the public. Parents were often ignorant of basic facts such as its causes, available treatments, and their children's capabilities; consequently, they were sometimes ashamed of their children. Goldenson wanted to refute stigmas against "spastics." Some myths "whispered" that venereal disease or "bad blood" caused the condition. Others said that evil spirits possessed children or that some ancestor's sin had provoked divine punishment. These superstitious attitudes fueled bigotry, which led to confining some people with cerebral palsy in harsh institutions that Goldenson's wife Isabelle likened to Dante's "Inferno." Many others were kept hidden at home, literally locked away in a closet or a basement. "We've got to free these people from their guilty feelings," Goldenson said. He believed the UCP Telethon "had a very strong, very dramatic impact" in changing perceptions.[46]

Though most modern Americans could apparently be persuaded that the physiological process of disease was not linked to sin, many continued to view illness and disability as psychological and social experiences charged with moral significance.[47] If someone with a disability failed to cope appropriately, if they succumbed to self-pity, if they manifested bitterness or undue anger, they would be labeled as moral failures. Telethon sympathy entrepreneurs forestalled both forms of stigma by enlisting sentimentalism, that is, presenting their clients as not only innocent of having caused their conditions but also indomitable in their struggles to overcome them. That made them worthy of sympathy. Blameless victims of bad luck, their courageous perseverance in facing personal adversity made them worthy of sympathy and merited the community's benevolence.

These brave innocents also verified their moral worthiness by serving as role models of saintly endurance and vehicles of their benefactors' moral and social redemption. They had real-life counterparts in charity fundraising from nineteenth-century benevolence to late-twentieth-century telethons.[48] Young Helen Keller—her unruly behavior depicted as a child in the 1962 movie *The Miracle Worker* notwithstanding—was widely publicized as "the perfect Victorian child," "unselfish, self-sacrificing, empathetic, devoted to others, forgetful of self, a born philanthropist, filled with unfailing love and sympathy." Meanwhile her deaf-blind predecessor at the Perkins School, Laura Bridgman, had captured Americans' popular imagination in no small part because of her religious piety and morally upstanding conduct. Images such as these offered an antidote to the Gilded Age's harsh materialism.[49] Real-life figures such as Keller and Bridgman, along with fictional characters such as Tiny Tim, helped to neutralize the old stigmatizing moral blame inflicted on sick people and people with disabilities. At the same time, this framing enforced an alternative assessment of character that was equally rooted in moral judgment.[50]

Voyeurism, Social Distance, and Pleasure-Taking

Even while sentimental spectatorship sought to awaken fellow feeling, it induced—indeed, it relied on—the opposite emotion: dramatizing the difference between sympathizers and the objects of their sympathy. This distinction encouraged them to dwell on and celebrate their own emotional and moral sensitivity while widening a gap to reassure themselves of their own safety and security. It even authorized them to find pleasure in the spectacle of suffering.[51]

Sensibility's conventions urged would-be sympathizers both to imagine other people's misery and to carve a social gulf between themselves and the sufferers. Despite Adam Smith's appealing picture of individuals fancying themselves in another person's situation, sympathetic spectatorship depended as much on psychological and social distance as on identification. In 1712, a generation before Smith, ideas regarding a cult of sensibility were beginning to gain traction. This intellectual climate led the politician and essayist Joseph Addison to formulate the central function of difference and distance. Compassion "refines and civilizes Humane Nature," he said, because it "knits Mankind together, and blends them in the same common Lot." Yet it also allowed sympathizers to separate themselves from sufferers. Writing in the *Spectator*—one can't help but take notice of the appropriateness of that name—he noted: "When we read of Torments, Wounds, Deaths, and the like dismal Accidents, our Pleasure does not flow so properly from the Grief which such melancholy Descriptions give us, as from the secret Comparison which we make between our selves and the Person [who] suffers. Such Representations teach us to set a just Value upon our own Condition, and make us prize our good Fortune, which exempts us from the like Calamities."[52]

Historian G. J. Barker-Benfield points out that this distancing comparison was both psychological and socioeconomic. Swelling prosperity in key regions of Britain's eighteenth-century empire, including its American colonies, enhanced the middling classes' material comfort. It also increasingly removed them from the hardships of those whose labors made their affluence possible but who were denied prosperity's benefits—lower-class British workers, colonial indentured servants, and slaves. Bourgeois compassion rested on economic privilege. Addison claimed that cultivators of sensibility secretly compared themselves to those in misery, but, in fact, they openly celebrated their advantage. Aware of their insulation from suffering, bourgeois sympathizers savored their feelings of pity, congratulated themselves on their sensibility and virtuousness, and "prize[ed the] good Fortune" that exempted them from such "Calamities." The pleasures Addison advocated, says Barker-Benfield, "were largely those of relief, complacency, and a sense of safety, adequately remote from a pain on which they depended for 'secret comparison.'" Such feelings lay at the heart of the culture of sensibility.[53]

Appealing to sentimentalism's traditional middle-class audience, tele-thons perpetuated certain bourgeois functions of savoring distance from those deemed less fortunate, while not fully escaping the threat of finding themselves cast down. The programs thus invited nondisabled spectators to celebrate publicly their own fortunate status while always reminding those viewers that they hovered titillatingly close to danger. Jerry Lewis talked about a man with myasthenia gravis who had appeared earlier on the MDA show with his wife. Lewis wondered why he and the audience had applauded them so vigorously. "There's a stigma here that bothers me," he said. "Are we applauding 'There but for the grace of God go I?' or are we applauding their courage? Yes. Without question," he decided emphatically, "we're applauding their courage."[54]

Yet Lewis had, however unwittingly, acknowledged a major theme of his and all telethons. On another MDA telecast, New York host Ben Vereen, backed by a choir, reverently suggested, "While we're singing this song, I want to ask everybody to please take a moment and reflect and think about it, 'There but by the grace of God go I.'"[55] On the UCP show, the actress and singer Pearl Bailey sat beside three children with cerebral palsy as she sang "What a Wonderful World." Then she instructed one of them: "Say, 'What a wonderful world.'" "What a wonderful world," repeated the child. Looking into the camera, Bailey asked: "Now if this guy thinks this is a wonderful world, what in the world out there have you all got to think about?"[56] To repeat the words of Addison, the example of socially invalidated children taught viewers to "make us prize our good Fortune, which exempts us from the like Calamities."[57] "There but for the grace of God go I" was a central theme of sentimental spectatorship. The unspoken, perhaps unconscious, tenet was that God—or some higher power—graciously preserved charitable spectators because they had shown that they deserved his—or its—protection. In this way, spectatorial sympathy often mixed genuine compassion with a sense of safe distance from suffering and even a morally smug attitude about it.

But sympathetic spectatorship also encouraged a more troubling activ-ity: the vicarious experience of someone else's suffering as a source of pleasure. In addition to Smith's compassion and Addison's formulation of difference and distance, it may be useful to consider another eighteenth-century thinker, the political philosopher Edmund Burke. As Addison pointed out, separation made it possible to enjoy the experience of anguish at a distance.[58] Burke sim-ilarly observed that "when danger or pain press too nearly, they are incapable of giving any delight, and are simply terrible; but at certain distances, and with certain modifications, they may be, and they are delightful. . . ."[59] Sentimental representations interposed a written text, a canvas, a stage performance, or, in the late twentieth century, a televised image "between the virtuous spectator and the (imaginary) suffering victim."[60] Those arts instituted the "modifications" that sustained the physical, emotional, and social distances necessary for spectatorial sympathy to work. Secure in their superiority but with just a frisson of danger, spectators could savor their feelings of pity.

Addison called pity "a kind of pleasing Anguish."[61] Other eighteenth-century writers described "the sweet emotion of pity" as a "dear delicious pain" and an "exquisite pleasure." They invited readers to indulge in "the luxury of grief." Historian Karen Halttunen notes that this pleasure-taking was always integral to spectatorial sympathy. In making "ethics a matter of viewing the pain of another, the literary scenario of suffering . . . lent itself to an aggressive kind of voyeurism" that she calls pornographic. This "pornography of pain" that took shape in the late eighteenth and early nineteenth centuries was, she concludes, "not merely a seamy sideline to humanitarian reform literature but rather an integral aspect of the humanitarian sensibility."[62]

The traditional rhetorical devices, laudable purposes, and self-centered gratifications reappeared on telethons. As throughout the history of spectatorial sympathy, ostentatious sentimentality was more than a stratagem to extract donations. It was a pleasure to be taken. Even when Jerry Lewis might distinguish between "going for the jugular" and "try[ing] to entertain and keep you glued to that set," the heart-touching and emotion-wrenching were inextricably part of the sentimentalized entertainment. The central performances on telethons were the displays of people with illnesses and disabilities, tragic and sad, sentimental and poignant, inspirational and heroic.[63]

On one early MDA telecast, host David Hartman epitomized the genre. He interviewed a man with a degenerative condition whose brother had already lost his life to the disease, which made it likely that he would also die of it. A TV critic described the encounter: "Hartman fished for grief with the usual pointed, morbid questions ('How did you feel when your brother died?'), at one point asking, 'What does "humanness" mean to you?' [The man] answered that it means being considered a person, not just someone diseased. Ignoring this answer, Hartman continued his interrogation, finally hitting pay dirt as [the man] began to cry. ... The sick man suddenly stopped moving. It was not actual death, or further paralysis, but a freeze-frame; and then that image of the immobilized [man] appeared on a huge video screen on-stage at the Sahara, with Jerry Lewis, his back to the camera, standing motionless, looking at the image, broadly 'moved,' yet unmoving." It was a classic moment of telethon pathos: "the victim, forever sad and damaged; the 'caring person' [the sentimental narrator] fixed in his concern; ourselves [the sympathizing spectators] still and staring, with our mouths hanging open."[64]

As one disabled man put it: "I think it is intact people who like to experience the feelings of sorrow and loss and bitterness over and over again—and who always ask injured people about these feelings, to conjure them up and experience them vicariously."[65] His words were self-stigmatizing, but his insight was on target. Just as Victorian readers of sentimental novels or humanitarian reform literature could be moved to tears by the plight of both fictional and actual sufferers, modern viewers could watch telethons for the pleasure of vicariously experiencing someone else's anguish. They could peep through their video windows at the telethonic Cratchits. On telethons, the spectacle of human suffering and striving was the most noteworthy form of entertainment.

Pleasure-taking and social distancing also came from ridicule. "There is, in fact, a certain reassuring air to the proceedings that confirms all is right with the world," entertainment critic Ray Richmond explained in a 1993 *Los Angeles Daily News* article. "We know that Jerry will showcase a head of hair that appears to have been marinated in Valvoline. We know that as the tote board rolls along to yet another certain all-time record, Jerry will greet the tote-changing timpani with his trademark, 'Oh yeah ... oh yeah ... OH YEAH!' We know that a succession of executives representing the Southland Corp. will emerge and hand Jerry checks in excess of $1 million apiece and then be moved to observe. . . . And there's plenty more where that came from."

Another journalist described her annual party: "Our gang usually wagers how long it will take Jerry to start crying once he begins his final number, 'You'll Never Walk Alone.' The winner calls in the pledge or goes out for more beer. ... In the early morning hours ... you and your guests may want to debate whether combining show business and muscular dystrophy is vulgar exploitation. The filmed segments of stricken children and their parents are often sadly tender and moving. But then, we're whipped back into Jerryland, watching the hardest working hair in show business schmooze and shtick his way across our living room."[66]

Because of the cult of sentimentality's emotional excesses, a critical countertradition rose up almost from the beginning. Literary scholar Michael Bell explains that sentimentalism began as an attempt "to base the moral life itself on feeling," but was often "so simplistic and overblown as to come into discredit even at the time."[67] Some eighteenth- and early-nineteenth-century critics questioned spectators' alleged virtue, condemning their sympathy as egocentric voyeurism. Poet John Keats and critic William Hazlitt indicted the poetry of sensibility for showcasing "not the feelings of the imagined sufferer but the feelings of the spectator watching that sufferer. . . ."[68] By the early twentieth century, notes Bell, the word "sentimental" had become "a term of near abuse referring to mawkish self-indulgence and actively pernicious modes of feeling."[69] TV critic Tom Shales complained that "one cult of telethon viewers has always watched [the MDA Telethon] mainly to ridicule—not the cause or the kids, but the crudeness of Lewis and the prevailing aura of vulgar kitsch. For this contingent, as the show has gotten tamer and less appalling, it's gotten worse."[70] Yet ridicule rested at the heart of this cynical detachment that only thinly masks mocking of "Jerry's kids." Sentimental spectatorship lent itself to not only voyeuristic indulgence in pity, but also a smug sense of superiority that diminished people with disabilities portrayed on the show. Even as nondisabled people often publicly expressed favorable attitudes toward people with disabilities, their "deeper, unverbalized feelings were frequently rejecting."[71] After all, as anthropologist Ann Douglas explains, sentimentalism "asserts that the values a society actively denies are precisely the ones it cherishes. . . ."[72]

Insider Versus Outsider Perspectives

Sentimental imaginings confirmed the status, privilege, and power of nondisabled spectators by substituting stereotypes for the lived experiences of people with disabilities. The extravagant and tearful responses out of pity or inspiration that had come to seem so natural and normal during the twentieth century often crowded out the varied emotions that would arise by sharing a social world with actual disabled people. Of course, people with disabilities experienced sadness and difficulty at times. Some had a larger share of physical pain and functional complications than most nondisabled people. And a small number had progressive conditions, some of which were fatal. Nonetheless, like all modern discourses of disability, telethons shaped sentimental narratives, conveniently ignoring disabled people's varied, complex, and rich perspectives. Individuals featured on telethons were chosen because their view of their lives matched prevailing attitudes. Moreover, telethon sympathy entrepreneurs, like Victorian humanitarians, coached disabled individuals to frame their experiences within a "rhetoric of affliction."[73] Live interviews and filmed vignettes squeezed the maximum pathos out of the persons they made available for gazing. Telethons distilled their stories into a poignant concentrate that conformed to the cult of sentimentality's conventions even while they reinforced the medical model of disability that promised to decouple disability from morality and sin.

These oversimplified framings persisted despite research on the actual experience of disability that revealed considerable nuance and complexity. Psychologist Nancy Weinberg and her colleagues found that disabled people's self-assessments ranged from seeing their lives as completely ruined to a positive incorporation of disability into their identities. It is especially important to note that those perceptions were not simply based on individuals' physical conditions but were often strongly affected by the socially constructed circumstances within which they had to live, such as dealing with architectural inaccessibility, limited job and health-care prospects, as well as prejudice and stigma. Furthermore, their views were seldom fixed. Fluid and changing over time, they were apparently influenced by both internal attitudes and social experiences.[74] Weinberg concluded, "We need to question the assumption that physical limitations are directly related to happiness."[75] Subsequent surveys bore this out, with results showing that disabled persons' perceptions of their quality of life appeared to have much to do with the adequacy of social and economic supports and the degree to which they had control over their life choices.[76]

Other studies reported a sharp disparity between "insider" and "outsider" views of the experience of illness and disability. Researchers repeatedly found that, as with other "devalued groups," while disabled people did not see themselves as "unfortunate," nondisabled people easily ascribed that label to them. For example, physically disabled people at a rehabilitation center "rated themselves as individuals at least average in terms of how fortunate they were," whereas others ranked them "below average." Beatrice Wright, a leading social psychologist studying disability, explained that "outsiders" attached a label that picked "the salient aspect to be observed and little else."[77] The limited cultural framing of disability made it possible for outsiders to latch onto a single negative trait that engulfed the entire person: That child cannot walk. That woman suffers from arthritic pain. That man breathes with a ventilator.

In contrast, insiders took into account the full range of their experiences, often emphasizing the positives.[78] It was not just that they grew accustomed to disability and learned how to deal with it. Rather, disability became part of their personal histories and identities. Nondisabled people often assumed that disabled people were putting the best face on their bad lot in life, yet according to researchers, many saw their experience as yielding much that was positive, even allowing them to incorporate their disabilities into their sense of self.[79] Unfortunately, what Wright describes as a "fundamental negative bias" steered perceptions, thinking, and feelings so much that observers often perceive positive elements and qualities in disabled people's experiences as negatives.[80] The telethon context provided little to challenge such negative views of disability—if anything, it played them up as part of its unrelenting sentimental narrative of pain and suffering.

The medical model's inherent undermining of disabled people's lives offered a particularly destructive example of fundamental negative bias. In this case, the outsiders, health-care professionals, disregarded social context, attributing "quality of life to the type and degree of physical and cognitive disability." They often believed that someone with a significant physical or cognitive disability "would want to be 'cured,' or ... might not want to be alive because," the professionals assumed, "their quality of life [was] poor."[81] While there is no doubt that many doctors and telethon producers acted out of sincere feeling for what they saw as the suffering of people they truly cared about, the sentimentalized sympathy in which they were steeped impaired their understanding. The medical model's pathologizing of disabled people's lives meant that they could see only functional difficulties, physical limitations, deterioration, and death. Such perceptions colored how most nondisabled people—the group most health-care providers saw themselves belonging to—thought about everything related to disability, from medical devices such as ventilators to basic life satisfaction.[82] Contrasting research by health professionals and by people with disabilities themselves, psychologist Carol J. Gill noted, "The gap is consistent and stunning."[83]

Attitudes toward medical devices reflected the stark insider–outsider divide. Tapped into medical views of disability, telethons gave no indication that many disabled people lived meaningful lives using the very tools that nondisabled society equated with a living death. On one MDA show, a woman told of her father, a very big, very strong man who never let anyone do anything for him and who grew progressively weaker from ALS (often referred to as Lou Gehrig's Disease). "I think the hardest thing for him was getting into that wheelchair," she said. Her mother said that he signed a form saying that under no circumstances did he want a ventilator. He felt that living on machines would not be living for him. It was his time to leave us, she said. She didn't want anyone else to go through that. "I never want another child to not be able to walk," she declared, nor did she want a child to wake up in terror each morning, fearing that his or her father might have died during the night. Her voice breaking, she asked viewers to donate in order to help Jerry make a miracle "for his Kids."[84] But in reality by the early 1990s, when more doctors were prescribing ventilators, increasing numbers of young men with various neuromuscular conditions were living into their early thirties and beyond. And by 2010, quadriplegic ventilator users with conditions such as DMD could celebrate their 50th birthdays and continue to work. Medical advances partly funded by MDA helped make this productive longevity possible, even as many medical practitioners themselves clung to older views.[85] The persistence of a sentimentalized image of disability and disabled people helps explain why the telethon's producers failed to inform sympathetic spectators that by using ventilators many people with ALS and DMD and other respiratory conditions shared a longer time with their loved ones and enjoyed a rich quality of life. Instead, the telethon upheld the belief that breathing on a ventilator—or even riding a wheelchair—was too horrible a fate to contemplate.

Telethons operated within this cultural tradition. They interpreted bodily differences as signifying interior states of being. Disabled people's lives were presented as existing within a narrow range of emotional extremes. They fostered in nondisabled spectators similarly restricted, oversimplified, and excessive emotional responses that came to be seen as the natural reactions to disability. Rather than confronting nondisabled spectators' ambivalent, rejecting, and even hostile attitudes and behavior, these simplistic melodramatic depictions covered conflicted and negative feelings. Emotionalistic narratives reverberated so intensely, so loudly, that they influenced and even drowned out other ways of understanding disability. Sentimentality shaped not only charity fundraising and media portrayals but also public policy making, social services, and medical practice. Yet modern criticism usually left this emotionally disproportionate framing unexamined, unquestioned, and therefore invisible.[86] As a result, the consequences for people with disabilities could be the opposite of the happy future promised by telethons.

"Look at Us We're Walking"

CURE-SEEKERS, INVALIDS, AND OVERCOMERS

Telethons made medical needs the overriding concern of people with disabilities in a system devoid of universal health care and with an unraveling safety net. The shows dwelt on the quest for cure—or quasi-cure of overcoming disability through rehabilitation—but the framework involved more than medical matters. It also defined the social roles and identities available to people with disabilities. Without cures that would make them socially normal, they would be "invalids" or must become "overcomers." For many, these became their primary social identities. As we will see in chapter 13 below, beginning in the 1990s, disability rights activists condemned telethons for propagating an ideology that medicalized and pathologized disabled people and their families. Yet at the same time, telethon talk about cure, invalidity, and overcoming obscured efforts by the charities that indirectly undermined that medical model. More than simply seeking cures, agencies such as UCP, Spina Bifida Association, and Easter Seals came to embrace an approach that encouraged their clients to enhance their health and quality of life, thereby undergirding their family relationships, productive employment, and participation in the community. This implicitly supported a new positive late-twentieth-century identity that competed with the invalid and overcomer identities: "people with disabilities." Insofar as telethon messages registered that development, they became increasingly contradictory, relying as they did on infantilizing images of the individuals they helped.

The Quest for a Cure

As part of their medical focus, most of the telethon-producing charities portrayed the quest for cure as central to their missions. Charity professionals began making bombastic promises when the March of Dimes pledged that children "crippled" by polio would walk and anyone who contracted it would one day wake up free of the disease. The NFIP billed its campaign "as a kind of holy quest,"[1] despite the fact that scientists and physicians knew that such promises were vastly overblown. NFIP executives believed that for the crusade to succeed, "a certain amount of flamboyant publicity was absolutely necessary and they must go along with it."[2]

Like the NFIP, the Arthritis Foundation, MDA, and UCP Telethons talked frequently, even extravagantly, about the quest. The host of the Arthritis Foundation's San Jose, California, show described a roomful of grant proposals submitted by scientists who were "trying to find the cause of arthritis." Never mind that it was the amalgamation of over one hundred connective-tissue diseases, making it impossible to find a single causative agent. "Somewhere in that room," he declared, "there may be the cure for arthritis."[3] Year after year on the MDA show, Jerry Lewis announced breakthroughs related to muscular dystrophy, while local MCs promised that a cure was near. In 1994 a Denver host repeatedly asserted that "this may be the year," a claim MDA's San Jose, California, host had made a year earlier using the exact same phrase. (He was, by the way, the same MC who talked to the Arthritis Foundation Telethon audience about a single cure for arthritis.) Though just nine of the more than forty neuromuscular conditions MDA addressed were forms of muscular dystrophy, the rhetoric often conflated all of them into a single disease. That melding, like the many conditions that constituted arthritis, surely made it easier to expect medical science to come up with the miracle of a single, all-encompassing cure for the entire lot.[4]

But as with the scientists and physicians who had studied and treated polio, researchers and doctors specializing in neuromuscular conditions were much more circumspect. The MDA website's "Ask the Experts" section allowed visitors to query those specialists about neuromuscular conditions and treatments. Disability activist and telethon critic Laura Hershey reported lots of questions about a cure. But "in almost all cases, the doctors responded with great caution. They said things like: '... it is very hard to predict the exact pace that expected advances will take'; and 'This is something that cannot be predicted with certainty'; and 'Gene therapy faces serious technical problems. It is very hard to say when these will be solved. Scientific discoveries are hard to predict. . . .'" Hershey concluded that "the information provided [on the MDA website] doesn't support the overblown claims of imminent, dramatic cures which are made on the Telethon." She called telethon cure talk "strictly a marketing ploy."[5]

The UCP telecasts seemed to make the most intemperate promises. In 1989 a guest star told viewers that research "has done a lot to curb this dreaded disease," while another said that research could "help prevent the spread of this dreaded malady." As with so many disabling pathologies, cerebral palsy was a catchall term for a number of conditions rather than a single disease.

Indeed, it was not a disease in the sense in which most people used that word. Although it was not contagious, over the years some UCP stars promised that research would stop its spread. As late as 1996, MC Dennis James was talking about the possibility of finding a cure.[6] Even though 25 percent of UCP spending that went to medical research focused on prevention and rehabilitation, UCP's producers prompted the hosts to make astonishing claims. In 1992, one MC predicted: "[By] the year 2000 cerebral palsy will be eliminated," and the following year Dennis James forecast "there will be no child born with cerebral palsy by the year 2000." By 1995 he was proclaiming that with the help of television viewers "the next great step for people with cerebral palsy and other disabilities [will be] a future where the word 'disability' will one day be eliminated from our vocabulary." UCP propaganda, in effect, enlisted donors, not just to prevent cerebral palsy, but in a chimerical crusade to eradicate all disabilities.[7]

Unable to fulfill such promises but continuing to tout possible cures, the MDA, Arthritis, and UCP Telethons focused on prevention as well as health management, support services, and rehabilitation. In fact, much of the research supported by MDA did not aim at a cure.[8] Some of it led to genetic screening that, rather than curing diseases, made possible their prevention through abortion. One such disease was spinal muscular atrophy (SMA). Living with the condition, disability activist Laura Hershey drove a power wheelchair and used a ventilator. She also enjoyed a career as a writer and was raising a daughter with her partner. She rebuked MDA's telethon for portraying life with disabilities like SMA as an unmitigated tragedy and condemned the organization for proudly publicizing genetic research developments that "allow[ed] prospective parents to decide not to give birth to a child with SMA."[9]

In fact, most of the genetic, pharmacological, and other MDA-funded research made great strides in treatments that enhanced the health and functioning of people with neuromuscular disabilities, significantly increasing the longevity and quality of life of many. For example, a telethon film from 1990 showed three women who walked more easily because an MDA-supported scientist came up with a new treatment for myasthenia gravis and related diseases.[10] Indeed, MDA put far more money and effort into services than research, with its 1993 telethon reporting that less than a quarter of funds went into research while around 57 percent went to patient services. That medicalized label referred not only to clinics, but also devices such as wheelchairs and programs such as support groups and summer camps, a far cry from the rhetoric of cure on its telethons.

Meanwhile, the National Easter Seals Society, one of the largest providers of rehabilitation in the United States, promised neither prevention nor cure; it touted treatments such as physical therapy to help people "overcome" their disabilities. UCP's Telethon also made overcoming through rehabilitation a major theme. Constituting a kind of ersatz cure, overcoming was, as we shall see, problematic, too. In reality, UCP's programs mostly supported rehabilitation, education, independent living, and employment for people with cerebral palsy.[11]

Unique among telethons, the Arthritis Foundation helped to produce innovative treatments that did not cure people but instead enhanced their health and functioning: Advanced, nonnarcotic anti-inflammatory drugs managed pain with fewer side effects and new exercises increased range of motion and prevented overuse of joints. Those exercises, along with new surgical techniques, boosted physical functioning and general health. These many treatments sought not only to slow or stop the progress of connective-tissue diseases, but also to help individuals improve their quality of life.[12] From its start in 1948, the Foundation provided rehabilitation to aid people with arthritis in managing their conditions, returning to work, and living their daily lives. Literally embodying those goals, its first national chair was Atlas Corporation Board Chairman Floyd Odlum, who had rheumatoid arthritis.[13] In the 1990s, the telethon still pursued those goals. A film assured, "Having arthritis doesn't mean that you have to stop what you do, but rather learn ways to modify how you do it." Segments like this one showed people doing daily activities with devices for reaching, picking things up, and turning doorknobs. They also offered tips on inexpensive ways to adapt one's home environment. Meanwhile, the Foundation's agenda exemplified the movement urging individuals to play an active part in their own health care: Learn as much as you can about your condition. Ask specific questions of your health-care providers. If you don't understand, ask them to explain it again in language you do understand. Take charge of your health care. "Remember," urged a film, "it's you and not your doctor who makes the daily decisions concerning your health." The telethon's slogan summed up the message: "Stay in charge! And live well with arthritis."[14]

While telethons reported on many of these activities, propaganda about cure or prevention completely overshadowed them. Put another way, the airtime devoted to promising a cure was vastly disproportionate to that which discussed what many of the charities actually accomplished. This obscured one of the great achievements of modern medical science and thus of the telethon-producing charities. Rather than curing people, medicine more often boosted the health and functioning of those who lived with a wide variety of health conditions, in some instances extending the longevity of people who had theretofore life-shortening diseases. For the first time in human history, people who would have perished or languished, now not only survived, they thrived. The charities could take some credit for development of those treatments. They played an even bigger role in reframing moral perceptions and social values to convince Americans that providing that medical care—not only through private donations but also government expenditures—was a societal obligation and imperative.

MDA's official magazine was equally progressive when it came to disability, as Hershey discovered much to her surprise. In 1991 she found articles "about job-seeking strategies; profiles of successful individuals who have neuromuscular diseases; honest and thoughtful pieces about families of children with neuromuscular diseases; lists of useful resources; and clinical updates."[15] Hershey, one of the most articulate disability rights critics of telethons, praised MDA's magazine as "a high-quality forum for education, information, and the sharing of experiences," and noted its "realism and insight," "positive, realistic tone," and use of "respectful and appropriate language." The phrase "'people with disabilities' was used at all times—never 'victims,' or 'sufferers,' and certainly not 'cripples.'" In contrast, the telethon traditionally depicted people with neuromuscular disabilities as doomed and desperate. It struck her that these were "two very different presentations, intended for two very different audiences." The magazine served "people with neuromuscular diseases and their families." The telethon aimed fearsome images of tragedy at prospective donors, who were apparently presumed to be nondisabled.[16] Hershey's comments on this discrepancy could have been applied in one way or another to the other charities and their telethons. Even while the charities supported the efforts of their constituents to live fulfilling lives as "people with disabilities," their telethons propagated a contradictory ideology that pathologized them.

Given the momentous difference that medical advances and rehabilitation made that allowed so many people to live worthwhile and productive lives, why did three of the four telethons put such emphasis on cure or prevention? Why did they try so strenuously to raise expectations that sovereign remedies were at hand? On one level, the charities were shrewdly copying the March of Dimes' flamboyant but highly successful publicity. Trumpeting a quest-for-cure narrative, they recruited donors to a crusade far more dramatic than merely supporting the health and functioning of people with chronic conditions as they lived ordinary daily lives. Furthermore, pledges of cure or prevention appealed to donors' self-interest. If "this" could happen to you or your family, as the telethons so often warned, the prospect of conquering illness offered charity-givers personal protection. Also, as a later chapter will show, these false promises fed the desperate hopes of some parents that their children who had disabilities could be made over into "normal" kids.

Meanwhile, unspoken on the telethons but present in public discourse, cure would eliminate disability as a social problem by making disabled people virtually disappear. Such "success" supposedly would relieve the financial burden of long-term personal assistance services. It would also turn aside the political demands of disabled people who were becoming increasingly activist. It would obviate the need for civil rights measures that ensured access and reasonable accommodations and barred discrimination in education, employment, and public services. If people with disabilities got better, non-disabled individuals would not have to grapple with their personal biases and society would not have to rectify its institutionalized exclusionary practices.[17] Hershey called cure "a simple, magical, non-political solution. ... The other solutions we have to work for, even fight for; we only have to dream about the cure."[18] In other words, the search for a cure was understood to be above politics and beyond reproach.

An American penchant for such dreams was central to this quest for cure. The fanciful promises tapped into a boundless faith in modern science. Science could—one day it would—eliminate not just some diseases and disabilities but all disease and disability. The pledges of cure or eradication also reflected many Americans' insistence on total and unconditional victory.[19] Anything less they considered de facto defeat. The charity professionals surely shared these fantasies with the donors. And so both they and the public demanded complete triumph. In a sense, it did not matter that the cures never came. What counted was the quest and the belief that Americans would in the end master fate. Cure would erase the visible presence of people whose health conditions, modes of functioning, and appearance threatened, as we shall see, American myths of control of individual and collective destiny.

Invalids

In making their pleas to nondisabled donors, telethons deployed extreme images of people with disabilities that conformed to the rhetoric of sentimentality discussed in the previous chapter. They portrayed a few as doomed to physical death and all as condemned to social invalidity, which is to say, social death. At the same time, the shows presented many as striving to escape invalidity by overcoming their disabilities, that is, transcending their physical limitations and more important the social defects assumedly inherent in disability. These depictions consigned people with disabilities to one of two restrictive but, in an ironic way, complementary social roles and identities, that of invalids or overcomers. We shall examine each in turn.

Telethon viewers unconsciously absorbed charity fundraising messages that defined what it meant to be an invalid. Activists like Hershey scorned shows that portrayed life with a disability "as a fullblown tragedy ... [that] invalidates—literally, makes invalids of—people with disabilities and the hardwon perspectives we can offer."[20] Programs presented these framings as factual statements of biological and social reality, but, in fact, they naturalized cultural constructions of disability. As depicted on telethons, *in-valids* could not satisfy any valued social role.

Despite improving portrayals of people with disabilities such as those mentioned above, telethons fell back on old stereotypes, such as presenting invalids as incapacitated for work. On the Arthritis Foundation's 1989 Telethon, former talkshow host Sarah Purcell told of a young woman who enjoyed a professional career until diagnosed with arthritis. After that, her life allegedly "revolved around arthritis."[21] Likewise, the MDA show frequently asserted that people with neuromuscular diseases could not go into the workplace; in fact, they could do nothing. Because prevailing opinion believes that having a disability precludes doing any kind of work, surely more than one person with a disability has shared Hershey's experience of having her "occupation" listed on her medical records as "disabled."[22]

Moreover, telethons suggested that as invalids, the disabled were unfit parents. One host assumed that arthritis caused poor parenting. "An adult deserves a chance to be a good parent," she said, "and to not have to walk in a walker, or to be maybe irritable or cranky because they hurt."[23] An Easter Seals MC talked about a woman who had sustained a back injury. In bed for a long time, she "could not take care of her children." But Easter Seals got "her back on her feet. We had her doing all of the things at home that moms do to take care of their families, and now she is the mother of her family again." As long as she could not walk or do physical chores, a woman could not be a real mother or satisfy a traditional gender role.[24] On a broadcast of the MDA Telethon, parents with disabilities worried that they would not be able to pick up their children, "as if someone in a wheelchair could never provide children with affection, discipline, or moral or financial support."[25]

According to telethons, invalids were also unsuitable romantic partners. The MDA program brought on a father to say that his teenage daughter would never "be asked to the prom."[26] Meanwhile, an Arthritis Foundation film narrated the life of Alice Bradley, a woman with rheumatoid arthritis: "Arthritis escorted Alice into her teenage years. It graduated from UCLA with Alice. Ultimately, arthritis married Alice, till death do them part." Arthritis was Alice Bradley's lifelong lover and companion, an incubus, whose nightmarish embrace she could not escape.[27] These segments upheld the bias that people with physical disabilities—especially women with physical disabilities—were incapable of romance or marriage.[28]

Telethons also suggested that invalids could not enjoy ordinary personal interactions. "Look at me," said an Easter Seals host as she bustled in front of the camera. "I can walk across the set here, and I can kind of tease with these folks over here [the phone operators]. … [T]here's a lot of people who can't do that. They need to have a wheelchair or crutches or someone actually help them." People who used wheelchairs or crutches, she absurdly implied, could not banter with friends.[29] An Arthritis Foundation host declared that arthritis "is not just crippling physically" but "crippling emotionally."[30] Disability allegedly made real relationships impossible.

Such exclusions seemed inevitable given how most telethons framed the incomprehensible suffering that consumed invalids' lives. *Normal* people could not conceive just how much invalids struggled, even as sentimental spectatorship invited them not only to try, but also to take pleasure in it. "You know, most of us have no idea of the pain these people with arthritis are going through," lamented a telethon MC, her voice almost breaking.[31] For invalids, life was always downhill. "I guess," conjectured Leeza Gibbons, a national MDA host, "there's the knowledge that today is the best you've got."[32] And so invalids presumably feared for the future. "Often there is something beyond the pain," asserted Arthritis Foundation host Mickey Gilley. "It's a sense of fear from [*sic*] the future or even the present. It is that feeling of not knowing what may happen."[33] Neuromuscular disabilities were "uncertain and frightening," declared Jerry Lewis. To confirm that claim, the telethon's producers selected parents who described their children as counting up losses rather than accomplishments. Life, they kept saying, only gets worse. "It never gets easier," said one mother. "It gets harder every year. It gets harder for her physically. It gets harder . . . socially."[34]

Invalids hung on in a state of suspended animation, looking to doctors to help them endure day to day, hoping against hope that one day the miracle cure would happen. "Sometimes," asserted Arthritis Foundation MC Larry Van Nuys, "all you have to get through another day is the kind of hope" the Arthritis Foundation offered. He claimed that 37 million Americans with arthritis "dream[t] about" the moment they would learn that "the cure had come."[35] Year after year, the UCP Telethon's Dennis James described hopeful parents imagining their "cerebral palsied" children walking and talking, as if those abilities were lost to everyone with the condition. It was a phantasm of normality, of social authenticity, that, according to telethons, ceaselessly occupied invalids' minds. A performance of the pop song "One Moment in Time"—made famous by Whitney Houston—on the Arthritis Telethon reinforced that fantasy, as it was sung to a young girl, "I want one moment in time / When I'm more than I thought I could be."[36]

The drama of suffering could be heightened by contrasting a "normal," presumably "healthy," state and an assumed unhealthy disabled one. Telethons sometimes had actors contrast their temporary performance of fictional roles as disabled characters with disabled people trapped in the permanent role of the invalid. In 1990 the then-teenaged actor Fred Savage starred in a TV movie "When You Remember Me" about a disabled youth who fought for nursing home reform.[37] On the MDA show, he spoke briefly about that battle for justice and dignity, but, following the typical telethon script, he dwelt mostly on the invalidating limitation supposedly inevitable with a disability. "Doing the movie, what is the most important thing you learned about someone suffering from muscular dystrophy?" asked Lewis. He learned about all the things they could not do, said Savage. "Tell them about being an actor," instructed Lewis. "[F]or a little while you get to become somebody else," read Savage dutifully. But "when I go home at night, I can be myself again. I can, you know, call my friends on the phone. I can participate in sports." The scenario contrasted the young nondisabled actor with the nonprofessional, disabled actors who played the other nursing home inmates. They were actual wheelchair riders. That apparently meant they could not participate in sports (not even wheelchair sports?) or "call [their] friends on the phone." Supposedly confined not just to their wheelchairs but to the invalid role, they could not "be" themselves—or rather, socially legitimate selves.[38]

An Arthritis Foundation show prompted actor Alan Rachins, then starring on NBC's popular LA Law, to mark the same invalidating difference. "One of the nice things about being an actor is having the opportunity to totally lose your identity and become someone else for a brief period of time," he said. "For 37 million Americans though, there is no escape, not even on a temporary basis, from the physical and emotional struggles of living with arthritis." When at last the cure came, they would no longer "want to escape the reality of their own life."[39] Likewise, UCP enlisted Broadway and TV star Jerry Orbach to contrast acting's playful escapism with the inescapable grimness of an invalid identity. "You know, getting to play a character every night enables me to create another identity, another kind of a personality. But I know once the camera clicks off, that's it, and I get to be me again. Now, a person with cerebral palsy, the scenario is quite a different case. Personality, character, disability are constant. It never changes: the affected speech, the involuntary movements [he twitched as he said this], the irregular gait."[40] Cerebral palsy allegedly ensnared people in both an unacceptable body and an invalidating "personality" and "character."

Such telethon laments created a gulf between a presumably healthy nondisabled "us" and the ghastly suffering of a disabled "them." They reinforced the view that people with disabilities were caged in an identity-defining, identity-devouring social role, one created largely from the imagination and dread of the nondisabled. Arthritis Foundation hosts and guests said that people with arthritis were "trapped," "imprisoned," "condemned."[41] Disability engulfed their personhood, precluding any positive role or identity.

That verdict was implicit in MDA's depiction of "Jerry's kids." The telethon focused viewers' attention on certain kinds of MDA "patients." It featured many adults with ALS and boys with DMD. But MDA's own figures showed that persons with those diseases were unrepresentative of the million Americans with neuromuscular conditions. Some 20,000 had ALS, yet they were a lopsided percentage of adults on the telethon.[42] Although the telethon portrayed all such children as doomed, respiratory assistance—once MDA-supported doctors began to prescribe it—enhanced the longevity and quality of life of many of them.[43]

MDA Telethons had valid reasons for depicting virtually all of "Jerry's kids" as perishing. The programs expressed genuine concern for children, some of whom did, in fact, have terminal illnesses. At the same time, dying people evoked greater sympathy and drew more donations than those with chronic conditions. People with life-shortening illnesses had a right to the medical care they needed, especially given the fact that government-run health care wasn't always up to the task. But by conflating these children with people who had long-term conditions, the telethon made it seem that most people with neuromuscular disabilities were doomed, on the verge of imminent death. Yet more was going on here than profound empathy mixed with fundraising pragmatism. A close reading of charity image-making disclosed that *all* people with disabilities were, in a sense, doomed. As an Arthritis Foundation Telethon host warned ominously, "Time is running out for people who have arthritis."[44]

US health charities had long used fear to motivate donations.[45] Taking it to a new level, telethons warned that you or someone you loved might, in the blink of an eye, be transformed into an invalid. "All of us are just an accident or a stroke or a disease away from getting the help of Easter Seals," admonished a Los Angeles MC. "[I]t can happen to anybody," cautioned an overnight host of the Easter Seals' regional Chicago broadcast, even "God forbid, in your own family."[46] Arthritis Foundation Telethon hosts and stars said over and over how frightening they found the possibility of having arthritis. An actress said that a few years earlier she suffered a couple of weeks of "hell" because of a mistaken diagnosis of rheumatoid arthritis. During those days of anguish, she kept thinking, "Oh, my God! I'm going to be crippled for life!"[47] Dennis James asked the parents of a boy with cerebral palsy, "Now, you've been watching the telethon in years past? Did you ever think it would happen to you?" "No," replied the mother, "never."[48] Raising that specter, Jerry Lewis warned, "A dystrophic child happens either at birth or when he's six or seven, just like that, overnight. Your healthy child can go to bed tonight fine and wake up tomorrow and be one of my kids. Think about it coming into your home." He does not want "you" to be "one of the million neuromuscular problems in the world today."[49]

Lewis and the Easter Seals, Arthritis Foundation, and UCP hosts were not just cautioning that viewers or their children might suffer the physical and financial hardship of a disease or injury. They were signaling the more terrifying threat that one's social identity might undergo a sudden and catastrophic transfiguration. "It" could come into "your home." You or your child could become an invalid. Invalids were patients, clients, objects of charity. They were dependent and passive, acted upon rather than acting. They could play no positive social role. Pathology, defect, and deviance defined their identities. In *The Unexpected Minority*, John Gliedman and William Roth wrote that the reigning ideology stigmatized people with disabilities as "incapable

of assuming any normal social function, even the most humble and demeaning." Denying them "any positive social persona" and "any place at all in normal society," this "exclusive negative social identity [was] psychologically and
socially synonymous with denial of any human identity whatever." It was "the
most radical act of social declassification possible."[50] The theme of invalidity was central to the Arthritis Foundation and MDA shows and significant
on the UCP fundraisers. Easter Seals implicitly warned that unless their clients were enabled to overcome their disabilities through rehabilitation, they
would be invalids.

Overcomers

For people with disabilities who wanted to break free of invalidity, the medical model—grounded in the notion that disability should be understood as
an individual's pathological state—prescribed overcoming as the only alternative. An Easter Seals host described a disabled radio newscaster as "a man
who knows very well what it means to be an overcomer." The man himself
said that with Easter Seal's help, he learned "that wheelchair and all, I am still
a valid person, not an *in*valid or in*val*id person."[51] While often celebrated in
the media and especially on telethons, when subjected to scrutiny, overcoming turns out to be far more complex and problematic.

The telethon rhetoric of overcoming grew out of postpolio and disabled
veterans' rehabilitation of the 1930s, 1940s, and 1950s; Franklin Roosevelt's
carefully fashioned public persona; and March of Dimes propaganda.[52] The
Arthritis Foundation and MDA Telethons sometimes invoked it.[53] The UCP
and Easter Seals programs perfected it. In late-twentieth-century America,
overcoming was the dominant approach in medical and vocational rehabilitation and significant in special education. In the culture at large, it was the
requisite mode of individual coping with disability under the regime of what
disability studies scholar Robert McRuer has called "compulsory able-bodiedness."[54] Overcoming entailed contesting a disability's physical limitations,
resisting the presumed likelihood of self-pity by displaying cheerful indomitability, and striving toward physical, psychological, and social normality. It
did not ensure the complete social validity imagined as produced by cure. It
pledged instead that people with disabilities who battled toward a semblance
of normality would be granted provisional social legitimacy and partial social
acceptance.

Although overcoming could achieve no more than an approximation of
normality, hyperbolic telethon rhetoric sometimes depicted it as virtual cure.
UCP's Dennis James often talked as though the charity and its contributors
had supplied the fantasized outcome. "You've made a lot of able-bodied people
out of disabled people," he congratulated viewers. "I've seen youngsters like

this grow up to be able-bodied men and women, out into the business world, just making a good living on their own, and having families of their own." "[Y]ou have it within your power and grasp to get those kids off those [wheel] chairs and out of those braces and off those crutches and back into society, to be whole again, to be able-bodied," asserted James. He promised that year-by-year viewers would see children progress toward normality. Instructing one boy to walk across the stage to his father, he promised viewers, "Next year, that boy will be riding a bicycle, probably roller skating. Now, that's a miracle only you can perform. ... You can give a life to the youngsters." Without the treatments, he warned, "they don't progress. They don't become part of society."[55] They would stay stuck in the invalid role, socially dead. "A lot of them won't be able to get that far," James admitted, but they should try because the most important thing was to strive toward the ever-elusive but compulsory goal of able-bodiedness.[56]

UCP's New York City Telethon promoted this view in its memorable segment that displayed children with cerebral palsy along with a song that suggested their yearning for physical and social normality: "Look at us, we're walking, / Look at us, we're talking, / We who never walked or talked before," they sang. Presumably telethon viewers were to provide funds that would allow all children to escape invalidism, but within restricted normative roles that excluded riding wheelchairs or using interpreters or assistive devices to communicate.[57]

More than any other activity, walking became the chief expression of overcoming. Telethons dwelt obsessively on disabled people standing up and walking. Those physical efforts supposedly made it possible for them to feel proud and served as a powerful, dramatic symbol of cure. On one Easter Seals telecast, for example, a 9-year-old boy with cerebral palsy used a wheelchair when he had to go any distance, but the MC stressed that he got physical therapy every week because "he wants to get out of that thing."[58] Another program showed Dennis James asking a little girl to stand up wearing her leg braces. He asked: "Are you proud to be standing up?" When the beaming little girl followed her mother's cue to "say yes," the studio audience applauded.[59] After a boy with juvenile rheumatoid arthritis had gone through weeks of physical therapy to prepare for his appearance on the Arthritis Telethon, the host informed the audience how proud the little boy was to be walking around the stage without the leg braces he usually wore.[60]

Such images were not limited to children, as the story of a student on the Easter Seals Telethon made clear. After announcing that he had graduated from college "in my wheelchair," the young man's voice was replaced by a narrator who exclaimed: "But for his Master's degree, he decided to do something special which would crown his educational achievement." He would "walk across the stage with braces and crutches," thanks to physical therapy provided by Easter Seals. A home video showed him at the graduation ceremony wearing long leg braces and using crutches as he moved laboriously across the stage. The audience gave him a standing ovation. He proclaimed to them, "Our spirit cannot be held down by anything." But as he told his story on the telethon, he was, in fact, sitting on his wheelchair. And in later appearances as an Easter Seals National Adult, he was riding it.[61]

Apparently, the impulse toward overcoming could start at an early age. A filmed profile of an Easter Seals National Child described how she "was walking with a walker at eighteen months." And then a year and a half later, she amazed her therapist when she gave up her walker altogether and started walking on her own. But while the film showed her using crutches and wearing leg braces in one scene, in others she rode her wheelchair as she practiced in karate class and played wheelchair tennis and golf.[62]

Viewers might have wondered about the discrepancy between telethon stories of disabled people standing and walking and the apparent fact that these young people usually rode their wheelchairs or wore leg braces. For many people with disabilities, riding a wheelchair was functionally more efficient, a smarter use of their energies. But walking, though enervating and in the long run even physically harmful, reflected the cultural imperative to strive toward a semblance of normality. If being "confined to a wheelchair for life" was the emblem of the invalid, walking was made the epitome of overcoming disability and escaping social invalidation.

There were also unacknowledged practical reasons to push for walking. The built environment with its many steps and narrow passageways is still largely inaccessible to wheelchair users. Parents might hope that if their children can walk, they will be able to enter businesses, homes, and other places such as parks and gardens that are the exclusive preserve of people who walk. They might want to believe that walking could ensure their youngsters' assimilation and integration into the larger society that bars them from taking certain jobs, visiting certain friends or family, and participating in certain outdoor activities. But the fact is that these young people will always have mobility impairments. They will never be able to walk with the ease that will make that environment readily usable by them unless they compromise by pushing themselves to exhaustion. These exclusive environments and the prevailing assumptions that go along with them will always make these struggling walkers awkward, provisional visitors rather than true residents. By pushing someone to overcome his or her individual disability, the telethons ignored the situations that made not being able to walk problematic. But given the prevalence of sentimentalizing stories and the accompanying medical model, hosts were not likely to urge viewers to insist on making more spaces accessible to more people by championing an architectural cure.

Ultimately, the desire of families, doctors, and therapists that a person should walk at almost any cost rested on cultural values about what constituted a whole person in modern America. People in wheelchairs are looked down upon, literally and figuratively. "Wheelchair-bound" means identity-bound. If you are "confined to a wheelchair," you will be consigned to being an in-valid. Use a wheelchair, go to stigma-jail.[63] Since no loving parents want that for their son or daughter, they urged their children to pursue the only obvious alternative: constant therapies and repeated surgeries to correct their bodies and, even more, to try to correct their identities. To escape from the invalid role, they are led to believe, they must throw themselves into the overcomer role, the futile quest to become normal.

Walking was but an obvious example of the pervasive American goal to be independent and as self-sufficient as possible. "The Easter Seals touch," proclaimed actor Ricardo Montalban, helped people with disabilities "live and work and get along on their own, so they once again will say with pride, 'I can do it myself.'"[64] The mother of an Easter Seals National Child declared proudly that "when [people] try to help her, she says, 'No. I can do it.'"[65] Asking for help veered dangerously close to invalidism. No wonder that so many individuals with disabilities strained toward "independence" even when it proved detrimental to their health.[66] They knew that insofar as they required assistance, they would be classified as dependent and socially discredited.

Physical overcoming had a perhaps more important mental corollary in what might be called "an overcoming mindset." The rhetoric of overcoming promised that even people who had extensive physical disabilities such as quadriplegia could partially compensate for their invalidating dependency by displaying relentless inner resolve and cheerfulness. Easter Seals pictured physically strenuous rehabilitation as "building character, instilling confidence," and "building self-esteem."[67] In fact, what undermined the struggles of people with disabilities to believe in themselves was the incessant cultural message that they were inadequate and incomplete as they were. Nonetheless, Easter Seals selected National Children and Adults who incarnated sunny indomitability. A filmed profile described one as "a doer," who "doesn't let [cerebral palsy] get her down." The next year's National Child was also "a doer" who was "optimistic" with "grit" and "determination." "Because her family and her friends at Easter Seals have taught her to be all she can be, [she] doesn't let anything stand in her way—not even spina bifida."[68]

Overcoming was not rooted in a scientific understanding of what made bodies healthy or a realistic assessment of the most efficient ways to function with a disability. It grew out of cultural imperatives. Many Americans believed that individuals who worked hard could achieve success against any obstacles and that failures typically stemmed from personal faults.[69] Telethons did not blame individuals for bringing their disabilities on themselves. Quite the contrary. But they did restate culturewide beliefs by making personal success or failure in coping with a disability a matter of individual will. Overcoming located the problem of disability in the bodies and, more important, the character and attitudes of people with disabilities. It then defined the solution in terms of individual adjustment. Easter Seals invited right-wing radio talk show host Rush Limbaugh to link overcoming to basic American values. "My friends," he asserted, "what makes America great . . . is our rugged individualism. Once we have our independence, the possibilities for achievement are limitless."[70] Channeling such a message through Limbaugh signaled overcoming's social and political implications.

Invalidating Overcoming

While each telethon's narrative emphasized either the invalid or overcomer roles, all propagated the medical model. Charity professionals promoted that ideology, but they had not invented it. The medical model and the invalid and overcomer roles it prescribed originated and were most powerfully institutionalized in public policies and health care, educational and social service professions and programs. Social welfare policies required millions of people with disabilities to present themselves as incapacitated for productive work or any other valued social role in order to qualify for health insurance and support services that they could not obtain in the private sector. At the same time, rehabilitation and education policies and programs focused on fixing individuals by correcting their physical and social functioning. Furthermore, whatever the setting, a clinic or a classroom, a Social Security office or a services center, the dominant ideology defined people with disabilities as incompetent to manage their own lives and enforced their submission to professional or bureaucratic authority. Public policies and professional practices repeatedly compelled them to comply with the invalid and overcomer roles.[71]

Meanwhile, arrangements in other social spheres reinforced those roles. Architecture and technology traditionally designed spaces and products that inconvenienced or completely excluded people with disabilities. Dominant ideologies in both design and disability took the built environment for granted as normal, disguising that it was contrived to accommodate nondisabled people. Instead of seeing inaccessibility as caused by design flaws, ideology attributed it to flaws in disabled people's bodies. Given the general lack of access and accommodations until near the end of the twentieth century, environments and products fashioned for nondisabled people became for people with disabilities another expression of compulsory able-bodiedness, another mandate that they must overcome.[72]

Likewise, the mass media depicted people with disabilities as violating normal social role expectations because of their physical flaws and psychological and social deviance. At the same time, the media lauded successful disabled individuals for triumphing over personal adversity. Some were rewarded for performing the overcomer persona as a public career, with the corporate system deploying them to prove that in America all things were possible for those who tried harder. The rhetoric of overcoming masked the inequities that kept down most people with disabilities.[73]

In fact, most working-age adults with disabilities were barred from productive employment by pervasive discrimination in the job market and work disincentives in public policies. Many were shunted into a separate economic sector where they were permanent patients and clients, profitable to vendors of treatments, services, and devices.[74] Rendered unproductive, dependent, socially incompetent, and in fact schooled in incompetency, their socioeconomic situation confirmed the invalidity ideology had already decreed. "No wonder few of us find it strange that tens of millions of . . . disabled people are segregated from the mainstream of daily life," said Gliedman and Roth in 1980. "We simply don't expect to find them among us."[75] Those who seemingly escaped marginalization were lauded for a ruggedly individualistic perseverance that set them above invalids. In every sphere—public policies and professional practices, the built environment and technology, the economic system and media representations, including telethon framings—US society so relentlessly enforced the invalid and overcomer roles that one or the other became many individuals' primary identity.

Nondisabled Americans remained largely unaware of these realities because ideology substituted fictive images that effectively rendered real people with disabilities invisible. That displacement included telethon portrayals of them as socially invalidated by medical conditions and either longing for cure or striving to overcome their physical and sociological shortcomings. Disability rights activists criticized the impact of those ideas. "We are read as avatars of misfortune and misery, stock figures in melodramas about courage and determination," said disability rights lawyer Harriet McBryde Johnson, who had muscular dystrophy. "The world wants our lives to fit into a few rigid narrative templates: how I conquered disability (and others can conquer their Bad Things!), how I adjusted to disability (and a positive attitude can move mountains!), how disability made me wise (you can only marvel and hope it never happens to you!), how disability brought me to Jesus (but redemption is waiting for you if only you pray)."[76] Nondisabled people, said Dai R. Thompson, who published on deinstitutionalization, "tend to view us either as helpless things to be pitied or as Super Crips, gallantly fighting to overcome insurmountable odds. Such attitudes display a bizarre two-tiered mindset: it is horrible beyond imagination to be disabled, but disabled people with guts can, if they only try hard enough, make themselves almost 'normal.'"[77]

Having framed the problem of disability in terms of individual physiological and sociological pathology, this ideology set a moral and social standard for nondisabled people to guide them in how to deal with disabled people. Ideology influenced not only nondisabled people's perceptions but also the self-concepts of people with disabilities. To what degree would they internalize

or resist its definition of their identities? Would they see themselves as invalids hoping for cures or overcomers struggling to transcend their fate? Or
would they redefine themselves outside that framing? Individuals engaged
these questions with varying levels of awareness and varying degrees of compliance or resistance, but in one way or another everyone with a disability had
to grapple with them.

On telethons, some people with disabilities spoke of themselves as invalids and others as overcomers. Some felt disability had ruined their lives and
invalidated their selves. Others believed a can-do attitude could surmount
the physical, psychological, and social distortions presumably caused by
a disability. Parents on telethons applied one or the other of those views to
their children. The charities chose these individuals to appear on the shows
because their perceptions matched the fundraisers' messages and the ideology underlying them.

Many other people with disabilities who were not featured on telethons
saw themselves differently. For example, there were varying opinions about
the quest for cure. To activists such as Laura Hershey, false hopes about cure
deflected some people from positively integrating disability into their sense of
self and also undermined public support for civil rights enforcement, accessibility, and personal assistance services.[78] Other people with serious medical conditions expressed unexpectedly complicated thinking about cure.
Philosopher Susan Wendell, who had myalgic encephalomyelitis, also known
as chronic fatigue syndrome (ME), objected to the constant "emphasis on
possible 'cures' in biomedical talk and charity talk (and indeed most talk)
about disability, and so little recognition of the potential and value of disabled people's actual lives. ... The widespread message that they are not good
enough until they are 'cured' places the self-respect of people with disabilities
in conflict with any desire to be 'cured.' I find that my own resistance to the
attitude that I need to be 'cured' in order to be a whole or fully acceptable
person infuses my desire for a 'cure' with ambivalence. I want to have more
energy and less pain, and to have a more predictable body; about that there is
no ambivalence. Moreover, I feel heartsore when I hear about someone being
diagnosed with ME; how could I not want a cure for everyone else who suffers with it. ...." Yet "I cannot wish that I had never contracted ME, because
it has made me a different person, a person I am glad to be, would not want
to have missed being, and could not imagine relinquishing, even if I were
'cured.'" Summing up her thoughts, she said, "I would joyfully accept a cure,
but I do not need one. If this attitude towards 'cures' were taken for granted in
my society, then the search for them would not be accompanied by insulting
implications, as it often is now."[79]

Wendell's view was not some saccharine triumph over adversity, or making the best of a bad lot. Rather, like other disabled people (see chapter 7), she
spoke freely of the difficulties and, in her case, the suffering inherent in her

situation. But, embracing the totality of her experience, she prized the changed values, the enriched relationships, the complex maturity it had brought to her. She and others desired health-enhancing treatments, but these should not come at the cost of their dignity or recognition of the meaning and value of their lives, not despite their disabilities, but as persons with disabilities. Many people with and without disabilities found these views hard to fathom, especially because of the medical model's impact on their perceptions.

While these thoughts about cure were surprisingly complex, the responses of many disabled people to the invalid and overcomer roles were not only complicated but also troubled. So deeply entrenched was the invalid role in the social structure, interpersonal relations, and personal consciousness that even highly accomplished, independent individuals sometimes reflexively complied with it. "As soon as I sat in a wheelchair [as a participant observer] I was no longer seen as a person who could fend for himself," reported the distinguished sociologist Irving Kenneth Zola, who usually wore leg braces and walked with crutches. "Though [a colleague] had known me well for nine months and had never before done anything physical for me without asking, now he took over without permission. Suddenly in his eyes I was no longer able to carry things, reach for objects, or even push myself. Most frightening was my own compliance, my alienation from myself and the process."[80] Within many people with disabilities lurked the fears that nondisabled people would take over without permission, controlling them, dominating them as though they were invalids, or that they themselves might unthinkingly and automatically allow this to happen, willy-nilly slipping into the invalid role. Every encounter with a nondisabled person in one way or another carried the risk of invalidation.

Overcoming was fraught with danger, too, for it involved the pretense that one wasn't really disabled or that one's physical difference was unimportant both functionally and sociologically. Overcoming was a kind of passing. Its "try harder" mindset and mode of self-presentation imposed an enormous cost by requiring denial of the real differences and difficulties of living with a significant physical disability. One must never admit to weakness or fatigue, never ask for help, never say "I can't." To do so would be to confess to invalidity. Furthermore, one must never complain about prejudice, discrimination, and inaccessibility and never expect accommodation of one's disability. And in striving to assimilate into the majority culture, one must avoid association with other people with disabilities, especially political affiliation.[81]

But things were changing. Psychologist Carol J. Gill observed in 1998, "Twenty years ago many activists focused on simple barrier removal. ... Now, [they] have stopped apologizing for being different and, instead, criticize society for failing to respond adequately to disability." They were joining in supportive, politically engaged communities. And many—including people like Susan Wendell who had serious medical conditions—were affirming disability as a source of positive identity and alternative values. For those imbued with the overcoming ethos, this new consciousness might seem not only anathema but also deeply threatening to the identities they had been taught to construct. Gill urged them to escape "the treadmill of overcoming." She continued: "[E]mbracing those disabled parts we have tried so hard to overcome and ultimately learned to hide is an exciting promise of personal integration." Relinquishing "the strain of trying to be nondisabled," letting "go of it deliberately, in celebration, not in disgrace, is a truly liberating idea," she said. "Far from giving in or giving up, self-acceptance is an empowering process."[82]

Most disabled Americans did not become political activists, but as we shall see, there were numerous indications that in the late twentieth century many were asserting their rights to access and accommodations, declaring their membership in a minority group, and identifying themselves in positive ways as people with disabilities. They were also groping to fashion a discourse that would refute the dominant ideology and express this new consciousness.[83] Cure, invalidity, and overcoming continued to dominate telethon discourse, but contradictory telethon messages and the charities' actual services at times supported those affirmations and efforts.

Every Labor Day from approximately 1990-2005, Paul Longmore enlisted the help of friends and colleagues across the country to record and send video cassettes of the telethons that aired in their local markets. This insert includes screen captures to give a sense of what Longmore and millions of viewers encountered when watching scores of these programs year after year. Special thanks to Kevin Gotkin who viewed and provided screen captures from various cassettes from the Paul K. Longmore Papers housed in Special Collections and Archives, San Francisco State University.

PAIRING 1 *Telethons were over-the-top splashy "show biz" spectacles designed to keep viewers glued to their sets. Top: MDA Labor Day Telethon Logo with a cartoon of Jerry Lewis from the 1997 telecast in Chicago. Bottom: Balloons fall from the ceiling on a stage of people in wheelchairs, others standing, and volunteers in tiered phone banks at the conclusion of the local 1999 Bay Area telethon in Oakland.*

PAIRING 2 *The specter of disability haunted many aspects of the telethon-watching experience. Top: On one side of a split-screen a father talks about his disabled children shown on right, as they are pushed in their wheelchairs on the 1997 broadcast from Chicago. Bottom: A shot of a child who is limping along down a dark hallway toward the light, the concluding part of an often-repeated segment from the 1992 broadcast about the good work of MDA. Note the ubiquitous telethon convention of the local telephone pledge number appearing prominently on screen.*

PAIRING 3 *Telethons meant big money from individual and corporate donors. Top: National co-host Jerry Springer at the 1997 telethon in Chicago, surrounded by the logos of major credit card companies, having just told audiences they can use any of them to make their donation. Bottom: Jerry Lewis shakes the hand of an executive from 7-Eleven, whose logo is on a large screen behind them.*

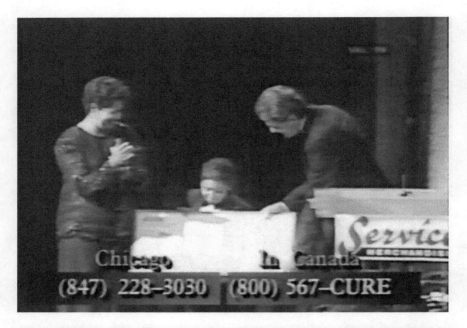

PAIRING 4 *The "oversized check," a recurring publicity gimmick of telethons, which originated from the genre's popular precursor, Franklin D. Roosevelt's Birthday Balls, launched to raise money for the National Foundation for Infantile Paralysis, later renamed the March of Dimes.*

PAIRING 5 *Telethons reflected the American love of scorekeeping with large tote boards constantly updated with the latest total in contributions. Top: Tote board showing total of $18,181,133 and a screen below it with the 1999 MDA logo. Below: Wide shot of the audience, stage, and tote board from the 1999 MDA telecast. Note the prominent display of a phone number to make a pledge.*

PAIRING 6 *In the era before online donations, modern soliciting meant receiving contributions by phone. The yearly programs made much of the volunteer operators waiting to receive calls. Top: The Bay Area 1999 call center volunteers, sitting in tiers on the stage of the local broadcast, were part of the show. Bottom: Close-up of a woman volunteer wearing an American flag visor and talking on the phone.*

MDA 1-800-805-3149

MDA 1-800-805-3149

PAIRING 7 *More than one telethon lured in donors by asking them to pay a celebrity's way out of jail. Being a prisoner of one's disability offered a provocative subtext.*

**Vacaville
(707) 446-2122**

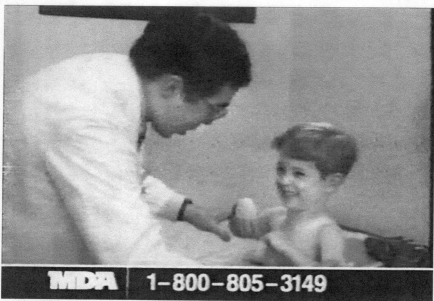

MDA | 1-800-805-3149

PAIRING 8 *Telethons subtly conveyed the power dynamics between people with and without disabilities. Top: Lewis looks down on a woman in a wheelchair as he speaks into a microphone and then holds the mic to her mouth (MDA 1992). Bottom: A doctor touches the arms of a shirtless boy who is smiling widely.*

MDA '92
[415] 358-4000

(213) 856-8888
Ventura (805) 650-1992

PAIRING 9 *Civic buy-in (quite literally, as suggested by the local call-in numbers displayed on screen) was important for showing how telethons were part of the community. Top: Jerry Lewis shakes the hands of representatives from the International Association of Fire Fighters, who are presenting a check to MDA. Bottom: Lewis and the head of the National Association of Letter Carriers with the organization's logo on a large screen behind them.*

PAIRING 10 *Not all people with disabilities accepted the telethons; a passionate minority organized protests against what they saw as patronizing, even mean-spirited treatment. These are images from Los Angeles outside the Oscars ceremony in 2009 where Jerry Lewis was receiving a humanitarian award. Photos: courtesy of Robin Stephens.*

American and Un-American Bodies

SEARCHING FOR FITNESS THROUGH
TECHNOLOGY AND SPORT

In fully embracing the medical model of disability, telethons both drew on and transmitted distinctly American notions of embodiment. Having roots in western Europe's "civilizing process," an increasingly powerful web of social rules and mores sought to domesticate every aspect of the human body. This included physiological functions such as elimination, perspiration, and sexuality, expressions of emotion such as anger and exuberance, as well as social activities, including the use of time and organization of work. Bodies came to be seen as manageable tools. The power to define and regulate socially appropriate bodies shifted from religious institutions to nation-states, workplaces, medical facilities, and, in late modernity, various cultural sites of body expertise regarding fashion, fitness, and sport. How television presented bodies on programs such as telethons reflected these imperatives and also played a part in shaping them.[1]

Modern authorities often exercised their powers indirectly and invisibly by instilling in individuals internal mechanisms of self-control. Management of one's body became synonymous with mastery of oneself. Societies throughout history prescribed appropriate bodily self-expression, but modern cultures instituted dominion of unprecedented depth and detail. If civilized bodies were necessary to the smooth and maximally productive operation of modern states and capitalist economies, regulation of one's own body was essential to full functioning as a legitimate citizen and contributing economic unit.[2] Given this scrutiny and superintendence, social constructions of disability became central to modernity. Late modern body ideology interacted with the medical model, the charity tradition, and American myths of the sovereignty of the self to frame the bodies and identities of people with disabilities as the negation of appropriate modern bodies/selves.

Bodies as Bearers of Meaning

In the late twentieth century, the era of high modernity, focus on the human body intensified and assumed enormous popular importance. Sociologist Bryan S. Turner described a " 'somatic society,'. . . within which major political and personal problems [were] both problematized in the body and expressed through it." This shift appeared in two ways especially pertinent to the identities and social status of people with disabilities. On the one hand, whereas industrial capitalism in the second half of the nineteenth century had linked economic productivity to ascetic self-discipline, late capitalist consumerism of the post–World War II era promoted hedonistic self-gratification. Consumerism held up certain types of bodies as signifying both the good life and individual cultural capital.[3] Meanwhile, modernity displaced traditional religious worldviews with secular ones. But secularism did not supply collectively shared core beliefs that joined individuals in moral community, set forth a larger meaning for their lives, or that guided them in daily living. Instead, cultural fragmentation led each individual to cobble together personal frameworks upon which to construct coherent identities. Ultimately, personal values converged with consumerism's focus on the body as a bearer of meaning. "The exterior territories, or surfaces, of the body," said sociologist Chris Schilling, came to "symbolize the self." More than that, high modern cultures regarded a person's body as not only reflecting his or her interior self, but also constituting it.

At the same time, advances in technology made it possible to fundamentally alter one's body. Feminist theorist Susan Bordo quickly understood this "freedom" as offering the paradoxical constraint that once one can alter the body, one has a certain obligation to make it adhere to ever-restrictive norms. "The very advertisements whose copy speaks of choice and self-determination," she explains, "visually legislate the effacement of individual and cultural difference and circumscribe our choices." Adrift in the moral and social uncertainties of the late twentieth century, growing numbers learned to seek in the body's physicality a solid basis on which to build a cohesive and stable sense of self. Even as possibilities for making modifications proliferated, fashioning one's body became a project of making one's self within a narrowing set of parameters.[4] Such expectations would influence how people with and without disabilities thought about the possibilities for bodies and the responsibility for adhering to certain norms.

Beginning in the late 1950s and early 1960s—just as telethons were becoming a prominent fixture in US culture— fixation on the human body appeared everywhere in the mass media. Magazine and newspaper articles along with television programs teemed with stories about "body image, plastic surgery and how to keep the body looking young, sexy and beautiful. . . ." Weight loss and fitness programs burgeoned as multimillion-dollar businesses. Consumer culture focused "on the body beautiful, on the denial of the aging body, on the rejection of death, on the importance of sport and on the general moral value of keeping fit." Bodies were the focus not only of commercial marketing and advertising, but also both social stigma and personal self-promotion. More and more people became preoccupied "with the health, shape and appearance of their bodies as expressions of individual identity."[5]

Obsession with their bodies was, it seemed, not so much individuals' private choice as an approach to living produced within the conditions of high modernity that dominated in the 1970s and 1980s. If their bodies became "increasingly central to [many people's] sense of self-identity," that view was shaped by a social order that read their bodies as autobiographical and cultural texts, which disclosed the essence of who they were.[6] Critical bodily assessments, argued Shilling, implemented cultural definitions of "what count[ed] as a legitimate body, and the legitimate use of the body in society." They also passed judgment "on whether certain bodies or bodily practices should even exist." Those evaluations reflected deeper "struggles over the power to develop, define and appropriate bodily forms" considered "of most value in society at a given time." In one respect, efforts to enforce acceptable bodily forms and exclude or eliminate illegitimate ones played out socioeconomic and political contests about the allocation of material resources, while facilitating for certain classes "the production and realization of physical"— which was to say, cultural—"capital."

Meanwhile, body management regimes demonstrated the important role in high modernity of a loose eclectic category of social actors Shilling called "body experts." Operating in a wide range of milieus such as health, education, sports, and fashion, they set forth criteria for determining which bodies and bodily practices were legitimate and which were deviant. They schooled individuals in how they should regard and regulate their bodies, indeed, how they should experience their bodies. Body experts also taught them how to judge whether other people's bodies and bodily practices were "'right' and proper or in need of control and correction."[7]

The bodies of people with disabilities were used to reinforce modern body ideology. If individuals' bodies could serve as revelatory autobiographical texts, those texts could be read in reference to one another. Thus, in a world where assessing and comparing bodies played such a huge role, those that appeared to be different helped to underscore what it meant to fit in. And if people's bodies not only reflected but also constituted their interior selves, the discrepant exteriors labeled "impaired" or "whole" would indicate which selves were socially deviant and which legitimate. Thus, some people could show that they fulfilled the somatic society's imperatives by contrasting their bodies with the bodies of people with disabilities. If bodies formed selves, ascriptions of disability disclosed not only which bodies/selves were culturally flawed and unacceptable but also, reciprocally, which were socially normal and valid.

In the historical moment when the disability rights revolution was making people with disabilities an increasingly visible public presence, American culture was placing unprecedented emphasis on the need for physical and bodily control.[8] "It is no longer enough to be thin," noted a disabled feminist, "one must have ubiquitous muscle definition, nothing loose, flabby, or ill defined, no fuzzy boundaries. And of course, there's the importance of control. Control over aging, bodily processes, weight, fertility, muscle tone, skin quality, and movement."[9] These imperatives fell particularly hard on women with physical disabilities. "[R]egardless of how thin" they were, they still lacked "full bodily control." Another feminist writer observed that the cultural obsession with control deployed "the disabled body," a "body out of control," to stand as "the social antithesis" of an appropriately managed body.[10]

Disabled Enablers

Charity professionals who propagated the medical model of disability operated as unrecognized "body experts." At first glance, charity events seemed merely devices to draw donations. But a closer look revealed that most were designed to set apart *able-bodied* benefactors from *abnormally embodied* charity recipients, to distinguish whose bodies/selves were legitimate and whose were deviant, putting these human oddities on display. Scornful observers laughed, but the intense physicality of fundraising events reflected deep-seated cultural anxieties and imperatives.

Fitness and athletic programs differentiated the physically and socially valid from the invalid. Exhorting newspaper readers to "Work Out for Easter Seals," Nautilus Fitness Centers' ads pledged that it would donate part of new enrollees' fees to the charity. A photo of the Easter Seals National Child accompanied the slogan "Help Others While You Help Yourself." The ad implicitly contrasted those whose bodies needed "control and correction" from those whose bodies could be considered "'right' and proper."[11] On the UCP Telethon, "Team Reebok," sponsored by the athletic shoe company, performed a dance workout. An MC called them "incredibly energetic fitness and dance professionals who are causing a sensation wherever they appear across America." On the MDA show, the Universal Cheerleaders Association and Universal Dance Association performed and then presented a $50,000 check. "Each year," said their spokesperson, "we train many of America's most energetic and athletic young people. And we're real proud to be a part of your team and share in your dream that one day all young people will be able to participate in cheerleading or any other athletic activity." These performances not only marketed fitness programs, they also marked off those who matched a modern cultural ideal of physicality, youthful energy, and social fitness from those who literally embodied its opposite.[12]

It seemed that every health and disability charity in late-twentieth-century America put on vigorously physical fundraising events. There were walk-athons and aerobathons and hopathons and bikeathons and danceathons for the March of Dimes, the UCP, the American Cancer Society, the National Multiple Sclerosis Society, AIDS groups, the Cystic Fibrosis Foundation, the Leukemia Society, the Heart Fund, and more.[13] The polio-related "Paralysis Dances" of the 1930s had raised money by contrasting those with fit and unfit bodies.[14] Copying that precedent, MDA enlisted students from four Southern California high schools to frolic at a "super-dance," while the Arthritis Foundation arranged for the Santa Cruz, California, YWCA to hold a dance-a-thon and Beverly Enterprises, the corporate nursing home chain and Arthritis Telethon sponsor, hosted "sock hops."[15] The March of Dimes Birth Defects Foundation conducted WalkAmerica events in cities across the United States. It also organized Wonder Walks to get children aged 3 to 8 ambulating to raise donations. The stated purpose was to introduce youngsters to charity volunteerism, but that mode of solicitation implicitly instructed them in how different kinds of bodies constituted socially valid and invalid selves.[16]

That was the lesson at least some nondisabled adult participants took from intensely physical fundraising. MDA corporate supporter 7-Eleven convenience stores sponsored the "Desert Dash" bicycle team, nine young men who rode overnight through the desert from Los Angeles to Las Vegas to appear on the telethon. Their spokesman summed up the meaning of philanthropic physical-ity. There is a point as you are riding when you cannot see "the light at the end of the tunnel," he philosophized, "but then you think about the less fortunate people. It really gets us through, because we are fortunate. We can walk. We can pedal our bikes. We can run. And we shouldn't take that for granted. There's a lot of people who envy what we have."[17] Athletic fundraising ritually enacted the gulf between those who usually took for granted their physical competency and social validity and those who envied them their normality.

Some benefactors dashed through the desert to track the contrast, others dove underwater, then resurfaced to announce it. The Professional Association of Diving Instructors raised funds for MDA with an underwater Monopoly game. Scuba instructors also dropped in at MDA camps to spend time with "these special children." This enabled them to discover, said a representative, that they could go to the greatest depths they would ever know, the depths of their own hearts. These stunts and stop-ins also served to distinguish the scuba divers from the "special children." The plunge in full scuba gear aque-ously differentiated disabled kids from able-bodied altruists.[18]

Likewise, telethon programs drew upon and promoted explicitly American values. Given that automobiles represented the ultimate expression of the autonomous self within US consumer culture, discussions of them helped bolster the telethon's underlying messages about appropriate bodies. The 1990 Easter Seals Telethon had hunky TV star Lorenzo Lamas talk about his passion for auto-racing. He loved "more than just the speeds of 150 or 200 miles an hour. It's the fact that I'm surrounded by one of the most perfectly designed pieces of equipment anywhere. Every piece of metal, each part of that high-performance engine, everything down to its minute detail, has been created for one sole purpose, and that's to make that car go fast and to be first at the checkered flag." He contrasted this "wonderful" but largely "unknown" world of auto-racing with the "equally unknown ... world of the disabled. It's a world of children with epilepsy and speech disorders, a world of adults who are putting their lives back together after a stroke or an accident. It's a world of mothers and fathers constantly asking each other the same question over and over and over again: 'Why our son? Why our daughter?' "[19]

The telethon script read by Lamas contrasted finely tuned racing cars with people who needed total repair of their allegedly wrecked lives. The imagery juxtaposed a series of modern bodily opposites: perfection of design versus damage and flaw, high performance versus incapacitation, speed instead of immobility, competitiveness rather than marginalization, triumph in contrast to despair. The antipodal traits reflected American dreams and nightmares. For people with disabilities, dependency and invalidity were inherent, inevitable, identity-devouring. They were sidelined, not by institutionalized social practices or inaccessibility, but by their own bodies. Easter Seals pledged to restore their "independence," which was to say their valid modern identities, by fixing their bodies.[20] Like cars, motorcycles were extensions and expressions of independent bodies and autonomous selves. MDA corporate supporter Harley-Davidson sponsored motorcycle runs that embodied big bikes' cultural and psychological symbolism. Harley's rep declared: "The freedom that the riders get on their motorcycle, we want these children to experience that same freedom."[21]

If legitimate bodies ensured freedom, the misbegotten bodies of people with disabilities held them captive. Their bodies had long been described as prisons in which they dreamt of liberation and from which they needed rescue.[22] When a group of California convicts raised money from their prison earnings to help buy a computer for a girl with cerebral palsy, UCP's annual telecast had its host, the sitcom actor Henry Winkler, ask: "You know why they did it? They're in prison and they couldn't get out. And they felt this little girl was in prison, and she needed to get out."[23] The Arthritis Foundation Telethon described people with arthritis as trapped and imprisoned in their bodies. It dramatized that bondage in a film that showed a bedraggled man held in a dungeon. Sneaking past the guards, he escapes. A narrator says: "Until recently, arthritis was a life sentence. Because of the Arthritis Foundation, more Americans are escaping the pain everyday."[24] In 1993 the

Denver Post reported that the National Multiple Sclerosis Society had introduced an advertising campaign "aimed at distinguishing itself and generating donations." The "shocking new TV commercial" showed a woman being attacked by a serpentlike barbed chain that wraps around her eyes, her legs, her hands, as a voice-over notes that one month, one symptom occurs, but another month reveals a different symptom. Another print ad displayed a mother wrapped from head to toe in chains, as an infant sits at her feet, with the message, "If you had to pick the days you could hold your child, which would it be?"[25]

Within this ideology, disabled people's imprisoning bodies stole the natural freedom that was Americans' birthright. The Arthritis Foundation Telethon saw veteran movie star Cesar Romero talking about the un-Americanness of disability. "You know what makes our country great is the individual freedom she offers. . . . But," he declared as he made the crucial distinction about people with disabilities, "someone suffering with arthritis has lost this freedom. . . . We were taught as children that every American is guaranteed their personal freedom, but arthritis has stolen freedom away. Now is the time to work as a nation to cure this disease, because right now, right this very second, more than thirty-seven million Americans are being held captive."[26] The 1988 telethon script, in effect, likened people with arthritis to the American hostages who were at that moment held by terrorists in Lebanon.

Other cherished American values were threatened by physical disability, namely self-determination, self-control, as well as independence and autonomy. Historian Robert Dawidoff observed: "Beyond race, gender, ethnicity, sexual orientation, disability is a culture-wide metaphor for the vulnerable, the pitiable, the weak and thus unacceptable and panicking in an American culture in which identity is formed in constant fear of the loss of autonomy." Of course, the fear of autonomy's loss is the strongest evidence for autonomy's existence. Within the telethon system, as in American culture at large, people with disabilities were in Dawidoff's words, "available . . . to fuel the self-absorption and self-interest of the able-bodied. Just as black creates white . . . disability creates the able-bodied. . . ."[27] Presented as an example of all that was un-American, people with physical disabilities instructed and reassured nondisabled Americans regarding what constituted appropriate values.

The availability of people with disabilities—or rather the cultural handiness of their bodies—as metaphors of the loss of autonomy predated the telethons and operated outside them. But in the late twentieth century, those shows, more than any other cultural institution, propagated the notion that people with disabilities literally embodied some of Americans' deepest fears: overthrow of individual liberty, helpless dependency, cultural and social invalidation. In a historical moment when many feared they might lose—or already had lost—control of their lives, the ritualistic contrast with disabled people's bodies reassured them that their bodies/selves were still free, still autonomous. An Easter Seals broadcast had former Chicago Bulls Team Captain Norm Van Lier spell it out for viewers: "You can celebrate your independence as a person right now by helping to give the gift of independence to someone with a disability."[28]

To demonstrate disabled people's physical (and social) incompetency, some telethons used a common instrument of daily life, the telephone. An Arthritis Foundation public service announcement shows a telephone in close-up as an announcer declared: "Supporting the fight against arthritis is as easy as picking up the phone." The hands of someone with rheumatoid arthritis struggling to raise the receiver were then shown. "Unless of course, you have arthritis," the announcer intoned solemnly. "If you have a healthy hand, go to that phone," an Arthritis Telethon MC directed, "and use those healthy fingers to dial the phone." An MDA host issued the same order: "Pick up a phone and pledge for all those who cannot pick up a phone."[29]

A mundane physical act, picking up a receiver and dialing a number, was used to distinguish the normal from the invalidated. Phoning in a pledge operationalized the difference in a particularly terrifying way by hardwiring it into a routine act that nearly everyone performed. The manner in which people's bodies functioned established and expressed their interior as well as their social selves, their social legitimacy or deviancy. Like the sports events that helped raise money for charity, these quotidian tasks underscored a gulf between nondisabled and disabled Americans, all while explaining exactly what it meant to be a true American.

Bodily Control

The convergence of high modern ideology with American mythology made repairing the bodies of people with disabilities imperative. Historian Thomas Haskell has argued that in early national and antebellum America, a revolution in thought asserted the malleability of the human condition. That transformation spurred benevolence and reform movements but also fostered "exaggerated pride" in human beings' ability to shape the future to their own will.[30] Crusades both radical and conservative shared a belief in individuals' power to change society by exercising sovereignty over their selves.[31] America's emblematic philosopher Ralph Waldo Emerson "enshrined psychic self-sovereignty as the essential manly virtue."[32] Self-making and control of one's destiny came to include dominion over one's body, command of one's health. Antebellum reformers assumed that individuals could not act in morally responsible ways if bodily infirmity corrupted their selves. Moreover, according to literary scholar Susan M. Ryan, benevolence played an important role in reinforcing ideas of a healthy citizen because the ability to give to others helped solidify an economic status already conveyed by class standing and property ownership, which of course were linked to one's race, gender, and nativity.[33] This notion of embodiment's moral and social meaning persisted in American culture from then on. Health and fitness evidenced the sovereignty of the self. Their absence indicated incompetency to participate in a democracy of free choices.[34]

In the late twentieth century, the discourse of self-sovereignty interacted with the high modern view of the body as a project in self-making. Medical-model framings of disability were integral to these American beliefs. Modern medicine ostensibly forbore moral judgments, depicting disease and disability as biological processes, not divine chastisements. But moralizing about illness and disability persisted in medical and social discourse.[35] If premodern cultures and religious worldviews took health or illness as signs of divine favor or displeasure, modern American culture, whether secular or religious, saw them as emblems of fulfillment or failure in meeting the demands of democratic individualism. Unfitness was a modern form of moral failure. It was delinquency in practicing individual self-control. The twentieth-century ideologies of individualism and the human body asserted a corollary moral premise: Even if individuals were not culpable for their conditions, disabilities rendered them incapable of exercising the sovereignty of the self. So whether morally blameable or hapless victims of accidents or diseases, they were unfit to participate in the democracy of free choices. Disability evidenced unwillingness or incompetency to practice self-determination.

Personal health had consequences for not only individual lives but also society. If unfitness evidenced individuals' moral shortcomings, that negligence threatened the viability of American freedom. If disability was a misfortune that befell ill-fated souls, it subverted the very idea of a society of individuals in control of their personal destinies. Either way, the health of individuals would impede, perhaps even sabotage, American social progress. Any dereliction of personal sovereignty or incapacity for self-determination called democratic individualism into question. The presence of impairment raised a terrifying prospect: Human beings might not be in control of their destinies after all. Disability imperiled the American myth of the sovereignty of the self.[36]

To sustain the belief that Americans could control their destinies, the telethon ritual invalidating people with disabilities as the inversion of authentic American identity must also attempt to revalidate them, thereby reconfirming the capacity of Americans to master fate. *Washington Post* television critic Tom Shales captured that function of telethons in his review of one MDA show. "The telethon is about conquering not just one disease, nor even every one of the 20 neuromuscular diseases covered by MDA," he wrote. "In spirit, it's about conquering all disease, and it celebrates a stubborn human hope that we can defeat forces that conspire against us. The telethon endorses the idea that obstacles are surmountable. . . ."[37]

UCP host Dennis James made the same point in 1994. The Northridge earthquake had made a shambles of his and his son's homes. "How unpredictable life can be," he said, "and how the forces of nature are at times so unexpected and so unaccountable." But when the telethon displayed the accomplishments of people with cerebral palsy rehabilitated by UCP, "I realize that it is literally within our power to do something about a force of nature which contributes to the birth of a brain-damaged child." The next year, he spoke of the Northridge quake, a devastating earthquake in Kobe, Japan, and the recent torrential rains and mudslides in Southern California. "It points out how unpredictable the forces of nature can be. ... Now look, I'm not comparing an earthquake or a flood to the birth of a brain-damaged child," which, of course, was exactly what he was doing. "[T]he need for help and support ... shows me that we do have the power to do something about the force of nature, even with the birth of a brain-damaged child. When we meet the children, the young people and the adults, with cerebral palsy, you'll be thrilled to see their levels of accomplishment . . . because of you." Able-bodied donors could control nature and master fate.

Seemingly intractable social problems left many Americans feeling even more powerless than during natural disasters. "When we read the newspapers or watch the news on TV," said a UCP host, "we sometimes feel overwhelmed by problems that seem to have no solutions. It's a terrible helpless feeling." But UCP "offers everyone who wants to make a better world a way to solve problems that can be solved."[38] People with disabilities could be a means for Americans to escape the mood of futility and fatalism that had overtaken many. In a moment when the myth of the sovereignty of the self and American dominion over destiny was in danger, the "power to do something about a force of nature," disability, reassured Americans that they could still beat fate.

"Technology Means Equality"

Meanwhile, developments in technology and disability rights were making it possible for people with disabilities to beat fate on their own terms. In the early 1990s, the MDA Telethon profiled a woman who had an advanced degree and was pursuing a professional career. Nonetheless, her mother said she was afraid to leave her daughter alone in the house because she couldn't use the telephone or answer the doorbell. Disability rights activist Laura Hershey wondered why the woman did not have "relatively simple and inexpensive devices" such as a hands-free telephone or a doorbell intercom. The telethon made the woman seem helpless. In fact, said Hershey, common, real-life, problem-solving strategies involving adaptive equipment, access modifications, and personal assistance could help someone with her disability function more independently.[39]

The era of telethons, roughly the second half of the twentieth century, also saw a technology revolution that challenged the medical model by bringing about major changes in disabled people's bodily experiences. Manufacturers catered to a new disabled consumer market with a proliferation of products. Cars and minivans and full-size vans had hand, foot, and voice controls, as well as electrically powered ramps and lifts. Deaf and hard-of-hearing TV viewers read captions; blind and vision-impaired customers banked via talking automated teller machines. People with physical disabilities operated lamps and other appliances with voice-controlled switches, while people with vision disabilities managed their daily schedules with speech output clocks, watches, pagers, and calculators. As with many nondisabled people, people with disabilities worked and learned and played on personal computers. Their computers had sticky keys and zoom-text and picture-based keyboards. Text could be translated into speech, and speech into text. Deaf and hard-of-hearing people accessed the telephone system with telecommunications devices (TTYs and TDDs), volume-control telephones, and Nokia's Loopset for mobile phones.[40]

In this era, the engineering and appearance of wheelchairs underwent a radical redesign. Modern manual wheelchairs were half to two-thirds lighter in weight than traditional chairs, while power wheelchairs were computerized. Both manual and power chairs had a new look—sporty, high-tech, and available in vibrant colors. Supporting the active lifestyles of a new generation of disabled people, these wheelchairs reflected a new form of disability identity that began to emerge thanks to the disability rights movement in the 1960s, 1970s, and 1980s. No longer confining "wheelchair-bound patients," modern wheelchairs were marketed and used as means of mobility, self-determination, and active engagement with the world.[41]

All of this equipment facilitated the social integration of people with every sort of disability. But it was set apart by the labels "assistive" and "adaptive," terminology that marked it as in some essential way different from the devices used by "normal" people, which was simply known as technology.[42] These stigmatizing terms were heard most often from manufacturers and gate-keeping professionals who decided what devices many individuals with disabilities would get. Contesting both the dominance and discourse of vendors and professionals, disability rights activists redefined all such equipment as, not adaptations for "special" needs, but alternative means of doing ordinary daily tasks.

Technology's liberating possibilities became a theme of the UCP and Easter Seals Telethons. That was partly because it fit their rehabilitation agendas. But as these programs scaled down in the late 1990s, access to technology became part of the civil rights messages they began to include. The UCP's broadcast demonstrated voice synthesizers and announced plans for a high-tech center in Chicago.[43] Easter Seals showcased a Canon Communicator that printed the words typed by a child with cerebral palsy and an optical reader that translated printed words into refreshable Braille for blind and deaf-blind readers. It also profiled a quadriplegic man who drove a power wheelchair and used a computer in his work as a financial consultant. And it showed a young man with muscular dystrophy on his job as a data entry operator; he used a voice-operated computer and an electronic page turner. Easter Seals Vice President John Kemp, an amputee who wore prostheses, summed it up: "Technology means equality. It means opportunity. It means not being left out. Such images marked a sharp contrast with those of helpless invalids."[44]

But many disabled people could not afford these devices on their own and so they had to stay eligible for social welfare programs or seek private charities' help to buy the needed equipment. Institutionalization of the medical model meant that they could receive the technology only if medical professionals certified them as legitimate patients. That arrangement also protected vendors' economic interests by trapping disabled people in a state of dependency.[45] Challenging this setup, activists lobbied for policies guaranteeing disabled people's right to the new technologies in order to ensure them opportunities in school, work, and society.[46] Despite the financial and bureaucratic obstacles, the technology revolution transformed the bodily experiences of many. Meanwhile, growing numbers experienced their bodies and expressed themselves in unexpected ways.

Adventures in Embodiment

More and more people with disabilities engaged in dance, sport, recreation, and exercise both to enhance their bodies' health and functioning and manage the social and cultural meanings attributed to their embodiment. It seemed that many partly complied with high modern body ideology while also resisting it. Others challenged cultural verdicts on their bodily experiences by using those activities to express themselves creatively through their bodies.

Nowhere was this new ebullience more evident than in dance performance. In June 1997 for almost two weeks in Boston, the first International Festival of Wheelchair Dance brought together more than a dozen North American and European "mixed-ability" dance companies. A *Christian Science Monitor* writer reviewed the performances, describing "an art form [that] encompasses a wide variety of aesthetics, movement styles, and contextual concerns, with pieces ranging from the overtly sentimental to the political to the purely abstract." The reviewer understood disability as central but in a new way. "By and large, these companies want their work to be accepted as art, not novelty," she explained, extolling the virtues of AXIS Dance Company, particularly "William Shannon's delightful improvisations throughout the night [that] tied it all together. His jangly, isolated movement atop crutches, including a high energy skateboard romp, showed athletic virtuosity, a keen imagination, and a wonderfully skewed sense of humor."[47] The review pointed to profound changes in thinking and presentations of disabled bodies that inadvertently challenged telethon fare. For the first time, people with disabilities were, in the late twentieth century, coming to find enjoyment, beauty, and pleasure rather than suffering, ugliness, and dread. Now that some disabled people danced professionally and many more just for the fun of it, there were a wider range of options for understanding disabled bodies as powerful creative forces in their own right.

Yet most telethon segments languished in old ways of thinking that pathologized all disabled bodies regardless of what they did. For example, the 1993 MDA and 1995 UCP shows both featured actress/dancer Zina Bethune, founder of Bethune Theatredanse. Bethune, who had an unspecified disability, danced with a young girl who rode a power wheelchair. Jerry Lewis described Bethune's company as an "educational program" that had taught over a thousand "physically and mentally challenged children to learn and perform dance." Easter Seals likewise spoke of dancing as rehabilitation for children. Its 1994 San Francisco telethon introduced teenaged and younger girls involved in "movement therapy." The program's founder explained that its classes differed from regular dance classes in that they were team-taught by an artist and a physical or occupational therapist. "It's really important for everybody to have a chance to express themselves," she said, "and everybody has things to express with their body, and it's fun." Those notions that disabled people could say something with their bodies and even enjoy their bodies clashed with telethon dogma. But a key element of the presentation corrected that contradiction: The dancing was "therapy." Such pathologizing perspectives largely filtered out the creativity, exuberance, and physical eloquence of disabled people dancing.

As with dance, the charities propagated their traditional messages when showing the growing numbers of people with disabilities who enjoyed sports and recreation. Sometimes they engineered images of disabled people as invalids, helpless and essentially different from people depicted as able and autonomous. MDA corporate sponsor Brunswick Recreation Centers filmed a child "ambassador" bowling against two professionals. Seated on his wheelchair, the boy used a device designed for bowlers with disabilities. The audience groaned as his ball veered into the gutter, then applauded when the rigged pins all toppled anyway.[48] Such depictions of the sport transformed it into a feel-good moment, eclipsing the possibility for viewers—and perhaps for the bowler himself—that someone with a disability could be a competent bowler and should expect to win or lose like anyone else.

Even while some segments perpetuated the old contrast between invalids and "normal" people, Easter Seals and UCP introduced young people with disabilities who demonstrated overcoming through athletics. Easter Seals featured programs that reflected its rehabilitation objectives: to bolster self-esteem, instill confidence, build character, teach independence, and encourage youngsters to overcome their disabilities. The telethon showed young people with spina bifida, cerebral palsy, congenital amputations, and other disabilities engaged in many sports: swimming, snow skiing, and karate as well as wheelchair sports such as archery, basketball, bowling, racing, and tennis. The UCP Telethon featured Paralympic athletes who delivered the same message of overcoming. New York sportscaster Sal Marciano summed it up: "You know, the will to win can overcome any handicap. ... [It] comes from within. The heart and the mind provide the inner power to race greater distances, to lift heavier weights, to exert superior stamina. ... Never mind the diagnosis. No matter what the physical obstacles, there is no disability in the soul of an athlete."[49] At first glance, overcoming would appear to be a direct challenge to older views of people with disabilities, particularly since it replaced the passive invalid with someone far more active and dynamic. Yet, as we saw in the previous chapter, overcoming proved problematic by insisting that success resided within the individual who would somehow push past his or her problematic body to become more normal. In doing the unthinkable, these youngsters were expected to deny their disabilities, which was of course impossible and, as a result, left them feeling further stigmatized.

Whatever the motivation, athletics was becoming increasingly important as a force in the lives of people with disabilities. In the second half of the twentieth century, disability sport and recreation organizations multiplied, reflecting the athletic and recreational interests of people with every sort of disability and across the talent spectrum. Some had national and international governing boards that sponsored competition among elite athletes, while others participated in Olympic-level competition. At the highest levels, such as the quadrennial International Paralympic Games, which eventually affiliated with the Olympics and were held in Olympic host cities, athletes with disabilities competed in a full range of sports comparable to those nondisabled athletes played. By the end of the twentieth century, the Paralympics were the second largest sporting event in the world.[50] And some disabled athletes even competed against nondisabled athletes at the highest levels, including the Olympics.[51]

Of course, as with the nondisabled, the vast majority of disabled people participating in sports and recreation were not elite athletes. The disability sport and recreation movement was a largely unrecognized contingent of the disability rights movement as it opposed discriminatory exclusion and demanded equal access to programs, venues, and events.[52] Perhaps a sign of this success, in 1996 Easter Seals presented disabled sports as simply standard athletics. Sportscaster Al Michaels interviewed elite disabled athletes, asking questions he would have put to nondisabled athletes, questions about training and coaching, equipment and competition. And the interviewees responded matter-of-factly to his questions about both sports and disability.

Such matter-of-fact presentations of sports no doubt helped steer more and more people with disabilities to participate. During the last decades of the twentieth century, sports and recreation at all levels began cropping up for the growing numbers of people with disabilities interested in both fitness and play. Team sports proved especially popular, some thanks to rehabilitation efforts and some invented by disabled people themselves. For example, there was goal ball for blind athletes, an intense game that required two teams of three members to play blindfolded, which ensured that all team members played without sight. The object was to get a large heavy ball with a bell inside across a basketball court marked off with heavy tape. Team members communicate with sounds and tapping on the wooden floor, using their whole bodies to block the ball. The sport requires agility, skill, and extreme concentration.

Power soccer, the first sport designed for people who drove power wheelchairs, was popular among men and women with mobility impairments, including quadriplegics. "Power" referred to players' electrically powered wheelchairs. Invented in Vancouver, Canada, in 1982, the sport spread around the globe in the following decades. Four-member teams usually played it on indoor basketball courts where, as in standard soccer, players maneuvered (a larger) ball across the opposing team's goal line while defending their own goal. They moved the ball with heavy-duty, plastic guards that wrapped around their wheelchairs' footrests. Teamwork, according to MDA's *Quest* magazine, involved intricate offensive and defensive strategies: "positioning, blocking [shots], setting picks and screens, and controlling the ball." *Quest* described play as often intense, with the ball "slammed around by people piloting high-speed metal chairs" that weighed "300 pounds or more" as they blocked shots "by interposing the chair (or themselves) in the ball's path." But for the players, explained *Quest*, "the action and contact [were] just part of the thrill. Speed [was] also a big draw" and essential to top-flight play.[53]

Competitions such as goal ball and power soccer were vigorous sports, ones that ran right over all of the stereotypes about people with major physical disabilities.[54] In general, though, Easter Seals, MDA, and UCP Telethons presented sports stories without acknowledging them as an important development in the bodily and social experience of disabled people. Reasons for participating were complicated and even contradictory, sometimes upholding, sometimes resisting both medical-model framings and late modern body ideology. Most said that these physical activities enhanced their health and fitness. Many also believed that sport and exercise refuted stereotypes of their dependency and physical incompetence. They turned to athleticism and exercise as tools of stigma management, means to prove that they, too, could match the imperatives of high-modernity's body regime.[55]

   Telethons enlisted people with disabilities to perpetuate a particular set of American values. In a society that equated body and self, the message was clear: A valid person was autonomous, fully in control of his or her body and environment. In contrast, a disabled body inevitably produced a dependent self, a self at the mercy of others and the social and physical world. And yet, as the examples of disabled dancers, athletes, and recreational sports enthusiasts revealed, people with disabilities suggested new ways of thinking about bodies. Both individually and in organized efforts, growing numbers challenged dominant notions about what their bodies could do and what they should do with their bodies. At times embracing, at times refuting modern body ideology, and at times rejecting the medical model and charity tradition, they reframed their embodiment. In the process, they went beyond expressing their physical selves to create a sense of possibility and audacity that flew in the face of prevailing stereotypes of shut-ins trapped in inferior bodies. Contrary to dominant cultural framings, social biases, and other people's expectations, they took pleasure in their bodies and celebrated this pleasure with anyone in the public who dared to take notice.

Smashing Icons

GENDER, SEXUALITY, AND DISABILITY

Ideologies of disability and the body intersected with ideologies of gender and sexuality to define the identities of not only people with disabilities but nondisabled people as well. In an era when gender ideologies and identities were in flux, telethon framings of disability implicitly tried to stabilize traditional conceptions of heterosexual masculinity and femininity in two ways.[1] Consistent with the charity tradition, telethons contrasted disabled people—especially children—with nondisabled adult male and female benefactors who embodied dominant standards. At the same time, the agendas of cure or rehabilitation tacitly promised to make disabled children into suitable adult women and men and to ensure disabled adults of normal, which was to say normative, gender roles and identities. Meanwhile, many people with disabilities battled social prejudice in their efforts to fashion positive gender and sexual identities. One telethon eventually backed their struggle.

Disability to the Rescue: Gender Norms for the Nondisabled

In the 1990s, when traditional framings of heterosexual American masculinity and femininity were being challenged by scholars and within popular culture itself, telethons and their corporate sponsors implicitly bolstered those ideologies by presenting patriarchal nondisabled males and nondisabled females who matched reigning standards of feminine body beauty as benefactors of deviantly embodied girls and boys. The 1992 MDA Telethon's opening projected an iconic image of philanthropic patriarchy. A lone violin played "When You Walk through a Storm" as Jerry Lewis and a child approached one another in silhouette before a night sky. Lewis embraced the child without bending. This put the child's face against his stomach. The poignant image emphasized his masculine adult size and the child's small-ness and dependency.

If Lewis was the quintessential telethon patriarch, corporate sponsors' male executives were patriarchs of their companies' "families." Almost all of them white and middle-aged (and to all appearances able-bodied), they became surrogate fathers to poster children. A significant minority was female, but they held lower-ranking positions. By rescuing Tiny Tim's metaphorical sib-lings, business *men* became, like Ebenezer Scrooge, "second fathers" to the disabled children who ostensibly depended on their fatherlike concern. At a time when patriarchy and "corporatocracy" faced intense criticism, telethons validated capitalist patriarchs' benevolence and the paternal beneficence of the economic system they headed.

Meanwhile, telethon-linked advertising marketed children with disabili-ties as a means for other men to display their patriarchal brawn. One Miller Brewing Company ad in an alcohol-beverage industry magazine showed a man's hand gently clasping a child's fingers. Above the picture was the slo-gan: "Help Miller Give United Cerebral Palsy a Hand for the Holidays." Another Miller ad urged beer drinkers: "This February Lite beer for you could mean a better life for them." The ad showed a girl and boy with cerebral palsy surrounded by a group of men. Most were celebrity athletes, but among them stood hard-boiled detective story writer Mickey Spillane, who, attired in his trademark trench coat and fedora, was the *reductio ad absurdum* of American *machismo*. "[R]emember," the ad intoned, "to give them a chance, the rest of us have to take the first step." Here were the counterpointed ste-reotypes: masculine strength and childish dependency, proxy fathers looking after unfortunate youngsters.

This image of gentle patriarchy was not just for celebrities and CEOs. It could work for average American men, too. Motorcycle manufacturer Harley-Davidson used "Jerry's Kids" to bolster precarious male identities, part of its plan to reinvent the image of biking for a new middle-class, mostly male mar-ket. In the early 1980s, the legendary company, facing bankruptcy, signed on as an MDA corporate sponsor. By the mid-1990s, its marketing campaign had retooled motorcycling's demographics. In 2001 the median age of new bik-ers was 45.6, they enjoyed a median household income of $78,300, and more than 9 out of 10 were male. In March 1994, *Today* show "Gadget Guru" Andy Pargh explained that Harley succeeded with these customers by merchan-dising the "Harley lifestyle," which included not just motorcycle riding but "motor-clothes" and accessories: boots, leather jackets, leather pants, gloves, decals, jewelry, and chains. Many customers bought just the clothes.[2]

One customer, a 52-year-old man, explained the appeal, which in many respects was the antithesis of the disabled invalid: "It's such an incredible rush. It's the legend. The mystique. The power. The macho image. People are drawn to that. That power is so addictive." "It stands for freedom," said another man, "for getting away, and just having a good time." The Harley dealer thought there were "a lot of parallels with the Wild West and with cowboys." Another part of the image, announced Senior Vice President Willie G. Davidson, grandson of one of the company's founders, was "the rebel thing." Posing for reporters at Harley's 100th anniversary in 2003, he wore a black bandanna and Harley-Davidson sunglasses as he leaned against his motorcycle. "That's my body," said the 70-year-old Davidson. "Inside I'm about 35." "I gotta tell you," exulted *Today's* Andy Pargh, "this is really the ultimate cure for the mid-life crisis. ... It's kind of like testosterone on wheels."[3] The new Harley image was "mainstream America," though, assured Pargh. One T-shirt proclaimed: "We're all born to be wild," adding, "At least for a few days." Accommodating some bikers' middle-aged avoirdupois, that T-shirt came in XL, XXL and XXXL sizes. "The Hell's Angels image is really going away," said Pargh.[4]

But that image, what Willie Davidson called "the rebel thing," must not go too far. If it disappeared entirely, motorcycle riding could not cure American male mid-life crises. In order to resolve symbolically the complex situation of men in late-twentieth-century America and the contradictory expectations embodied in current notions of American manhood, the Harley image must mimic Wild West freedom without evoking *The Wild One's* terrifying anarchy. Biker liberty must be tempered. The roar of testosterone should be only a metaphorical sound from an exhaust pipe, not the feral bellow of a hoodlum biker. Harley had to replace the Hell's Angels image with a more complex persona of supposedly unfettered but ultimately unthreatening individualism. And that was the point at which "Jerry's Kids" and other charities' clients proved useful for Harley's marketing and for propping up American masculinity.

On the 1994 telethon, Harley's CEO effected the transformation from biker gang to motorcycling "family." "It's a pleasure to represent the worldwide Harley-Davidson family of employees, dealers, and enthusiasts," he told Lewis. "Raising money for your kids is a priority at Harley-Davidson. And we've developed many creative ways to combine the two things we love to do most, ride motorcycles and MDA." An MDA executive explained the link between motorcycle aficionados and children with disabilities. "Harley-Davidson is all about freedom, and that's what the Muscular Dystrophy Association is about," she said. "We're both about giving people an independent life."

This vaunted parallel obscured the essential dissimilarity that was the real point. Pictures of Harley riders helping "Jerry's Kids" furnished the balanced image of bikers the manufacturer and their middle-class, middle-aged, male customers were looking for: mythically rebellious but actually responsible, ostensibly free-wheeling but in fact paternal, still autonomous rather than helpless.[5] The emotional sensitivity, sympathy, and sentimentality displayed in the "care work" of looking after "Jerry's Kids" were traditionally regarded as feminine traits. In the last decades of the twentieth century, many American women and especially feminists criticized American men for lacking those virtues. This charity-related framing of macho motorcycling combined with fatherly tenderness reasserted manliness without endangering masculinity.[6]

This masculine makeover evidently worked. In the late 1980s and early 1990s, Harley-Davidson roared back from bankruptcy's brink. While production grew by 15 to 20 percent each year, the volume of orders swelled so much that customers sometimes had a four- to nine-month wait to get their bikes. In 1993 the company grossed a billion dollars. The "Harley lifestyle" was a hit, too. By the mid-1990s, the merchandising brought in more than $200 million a year. By 2001 Harley had registered record sales for seventeen straight years and stood as the number one peddler of heavyweight motorcycles in North America.[7] Harley's mythology of motorcycle riding promised to rescue endangered American manhood. Its cause-related marketing succeeded, in part, by contrasting putatively free, nondisabled, middle-aged male bikers with disabled children who assumedly needed their patriarchal compassion.

If telethon images of benevolent patriarchs bolstered what feminist scholars called hegemonic masculinity, disability-related depictions of charity-minded females propagated a complementary image of femininity. In the late twentieth century, the exemplary American woman was slender, fit, and sexy. More than anything, weight measured female social worth or invalidity. Here again, people with disabilities—girl children, in particular—were made the inverse of the cultural ideal. In order to market exercise and weight-loss programs, telethon-linked advertising contrasted disabled girls with slim, toned, culturally legitimate adult women. Nautilus Fitness Centers' 1992 print ads announced it would waive its enrollment fee for customers who gave Easter Seals a minimum $25 donation. Below the slogan "Workout for Easter Seals" were side-by-side photos of a shapely, young blonde woman hoisting a hand barbell and the Easter Seals National Child, a girl wearing leg braces and leaning on crutches.[8] Female fitness versus female dependency, womanly sex appeal juxtaposed against disabled asexual little-girlness.

Jenny Craig Weight Loss Centers, a new Easter Seals corporate sponsor in 1992, launched a promotion exploiting that antithesis. In a TV spot, Ms. Craig announced: "If you've been thinking about losing weight, now you can do it and help others at the same time. Because this month you can join our Introductory Program for only $19.00, and we'll donate that entire amount to Easter Seals. . . . [Y]ou'll be helping people with disabilities do many things most of us take for granted." Spelling out the difference between disability and ideal femininity, film footage showed a girl in physical therapy practicing walking between parallel bars, a man riding a power wheelchair, a boy on a wheelchair batting a baseball helped by a woman who pushed the chair, and a girl on a wheelchair with a nondisabled girl next to her who hugged her. Print ads pictured Ms. Craig hovering over the Easter Seals National

Child. Disabled child recipients of charity, most of them girls, were contrasted with fit (more accurately, would-be fit) adults, mostly women, who
were both Jenny Craig customers and Easter Seals donors.[9] As with the MDA/
Harley-Davidson partnership, Jenny Craig likened her business to the work
of the charity. "Jenny Craig Weight Loss Centers and Easter Seals, what a
great combination," she gushed on the telethon. They shared "the same mission: to help people improve their lives."[10] This promotion not only contrasted
supposedly fit and standardly attractive nondisabled women with disabled
girls; as important, it implicitly compared toned slender females with women
who violated the requirements of feminine body beauty.[11]

The modern American ideal of femininity was incarnated in, not just fitness, but fashion and beauty. The charities got "beautiful" women and girls
to show compassion toward folks whose unacceptable bodies spoiled their
identities. Like the March of Dimes long before, some Arthritis Foundation
chapters hosted fashion shows. In 1989 the San Fernando Valley branch sponsored "Applause," "a children's fashion show, where healthy kids help kids
suffering from arthritis."[12]

Though feminists condemned beauty contests for pushing oppressive standards of appearance, some telethons tapped into those spectacles and their
gender ideology. Both the Arthritis Foundation and Easter Seals shows brought
on Miss USA 1994. Arrayed in her Miss USA sash, she pitched for donations.
Other telethons displayed beauty pageant winners' cultural appropriateness
in a bid to fix girls who fell short of required feminine attractiveness.[13] On the
1993 UCP program, Dennis James introduced a panel of gorgeous actors and
models who were answering phones. Of one, he said: "She's on the cover of this
month's *Better Bodies* magazine. And I'm not going to ask her to get up and
show her body, but she apparently has one tremendous body."[14]

It might have seemed contradictory—or at least ironic—that telethons,
which ostensibly aimed at reminding viewers of the humanity of people with
disabilities, would buttress gender-based norms of physical acceptability. By
focusing on female bodies, the charities reinforced gendered ideas of social
worth. This emphasis on looks pressured American women and girls, nondisabled and disabled alike, to try to match up to dominant standards of feminine appearance.

The triad of patriarchal nondisabled males, "beautiful" nondisabled
females, and children with disabilities, particularly girl children, helped
enforce gender norms for everyone. Feminist disability studies scholar
Rosemarie Garland-Thomson explains that "the normative female, the figure
of the beautiful woman," served historically as at once the negative opposite of the ideal male and the privileged opposite of "abnormalized" females.
"Within this scheme, all women are seen as deviant, but some more so than
others. Indeed, the unfeminine, unbeautiful body defines and is defined by
the ideal feminine body. This aberrant figure of woman has been identified

variously in history and discourse as black, fat, lesbian, sexually voracious, disabled, or ugly. … [T]his figure's deviance and subsequent devaluation are always attributed to some visible characteristic that operates as an emblem of her difference, just as beauty has always been located in the body of the feminine woman."[15]

Images of benevolent beautiful females along with portrayals of compassionate patriarchal males helped to defend hegemonic gender ideology in a historical moment when it was under siege. Garland-Thomson explains that in this scheme, "women who possessed valued traits" regarding their appearance and therefore had higher status and power "patronized lower status women." This paralleled a "masculine economy of benevolence" in which "money and public power" rather than appearance "are the currency."[16] The telethons used these images to highlight not just the advantages of able-bodiedness but also the imperative to embrace the norms associated with this privileged status. Far from being a marginal, even invisible status, disability proved essential to maintaining existing ability *and* gender hierarchies.

Striving for a Gender Cure

Similar, sometimes more complex messages applied to children whose identities were still being formed. In addition to telling the nondisabled how they could—and must—maintain appropriate gender and sexual identities, telethons also taught children and adults with disabilities what they needed in order to match up to cultural expectations. The shows informed participants—and nondisabled potential donors, too—that without cure or correction of their bodily differences, they could never fulfill those requirements. Gendered standards of embodiment interacted with the medical model of disability; as long as children with disabilities were regarded as physically flawed, they could never be appropriate American boys or girls and could never become culturally acceptable, heterosexual grown-ups. MDA exhorted, "Let Jerry's Kids Just Be Kids." But what did it mean to "just be" a kid? As the MDA and other telethons explained, it meant matching cultural definitions of appropriate boyness and girlness.

Children with disabilities could realize these gendered dreams, telethons claimed, only if they were cured or rehabilitated. On the 1989 MDA Telethon, Jerry Lewis put that message to music, with lyrics that contrasted "your" normal kids with his invalid ones. Set to "My Boy Bill," a tune from the musical *Carousel* that invoked strict gender and body norms, the lyrics describe a little girl as "Perfection in every way" and, similarly, a nondisabled young boy who would "rule the world some day." These presumably nondisabled children provided a sharp contrast to "Jerry's Kids" who couldn't fulfill these "normal" expectations. They had only "pain" and "misery" and doom. So, the song went on, with an emphasis on the need for donations to fund the care and treatment necessary to find a cure. With this accomplished, "Jerry's Kids" could live "normal" lives, "With their heads held high / And their feet planted firm on the ground." In other words, they wouldn't ride wheelchairs.

Deprived of the symbolic trappings of American boyhood, boys with disabilities implicitly fell short of traditional expectations. On the 1988 MDA Telethon, actor Robert Young—most famous for his portrayal of a fictional doctor on the medical drama *Marcus Welby, M.D.*—showed viewers a set of roller skates and asked if they remembered their first pair. Did they remember their first baseball glove? But some kids, he said, "some very special kids," use a different kind of equipment: leg braces and wheelchairs. "That's what kids with muscle diseases use, and it isn't fun and games kind of stuff. It's serious, very serious." "Come on," urged Young. "Let's all help to get these kids to where they are going, onto skates, playing baseball and basketball." No doubt many American boys with physical disabilities did wish they could roller skate and play basketball and baseball. But that was not all they wished for, and they *could* do many other boyish things, especially once the sports opportunities described in the previous chapter became more common. Nonetheless, MDA had Young announce that children with disabilities, especially male children, must be remade into *real* kids. So the leg braces and wheelchairs had to go. To become truly American boys, they would have to slip on baseball gloves or shoot hoops.[17]

Girls with disabilities also fell short of a modern standard of fit female embodiment. The father of a girl named Miriam told the Arthritis Telethon audience, "Well, I hope that it does go into remission, and she can have a full life. There's a lot of things that little girls like to do, cheerleading and sports and stuff. And I hope she's not held back with this." An MDA video featured a girl who dreamt of dancing as a ballerina. But instead of ballet shoes, she put on short leg braces. "That's not easy to watch," decided a local MC.[18] His statement was not merely a personal observation but implicit tutelage of the audience in the gendered meanings of childhood disability.

Disabled children's supposed gender incompetency not only kept them from living up to these cultural expectations. It also thwarted their parents' American fantasies about them. On a broadcast of the Arthritis Foundation's show, a mother who "dreamed" of a cure for her daughter imagined seeing "her walk down ... that ramp in her pageant dress, just like all the other seniors, be the Miss High School, whatever high school it may be." In contemporary American culture, it was inconceivable that a teenager could "walk down that ramp" on crutches or roll down it riding a wheelchair and be regarded as lovely. On several Easter Seals Telethons, the mother of a girl with arthritis described her own reaction to a major flare-up of her daughter's condition: "That was about the time when it hit me that my daughter was not going to be maybe all the things that I was or that you envision for your child.

That's the time when I realized, you know, she will never be a cheerleader. She will never play competitive soccer. You know, she is not going to be Miss America . . . right now our major concerns are to build up the muscles in her legs and to get her walking as normally as possible. I would do anything in the world to get her running around like a normal kid, but, you know, I can't right now, so I just have to deal with, deal with what we've got." The woman was almost weeping.[19]

The message from the mothers and the telethons was that these girls must overcome more than the pain and functional limitations of arthritis. The telethons taught that disability limited their capacity to satisfy contemporary cultural standards of femininity. Just as MDA lamented that disabled boys couldn't play baseball or basketball, the Arthritis Foundation and Easter Seals along with their mothers deplored that these girls would never be cheerleaders or beauty contest winners or Miss Americas. They wouldn't play soccer and become athletic golden girls. These disappointed mothers had "to deal with" daughters who could not match late-twentieth-century American cultural definitions of girlhood or womanhood. No wonder the second mother was close to tears.

According to the telethons, young people with disabilities deviated so far from cultural expectations about gender and sexuality that, unless they were medically fixed, they would never know love or romance or sex. Conventional thinking in rehabilitation had long warned that a disability was likely to distort the development of normal sexuality. For example, mid-twentieth-century professionals propagated fear that postpolio disability would unsex males and turn teenage boys into homosexuals.[20] Four decades later, MDA corporate sponsor 7-Eleven convenience stores more obliquely promoted fear of the desexualizing and demasculinizing impact of disability. A film showed two boys about 12 years of age. One rode a wheelchair. The narrator explained that this boy dreamt about "basketball, baseball, and, of course, girls." The spot showed him hanging out with his nondisabled pal, then swimming in a pool. He and his friend teased one another about girls, too. He admitted liking a girl named Ann. "But for [his] dreams to come true," asserted the announcer, "he'll need a miracle." On another show, the father of a teenage girl told MDA viewers: "Here's a kid who won't be asked to the prom, who won't be asked to go spend the weekend with her buddies at the beach, who won't be asked to go out on a Friday night for a pizza."[21] These segments implicitly reinforced heterosexuality as the norm and explicitly upheld the bias that a young fellow who rode a wheelchair could only dream about romance, that a young woman with a disability would never have a date or even socialize with friends. They would never experience love or—unmentioned but undoubtedly in the back of everyone's mind—sex. Their gender-inappropriate bodies, not cultural devaluation and social prejudice, would shut them out of those experiences.

Inauthentic Women and Feminized Men

As with children, adults with disabilities needed cure or rehabilitation if they were to meet American culture's gender requirements, while telethons sometimes pictured adults as incapacitated for the role of parent. When applied to mothers, those images reflected common prejudices about women with disabilities. A 1986 survey of nondisabled college students asked them to list words they associated with the terms "woman" and "disabled woman." They linked "woman" to the roles of "wife" and "mother" and to work ("intelligent," "leader," "career") and sexuality ("soft," "lovable," "orgasm"). But "disabled woman" evoked images of helpless dependency ("crippled," "almost lifeless") and of isolation, disgust, and pity ("lonely," "ugly," "someone to feel sorry for"). The respondents did not connect "disabled woman" with "wife," "mother," or "worker." One 35-year-old married mother of two children, who had polio as a child, repeatedly felt the sting of bias within her own family. "Each time I announced I was pregnant, everyone in the family looked shocked, dropped their forks at the dinner table—not exactly a celebration."[22]

Disabled feminists decried telethon images. "Smashing Icons," an essay in the pathbreaking disability studies anthology *Women with Disabilities: Essays in Psychology, Culture, and Politics* (1988), compared telethons with beauty pageants. If the pageants propagated a hegemonic femininity that elevated while still restricting "beautiful" nondisabled women, telethons, said the authors, bolstered the belief that a woman with a disability was incapacitated for any adult social role whatever. Because of social bias, reported the authors, women with disabilities were "less likely to be married, more likely to marry later, and more likely to be divorced than non-disabled women," while fewer than 1 out of 4 had wage-earning jobs. Discrimination and devaluing cultural representations decreed that a woman with a disability could not be "a mother or a sexual being."[23]

On telethons, the vast majority of mothers were nondisabled parents of children with disabilities; the vast majority of wives were nondisabled partners of men with disabilities. If a disabled woman on a telethon had a wage-earning job, she was likely to have a developmental disability and to work in an Easter Seals- or UCP-supported employment project. A handful of married working mothers appeared on some telethons in the 1990s after activists stepped up their protests against stereotyping.[24]

Meanwhile, some physically disabled men talked about how male gender stereotypes restricted them. In his 1982 memoir *Missing Pieces: A Chronicle of Living with a Disability*, sociologist Irving Kenneth Zola recollected obstacles he faced in dating as a young man. "Almost inevitably, if [he and a woman] saw each other more than once, I would hear about a certain parental concern ranging from earning capacity to life expectancy to 'marital responsibility.' Occasionally I felt I should carry a medical affidavit with me." Each of these "concerns" reflected traditional notions of normative American masculinity. A man with a physical disability, it was assumed, could not be an adequate breadwinner, family man, or lover.[25] "Disability" not only made females inauthentic women, it also feminized males.[26]

On several occasions, MDA showed how disability threatened men's capacity to be proper husbands and fathers. One of those men was a medal-winning wheelchair basketball player whose condition had progressed to the point that he could no longer perform as he once had done, so he had become his team's coach. He and his wife had recently bought a house and were about to have their first baby. Both the house and the baby would require a lot of work, said the wife, but they were not going to let his disability stop them from doing anything they wanted to do. She also said it was "very very unfortunate" that he wouldn't "be able to do the things that everyone else does with their children." He himself thought he would be "a good father," though he did "wish I was able to stand up and, you know, walk with my child. I won't be able to do that. So my child will just have to learn that, you know, his or her father uses a wheelchair to get around." He also worried about possibly reaching a point where he wouldn't be able to earn an income and "support my family." His wife added that "the things that I compensate for will become greater and greater as . . . as time goes on, when he no longer can put his socks on and button his shirt."[27]

Later MDA telecasts carried the same message: Disability endangered an American man's efforts to be a breadwinner, partner, and parent. That point was repeated in profiles of two men, both driving power wheelchairs, both married, both working as computer programmers, both with SMA. One was a young man married for five years to a young nondisabled woman he met when she was a volunteer at an MDA camp. The wife described her husband as "an extremely thoughtful person, very caring," who faced "discrimination through the years, people not wanting to give him a chance because of his disability. But he hung in there and let people know that he was able to do it. And it might be a little different than everybody else, but he's still able to get things done." The young husband praised MDA as the "vehicle" for him to achieve independence. The other man was middle-aged, the father of four children. Like the first man, his wife helped him get dressed in the morning. It took two-and-a-half hours, said the wife. The telethon's filmed profile also pictured her feeding her husband. This was puzzling since other shots showed him handling a computer mouse, talking on the cell phone he was holding in his right hand, and driving his van. His wife said his needs put a strain on their marriage and children. And he expressed his anger at having to deal with this disease. Both men urged the importance of medical research to cure or alleviate SMA.[28]

These three profiles were not simple and straightforward but complicated and even contradictory, for MDA and the couples themselves shaped their experiences and feelings to fit the telethon's rhetorical argument. Genuine appreciation and admiration were mixed with devaluation. The serious difficulties were real, but at times overstated and, in important ways, misunderstood. Clearly, SMA caused significant functional restrictions and physical hardships that had an impact on these men's relationships. Their sense of loss and their fears about the future deserved empathetic respect. But at the same time, the emphasis on their physical limitations underrated the greater importance of emotional reciprocity in a marriage and emotional nurturance and role modeling in parenting, actions all of these men were obviously capable of. Putting on his socks didn't make a man a caring husband. A good father could ride a wheelchair instead of walking.

Meanwhile, the focus on how much their wives assisted these men implicitly argued that disability stole the physical autonomy that was assumed to be a hallmark of American manhood. As a result, their disabilities overburdened their wives, distorting traditional marital relations. But this left out important elements in the situation of couples and families like these in the latter decades of the twentieth century. This was information telethon viewers needed if they were truly to understand what life was like for those sorts of neighbors. Many American families in which a spouse or parent had a significant disability struggled with how to get personal assistance services. Disability activists called for publicly funded options to undergird marriages and families. But instead, disabled men such as these three—and disabled women, too—who were employed or married or both were often ineligible for government help. This played out in the case of disability and reproductive rights activist Barbara Waxman, who for many years was unable to marry Daniel Fiduccia because she would lose the government support of $36,000 to pay for the two ventilators and personal attendant care services she needed in order to survive—marrying the legal affairs consultant who also lived with a disability would raise her above the $256/month maximum she was allowed in order to receive health benefits. In essence, the system forced her to chose between health care and marriage. Disabled adults usually qualified only if they were spouseless, familyless, jobless, impoverished, and isolated.[29] Those policies—which were euphemistically called work and marriage disincentives—flew in the face of a vaunted commitment to "family values." Lack of support undermined marriages and families, while sapping the physical and emotional energy a person with a significant disability needed to go to work every day. This burden was a major but unacknowledged challenge to many disabled adults' strenuous efforts to perform the social roles ordinarily expected of American males and females.[30] At its most extreme, gendered telethon images pictured disease and disability as assaulting American manhood to the point that life became unbearable.

The unstated gendered point of segments such as these was that disease attacked not just a man's body but his identity as a self-sufficient American man. And the culture that had defined authentic masculinity for him, speaking now through the telethon, confirmed that he was right: His presumed emasculation made his life unendurable. If the situations of most other disabled men portrayed on telethons were far less dire, the implicit message on and off those shows was often that disability and disease could well make true manhood impossible.[31] Normative gender identities were to be achieved either through medical treatments and research or rehabilitation; without them, potential donors were told, American manhood was in danger.

Throughout history, human societies have typically organized work according to a gendered division of labor. The type of labor men and women did both reflected and defined their gender status. And so it was that modern US vocational rehabilitation (VR), focusing mainly on men, sought to restore them to not only productive employment but also normative masculinity. When it enrolled women, VR upheld traditional gender roles in seemingly contradictory ways. It often shunted them into non-wage-paying occupations, namely homemaking. When VR did train disabled women for paid employment, it apparently reflected the idea that they could not be wives or mothers.[32]

During the late twentieth century, Americans' ideas about gender and work began to change. Out of economic necessity and increased economic opportunity, more and more women took paying jobs outside the home. And because of evolving cultural expectations and women's rising aspirations, more and more of them sought personal fulfillment through jobs and careers. Economic productivity and social validation via paid employment became an element of the gender identities of not only men but also many women. Because of that socioeconomic and cultural shift, the capacities—or rather the assumed incapacities—of disabled adults of both sexes to function as paid productive workers shaped their gender identities in new ways. Telethon framings reflected that development.

Though the Arthritis Foundation Telethon did not make employment a major theme, it occasionally profiled adults who had jobs and careers. Sometimes it showed them at Foundation-sponsored workshops on work issues. The 1988 telecast included segments on "Arthritis in Prime Time," a symposium about such concerns as job site modifications, adaptive devices, and strategies to educate employers and the public. A woman with arthritis organized the project because she had trouble getting her boss and coworkers to understand her disability.[33] Meanwhile, UCP tried to refute the bias that men and women with cerebral palsy were incompetent or unable to hold down jobs by promoting its job training, coaching, and supported employment programs. Easter Seals explained its comparable services as well as adults' capabilities for paid productive employment. In the 1990s, Easter Seals, like UCP, sometimes raised the issue of job discrimination. Both charities attributed working-age disabled adults' high unemployment rates to bias and inaccessibility. But Easter Seals tended to approach the matter gingerly, typically airing those segments late at night. However, as will be seen below, UCP confronted job discrimination more emphatically.

It seemed that only the MDA Telethon, or at least Jerry Lewis, clung to the assumption of unemployability. As noted earlier, in 1991 Lewis responded to disability activist critics by claiming: "My kids, and my older kids, and those stricken with muscular dystrophy or neuromuscular diseases, cannot go in the work place. There's nothing they can do." Yet, contrary to his assertion, a year earlier the telethon featured adults with neuromuscular conditions at work, and even more significant, as chapter 13 will show, the year after those remarks were made, the telethon profiled dozens of men and women pursuing careers.

Whether they portrayed adults as incapacitated for paid employment or showed them working for a living, telethons usually propagated the notion that adults with disabilities had to be cured or rehabilitated if they were to match up to American gender requirements. Meanwhile, many people with disabilities engaged in even more strenuous labors to build positive gender and sexual identities and emotionally fulfilling relationships.

Flourishing Despite the Pressure

Some adolescent girls with disabilities searched for adult disabled women as role models. As a teenager during the early 1960s, blind writer Deborah Kent hunted for heroines in novels and plays. She sought characters who could give her reason to hope she would find emotional connection and romance, love and a committed partner. But instead, the stories available to her, even novels by feminist authors, depicted women with disabilities as helpless, dependent, useless, pitiable, and undesirable. Seldom did those tales explore the social stigma that caused so much pain—or even acknowledge that such bias existed. Kent's futile quest repeatedly taught her that "I was different from most other people, and that my differentness was a judgment against me."[34] It wasn't only heterosexual disabled women who were rejected as romantically unacceptable. Disabled lesbians told how they were "dismissed, shunned, or relegated to the status of a confidante rather than a lover. . .."[35] Male youths and adult men with disabilities, gay as well as straight, also faced disability bias in tandem with not only hegemonic masculinity but also dominant gay norms.[36] Certainly, most telethons gave little indication that disabled people might be sexual, let alone that some might seek pleasure outside the heteronormative American mainstream. Late-twentieth-century autobiographies of men and women with many kinds of disabilities and various sexual identities recounted their ceaseless exertions to form meaningful emotional and sexual connections, but those publications seldom reported intimate relationships.[37]

This absence of intimacy resulted from more than interpersonal rejection. It indicated the working out one-on-one of societal biases and institutionalized discrimination.

In late-twentieth-century America, discrimination by health-care professionals struck women with disabilities especially hard. Commonly viewed as unfit sexual partners or mothers, many complained of the lack of appropriate or adequate counseling for sexuality, birth control, pregnancy, and childbearing. Not only were few obstetricians, gynecologists, midwives, or rehabilitation professionals knowledgeable about their needs, few were willing to support them through pregnancies. Some were even hostile to disabled women who wanted a child. Some women were legally barred from motherhood: Early- and mid-twentieth-century state laws and court rulings prohibited women and men with certain disabilities from marrying and often allowed or compelled their sterilization. Throughout the century, women also faced discrimination in adoption and foster parenting, even if they were married to a nondisabled man, and in divorce proceedings some mothers found it hard to win custody of their children.[38] Yet, marriage disincentives in social welfare policies prevented, undermined, or broke up marriages of both women and men. Taken together, these socially created restrictions denied people with disabilities emotionally and sexually intimate partnerships, blocking them from sharing in and contributing to the nurturing and security of life in a family.

Corroborated by research, such dismissive responses to women with disabilities shaped women's self-identities. In the 1970s and 1980s, studies found that while social attitudes toward all people with disabilities were negative, girls and women faced even more hostility than boys and men. Internalizing this prejudice, many females carried a heavier burden of low self-esteem.[39] A woman with mild cerebral palsy made some admissions to the UCP's 1989 audience that they were not accustomed to hearing on telethons. She stated that when you have a disability, society tells you that you are "ugly." And so she grew up with a poor body image. But then studying to become a teacher of deaf adults, she learned sign language. For the first time, she did something beautiful with her body. It took a long time, but she finally achieved a positive body image, she said.

Both men and women with disabilities tried many strategies to counter the negative self-images inflicted on them. For physically disabled young men whose manliness was often questioned, involvement in sport, recreation, or exercise, as shown in chapter 9, could display traits of hegemonic masculinity: physical prowess and competitiveness, independence and dominance. Some women with physical disabilities believed exercise could help them normalize their bodies to approximate dominant standards of feminine body beauty. Both men and women said that sport and exercise improved their appearance and made them more attractive, more appealing sexually—in line with prevailing gauges of physical attractiveness.[40]

Some disabled women gave up on marriage and motherhood and instead copied traditional male norms of achievement through work and personal independence. But psychological studies and autobiographies suggested that such success might come at great emotional cost.[41] In many other instances, girls with disabilities were sheltered. Denied opportunities to develop their skills, a sense of validation through accomplishment, or feelings of identification with other girls and women, they felt "trapped and demoralized." Some women found themselves trapped in yet another way. At rates surely higher than those among nondisabled women, they stayed in abusive or exploitative relationships. They stuck it out to survive economically, avoid institutionalization, or stay clear of their abusive families. And no matter where they were—at home, in institutions, or elsewhere—significant numbers suffered sexual abuse and rape, again probably at higher rates than their nondisabled counterparts. Reliable statistics on the physical and sexual abuse of girls and women with disabilities—and boys and men, too—were hard to come by because, often ignored, it was significantly underreported. Disabled feminists complained that battered women shelters and programs for abused women were often inaccessible and lacked accommodations for women with disabilities.[42]

Yet some people with disabilities found ways to resist. Some males fashioned their own disabled masculinity as an alternative to hegemonic masculinity.[43] And some girls and women withstood both gender and disability stereotypes to forge positive identities that incorporated their disabilities. Michelle Fine and Adrienne Asch, the editors of the *Women with Disabilities* anthology, described a new generation of disabled women who emerged in the 1970s and 1980s. "Because of or despite their parents, they get an education and a job. They live independently, enjoy sex with men or women, become pregnant and carry to term if they choose, or abort if they prefer. ... Some determine that they will play by the rules of achievement and succeed at meeting standards that are often deemed inaccessible to them," including "societal norms of attractiveness." Others "disregard anything that seems like 'passing'. . . [and] demand that the world accept them on their own terms, whether those terms be insisting upon signing rather than speaking, not covering their burn scars, not wearing clothing to hide parts of their bodies others may see as 'ugly' or 'deformed,' or rejecting prostheses that inhibit and do not help."[44]

One of those women was a New Yorker with cerebral palsy named Harilyn Rousso. Her mother tried many times to get her to "go for physical therapy and to practice walking more 'normally' at home," but she "vehemently refused." "My disability, with my different walk and talk and my involuntary movements, having been with me all of my life, was part of me, part of my identity," she said. "With these disability features, I felt complete and whole. My mother's attempt to change my walk, strange as it may seem, felt like an assault on myself, an incomplete acceptance of all of me, an attempt to make me over." Rousso grew up to become a respected researcher and a psychotherapist who worked with disabled people, especially girls and women.[45]

"[S]ome disabled girls and women," concluded Fine and Asch, "flourish in spite of the pressures from family and the distortions and discrimination meted out by society." The essays in their collection testified "to both the travails and the victories of these women." Similarly, the editors of *With the Power of Each Breath: A Disabled Women's Anthology* (1985) described it as "a work of resistance against institutionalized silence. ... These pages are a journey into our lives as we survive in an inaccessible society, express our anger, grow up in our families, live in our bodies, find our own identities, parent our children, and find our friends and each other. . . . Our contributors cross the lines of race, age, class, sexual orientation, geographical location and type of disability. But we know there are more disabled women, young and old, third world and institutionalized, whose stories we need to hear." Fine and Asch urged, "We need to know much more than we do about what helps some disabled girls and women resist. . .."[46]

If disabled girls and women—and for that matter disabled boys and men—were to learn how to resist those oppressive pressures, they needed role models. Late in the twentieth century, some of them serendipitously discovered exemplars among the new generation of activists. Emily Rapp had been a March of Dimes poster child. Growing up, she struggled to fashion a positive identity for herself as a woman with a disability. Then one day during her senior year in college, in her school's library, she came across *With the Power of Each Breath*. To her surprise, she found "disabled women speaking honestly about their experiences. The stories read like recorded acts of resistance. For the first time, I understood how deeply the disability experience informed my identity and the identities of women like me. The three themes repeated over and over again were the shame of being different, colored at times by anger; the silence of alienation and isolation, with an effort to break it; and the active longing for a more holistic vision of the self. ... I felt the rush of discovery and hope, like looking in a mirror that reveals a new and unexpected reflection."[47]

But times were changing, at least on the UCP Telethon. Given that expressions of romance, passion, and sexuality on the part of people with disabilities made many nondisabled folks uncomfortable, pragmatic charities had steered clear of those topics. Then in 1989, UCP prompted little-known actors Darrell Larson and Laura Johnson to deliver a new message. Acknowledging that "what we're about to talk about may embarrass some people," Larson continued, "but we're going to say it anyway. ... [D]id you ever stop to realize that people with CP fall in love and are perfectly capable of expressing it? Young men and women with cerebral palsy feel the same sexual stirrings all young people feel." Johnson added: "They are as romantic, passionate, and sensual as anybody else. People with cerebral palsy get married and have children." Larson responded: "United Cerebral Palsy helps make it possible for men and women with CP to lead full lives . . . and to be as romantic and loving as everyone else."

These statements were a bold and risky move on UCP's part. Nondisabled prospective donors might feel uneasy at the thought of people with cerebral palsy having sex, getting married, or bearing children. Many had been taught that romance and sensuality were impossible for people with disabilities. To suggest otherwise might even seem repugnant, for in late-twentieth-century America, eugenic thinking about people with disabilities persisted in altered form, particularly in policies related to prenatal testing and forced sterilization of disabled people.[48] Nonetheless, UCP Telethons in the following years kept raising the issue.

Viewers met married couples with cerebral palsy. They heard from a sex therapist who worked with disabled people, a disability rights advocate, and a disabled man who ran a dating service. All of these guests talked frankly about meaningful romantic relationships and disabled people's capacity to express themselves sexually. In 1992 UCP had actress Stephanie Hodge sum up the message: "I'm here to tell you the glorious truth that men and women with cerebral palsy are perfectly capable of experiencing a full romantic life. And I mean all of it, the good as well as the bad. This means a woman with CP can meet her Prince Charming or a real first-class jerk, just like everybody else. . . . [P]eople with cerebral palsy are everyday people, no different than you or me or anybody else. They have everyday needs and desires."[49]

People with cerebral palsy not only had the same needs and desires as everyone else. "[J]ust like everybody else, they deserve to have those needs and desires fulfilled," asserted Hodge. "They have a *right* to [fulfill them]." But prejudice blocked them from exercising that right. "If I could make one wish . . . ," UCP prompted another actor to say, "it would be to wipe out prejudice and misunderstanding of people with CP and other disabilities. People with CP get married all the time, and they have the ability and the right to have children. Just because a woman has difficulty speaking or walking doesn't mean she won't make a caring and loving mother. It's time we cast aside our prejudice. . . . UCP is there for all the good mothers in America who have cerebral palsy and deserve the right to care for their own children. You can make a pledge to motherhood by making that phone call right now."[50]

This statement was a stunning departure from traditional telethon messages. UCP was recasting donation to be in support of disabled motherhood and human rights. That shift reflected a major social and legal transformation brought about by the civil rights movement of Americans with disabilities.[51]

"Heaven's Special Child"

THE MAKING OF POSTER CHILDREN

As many Americans of all ages knew, Tiny Tim was a little "crippled" boy whose sweetness and courage and pathetic plight melted the heart of miserly Ebenezer Scrooge. Scrooge's charity toward Tim secured his own redemption. Dickens's *A Christmas Carol* is a Yuletide staple. Between 1901 and 2009, the entertainment industry produced fifty-six live-action and fifteen animated movie and television versions. Many were available on video and were rerun on TV each December.[1] Book retailers sold illustrated volumes as holiday gifts.[2] Each December it seemed that every theater in the US staged the story as a play.[3] Consequently, Americans saw *a lot* of Tim.

But Tiny Tim was more than a character in Dickens's tale. He was a ubiquitous cultural figure. The annual return of *A Christmas Carol* did not exhaust his appearances or significance. He arrived not just seasonally but almost year-round. The Tiny Tim image was made into a constant and powerful cultural symbol, especially on telethons. Its main purveyors were the disability charities. Within both the charity tradition and the operation of the medical model, the fictional poster boy helped to shape the identities of millions of people with disabilities.

Tiny Tim's Siblings

Telethons, in effect, reenacted a version of *A Christmas Carol*. The hosts and audiences were huge Cratchit clans, with disabled children—and adults—playing Tiny Tim. Jerry Lewis on the MDA pageant, Dennis James in the UCP spectacle, Pat Boone on the Easter Seals show, and the other hosts, male and female, conflated the roles of the Christmas Ghosts and Bob and Mrs. Cratchit. They were moral preceptors to potential donors, instructing them in their duty to look after Tiny Tim's siblings. At the same time, the hosts and the givers were the Cratchits gathered around the sweet pathetic children. Viewers at risk of becoming Scrooges peered through their TV screens and learned that they could join the family by opening their hearts to the afflicted Tims. By looking after the "most weak," they could buy a place at the telethon hearth. Telethon Tiny Tims were not just *Jerry's* kids. They belonged to anyone who phoned in a pledge to any of the telethons. Some Easter Seals posters declared, "He's yours too." Easter Seals local hosts touted "Adopt-a-Child." As with charities for third world children, sponsors supported a particular youngster, who would write them a personal thank-you.[4] "Believe me," declared UCP's Dennis James, "we're all taking care of heaven's special child."[5]

Through much of Western history, disabled and sick children were central to the practice of charity. In early modern Britain—roughly from the 1600s through the early 1800s—children's hospitals drew more support than those treating adults with venereal disease. Though the latter were desperately needed, philanthropists feared they would be seen as supporting vice and debauchery. Beneficence to children instead associated them with innocent suffering. In any era, donation typically went to institutions that promised the greatest public approbation. Older people were much less likely to receive such relief and remained desperately in need until establishment of state pensions in the twentieth century.[6]

The eighteenth-century English artist William Hogarth may have pioneered images of children as a charity fundraising tool. A governor of London's first foundling hospital, established in 1737, he designed both a distinctive uniform for the infant inmates and "an affecting coat-of-arms" for the institution. The latter displayed "a new-born child flanked by the figures of Nature and Britannia, with the plaintive motto 'Help!'" He and other artists exhibited their paintings at the hospital, inviting wealthy patrons to buy them. This advanced Hogarth's aim to make British art competitive with Continental art in the British marketplace. It also anticipated twentieth-century fundraising that linked charity with commerce and patriotism in the United States.[7]

In 1930s America, the National Society for Crippled Children and Adults and the polio crusade invented child-based methods that became standard in disability-related soliciting. As the Society (founded in 1919) launched its 1934 drive, Finance Chair Paul King asked *Cleveland Plain Dealer* cartoonist J. H. Donahey to design a stamp supporters could purchase for a penny and place on envelopes and letters. That first Easter Seal pictured a boy wearing leg braces and leaning on crutches, his head bent sadly. Behind him was a white cross and—reminiscent of Hogarth's coat of arms—the words "Help Crippled Children." The design expressed clients' alleged plea "simply for the right to live a normal life." The huge public response eventually prompted the organization to rename itself the National Easter Seals Society. In 1952 it made the lily part of its logo. The flower explicitly represented spring, while implicitly referring to Easter, the season's religious holiday and the charity's quasi-religious tenor. The Society also held annual contests in each state to select children as the public faces of its affiliates' fundraising.[8]

Meanwhile, the polio campaign crafted its own child-centered strategy. As early as 1932, the Warm Springs Foundation enlisted illustrator Howard Chandler Christy—famous for his World War I recruitment posters—to design a poster featuring a disabled child. He also drew program covers for the president's Birthday Balls. Unlike later images, these drawings did not make the children's disabilities visible.[9] But as time went on, the drive began to stress those physical differences. In 1934, calling on his audience to support the Birthday Balls, nicknamed "Paralysis Dances," syndicated columnist and radio personality Walter Winchell invoked the image of a paralyzed child. "If you buy a ticket to dance," he said, "then some little child who can't even walk may be able to dance some day." Polio publicists blazoned the slogan "Dance so that a child may walk." They filled the nation's newspapers with studies in physical contrast, photos of nondisabled adult dancers alongside pictures of children "crippled" by polio.[10]

In 1937 strategists at the new National Foundation for Infantile Paralysis "shifted the main appeal" from paying tribute to FDR as a victor over polio to "unashamed exploitation of the pathetic appeals of crippled children." NFIP's March of Dimes hammered at the radical difference between *crippled* children and *normal* kids. Its first drive in 1938 featured nondisabled children wearing buttons that proclaimed, "I'm glad I'm well."[11] In 1946 it begat its first poster child.[12] Its ominous film *The Crippler* blended sentimentality and pity with terror, fear, and hope. "A figure leaning on a crutch—sinister in its invisibility—stalks the land like death itself . . . 'And I'm *especially* fond of children,' the voice-over intones with fiendish glee. . . ."[13]

The strategies contrived in the 1930s persisted over the next seven decades. Disability charities, as we have seen, drew on the cult of sentimentalism's traditional tropes as they focused public attention on the icon of the innocent, helpless child.[14] The agencies also used adults to illustrate their services, but the grown-ups got nowhere near the publicity beamed at the kids. Poster children were, by design, the most visible symbols of fundraising. At the back of their stages, the UCP, MDA, and Easter Seals Telethons displayed photos of children. Easter Seals' 1994 opening scrolled images from past programs; 9 out of 10 showed children. Later, there was a montage of forty-eight years of poster children but no retrospective of adult representatives. Besides "national" children, Easter Seals and MDA exhibited state and local poster kids. UCP had only local poster children, but its national telecasts were filled with images of youngsters.[15] Even the Arthritis Foundation Telethon used children to elicit alms. Of the 37 million Americans with connective-tissue diseases, 200,000 were kids or teens with juvenile rheumatoid arthritis. Still, the telethon showcased a disproportionate number of children.[16]

At a 1986 workshop on the how-to's of telethon success, Easter Seals officials told local chapter executives: "Children raise more money than adults." Youngsters were effective fundraising tools, they explained, because the public sympathized with images of "the most weak." They also reported that girls pulled in larger amounts than boys.[17] Of the forty-eight national poster children chosen between 1947 and 1994, 2 out of 3 were girls. For MDA, the gender pattern seemed the reverse, with boys—in particular, boys with DMD—attracting more money.

Easter Seals' marketing strategists also said that white kids drew more donations than children of color, though more nonwhite children would appear by the later decades of the twentieth century. The ethnic ratios on all telethons reflected that strategic judgment, even though disability prevalence rates were higher in minority communities.[18] Among those forty-eight Easter Seals poster children, just one—a girl—was African American, while another girl was born in India. The selections reflected historic patterns of discrimination in health care. During the 1930s and 1940s, African American community leaders criticized the Warm Springs Foundation and the NFIP for neglecting black polio patients and then treating them in segregated facilities. Following World War II, in response to the civil rights movement and Cold War race politics, the NFIP slowly began to fund integrated training programs and medical rehabilitation facilities. Concurrently, starting in 1947, a few African American children were selected as poster children for local, regional, and national campaigns.[19] Beginning in the 1990s, perhaps because of the growth of the middle class in minority communities as well as the impact of civil rights movements, more disabled people of color, adults as well as children, were featured on telethons.[20]

Given poster children's important function, their selection became an art. Fashions changed in the charity business, noted the *Los Angeles Times* in 1986, but choosing child spokespersons remained highly competitive. It had "earmarks of a beauty pageant: stage mothers trying to boost their youngsters to fame and fortune, children trying too hard to impress, and local Easter Seals officials going to great lengths to promote their nominees." One chapter "arranged for [national Communications Director Sandi Gordon] Perkins to be flown in on a sponsor's corporate airplane, gave her a party featuring California wine—and followed up with an angry letter when the chapter's candidate was not selected." Local leaders promoted their favorites as embodying sentimental stereotypes. Of one finalist, a functionary wrote: "His clear, sweet, high-pitched voice . . . together with his angelic face, breaks hearts." Another declared that a girl had "a special magnetism that will draw you near and steal your heart."[21]

Each charity chose youngsters who embodied its particular message. MDA and Arthritis kids were heart-tuggingly dependent; Easter Seals and UCP children were plucky overcomers. But all poster children had this much in common. Picked for "practical marketing reasons," they had to be congenial and presentable, as well as attractive and telegenic. "The national child doesn't have to be gorgeous," said Easter Seals' Perkins, "as long as they look OK." Poster kids must not look too different. According to the MDA Telethon's producer, Jerry Lewis "prefer[red] his poster child to be ambulatory. He says he doesn't want to bend over a wheelchair to raise a buck." But in fact, Lewis was often shown bending over his "kids" seated on wheelchairs. It was a tricky balance: They had to appear helpless but they couldn't be too disabled.[22]

These considerations were crucial because poster children did far more than appear on the telethons. The charities displayed Tiny Tim's siblings year-round. A blizzard of poster-kid pictures blanketed the nation. Their images looked out from drugstore and supermarket displays tied to Easter Seals and MDA promotions. Their photos were fixed on MDA and UCP "banks" beside restaurant and grocery-store cash registers. Newspapers and magazines featured stories about them. They went to charity fundraisers: bowl-a-thons, golf tournaments, and dinners honoring local business leaders. They posed with sports heroes and Hollywood celebrities. Over the song "You've Got to Have Friends," the Easter Seals Telethon screened a photo montage of national poster children with movie and TV stars.[23]

Poster kids were "seen and listened to by millions of Americans," noted the Los Angeles Times. Just halfway through his "reign" the 1986 National Easter Seals Child had flown tens of thousands of miles, everywhere from Washington, DC, to Las Vegas, to Puerto Rico. He had addressed conventions of everyone from realtors to truck drivers. And his image had appeared "on everything from Easter Seals' seals to Crayola crayons posters to Safeway delivery trucks." His image had been reproduced roughly 70 million times. And he still had six months to go as a poster child.[24]

These dependent children were introduced to the executives whose corporations were the charities' most prominent supporters. A review of hundreds of hours of telethons found a few segments featuring executives visiting therapy centers that served adults and just one that showed them meeting an adult with a disability in a business setting. Telethons did not present executives or their employees encountering disabled adults in situations that portrayed them as colleagues or even potential coworkers. But they met lots of children.

Poster children also had their pictures taken with elected officials—state governors and legislators, members of Congress, even the president of the United States.[25] In 1992 Easter Seals aired a medley of photos of its national children meeting every president from George H. W. Bush all the way back to Harry S. Truman, while viewers heard the song "Stand By Me."[26] "The poster child is our major ambassador to the public," explained a March of Dimes spokeswoman.[27] That icon influenced business executives' attitudes about the millions of adults they might have seen as customers, employees, or colleagues, instead of recipients of their charity. It instructed lawmakers as they formulated policies that affected disabled citizens. It defined who Americans with disabilities really were and what they really needed. They were portrayed as dependent objects of beneficence whose most important needs were medical. In late-twentieth-century America, the Tiny Tim persona was central to framing the cultural, social, and political meaning of disability: A disabled person was a vulnerable child, one of "the most weak."

Jerry's Kids

In a *Parade* article entitled "Seeing the Light in a Child's Eyes," Jerry Lewis explained his role as father to the multitudes. "So what's so special about 'Jerry's Kids,' as they've called themselves for lo, these many decades? Well, for one thing, of course, they are 'My Kids.' I've been working with them, and for them, for 42 years now. ... I'm not ashamed to think in such personal terms of the tens of thousands of young people—and hundreds of thousands of adults—afflicted with any of the more than 40 neuromuscular diseases. And they've asked me to call them 'mine'—because, in fact, the term 'Jerry's Kids' is their invention. I know where they're coming from, and they know what I'm trying to do. And when you relate to each other as intimately as we do, well, there's a special relationship."[28] Some of Jerry's "kids" were older than Jerry. Furthermore, other telethons sometimes spoke of adults with disabilities as though they were children. Actor Wilford Brimley dedicated a song "to the Easter Seals kids, however old they are."[29] By exploiting the Tiny Tim icon, the charities reinforced the obsessive infantilization of people with disabilities in American culture.[30]

Telethon hosts sometimes unconsciously deprived disabled people of adult status by referring to them only by their first names: On an Easter Seals Chicago segment, a doctor and a woman who worked at a group home for developmentally disabled young adults flanked a developmentally disabled man. Introduced as "David," he was not included in the conversation. On the UCP show, a woman with cerebral palsy who was a social worker and a disabled man who worked as a computer consultant were introduced and referred to only by their first names.[31] LA Easter Seals MC Ed Arnold interviewed a 19-year-old high school student named Joyce who had cerebral palsy and a mild intellectual disability. He reported that she liked horseback riding. "Do you have a horse that's kind of one of your favorites? Do you know what the horse's name is?" he asked as though she was so limited that she couldn't even remember such a simple bit of information. "We're so glad you came to see us," said Arnold, "because you are very pretty." Then he added, "What did I say I was going to do? I said I was going to slip a kiss on you, didn't I?" After kissing her on the cheek, he laughed as though teasing a little girl. "Ha, ha, ha. I did that. I snuck one in on you." People in the studio applauded. Arnold called her "this adorable lady."[32]

On one MDA Telethon, Jerry Lewis declared, "I have dedicated this program to children of all ages for forty-four years." On another telethon, he called Bob Sampson, a man with a neuromuscular disability who was an attorney and a United Airlines vice president, "one of my oldest kids."[33] While Lewis did not explain why he referred to adults like Sampson as "kids," the reason is not hard to find. As we've seen with our discussion of cause-related marketing, American sympathy entrepreneurs had learned that images of children with disabilities and childlike images of disabled adults pulled in donations. This portrayal reinforced disability as an infantilized social role and identity. The childish image instructed nondisabled people to treat disabled adults as though they were children. And it taught disabled adults that they had the status and social power of tots. In particular, the medical model enforced professional domination that took away the adult standing of sick people and people with disabilities. Illness and disability were often made occasions of social degradation. Hospitals were one of the primary institutional sites of induction into this demoted status. Staffers frequently treated newly disabled adults as though they were infants and then perceived them as regressing to childlike behavior. Arnold Beisser, who would go on to become an influential psychotherapist and author of *The Paradoxical Theory of Change*, was just finishing medical school when he contracted polio. Well into adulthood, he found that the "nurses and attendants often talked to me as if I were a baby. ... If I became soiled ... they were likely to say, 'Naughty, naughty,' or 'You've been a bad boy.'"[34] This sort of dishonoring was one reason so many adults fiercely fought against identifying—or being identified—as disabled.

And yet many people took on such roles and identities, accepting their abasement. One reason was, of course, that they were forced into it. Society, in general, and the "helping" professions, in particular, quickly deprived them of the means and markers of adulthood. But that did not fully account for their apparent acquiescence or their knowing performance. The explanation lay in their prior socialization. Everyone was taught the terms of those social roles even when they were not sick or disabled. They knew them by heart.[35] They knew what society expected, indeed required, of the ill and the invalidated. They must submit to the authority of experts, yielding to not only medical personnel, but also professionals in every occupation related to rehabilitation and social services. They must comply with the terms of the invalid role and must gratefully accept their new status as objects of others' charity. They must cheerfully strive to overcome their disabilities—that is, to recover their normality, thereby confirming the legitimacy of culturally prescribed, dominant normal roles and identities. Until they achieved social validity, they must bow to their loss of adult status and adult social power. Because many people with illnesses and disabilities could see no alternatives, they played their assigned parts. In one sense, the charity fundraising broadcasts functioned as instructional telecourses in the performance of those roles.

Telethons' demeaning of adults infuriated some disabled people who struggled against cultural devaluation and for social respect. Among her ten "Thon-Watching Tips for the Skeptical," former poster child Laura Hershey urged, "Don't weep for the children. This may sound like a heartless thing to say, but I'm speaking honestly from my own experience." She went on to explain, "I sensed that viewers were supposed to see me as cute but doomed and useless. I was bright and generally happy, but no one mentioned that on the Telethon. Instead of introducing you to real children, the 'Thon gives you sob stories."[36] Ben Mattlin, a Harvard graduate and writer with a neuromuscular disability, took Jerry Lewis to task in an open letter in the *Los Angeles Times*. "[Do] you know how hard it is to become, and be treated as, a self-respecting disabled adult in this society?" he demanded. He scorned "your ubiquitous 'Jerry's Kids'" as "never more absurd than when followed by 'of all ages.'" Lewis might argue that "Jerry's Kids" was "a term of affection, but you wouldn't refer to your late friend Sammy Davis Jr. as your 'boy.'"[37] To adults like Mattlin, the phrase "Jerry's Kids" was comparable to racist epithets that degraded adult people of color. In their view, the social acceptability of telethon practices that robbed people with disabilities of adult dignity showed how deeply American culture devalued them.

Not Different, Just Special

If telethons presented children as the representative type of disabled person, they also portrayed them as fundamentally unlike normal children. A UCP announcer assured viewers: "Children with cerebral palsy aren't different. They're just special."[38] But, in fact, the identity of children with disabilities was, in the world of the telethon, not specialness, but negation. Their childhood was the inversion of real childhood.

First of all, children with disabilities were not real children because, according to the charities, they could not play. An MDA-linked Rice Krispies commercial made the point. As elementary schoolchildren race to the playground, an announcer intones: "They're rambunctious, full of energy, and in constant motion. They're kids . . . Unfortunately, not all kids are like this." Jerry Lewis was then shown seated at a kitchen table with a bowl of Rice Krispies in front of him as he explained the Kellogg's promotion. Back on the playground, boys played football as the announcer contrasted real children and children with disabilities: ". . .[S]omeday we'd like to see Jerry's kids just be kids."[39] On rare occasions, telethon viewers got a glimpse of the reality of a disabled child's life. Four-year-old Michael could drive his power wheelchair at speeds up to 6 miles an hour. So his neighborhood pals tethered their bikes and trikes to the back of his chair, as Michael led them in playing crack the whip. His mother explained to Jerry Lewis and the MDA audience that he also liked to drive his chair among clothing stores' circular racks and set them spinning. This boy had decided that his wheelchair was not a confining piece of medical equipment but an exhilarating toy. Lewis and the studio audience laughed with delight at this example of a typical child's creativity. Lewis concluded that young Michael was "doing quite well," but he still wanted to "get him out of" that wheelchair.[40]

Children with disabilities were not "real" children because they failed to match a standard of juvenile physicality. But the telethons measured disabled kids against skillfully athletic youngsters, not physically average ones. The shows presented dancing or gymnastic children and youths as the yardsticks of normality. The UCP telecast featured the Cheers USA Military Dance Team, made up of teenage girls, and Cheers USA Junior Mascots, composed of little girls.[41] UCP also showcased teenagers from the California Academy of Rhythmic Gymnastics.[42] Both UCP and MDA repeatedly booked an act called "Four Boys and a Babe," later renamed "The Babe and her Boys," five children who danced. Jerry Lewis spelled out the contrast between these youngsters and his "kids": "They're all wonderful . . . and they're all healthy."[43]

Telethons also pictured children with disabilities as longing to be like those junior athletes. "Ask any little boy what he wants to be when he grows up," urged the narrator of an MDA film. Seemingly in reply, a boy declared that he wanted to become "a baseball person and a football and a computer man." But he was "in a wheelchair," said the narrator, so "unless something changes, he won't play baseball or football." "That little boy," Leeza Gibbons, one of that year's cohosts, charged viewers, "needs your help to realize his dreams." No doubt the lad did wish he could play baseball and football. His disability involved real physical limitations. Yet even at his young age, "his dreams" involved more than athletics. He also wanted to be "a computer man." The film showed this precocious 6-year-old playing chess on a computer. Yet according to telethon ideology, he would have to play sports to be a real boy. The possibility of his playing adapted sports such as those discussed in chapter 9 was not even mentioned.[44]

Children with disabilities were not real children because there was something fundamentally wrong with them. In 1973, "holding a child in his arms," Jerry Lewis declared, "God goofed, and it's up to us to correct his mistakes."[45] On another telecast, he entreated viewers: "You can help us change the mistake, somewhere along the way, when the genes got confused somehow and a child came out wrong. We do this show so that we right that wrong."[46] The Lord, it seemed, had not "been kind" to children with disabilities, so they had come out wrong. Behind these offhand comments lurked ancient, often unconscious notions about the cosmic causes of illness and disability.

It was a short step from seeing disabled children as physiologically wrong to perceiving them as morally flawed. Professional dogma and conventional wisdom throughout the modern era assumed that disability impaired a child's moral development. In the mid-nineteenth century, Samuel Gridley Howe described his deaf-blind pupil Laura Bridgman as physically and socially imprisoned by her disability. Because she was necessarily "in the less blessed situation of receiver, and seldom in that of giver," disability made development of her capacities for sympathy and benevolence more difficult. Behind this view was the belief that any disability fostered narcissism, for, said Howe, "any departure from the moral and healthy condition of the body; any ail, or pain, or deformity, or maim, is very apt to contract the circle of the sympathies, by forcing the thoughts to dwell on the centre of self." Yet Howe undercut this interpretation when he observed with some surprise that despite Laura's dependence, "it is most remarkable that she has not become very selfish and inconsiderate of others."[47] The ideology of disability shaping his perceptions could not account for the actual girl before him.

Disabled children's moral development was also supposedly impaired by their parents' alleged inability or unwillingness to discipline them. That stereotype appeared at the beginnings of special education and rehabilitation. In the antebellum era, superintendents of southern state residential schools for deaf children warned of the "fatal effects" of parents' "almost unrestrained indulgence." The educators claimed that those children became selfish, unbridled, and willful, passionate and obstinate, developed "vicious tempers and habits," and were "almost a certain source of misery to themselves and family," "a pest, if not a curse." They promised to instill in deaf pupils the self-discipline their parents had failed to inculcate.[48] That conception of childhood disability persisted in the first decades of the twentieth century. The rehabilitationists who ran "hospital-schools" for physically disabled children assumed that family and friends had dangerously coddled them. In response to that misguided sympathy, a New York physician declared in 1911: "A failure in the moral training of a cripple means the evolution of an individual detestable in character, a menace and burden to the community, who is only too apt to graduate into the mendicant and criminal classes." Guided by that sort of reasoning, hospital-schools made moral training central to their regimen for young "cripples," particularly boys.[49]

The ideology of postpolio rehabilitation in the 1930s, 1940s, and 1950s continued to admonish against coddling disabled children. Some facilities prohibited parents from visiting their children during the first month of hospitalization. Others allowed only restricted visiting during the months of rehabilitation that sometimes stretched into years. In the mid-1950s, one major postpolio rehabilitation center permitted children to see their parents for a total of four hours a week and barred them from seeing their brothers and sisters at all. Meanwhile, hospital staffers such as those at a Canadian facility were instructed to take an "objective" attitude and cautioned about the "danger" of "allowing one's natural sympathies to get out of hand." One study ascribed "severe cases of homesickness at the hospital . . . either to the child's 'abnormal' attachment to its mother" or to his or her own emotional instability. A few specialists recognized that this "management philosophy" intensified children's "anxiety, dependency, and hostility." They recommended that staffers instead respond empathetically to children's concerns and fears. But more often, rehabilitation experts practiced a kind of tough love in the hospital. And before sending disabled children home, they trained parents to avoid indulging and spoiling them.[50] This mode of rehabilitating and parenting children with disabilities reflected ancient prejudices about the moral defectiveness of disabled people. It also exemplified the modern medical-model project of overcoming. In enforcing this ideology, rehabilitation and education professionals inflicted on disabled youngsters what can only be termed child abuse.

As with approaches to parenting in general, this view of children with disabilities and their parents persisted in the era of the telethons. An Easter Seals executive expressed it when she referred to parents' "natural urge to coddle"[51] and UCP's Dennis James talked about how parents of a child with cerebral palsy who misbehaved "would certainly not scold or spank."[52] Many people who grew up with disabilities did not remember their childhoods that way. They recalled their parents disciplining them. But telethons instead reinforced the stereotype of the spoiled disabled child—the cute, manipulative, little crippled girl who got her way, the bratty disabled boy who escaped punishment when other kids, normal kids would have been chastised. Because parents allegedly could not or would not correct their disabled children, they could not control or properly rear them. That meant these children would never become appropriate grown-ups, self-disciplining adult men and women. Beneath assertions that children with disabilities were disorderly and uncontrollable lay the bias that disability distorted moral development.

"Disability Awareness"

Opposing the charities' and the medical model's depoliticization of disability, activists in the 1980s demanded attention to prejudice and discrimination, inaccessibility and denial of reasonable accommodations. Meanwhile, the charities fashioned disability awareness programs that continued to focus on an individual's problems and limitations brought on by their disability. Easter Seals got Nestlé to sponsor a disability simulation called "Kids Baking for Kids." Teenagers measured ingredients while blindfolded or put cookies into an oven while seated on a wheelchair. This exercise allegedly taught them "what it feels like to have a disability." Through donations and cookie sales, 30,000 adolescents raised over $150,000. And they gave some of the cookies they baked to disabled youngsters—"filling [their] hearts." Nestlé's spokesperson said the scheme helped "raise the consciousness of young adults toward people with disabilities."[53]

Some activists charged "awareness" programs with reinforcing ignorance and bias. One could not learn quickly how to "have a disability," they said. It took more than wearing a blindfold or pushing a wheelchair for an hour. Operating in environments designed for nondisabled people required a fund of expertise one could only gain over time. Living in a world organized in ways that excluded people with disabilities demanded particular disabled skills and shrewd strategizing—and style, too. Novices did not know—they could not know—how to handle situations people with disabilities managed every day. As a result, nondisabled simulators often concluded that living with a disability was inherently hard, if not impossible, that it was tragic and in many ways terrifying. Activist Valerie Brew-Parrish described one exercise in which airline personnel were blindfolded "to test evacuation procedures. … The results were disastrous." With "no training in mobility or orientation," they "erroneously concluded that blind persons could never safely evacuate a plane." By way of contrast, Brew-Parrish explained, "When I'm disoriented in a dark place, I let my blind husband lead the way!"[54] She and other activists proposed alternative consciousness-raising exercises.[55]

Social psychologists' research corroborated activists' criticisms of disability simulations. Studies in the 1970s and 1980s found that they were not only ineffective but often bolstered detrimental stereotypes. Fostering "little, if any, attitude change," said psychologist Catherine Fichten, they generated a great deal of "new negative affect." Participants learned "mainly about the frustrations, difficulties and limitations of having a disability." She criticized this "pity orientation" as "thoroughly undesirable for the integration of students with a disability."[56]

Simulations like "Kids Baking for Kids" also reinforced the belief that physical impairments were the main limitation on individuals' ability to function in society. These exercises did not arrange for nondisabled teens to deal with access problems in the built environment or show them that barriers could be reduced or removed through individualized accommodations, general accessibility features, and universal design that aimed to make spaces available to a variety of users with and without disabilities. Those disability rights concepts aimed to ensure equality of opportunity and social integration. Universal design principles spelled out how to make objects and environments usable by people who operated in a variety of ways. Setting forth a socially transformative blueprint, they envisioned a truly pluralistic society that planned for diversity, rather than merely paying lip service to it.[57] In contrast, simulation exercises such as the cookie baking scheme only strengthened ill-informed notions that physical differences were inherently and inevitably restricting.

They perpetuated the medical model's assumption that the constraints were located exclusively in individual bodies.

Furthermore, these adolescent bakers were not introduced to disabled peers in a context that fostered equality of esteem. They gave cookies to children half their age, as an act of charity. Prejudice reduction research showed that the *type* of contact between majority and minority group members was crucial. Encounters with disabled people of equal or higher status tended to lessen nondisabled individuals' bias. Situations that brought together disabled and nondisabled people on an unequal basis not only failed to reduce prejudice but could also fortify beliefs about disabled people's inherent inferiority. The most effective efforts promoted "cooperative interdependence," explained psychologist Rhoda Olkin, interactions that were "personal, mutually rewarding, ... intimate on both parts[,] and persist[ed] over time." Positive attitudes also tended to develop when disabled participants were seen as "socially skillful" and "competent in areas valued by the other." Structuring intergroup contact in these ways was vital because "the myths about disability are remarkably immune from data," persisting even "in the face of data that contradicts them." Prejudice reduction research was conducted during the telethon era, but the cookie baking project adopted none of these recommended features. The teenagers did not encounter disabled people on an equal, cooperative, and interdependent basis.[58]

MDA had what it called "a handicapped awareness program for youngsters": "hop-a-thons." Children solicited pledges for every hop they could perform in two minutes. Hundreds of preschools and kindergartens and thousands of children participated. On the telethon's local segments, champion hoppers were applauded for their physical ability.[59] This "awareness program" was designed to dramatize the difference between allegedly normal youngsters and "Jerry's Kids."

MDA corporate sponsor KinderCare Learning Centers, a national chain of some 1200 day-care and education programs for young children, held hop-a-thons and other fundraisers. These events taught parents and children to think of the centers' pupils as the valid opposites of the objects of their charity. A film showed KinderCare children making things with paper and paste. "These are the lucky ones," asserted an announcer, "the healthy kids, and they're giving their time and their developing talents to help 'Jerry's Kids.'" In another spot, KinderCare pupils recited in singsong: "'Jerry's Kids' are very special people." "At KinderCare we raised over $200 dollars at our sleep-over," chirped a little girl. "We gave it to the MDA because we like to help 'Jerry's Kids.'" Another shot in a separate space showed three children sitting on wheelchairs and a nondisabled woman who spoke for them. "'Jerry's Kids' really appreciate what KinderCare kids do for them," she declared. A third segment featured KinderCare children participating in fashion shows and hop-a-thons and other fundraising activities. The only youngster with a visible disability was the focus of their benefactions, MDA's National Poster Child.[60] No MDA Telethon spot showed a child with a disability as a KinderCare pupil.

Disabled kids were absent from the KinderCare segments because the nation's largest child-care provider discriminated against them. So did La Petite Academy, the second-largest nursery school corporation. Complaints to the US Justice Department by parents of disabled youngsters charged the two chains with violating the Americans with Disabilities Act. In out-of-court settlements in 1996 and 1997, both companies conceded that private child-care programs were covered by the ADA's Public Accommodations requirements. They agreed to drop their policies barring children with disabilities and provide access and reasonable modifications.[61]

"Where No One Is Staring"

Special camps run by the telethon charities were places where many of these conflicting ideas about disabled children were quite literally played out. In fact, they were among the charities' most appealing services. The Easter Seals Telethon in 1991 reported that it provided "a unique summer camp experience for over 25,000 children every year." The 1993 MDA show announced that some 70,000 youngsters went to its camps. The Arthritis Foundation and UCP each had camping programs, too. These camps often provided positive experiences for children with disabilities, but telethon segments promoting the camps marked those children as fundamentally different from normal kids. Those messages also clashed with the views and goals of disabled adult activists and activist parents of disabled children. Easter Seals and MDA camps drew the most attention.

Telethons described special camps as offering momentary escape from the supposed day-to-day imprisonment of disability. MDA national cohost Jann Karl suggested that camp gave kids with neuromuscular disabilities the chance "to forget" for a while. The 14-year-old girl she was interviewing inserted a bit of teenage reality by replying that camp gave her a chance to forget about her parents.[62] Telethons displaced actual adolescent experiences with medicalized and pathologized depictions. Easter Seals camps were "the one place apart from mom and dad where a child with a disability can feel safe, secure and protected, where counselors are trained to handle wheelchairs, give medicine, help a child hold a pen when writing home."[63] An MDA host described children with disabilities as "very need-intensive." "That's the term that professionals use," he said.[64] While some children had significant medical needs, most did not require the ceaseless monitoring the telethons implied. Moreover, as so often happened, modes of functioning that had nothing to do with medicine, for instance, riding a wheelchair or even writing a letter home, were labeled as forms of medical care.

The camps temporarily freed youngsters from distressing physical limitations that allegedly shut them out of play. "Too often children with spina bifida, cerebral palsy, and other disabilities are unable to take part in sports and other outdoor activities," declared an Easter Seals film.[65] Easter Seals camp, contended Pat Boone, was the "one place somebody in a wheelchair can stroll through a forest and play softball, even go fishing."[66] MDA camps, said national cohost Leeza Gibbons, "let kids be kids"—for one week.[67] Special camps offered fleeting moments of liberation. "Can you imagine what it must be like for these children being able to leave the wheelchairs and crutches behind at least for a little while?" mused a host of the 1991 Easter Seals Telethon.[68]

A local Bay Area segment on the 2008 MDA Telethon gestured toward the stigma and prejudice imposed on children with disabilities. "The world can often be lonely and cruel for a child with a disability," the narrator of a short promotional film explained. "They don't respect kids in wheelchairs," a boy with MD sitting on a wheelchair at camp explained. *Narrator:* "But Camp Harmon offers a safe haven." *Camp counselor:* "This camp empowers the campers. It lets them know that, 'yes, I have a disability, but that doesn't mean I can't do what everybody else does.'" Then back on the show the host summed it up: "For this one special week, these campers are no longer the minority, no longer different. They're free to be themselves, happy, strong, and confident."[69]

The charities occasionally conducted camps for adults with disabilities, because, according to a local MDA host, "adults like to be kids too sometimes."[70] But activists charged that at special camps disabled adults often found themselves infantilized. Jackie Koch, a wheelchair-rider, complained to the disability rights magazine *The Disability Rag* that at one Easter Seals camp a nondisabled counselor compelled her and other adults to lie in their beds during "nap-time." The counselor also refused to follow her suggestions about how to help her transfer from her wheelchair. "You're my charge," she declared. "You have to do it my way." Adults were not only thrown together with children but restricted in their social contacts with nondisabled staffers. "I'd hear the counselors sitting around the campfire singing, telling jokes," recounted Koch. "The kids were asleep around me. I wondered why I wasn't out there with people my own age, laughing and joking with the adults around the campfire." Another activist, Robert Ardinger, recounted the political past of Camp Greentop in Maryland, which he had attended as both a child and an adult. He was "one of the first 'allowed' to make the transition from camper to counselor." According to Ardinger, the camp had "a policy, up until 1970, that forbade disabled persons from being counselors. Up until very recent times, adult campers were told to go to bed by 10:30 p.m. so counselors could have a nighttime snack. When I first started to work as a counselor at the adult camp, I was not permitted to have nighttime snacks with the other counselors because I was disabled and it might have upset the other campers." Ardinger and other disabled people saw this as a political struggle, a struggle for power, one with significant costs.[71]

To illustrate the temporary freedom Easter Seals camps offered, an exposé on the 1989 telethon narrated the photos of one camper: "Now, as you can see, Lisa uses a wheelchair to get around, and sometimes that means that Lisa can't join in when her friends are playing games. Now, for a long time, she felt that she would always be on the sidelines. But Lisa has discovered a place where there are no barriers because she's in a wheelchair. And when she's there, there are no games that she can't play. It's a whole new world for her, a world of doing and achieving, a world of playing ball and camping out under the stars and waiting to catch that big old trout. . . . Now, when Lisa's at camp she has freedom. She has freedom to join in group games, to talk to her friends, to share experiences, or to be by herself getting her story ready about the one that got away."[72] No one explained why Lisa needed a special camp to talk to her friends and share experiences, let alone commune with herself. No one suggested that mainstream camping and recreational programs could have created integrated group games. Taking for granted that her disability blocked her from programs designed for everyone else, the telethon presented separate camps as the solution.

For most disabled children, the biggest obstacles to play and fun were inaccessibility and lack of accommodations in recreational programs and at summer camps. At times the telethons obliquely acknowledged those socially constructed limitations. Both MDA's and Easter Seals' Bay Area chapters used Camp Harmon in the Santa Cruz Mountains, proclaiming that its accessibility enabled disabled children and teens to experience recreational activities otherwise unavailable. On the 2006 telethon, the national child ambassador exulted that at MDA summer camps everything is accessible. Telethons depicted two worlds, the inaccessible and unaccommodating world of the larger society and the "whole new world" of the accessible special camps.

Special camps were described as social and emotional safe places in a hostile society. "The world can often be lonely and cruel for a child with a disability," announced a local telethon host, but MDA camp offered "a safe haven."[73] *Parade* magazine's publisher claimed in almost Dickensian terms that without MDA's camps "many of these children would be shut away, or what we used to call 'shut-ins,' in attics, in rooms, in other places, or in hospitals."[74] MDA camps meant that "for one week [disabled children] get to have fun where no one is staring."[75] "At [Easter Seals] camp no one stares or points a finger. No one feels left out. For one glorious week out of the year, no one says, 'You can't.'"[76] The segregated camps put children with disabilities at ease by assembling them with their own kind. MDA campers found "comfort in what they all have in common," while Easter Seals campers "feel that they belong."[77] Outside the camps, children with disabilities suffered fifty-one weeks of hardship. According to Easter Seals, segregated camps "help make up for the pain and frustration that these children feel all year long," pain and frustration that were not just physical, but social.[78] Disability rights activist Laura Hershey complained, "We see children frolicking at summer camp, while an announcer tells us how miserable those children are the rest of the year."[79]

But as time went on, some camp programs began to reflect the emerging minority-group consciousness. Disabled advocates worked to create accessible nonpaternalistic camping. In the early 1980s, staffers from one independent living center held a training for camp counselors. They and Easter Seals camp managers tried to develop a truly adult camping program. The disabled adult staffers aimed at more than recreation for themselves. They wanted to become camp counselors because they knew that disabled children needed them as role models in developing positive identities as persons with disabilities.[80] Likewise, a counselor at one MDA camp declared: "This camp empowers the campers. It lets them know that, 'Yes, I have a disability, but that doesn't mean I can't do what everybody else does.'"[81] Meanwhile, cultural practices such as the popularity of power soccer at MDA camps suggested that young people with disabilities could begin building a sense of community and common identity, likely with support from some nondisabled counselors. Finally, some camps such as those supported by Easter Seals Massachusetts offered youth leadership and self-advocacy training that included lobbying the state legislature.[82] All of these efforts developed despite the ideology propagated in telethon segments publicizing special camping.

At the same time, a growing number of parents pushed for integrated recreation, insisting on their children's right of access to mainstream camps and playgrounds. For example, parents in Mineral Point, Wisconsin, built an accessible playground that became "the envy of neighboring communities." The swing set included "a wheelchair swing." An octagon-shaped fort offered many means of access, including two ramps that meandered around the playground's perimeter. The children nicknamed a "wavy" section of the ramp the "earthquake bridge." Linda Rowley, one of the parents and the project's coordinator, expressed her satisfaction: "Finally my son, who uses a wheelchair, can be part of the action, instead of watching from the sidelines." Integrated recreation offered unforeseen benefits. "[T]he NDA [nondisabled] children love running and climbing the ramps as much as the children who need the ramps for access," said Rowley. "Making it accessible for all children also makes it more fun for all of the children."[83]

By the mid-1990s, at least some of the charities' chapters supported integrated recreation and camping. Easter Seals San Francisco Telethon explained that "many parents want their children to be accepted at integrated camps, or perhaps the children themselves want to hang out with their neighborhood and school friends." So, the local Society worked with

Bay Area recreational camps to accept more young people with disabilities and mainstream them.[84]

But separate charity camps continued to operate. Some activists said it was because of the segregated structure of mainstream recreational outlets and the poverty and powerlessness of many disabled people.[85] For that reason, disability rights advocates worked for access, not just at camps, but in recreation programs, local, state, and national parks, and other public places: theaters and concert halls and museums and restaurants and amusement parks. Activists saw to it that the Americans with Disabilities Act mandated access and reasonable accommodations in facilities open to the public. They demanded full and equal access as a civil right. They rejected separate programs such as the special camps as a form of segregation.[86]

As descendants of Tiny Tim, "Jerry's Kids"—and thousands of others like them—perpetuated the infantilization of adults with disabilities well into the twentieth century. By showing them as wards of medicine and reinforcing associations between helplessness and disability, the yearly programs held them in suspended animation. But because telethons revealed that disabled children were ideal for inspiring contributions from the American viewing public, it's likely that MDA and other charities needed these children at least as much as the children needed them. At the same time, by establishing camps that removed access, stigma, and other barriers to participation, the charities inadvertently raised disability consciousness outside of the medical model, thereby helping spawn future activists.

Family Burdens

PARENTS, CHILDREN, AND DISABILITY

Children with disabilities were seen as inauthentic children because they were in many ways unknown and invisible outside of being depicted on telethons. In *The Unexpected Minority: Handicapped Children in America* (1980), John Gliedman and William Roth wrote: "There is a crucial sense in which not only the society at large and the professionals entrusted with the handicapped child's care, but even his parents, do not know who he is."[1] Stereotypes pictured children with disabilities as devastating burdens who made their families socially abnormal and shattered their parents' dreams at a time when the notion of the American family was believed to be in crisis. Already understood by most to be a tragedy, the disabled child spelled disaster for all those around them. The minority-group analysis of disability challenged these framings, often leading to competing images on the telethons.

An Unexpected Minority

Beyond the imaginary family portrayed with corporate patriarchs and Tiny Tim's siblings on the yearly telethon broadcasts were actual families: parents dealing with the concrete social, economic, political, and emotional realities of late-twentieth-century America. Perhaps more than anyone, children and adults with disabilities and their families came under the sway of the medical model that dominated thinking on telethons. *The Unexpected Minority* reported that medical, educational, and social-service professionals bore responsibilities for the well-being of such families and wielded power over them unparalleled "for any other social group." Despite the good they generally did, professionals' enormous authority often undercut or overrode the self-knowledge of disabled adults and youths as well as parents. "Many thoughtful parents and professionals" worried about the need for services that were often oppressive. Making matters worse, scientific knowledge about children with disabilities was woefully inadequate. Ignorance and uncertainty touched everything from children's psychological and social needs to how to educate them. Gliedman and Roth's exhaustive five-hundred-page study identified the core problem as inherent in the medical model: professionals typically viewed disabled people in terms of deviance and social pathology.[2]

The two researchers concluded that children with disabilities, their parents, and even professionals were harmed by "the absence of a mature developmental psychology of handicap."[3] A voluminous "burden literature" within psychology typically assumed that a disabled child—or any family member with a disability—negatively affected "*all* areas of individual and family functioning." This caused generalized stress and emotional distress.[4] Because research based in the medical model typically started from the premise that children with disabilities were deviant and socially pathological, it also usually presumed that they detrimentally affected their families. That scholarship took several assumptions for granted without adequate empirical data. For example, textbooks again and again claimed that parents had to grieve for and let go of the idealized normal child in order to accept the "imperfect" one.

Research and clinical psychologist Dr. Rhoda Olkin, a successor to Gliedman and Roth in criticizing the conventional literature, charged that the *expectation* of mourning came to be enforced as a *requirement* to mourn. It was a variant of the unsubstantiated stage-model theory of adjustment to disability. Olkin pointed out an important fact that the traditional framing ignored: Although parents' first reactions to a disabled child's birth might be "stressful and negative," many "quickly exhibit[ed] coping behaviors."[5]

Worse still, the burden literature offered parents little positive counsel on how to rear children with disabilities in a culture that devalued them. Unlike the parents of other disadvantaged children, disabled children's parents did not share their sociological destiny. African American, Mexican American, and Native American parents could draw on rich cultural traditions to help guide them in raising their children, but handicapped children's parents, who usually had not experienced handicap themselves, had no such tradition to aid *them*. The main advice offered such parents was "negative—a destructive definition of the child as a perpetual patient whose 'childness,' whose ability to grow up," was "gravely imperiled" by the handicap. It seemed that American culture lacked "anything like a tradition for raising reasonably happy, and reasonably self-fulfilling handicapped children. . . ."[6]

Clearly, the study of disabled children's moral development required a fresh approach. Research needed to examine not just their biological and functional differences, but their distinctive social experiences. It needed to question the idea that the lives of children with disabilities should automatically be measured exclusively—and unfavorably—in terms of the nondisabled. For example, Gliedman and Roth warned that accepted theories of moral development might well misread the stereotypes discussed in the previous chapter that portrayed disabled children as undisciplined and disorderly. Instead, research must consider the social disempowerment and sense of injustice that came with minority status.[7] They urged investigation of the marginalization and social undermining of disabled people's morale because of able-bodied people's low expectations and prejudice so often reported in autobiographies written by men and women with disabilities.[8] "At least from middle childhood on," explained Gliedman and Roth, children knew "that despite the pretty words and good manners," others might well be defining them in terms of the stigmatized trait of handicap. Making their way through this murky and at times hostile social terrain required young people with disabilities to become "shrewd sociologists."[9]

Moreover too many parents put their children at risk physically and psychologically by urging them to look and behave as much like able-bodied peers as possible. In one study adult interviewees said their parents instructed them "to walk more normally or to hide disabled body parts with clothing." People who acquired disabilities later in life often heard similar messages of conditional acceptance. This view was hard to escape because it was reinforced by health-care professionals, social service practitioners, and special educators. In effect, they told young people that their disabled parts were bad and the only acceptable aspects of them were those unaffected by disability. "Most systems of personality development," explained Carol Gill, psychologist at the University of Illinois at Chicago, would view any "splitting of the self into acceptable and unacceptable parts . . . as pathological." It was troubling then that most disabled children grew up feeling "accepted and valued only conditionally—loved in spite of their disabilities, not with them, and required to fix or hide their disabled parts."[10]

Many adults also remembered their parents telling them that they were not disabled or at least not like other disabled children, and that they should avoid people with disabilities.[11] This not only cut them off from other disabled children, said Olkin, it deprived them of "role models and mentors with disabilities."[12] Gill noted that disabled children might "spend all of their childhood and adolescent years with no role models or peers with disabilities, surrounded by the nondisabled culture" and "feeling different from everyone around them." They were further isolated by "[d]ifficulties with access, transportation, economic barriers, and stigma." If they were separated from the disability rights community and remained convinced by the medical model that their disability was the result of a personal tragedy, they might see themselves as "the 'abnormal,' 'damaged' or 'inferior' one, . . . first in the family . . . then in the surrounding social environment." Internalizing "a sense of defectiveness," some were "incapacitated by shame or preoccupied with hiding the extent of their differentness." Others exhausted themselves "trying to prove their worth, warding off the fear that they [could] never measure up to people untainted by disability."[13]

When they did try to grapple with their social situation, their families might resist them. Encountering "discriminatory treatment or social rejection," said Gill, disabled children and teens turned "to the family for comfort and validation." But many families disputed such reports or diminished "the significance of the experience," refusing "to acknowledge the reality of disability prejudice." Disability, they insisted, made "no difference unless the young person allow[ed] it to make a difference." Olkin corroborated Gill: Parents often told their children that the disability was "a problem only if the child [let] it be a problem," that disability was "only a matter of overcoming in your head." These responses, said Gill, intensified disabled youngsters' loneliness and might well lead them to blame themselves and to "fear discussing such experiences in the family." Olkin added that they also unintentionally bolstered "the child's outsider position" as a deviant "on the fringes of the nondisabled world." Disability, she declared, was, in fact, "a highly stigmatized condition, subject to profound prejudice and discrimination in all aspects of life. . . .." Though social bias was often "heartbreaking" for parents, they "must nonetheless resist the temptation to shield and spare their child." Disabled children could not learn how to cope with that reality if their parents ignored it.[14]

Gill, along with Olkin, and Gliedman and Roth, represented a new generation of researchers and clinicians in the 1980s who began to put together an understanding of disabled children based on the minority-group analysis. Individuals and their families might achieve more positive outcomes if families were helped to, in Gill's words, "view disabled loved ones as members of a legitimate social minority community instead of victims of medical tragedy." To be sure, those parents—and the children—faced real difficulties, physical and financial demands as well as the anxiety of living with a perhaps unpredictable disease and prognosis. But the "pervasive message of burden" undermined harmonious family life by picturing the care and rearing of a child with a disability as radically and negatively different from raising a nondisabled child. "So much of what constitutes a 'child' is common to all children," reminded Olkin. "Focusing on the disability as if it altered that essence is a mistake." Like all children, those with disabilities needed "love, safety, security, attachment, sexuality, affiliation, separation and individuation, productivity, meaningfulness. . . . In most ways children with disabilities are ordinary children." Inverting the meaning of the familiar telethon slogan, she proclaimed that a child with a disability had a "right . . . to be a child."[15]

Gill and Olkin each proposed a bicultural framework for understanding children and disability.[16] They lived "in a mostly nondisabled world" but also belonged to a minority group: people with disabilities. The idea of biculturalism was a far cry from the notion of special camps and separate worlds. Olkin explained: "As a person of any minority group knows, there are different expectations, behaviors, and norms in the two worlds, and varying aspects of oneself are differentially manifest in the two arenas." Disabled children needed to affiliate with both disabled and nondisabled peers and move freely between the two worlds. Connections with the world of disabled people would teach "the commonalities of the disability experience" as well as practical living skills. Contact would also reduce isolation and "break down the denial of disability" practiced by parents who, with well-meaning but mistaken intentions, tried to raise their child as what they thought of as normal. Perhaps most important, association with other disabled people would provide positive role models and facilitate positive identities that incorporated disability. In pursuing these goals, parents and professionals should follow two guiding principles. They should work with disabled children in ways that did not pathologize them. They should focus "more on increasing resiliency than on correcting deficits."[17] They should replace the medical model with a minority-group model.

As with all children, the ultimate goal of parenting and professional support should be to help children with disabilities grow up to become, in Gliedman and Roth's phrase, "reasonably happy . . . reasonably self-fulfilling" human beings. But instead, the typical social situation of people with disabilities exacted an immense human toll in "frustration, demoralization, humiliation, anger, despair, and identity." It was, the researchers declared, "a national disgrace."[18] And it played out every Labor Day on telethons.

Parents as Victims

Largely ignorant of this minority approach to disability, telethons appeared more aligned with the extensive "burden literature" so deplored by psychologists. As a result, telethons often pictured children with disabilities as millstones around their parents' necks. A UCP telecast from 1989 had Christopher Hewitt, star of the then-popular ABC sitcom *Mr. Belvedere*, declare that a child with cerebral palsy was, "of course," a "financial burden." In addition, "just arranging transportation to school for a disabled child could be as complicated as planning the royal wedding."[19] One MDA Denver host called his family's recent outing "a simple thing." "Just think . . . about how much more it would take for a family with" a disabled child.[20] He overlooked that more than anything inaccessibility and lack of accommodations hampered family activities. And UCP failed to explain that inadequate transportation services were often what made getting to school so "complicated." Nor did its telethon acknowledge that the financial burden of disability weighing on many families resulted from the US health-care and social services system's disparities discussed earlier.[21]

The programs also asserted that disabled children were psychological burdens. "Running a household and raising a family nowadays can be a highly stressful occupation," read Hewitt from UCP's teleprompter. "But can you imagine what it is like for the parents of someone who has cerebral palsy?" There were "severe emotional problems, . . . guilt, anxiety, depression. . . .." So UCP provided counseling "to relieve the stress that may result from living with a disabled person."[22] He did not suggest that nondisabled relatives might cause disabled family members stress. It was also assumed that strain jeopardized parents' relationships with one another. Easter Seals picked one poster child because her parents' divorce "would illustrate" that a disabled child's "presence often puts pressure on marriages."[23] In fact, research showed that in distressed families, factors other than disability were frequently at work. Marital satisfaction was frequently low anyway. Psychological, social, and material resources were more often than not lacking. Families who coped more effectively had more "assets": greater interpersonal competency and skills, more family and community supports. It was not that the presence of disabled children inevitably undermined marriages and families. It was, once again, the absence of adequate resources.[24]

Disability activist Laura Hershey described how shows often reflected the burden literature where "each piece puts forward an archaic and gloomy picture of the disabled family member's role, and of the role of the family in a disabled person's life."[25] Not only were disabled children the opposite of normal ones, their families were abnormal, too. These youngsters caused more than frustrations and stress: Their presence was devastating. Having such a child was "like a death," one that caused grief not just at birth or initial diagnosis but endlessly. "If you have a child, or a relative in any way, that has cerebral palsy, you know what I'm talking about," declared Dennis James. "If you have a child that's able-bodied, maybe you don't know what I'm talking about. It's a 365-day-a-year job."[26] It seemed that parenting nondisabled children required only part-time effort.

Telethons prompted parents to contrast their disabled children with their putatively whole offspring. One mother said that, unlike her nondisabled boy, her disabled son could not play sports.[27] Siblings allegedly felt neglected and were, it was assumed, made to feel guilty. Their disabled brothers and sisters burdened them, restricting their opportunities for normal growth. "His younger brother, I believe, is impacted as much as any of us," asserted one father. "Instead of having an older brother to go out and play with or to follow around high school with, Art instead is a brother that Tom has to take care of." *Confined* to his power wheelchair, Art could not serve as any sort of role model for his younger brother. Telethons stirred the grievances nondisabled siblings were expected to harbor. When the family appeared on stage, Tom spoke, but Art did not. Did Art have nothing to say, or did he choose to endure his public humiliation in silence?[28]

Here again, telethons repeated the outmoded burden literature, which presumed that disabled children must have a negative impact on nondisabled siblings. It was telling that the research failed to ask about nondisabled siblings' impact on their disabled brothers and sisters. Moreover, said Rhoda Olkin, some researchers were "so intent on finding problems" that they reinterpreted "seemingly positive behaviors . . . as pathologic." Nonetheless, investigators consistently reported some positive effects on nondisabled siblings. Most noteworthy was "an increase in empathy and tolerance for differences." And like any siblings who can grow up to identify deeply with one another, nondisabled siblings sometimes developed "strong identification with disability issues." Perhaps it was because they saw firsthand the "misconceptions, stereotypes, stigmas, and discrimination" their disabled sisters and brothers faced.[29] Too often, research based on the medical model screened out those positive results.

Programs occasionally showed parents who represented what Carol Gill described as a new breed of parent: ones who recognized their youngsters' minority status. Though many were reluctant to see the importance of a disability community for their loved ones and might even feel threatened by assertion of that need, Gill found a small but growing number who recognized their children as members of Gliedman and Roth's "unexpected minority." They sought out disabled adults as mentors and sometimes got involved in disability rights organizations. As one mother put it, "My daughter needs to be with her disabled brothers and sisters fighting for her rights." Another mother, who saw a parallel between her child's need for a disability community and her own need for a women's community, described herself as "a majority culture parent raising a minority culture child." Gill found that children whose parents nurtured a bicultural identity were "among the most confident and expressive children with disabilities I have known." They grew up seeing themselves as entitled to equal inclusion in society and felt at ease with both disabled and nondisabled persons.[30]

Easter Seals appeared to be the most open to this "new breed." The charity picked its 1986 National Child "partly because his mother and father had fought to have him accepted into the local public school and to have him picked up each day in a specially equipped school van." The following year, one finalist as Easter Seals' National Child was an eleven-year-old boy with spina bifida. At his birth, doctors urged his parents to let him die, but as they explained in a *Los Angeles Times* article, they rejected such hateful, discriminatory advice.[31] Meanwhile, in 1990 Easter Seals presented a Dallas couple who at first felt deeply saddened when their daughter was born with Down syndrome. The mother said she felt silly that she had ever been sad because she now realized her daughter was beautiful. She had discovered that the hardest thing to deal with was prejudice and discrimination. In the end, this mother went to law school, because people with disabilities should "have the rights and equality that they deserve."[32] She enlisted in the ranks of a usually unsung contingent of "activist mothers of children with disabilities."[33]

Laura Hershey discovered another new breed of mother in the pages of MDA's official magazine. This woman described "the difficulties" her son faced "in coping with a progressively disabling condition." He told her, crying, that he could no longer climb a neighbor's tree. The mother let him feel sad and then helped him figure out how he could climb the tree with help. "Whereas the telethon would have used this situation to create pity," said Hershey, this mother focused "not so much on how" her son differed "from other children, but on how [she could help him] understand his disability, and on his own resourcefulness in adapting to it. The grief was not denied, but neither was it overdone." She "emphasized the boy's fundamental similarity to other children in struggling to understand and come to terms with himself and his world." She "portrayed [him] as a real child, full of humanity."[34]

This new breed of parents were victims not because of a personal tragedy inflicted on them by their child's disability. The biggest frustrations came from inaccessibility and lack of accommodations in stores and restaurants and theaters and from discrimination by social institutions such as schools. The financial burden resulted from the failure to fund national health insurance, technological aids, and adequate in-home assistance. Some families' "devastation" and others' "heroism" stemmed from their varying capacities to withstand prejudice that stigmatized those with disabled members as abnormal, the opposite of legitimate American families. The medical model misinterpreted or blocked out such social factors. Telethon depictions of parents and children as pathological coincided with a historic crisis in the American family and American childhood that would further add to the burden.

The Family under Siege

The telethon era coincided with a time when many Americans worried that the idealized nuclear family—married heterosexual parents living with their children in a single household—was disappearing. Commentators of every political stripe attributed this "calamitous decline" to various and contradictory causes. Some explained it in terms of the culture of narcissism and materialism: Too many parents were allegedly modeling self-centered consumerism to their children while slighting their moral upbringing. A related criticism ascribed neglect of children to working parents' physical and emotional absence, with the primary culprits being either fathers or mothers depending on the particular critic's political standpoint. Other observers blamed a rebellious youth culture and an undermining of parental authority borne of the 1960s cultural upheaval. Still others said that intrusive state institutions such as public schools had usurped parents' role in raising their children. Meanwhile, condemning the traditional structure and functioning of families as built on patriarchy and heteronormativity, feminists and gay

and lesbian activists began fashioning alternative forms of family life during
the 1980s and 1990s. Conservatives, in turn, accused them of attacking natural and normal marriage, parenting, and particularly motherhood.

Given these clashing value systems and conflicting analyses, the crisis
of the American family represented a particularly big problem for telethon
charities. Trying to appeal to everyone with feel-good messages that spoke
directly to traditional American values, they found themselves face-to-face
with a social problem that had become central to the culture wars that raged
throughout the latter decades of the twentieth century.[35] At such a fragile
moment when families were under siege, how would telethons—the promoter
of American and family values—find a place for children and parents who did
not easily fit in?

The problematic condition of American families grew out of major transformations that were simultaneously material and cultural, economic and social.
In many instances, disability would not just be affected by these changes but
would also shape their impact on individuals and families. In the post–World
War II era, the material base of the middle-class nuclear family ideal had
been a wage-earning husband and father supporting a stay-at-home wife and
mother who managed the domestic household and assumed the primary
tasks of child care. But structural changes in the economy—including the
decline in job-related health insurance covering the entire family[36]—forced
growing numbers of married women with school-age children into the labor
force. From the 1970s on, many families required two wage earners to uphold
a middle-class living standard. In 1950 only 1 out of 5 such mothers worked
outside the home, but during the following decades more and more of them
took jobs: 35 percent as of 1960, 45 percent as of 1970, 55 percent as of 1980,
65 percent as of 1990.[37]

If mothers' paid employment was necessary for many families, it also
enabled more women to reach financial self-sufficiency and leave unsatisfying
marriages. This shift in the economic basis of marriage coincided with a cultural shift regarding emotional expectations for marital relations. Emotional
gratification became the glue that held together many couples. These emotional and economic changes combined to boost divorce rates to unprecedented levels. By the mid-1970s, half of US marriages were ending in divorce.
And to the greater alarm of observers from across the political spectrum,
more divorces meant more households made up of a single mother and her
children living in or near poverty.[38]

At the same time, many commentators warned that mounting marital
breakups—which were often also, of course, familial breakups—damaged
children emotionally. Boys reportedly became more aggressive, girls at
greater risk of emotional distress. Even when families stayed intact, the
emergent emotional and economic features of family life made them "more
volatile," "more fragile." Heightened expectations of emotionally gratifying

family relations increased the potential for dissatisfaction, disruption, and separation. Meanwhile, external pressures from the changing economy along with parents' consumerist desires to "give their kids the very best" pushed or pulled many parents out of the home and away from their children. The late-twentieth-century US economy, suggested Joseph Illick, a historian of American childhood, may have harmed children even more than divorce.[39] The advent of a disabled child threatened to completely destroy this fragile edifice.

The worrisome situation of American families and children prompted a flood of hearings, conferences, and research, including a series of studies funded by the Carnegie Council on Children. In addition to Gliedman and Roth's *The Unexpected Minority* discussed at the beginning of this chapter, it published a final report, *All Our Children: The American Family Under Pressure* (1977).[40] But this was only one commission. Scholars, social observers, and political advocates differed sharply about both explanations and solutions, while agreeing that America's families—particularly middle-class families—were undergoing wrenching transformations.[41]

Not only was the condition of such families a major social problem in itself, the private family, as had happened many times before at critical moments in American history, was taken as standing in for the collective national "family." Following the debacle of the Vietnam War and facing the critical social and economic changes that emerged in the 1970s and afterward, the middle-class family was seen as both a manifestation and a metaphor of a larger national crisis. As the primary inculcator of middle-class values and the central site of economic consumption, the family was simultaneously culprit and victim. It played a major role in generating the perceived displacement of authentic community by a culture of materialism and narcissism. At the same time and paradoxically, it was the primary casualty of that decline. The American "family-under-siege" came to symbolize the "aggrieved" and "wounded" American nation.[42]

Not surprisingly, disability—and the numerous dangers associated with it—loomed large in the rhetoric linked to the family in crisis. Anxieties about dependency appeared in two public debates: concerns about materialistic overconsumption by middle-class, mostly white families and condemnation of poor families on welfare who were incorrectly perceived as most often black. Historian Natasha Zaretsky has shown that during the 1970s the term "dependency" expressed the increasingly prominent worry that "the white, middle-class family had failed as a source of moral authority and national character." The early 1970s oil embargo focused the fear that mass consumption and indebtedness had eroded the traditional capitalist virtues of self-discipline, thrift, and self-sufficiency by encouraging middle-class families toward hedonism and profligacy. As consumers, they were allegedly out of control. The link between consumers' "dependency on energy-intensive

commodities and the nation's dependency on Middle Eastern oil" emblema-
tized families' failure to inculcate the moral values that undergirded the
national character. A concurrent controversy over family dependency arose
regarding poor families on welfare. That debate implicitly contrasted black
family life as pathological with white middle-class family life as normative. It
appeared that "dependency was becoming a pervasive condition," explained
Zaretsky. Social scientist Daniel Patrick Moynihan's description of dependency in his controversial 1965 report *The Negro Family: The Case for National
Action* argued for welfare reform but had implications for the broader crisis of
the American family. He called dependency "an incomplete state in life: normal in the child, abnormal in the adult. In a world where completed men
and women stand on their own two feet, persons who are dependent—as the
buried imagery of the word denotes—hang."[43]

Moynihan's definition of dependency resonated with dominant understandings of disability. In the medical-model ideology, the term "dependent"
represented a cluster of states of being that Americans had always found terrifying: loss of control, loss of independence, confinement or regression to the
condition and status of a child, incomplete personhood, social abnormality.
At the same time, as discussed earlier, "dependent" people with disabilities,
both children and adults, were depicted as devastating to their families. The
charities described disability as "happening to the whole family." The professional literature rooted in the medical model devoted considerable attention to the impact of disability on nondisabled family members to the point
that the effects on nondisabled parents often seemed to be regarded as more
important than those on people with disabilities themselves. The greater
tragedy, it seemed, was that disability impaired nondisabled family members'
upward mobility and status.

At a time when many Americans felt their own families were disintegrating, telethon depictions of those allegedly rendered socially abnormal
by disability reassured viewers that they still belonged to families that were
physically and socially whole. Marking the invalidity of families with disabled children, MCs urged parents to donate out of gratitude that their sons
and daughters had escaped the stigma of disability. A host of the regional Los
Angeles Easter Seals Telethon, Marta Waller, a local news reporter, stood next
to a young man with a head injury as she exhorted viewers to give as a way
to "honor your own children who aren't disabled," seemingly oblivious to the
fact that she was dishonoring this young man to his face.[44] She also brought
out her daughters "to pay tribute to them. We are so lucky that they were born
without disabilities."[45] On the 1989 MDA broadcast, cohost Norm Crosby, the
Borscht Belt comedian known as "The Master of Malaprop," directed "every
mother and father who has a healthy kid, who can hear my voice right now,
who has a kid who can pick up a spoon and dress himself and go to school, in
honor of your kid . . . and Jerry's kids, to pick up the phone right now."[46] It was

difficult to understand how it honored disabled kids to inaccurately assert that if they could not feed or dress themselves, they could not go to school. Nor did it "honor" "Jerry's kids" to imply that they were the kind of children no parent would want. The social normality of these lucky families without disabled members was contrasted with the American families that were seen as in crisis and disintegrating.

Polio's Betrayal of the American Family

Because polio disproportionately affected middle-class American children during the 1950s and 1960s, its victims loomed large on telethons. The disease posed an especially acute danger to families where disability had long been seen as a betrayal of the American dream, striking in sociologist Fred Davis's words, "families whose life-style most vividly displayed core American values." It was perhaps not so much the disease itself as "crippledness" that Americans saw as attacking their values. More than a relative loss of physical mobility, "crippling" suggested "social abnormality, isolation, and, in the eyes of some, visible manifestation of inherent malevolence." The parents Davis interviewed for his study *Passage through Crisis* had "felt pity, or even repugnance, toward crippled persons." They now feared their own children might arouse such feelings in others and hinder them in friendships, vocational success, marriage, or even developing "a pleasant personality." They might be relegated to the "low-caste" role of "cripple."[47]

Disability attacked their expectations for their children while thwarting parents' own hopes. One father said, "We tell ourselves, 'My boy, I can see in him possibilities untold. He's quick minded. He's quick on his feet. He's quick with his hands. There's no telling what he'd grow up and do. . . . Polio kills that. It stops that dream. . . . [M]aybe he won't be able to be a good 100-yard-dash man, maybe he won't be able to swim as fast as his daddy, play table tennis, ride bicycles." This father spoke of his son's physical condition, but the subtext was that disability destroyed the American fantasy of limitless personal possibilities:[48] not just for the boy but for his father. According to literary scholar Marc Shell, who explored literature by and about the disease in his book *Polio and Its Aftermath: The Paralysis of Culture*, "Many polio narratives written from the viewpoint of parents of polios start off with some such words as these from Quebecker Paul Decoste: 'We had dreamed of handsome and strong boys.' He goes on to ask this question: 'How do I describe to what extent this test was able to murder our hearts as young married persons?' Another first person narrator quotes his father as writing that the son's crippling was 'the symbol' of all the father's familial failures."[49] Had they been able to gaze into a crystal ball, they would discover the disproportionately large number of people with postpolio disabilities who strove to realize the

American dream. Many were highly successful in their chosen fields, some becoming activists who campaigned for disability rights.

Meanwhile, many parents of children with polio struggled to explain to themselves "what it meant, socially speaking, to be handicapped or to have a handicapped person in the family." "Crippling" had an enormous impact on its self-image, its values and its identity. It violated a post–World War II idealized image. Disability meant that the family was no longer "like everyone else." The entire unit was made abnormal.[50] A child with a postpolio disability was "the cause of family shame," reports Shell in his thorough study of polio literature. The instruction to be silent about polio played a prominent role in these accounts. Many disabled youngsters got the message that it was not to be spoken of. Well into adulthood, they never discussed polio or their disabilities with anyone. Parents often reflected the community's ambivalence toward their children. And in some families, parents— particularly fathers—acted out their shame and rejection of their disabled children—especially their sons—with emotional and physical abuse. Like many commentators, Shell describes this as the parents' inability to accept a "crippled" child. A more complete explanation would recognize this physical and emotional violence as parents acting out society's most virulent prejudices against their children.[51]

During the mid- and late twentieth century, the charities and their telethons sought to shape and reinforce these communal attitudes by their views of disability. But even while they overtly rejected the silence about disability borne of social stigma, they implicitly and unintentionally reflected and bolstered the ambivalence. They stressed the middle-class ordinariness of the families they aimed to help. "They are just like you and your family." Yet by endlessly repeating that disability violated American dreams, they marked those families as radically unlike other families.

Conflicting Messages

Telethons usually selected parents who confirmed the tragedy of disabled children. But sometimes the offspring implicitly contradicted their parents. One needs to listen carefully to find this hidden beneath the louder messages, because as "shrewd sociologists," disabled children needed to manage life within complex, often fragile families. Twenty-two-year-old Joe and his mother told rather different stories on the 1991 MDA Telethon that offer a striking example. The mother painted a picture of sad burden. "Everything has to be adapted. Zippers are taken out, and Velcro put in. There are eating utensils that have to be changed to fit his hands. ... He can't get into the refrigerator. He can't see what's in the freezer. You have to do that for him. He can't get a glass of water for himself. You do that." Adaptive devices and other refrigerator models could have enabled Joe to do some of these things, but there was no mention of these on the telethon. A film showed her carrying Joe on her back, out the sliding glass door of their home, onto the patio, and setting him on his wheelchair. Did she always carry him, or had someone suggested she do it for the camera? Why hadn't they put a small, inexpensive ramp over the single step?

If his mother saw adaptive devices and personal assistance as causes of grief, Joe called them sources of independence. He did not downplay his physical difficulties, but he didn't think his life a tragedy. "To me it's a fight for independence," he said. "I got sick a couple years ago, and I lost a lot of strength. And now it's real hard and I have to have attendants to help me. But all I really need is like help with showering and getting dressed. But if I could, if I could have that independence, it'd be complete freedom. So to me, it's a fight for independence. And independence can come from just a little tool that helps me zip my zipper or button my button, all the way to finding that cure for all of Jerry's Kids."

But Joe was not waiting around for that elusive cure. The film showed him working as a disc jockey on what appeared to be his college's radio station. It was hard to tell because MDA did not explain the picture. In addition, not only did Joe push his wheelchair himself, he played wheelchair basketball. But again, the pictures, so inconsistent with his mother's words, were not explained. One began to wonder if Joe was as dependent as the explicit message. And even though his changing disability required more assistance, he did not take that as thwarting his goals. An international studies major, he said he was "headed" for the United Nations.

Joe's mother contrasted him with his sister, in effect, declaring that he burdened her too. "Her gym teacher called me when she was in the second grade and said, 'Your daughter can't ride a bike.'" The sister explained why. "We couldn't go and run and ride bikes and go chase each other and play tag with the neighbor kids because Joe's in a wheelchair." Her comments suggested that she had preferred playing with her big brother. Rather than the stereotypically predicted sense of sibling grievance, it was clear that she felt strongly attached to him. "He needs help with his shower and getting dressed and tying his shoes and doing his hair," she explained, "but it doesn't really matter because I'm helping my brother."

Still, Joe's mother grieved over his physical limitations. "I have been feeling very sad since Joe's illness a couple of years ago that he spoke about, that he couldn't hug me," she said. "And he's not been able to hug me for quite a while." She and Jerry Lewis embraced as she wept. But just then another incongruous thing happened. Raising his right arm, Joe shook Lewis's hand. And the film had shown him pushing his wheelchair and playing wheelchair basketball. And when his mother carried him piggyback, he had his arms around her. What kept him from hugging her?

Most troubling, as the film showed Joe sliding backward up the stairs in his family's home, his mother said in voiceover: "You buy a house that's got two stories, and all of a sudden you forget that this child can't go upstairs. And my son goes up on his backside like a two-year-old and he's 22." How did a parent "all of a sudden . . . forget" that a twenty-two-year-old "child" could not climb stairs?[52] Other disabled people reported that their families also bought inaccessible homes. They wondered why.[53] Had their parents and siblings somehow forgotten they were disabled? Or did this de facto exclusion reflect an unconscious, culturally conditioned devaluation of them?

Part of disabled people's socialization involved swallowing this sort of humiliation and soldiering on. Rhoda Olkin explained that for people with disabilities, as for racial minorities, expression of certain emotions, especially anger, was unacceptable, while other emotions, namely cheerfulness, were required.[54] An interview from 1992's Easter Seals Telethon offered another hint of conflicting message between parent and child. A mother told how she felt about her young daughter's disability—with the girl sitting next to her. Melanie was an honor student in a mainstream school. Despite her accomplishments, her mother said, "I think the hardest thing with Melanie's handicap is seeing another eight-year-old child beside her who is not handicapped." Watching and listening to this admission, Melanie had a puzzled expression on her face. Then when her mother glanced at her, she looked down. "I think it's much harder for me than it is for her, because she never seems to have a complaint about anything," said the mother. "Mom is the one that gets frustrated. So Melanie is a one in a million. She never gets upset about anything." Looking at Melanie, she prompted: "Do you?" Melanie shook her head, No. And then she smiled.[55]

Children with disabilities struggled against a force in American society far more limiting than any physical impairment: a tragic view of disability that engulfed their entire family. They battled to build a sense of self-worth in the very teeth of the bias that they were not valid as human beings. More than medical services and assistive devices, they needed affirmation of their full humanity. They needed their parents to reject society's prejudice and value them as they were. Instead, many of the children on telethons found themselves condemned by their own parents in front of a nationwide audience. And the charities deliberately called on the parents to issue those devastating verdicts. If the father of the little girl with arthritis thought it was "pretty devastating" to have, not a child, but "a child with arthritis," and if another father "cried a lot" because he thought his disabled child made his family abnormal, how did it feel to have your parents invalidate you before the world?

Jerry's Kids Grow Up

DISABILITY RIGHTS ACTIVISTS AND TELETHONS

At approximately the same time as the dramatic transformations in thinking about American families described in the previous chapter, people with disabilities started to push back against telethons. During the 1970s, the decade when the broadcasts shifted from separate local to national network telecasts, disability rights advocacy emerged more vigorously as a nationwide movement. From that time forward, many activists decried telethons for propagating the charity and medical-model ideologies that pathologized the lives of people with disabilities. They campaigned to replace those models with one grounded in a minority-group perspective. Some organized protests; others worked inside the charities to change telethon messages. And still other people with disabilities, clients of the charities, some of whom were advocates, accepted the messages grounded in the medical and charitable frameworks as accurate, or at least necessary. Activists' criticisms highlighted their reframing of "disability" and their social and political agenda, while also displaying the dilemmas of disability rights advocacy and ideology. For their part, charity professionals disputed activists' charges even while they modified their telethons' messages. The protests, the charities' responses, and the varying opinions among people with disabilities indicated that in the last quarter of the twentieth century and early years of the twenty-first, ideas about disability and the social situation of disabled people were undergoing a complicated transformation.

Talking Back to Telethons

The first disability rights protest against a telethon ostensibly took place on Labor Day weekend in 1972 outside the Americana Hotel in New York City during that year's MDA Telethon. "[A]bout two dozen demonstrators," some of them wheelchair riders and most of them people with neuromuscular disabilities, introduced what would become major themes of activist criticism of telethons and charities. They did not demand an end to the MDA telethon but instead condemned it for using exploitative negative imagery. The dispute also reflected a key issue for disabled activists: Who should have the power to decide what people with disabilities needed and what resources they would have access to? They accused MDA of excluding disabled people from policy boards and failing to hire disabled people in its staff.[1] Activists found those same faults in all organizations that had an impact on people with disabilities but were especially critical of voluntary health charities for discriminatory hiring practices. Nondisabled professionals, they complained, wielded great power over disabled people's lives while profiting from their dominant positions. This anticipated the later disability rights rallying cry "Nothing about us without us." In the 1970s, activists were already demanding that people with disabilities have a major voice in any organization, program, or policy that affected them.[2]

The demonstrators in that first telethon protest belonged to Disabled in Action (DIA). Founded in 1970 in New York City with counterpart groups soon forming in other northeastern cities, DIA was a band of young adults. Though most had physical disabilities, they espoused a cross-disability politics and used militant tactics to call attention to everything from employment and educational discrimination to architectural inaccessibility to forced institutionalization. Aiming to shift the public discourse of disability from charity to civil rights, DIA inevitably took on telethons.

On 1 February 1976 a score of DIA members picketed the New York UCP Telethon. Repeating the criticism made against the MDA Telethon four years earlier, they charged UCP with propagating a negative image of people with disabilities. A spokesperson described as a low point the UCP Telethon's "children's march," when children with cerebral palsy walked across the stage to show their progress toward normality while nondisabled celebrities sang, "Look at us, we're walking; look at us, we're talking; look at us, we're laughing. . .." Many nondisabled viewers remembered that song years later with nostalgia, but DIA condemned the ritual as degrading and exploitative. They chanted, "Look at Us—We're people." UCP, they said, could accomplish their fundraising goals without the demeaning stereotypes. DIA did not oppose the telethon per se. Rather, it protested the telethon's manipulative "abusive fundraising tactics." A telethon spokesman snarkily responded that UCP "officials were too busy counting the 'abusive money' to comment on the criticism."[3] In 1977 DIA again picketed the New York UCP Telethon.[4]

During the late 1970s, activists criticized the Easter Seals and March of Dimes as well as the UCP and MDA Telethons.[5] In his 1978 manifesto *Handicapping America: Barriers to Disabled People*, Frank Bowe, one of the era's most prominent disability rights leaders, summed up activists' view-point. "[N]othing in America today so flagrantly plays upon our feelings of pity and sorrow as the annual telethons sponsored by various charity groups," he said. "As long as we pity disabled people, we will continue to see them as objects of charity rather than as equals deserving a say in their own destinies." He contrasted that image with adults who demanded implementation of the Rehabilitation Act's Section 504, which barred federally funded programs from discriminating against qualified persons with disabilities. Officials under Presidents Richard Nixon and then Gerald Ford had stalled signing them into law. In April 1977, fearing that Jimmy Carter was doing the same, disabled people organized demonstrations in ten major cities across the United States, including San Francisco, where more than one hundred protesters with various disabilities and their allies occupied the fourth floor of the Federal Building for nearly a month in what remains the longest occupation of a federal building in American history. Meanwhile, in Washington, DC, advocates worked behind the scenes, at last securing victory. Now people with disabilities had a legitimate base for demanding civil rights. In Bowe's words, "the non-disabled public saw, not the dependent children telethons had accustomed them to, but independent, aware, law-abiding, and intelligent individuals who happened to be disabled."[6]

Objections to telethons came from moderate activists, too.[7] Leslie Milk, executive director of Mainstream, Inc., which promoted corporate hiring of people with disabilities, complained, "Generally speaking, I don't think the business community is interested in hiring the handicapped. Many managers fear the disabled worker can't do the job. ... Let's face it, the image of the handicapped in this country is that of a poster child." Meanwhile, the White House Conference on Handicapped Individuals in May 1977 involved leaders from organizations spanning the political spectrum.[8] The conference focused on multiple issues that included civil rights, physical access, affirmative action, health insurance, treatment, research, technology, employment, and education. Relevant for telethons, the final report recommended that "studies should be instituted to explore the frequency and manner in which handicapped persons are represented in the media and to recommend mechanisms by which handicapped persons can be presented more positively and realistically."[9] Perhaps because the conference included representatives of the charities, its "Findings" didn't substantively challenge the charity, invalid, and overcomer framings discussed earlier.[10] "The depiction of handicapped individuals presented to the public," said that final report, "is usually that of a person seemingly helpless, needy and neglected. It might also be of a handicapped person who, with extraordinary effort, has overcome obstacles seemingly contrived to defeat the person's achievement of a chosen goal. Neither of these images accurately represent [*sic*] the millions of handicapped individuals in our society."[11]

If the conference report gingerly alluded to telethon depictions, other activists envisioned taking over the charities,[12] while still others strategized how to reform telethons from the outside. Attorney Deborah Kaplan, who in 1976 cofounded the Disability Rights Center (DRC) in Washington, DC, with consumer advocate Ralph Nader, explained to MDA officials that DRC worked to ensure "disabled people ... high quality educational opportunities and ... equal access to ... housing, transportation, employment, recreation, etc. Without this kind of access," she said, "the value of the rehabilitation services offered by your organization and others is diminished." In 1979 and 1980, DRC negotiated with and then prodded MDA leaders to do away with the negative images in its fundraising, join the disability rights movement, and allocate some of its grants "to advocacy organizations such as DRC." Evan Kemp, who took over as director of DRC in 1980, would learn that after he published his piece critical of MDA in the *New York Times*, MDA hired a private detective to follow him around in order to find evidence that would discredit him.[13]

Kemp, who had a neuromuscular disability, was a recently converted Republican from a well-to-do Democratic family. He graduated at the top of his University of Virginia Law School class, but thirty-nine firms refused to hire him, often explicitly citing his disability as the reason. Shocked by that discrimination, he became a disability rights lawyer. In June 1980 he reminded MDA Executive Director Robert Ross that his parents were cofounders of MDA—his father had sat on the board of directors, his mother had produced one of the early telethons. "All my life I have had a close and warm relationship with MDA," he said. But he and other activists were increasingly incensed at the organization's claim that its charter limited it to medical research and services. In fact, its certificate of incorporation and subsequent published statements committed it to promoting "adjustment to normal living" of people with neuromuscular diseases as well as their "training, vocational guidance and occupational placement." Kemp requested to meet with MDA's board in an "attempt to resolve amicably our very real differences." He also warned that DRC would use all means to ensure that MDA met its legal obligation to pursue its stated social and economic goals for its constituents.[14]

But MDA refused to yield. And so in late summer 1981, DRC and the American Coalition of Citizens with Disabilities (ACCD) launched, not a single protest demonstration, but a full campaign to compel MDA to reform its telethon. American Coalition of Citizens with Disabilities, comprising 126 advocacy groups, had been formed in 1974 to lobby for the regulations that would make Section 504 an enforceable civil rights law. In August 1981 ACCD and DRC published a full-page ad in the show business newspaper *Variety* addressed to "Jerry Lewis and his guests." The ad began with what seemed an oddly obsequious statement: "We don't mean to be ingrates but. ..." It declared that "the picture of the disabled that you paint on the MD telethon isn't real—or wise."[15] ACCD and DRC also wrote to corporate sponsors and local TV station managers outlining their objections to the telethon.[16] While those letters and the *Variety* ad were moderate in tone, op-ed pieces by ACCD Executive Director Reese Robrahn in the *Washington Post* and Evan Kemp in the *New York Times* were more forceful.

Kemp and Robrahn charged that the telethon's "pity approach" fed prejudice against people with disabilities and undermined their campaign for social integration. Kemp accused MDA of dealing in stereotypes that "offend our self-respect, harm our efforts to live independent lives and segregate us from the mainstream of society."[17] By "depicting disabled people as childlike, helpless, hopeless, non-functioning, non-contributing members of society," declared Robrahn, MDA had "lost sight of its original goal" of restoring people with neuromuscular diseases to the mainstream. Both called on MDA to send a different message by showing disabled people's "very real accomplishments, capabilities and rights" in working, raising families, and participating in community life. It should allay parents' fears about the future of their children who had neuromuscular disabilities by emphasizing independent living (IL). And it should "inform the public of the great economic and human waste that results from policies and programs that promote and perpetuate dependence rather than those that permit and foster equal opportunity, civil rights and independence of disabled people." This new message would help solve "problems of economic waste, demoralization and segregation." "For the telethon to make this case," declared Kemp, "would be a service to the disabled and to the country."[18]

Disability rights advocates in Boston echoed Kemp's and Robrahn's views of the telethon, charging that it hurt disabled people more than it helped them, even as they underscored the program's potential value. James Brooks, spokesman for the Disabled with Dignity Coalition, told the *Globe*, "We are not objecting to the need for fundraising in support of research to cure muscular dystrophy." He even went so far as to urge people to donate. But, he explained, "Year after year, Mr. Lewis parades before the camera people with muscular dystrophy as examples of what you would not want your child to be." Describing Brooks as "confined to a wheelchair," the reporter nonetheless quoted his description of the yearly display as "embarrassing and demeaning to disabled viewers."[19]

As with earlier protests, the 1981 DRC/ACCD campaign aimed to reform telethons, not abolish them. All of these advocates wanted the charities to include disability rights messages in their fundraising pitches. The 1981 campaign did not criticize the private charity system that gave rise to telethons or say that the objectionable fundraising images were inevitable in charity solicitation. While Robrahn noted that "the appeals are glamorized with the appearance of Hollywood and television stars," he did not suggest that there was a problem in relying on celebrity-generated private donations to pay for health care. Neither he nor Kemp condemned this approach for neglecting people with medical conditions that failed to attract a media star's interest. And they did not point out that the private charity fundraising system pitted people with different conditions against one another in competition for limited financial resources. Most significantly, they did not present their criticism of telethons within a broader critique of the US private–public health insurance/health-care system or offer proposals for its reform. The DRC/ACCD campaign particularly criticized MDA for positing cure as disabled people's primary need. That became a major theme of telethon protests.

In response to the DRC/ACCD campaign, an MDA spokesperson countered that "far from evoking pity," the telethon "seeks to profile adults overcoming their difficulties in ways that are 'meant to evoke admiration.'" Besides, he added contradictorily, "Many disabled people are desperate, and it makes no sense to worry about an image rather than a question of survival." Defenders of telethons and charity fundraising would throw this rejoinder back at disability rights activists again and again: Disabled people who needed medical and other services and had no other options but the private charities should not complain if fundraising methods purveyed pathetic images of them. MDA also mobilized a filmmaker to refute Kemp's "claim that the telethon 'focuses primarily on children.'" During the past two years, she had "produced seven filmed inserts" for the program. Six of the seven profiled adults, four of them "were employed full-time in positions of responsibility," two "were accomplished artists." That averaged out to two employed adults per telethon. As time went on, the MDA and other telethons—largely because of activists' criticisms—did increasingly feature adults, some of whom were shown working productively. But children remained the main fundraising tool, and on the MDA show they were still portrayed as doomed.

To mollify its critics, MDA invited Kemp to appear on the telethon in 1982. Militant activists were puzzled when Kemp, known for his strident criticisms and ardent calls for reform, delivered a mild-mannered, conciliatory message on the broadcast. He endorsed the fundraising effort by seeing it as partly matching the activists' agenda. "This Telethon introduces you to people . . . who represent the thousands of achievers among handicapped people," he said. "Your pledge can help create meaningful, productive lives for many. It can also help save the lives of others." Kemp was describing people with neuromuscular disabilities as overcomers rather than invalids. He was also apparently trying to bring together medical needs and civil rights.[20]

During the rest of the 1980s, activists organized no protests against telethons. Instead, they debated among themselves about telethons and charities. Many condemned them for reinforcing stereotypes that undermined the disability rights struggle. But some pragmatically defended telethons as necessary because they funded vital health-care services. That debate stayed largely within the disability rights community.[21] At the same time, some advocates continued to lobby inside the charities to change telethon messages and images.

Meanwhile, the crusade for disability rights was heating up. In March 1990 the *New York Times* described a "striking" picture: "Children paralyzed from the waist down crawling up the steps of the [US] Capitol,"—there were many adults, too, but the reporter overlooked them—"and more than 100 protesters, most in wheelchairs, being arrested by police officers in riot gear after a raucous demonstration in the Rotunda." They were demanding "enactment of the Americans with Disabilities Act, a comprehensive civil rights bill [to expand] to physically and mentally disabled individuals the same protections against biased treatment in employment, transportation and public accommodations now accorded women and minorities." The demonstration and the Americans with Disabilities Act (ADA), said the *Times*, reflected a major shift. "For years ... organizations like the March of Dimes and the Easter Seals Foundation" had set the agenda. But "in the last two decades," disabled people had "shifted from being passive recipients of institutional largess and paternalism to demanding a full role in society." Demonstrating outside the White House, disability rights leader Bob Kafka of Austin, Texas, declared, "We're not Tiny Tims, or Jerry's kids."

On 26 July 1990 President George H. W. Bush signed the ADA into law. An MDA press release issued the same day said that National Chairman Jerry Lewis hailed this as "a tremendously significant moment in the lives of the millions of Americans who are affected by disabilities. ... The ADA finally makes good for disabled persons on the promise made over a century ago by the Fourteenth Amendment to allow all Americans to participate fully in our society."[22] Then just five weeks later, Lewis took an opposite stance and triggered a firestorm of activist outrage.

Half a Person

Each Labor Day weekend on the first day of the MDA Telethon, *Parade* magazine, an insert in millions of Sunday newspapers, gave Jerry Lewis its cover article to talk about MDA's work. For his 1990 piece, he decided to imagine what it would be like "if I had muscular dystrophy."[23] He engaged in the sort of sympathetic spectatorship Adam Smith described two centuries earlier as "the source of our fellow-feeling for the misery of others." As noted in chapter 7, the Enlightenment political philosopher failed to consider how differences in status, power, and advantage shaped perceptions of other people's experiences, particularly people labeled deviant. He also overlooked the stereotyping that displaced the lived experience of people seen as objects of charity. These gaps distorted his understanding of how benevolence and charity actually worked as social practices.[24]

Falling into the same fallacy, Lewis assumed that he could imaginatively change places with people who had neuromuscular disabilities and "put myself in that [wheel]chair." He believed that "none of what I write is fantasy or assumption," because "I have lived with 'my kids' for 41 years now, and I've seen it all, maybe with one exception—getting into that chair." Despite his certainty, he was, in fact, coming from outside the experience of disability. More importantly, his essay failed to recognize the extent to which the dominant ideologies of disability and charity controlled his perceptions. This is not to deny the genuineness of his sympathy for people he saw as suffering. People with neuromuscular diseases repeatedly attested to his compassion toward them. But because of the determining influence of ideology, his essay perceived their lives as overwhelmingly and radically negative. The *Parade* article said little about medical treatments. Instead, it dwelt on the interpersonal and social hindrances of living with a disability. Their lives were a negation. They suffered from a "curse that attacks children of all ages. . . ." The rhetoric unconsciously invoked the ancient language of moral stigma. Though not personally at fault, disabled people embodied the human condition after the Fall. And by calling them "children of all ages," the essay implicitly asserted that neuromuscular disability reduced adults to childlike status. Historically more significant, the rest of the article indicated complete ignorance of the burgeoning disability rights consciousness. For example, it referred to wheelchairs as "that steel imprisonment," while in contrast, growing numbers of wheelchair riders described them as means of mobility, self-determination, and social integration. As one wheelchair rider had declared: ". . . To me, a wheelchair is a solution, not a sentence."[25] The essay also assumed that wheelchair riders who lacked full use of their hands had to be "pushed." Although Lewis said that he had "seen it all," the ideology that controlled his perceptions apparently screened out the widespread use of motorized wheelchairs.

The piece was equally dismissive of social and economic factors outside of the individual's disability, factors that many activists pointed out often created more difficulties than the disabling condition itself. For example, IL and personal assistance services (PAS)—that is, support provided in the home or workplace designed to assist an individual with a disability to perform daily living activities—still posed considerable challenges. By 1990 the IL movement had been campaigning for almost two decades for the right of people with significant disabilities to self-directed PAS. It also affirmed the fundamental dignity of people who used those services to chart the course of their daily lives. Yet Lewis's essay focused instead on dependency and "additional indignity, [in] being dressed, being fed, being everything you wouldn't have to be if you only had the use of your hands." Lewis and the activists also parted ways over architectural accessibility. While he was right to bemoan lack of access that still plagued too many hotels, restaurants, and spectator sport facilities, he was not demanding that US society guarantee equal access as a civil right.

To him, accessibility represented the efforts of "caring people" in "assisting the handicapped."

Jerry Lewis's decades of devoted labor and the testimony of many people with disabilities made clear the earnestness of his compassion. But he, like so many other genuinely sympathetic spectators, did not realize the extent to which the dominant ideologies of disability and charity distorted his perceptions of people with disabilities. He—and they—could only imagine the lives of people with disabilities as filled with indignity. They were convinced that having a disability meant being "half a person" and a perpetual object of charity. The closing paragraphs of his *Parade* article suggested an intriguing alternative possibility. If he could have broken free of the outdated confining ideologies of disability and charity, if he could have seen the health services he worked so hard to provide as integral to the civil rights of people with disabilities, he would have been a powerful ally.

Jerry's Orphans

In the weeks following Lewis's *Parade* article, newspaper columns and stories reported activists' outrage. Some criticisms were ad hominem. There was the absurd charge that Lewis was trying to make up for his original goofy kid persona because it supposedly mocked people with disabilities. There were claims that he profited from his charity work or was trying to salvage his waning career. In fact, he had been raising money for muscular dystrophy research and treatment since 1949, without compensation. But if some criticisms were fatuous, most were substantive. Some condemned him for arrogantly assuming he could speak for people with disabilities. Some scorned his stigmatizing language—"steel imprisonment," "cripples," the latter offensive to most people with physical disabilities, equivalent to the "N-word." Some were "appalled by what they saw as an inaccurate and insulting portrayal of life without hope, prospects or self-respect." They condemned him for dehumanizing bigotry: "half a person." Noting that his attitude conflicted with MDA's official view, disabled syndicated columnist Dianne Piastro quoted an MDA press release: "MDA promotes independence and self-sufficiency for people who are disabled. Remember that difficulties the person may be facing may stem more from society's attitudes and barriers than from the disability itself." The head of New York's Mayor's Office for People with Disabilities said Lewis "could do a great deal to change attitudes about disabled people as forever dependent, forever recipients of charity, forever children." He could, said other critics, promote civil rights and accessibility and the ADA. They were dismayed, as Chicago activist and former MDA poster child Cris Matthews put it, that his "description of airport security checkpoints, restaurants and stadiums that do not accommodate wheelchairs is woefully out of date."

Missing the point, Lewis "snapped," "Let her try getting off a plane in Akron, Ohio." He dismissed the criticisms as coming only from "'the activists'—he said the word derisively—with whom he has long been at war."[26]

A year later, Matthews and her brother Mike Ervin, who also had muscular dystrophy, launched a boycott of the 1991 telethon. Like the 1981 DRC/ACCD campaign, they aimed to reform the telethon, not abolish it. Objecting to it "in its present form," they hoped to persuade corporate sponsors and individuals to contribute to MDA outside the telethon until it made the changes they demanded. They wanted "the negative, degrading" "pity appeal" replaced with a realistic positive message about capability and independence. They suggested the United Negro College Fund Telethon as a model because of its dignified approach. Their protest differed from the 1981 campaign in two notable ways. First, Jerry Lewis must go. They called themselves "Jerry's Orphans." The name rejected paternalism. It also lent itself to misinterpretation that as a *Businessweek* headline put it, "Some of Jerry's Kids Are Mad at the Old Man," which left him a patriarchal figure and them children.[27] Second, unlike the 1981 protest, they did not criticize research to find cures "or the individual's desire to be cured." Instead, they disparaged the size of MDA research grants, condemned its policies limiting the services covered, and criticized cuts in payment for equipment such as motorized wheelchairs and ventilators. (MDA had said the cutbacks were due to "spiraling costs.") The activists did not reply that such limitations and reductions were inevitable in a charity system. Nor did they frame their criticism of the telethon within a critique of the health insurance/health-care system.[28]

On 1 and 2 September 1991 uncoordinated protests loosely associated with "Jerry's Orphans" picketed the telethon in Chicago, Las Vegas, Denver, Charleston, Los Angeles, Detroit, Boston, and Minneapolis/St. Paul. Repeating activists' common criticism of nondisabled professionals, Denver's "Tune Jerry Out Coalition" alleged that highly paid MDA executives profited from disabled people. They also rejected the poster child image. "[T]wo thirds of 'Jerry's Kids' are adults," they said, and want "to be treated that way." And they decried Lewis's *Parade* article. Ex-poster child Laura Hershey indignantly declared, "I'm here to tell Jerry, I'm a whole person." The protesters also introduced a new argument to telethon protests: Charity and civil rights were incompatible. A placard demanded "Dignity Not Charity" as the demonstrators chanted, "He sells pity day and night! Equal time for civil rights!"[29]

For the next several years, those activists held protests during MDA Telethons. In 1991 they demonstrated in eight cities; in 1992 their protests expanded to twenty. As was typical of most disability rights actions, the numbers of demonstrators in any particular protest were small, anywhere from half a dozen to two dozen. MDA said that showed that the critics represented only a handful of dissidents. Activists responded that mobilizing people with disabilities always posed distinct logistical problems and that the numbers turning out for most demonstrations never reflected the true extent of support on any given issue.

Most of the telethon protest leaders were veterans of ADAPT, arguably the most militant US disability rights group. In the 1980s, ADAPT had used civil disobedience to compel public transit systems to make buses accessible. For example, ADAPTers slid down out of their wheelchairs to lie in front of buses' wheels. In the early 1990s, they employed such tactics to end the "institutional bias" in public policy that trapped disabled people in nursing homes and institutions. On Labor Day 1992, activists demonstrated in at least eighteen and perhaps as many as two dozen cities.[30]

Responding to his critics as he opened the 1991 telethon, Lewis, like some activists, asserted a difference between "disabled" or "handicapped" people and "sick" people. "Never once . . . did I ever say, 'Please send your pledges, call in your pledges and then send your checks, for the disabled and for the handicapped.' I never did that. I've never used those terms. I said, 'Please help me eradicate a devastating disease known as the neuromuscular problem, forty neuromuscular diseases that are destroying the future of our world.' I'm begging for survival. I want my kids to live. I want them to survive. There are handicapped and there are disabled that are in the work place, that work damn hard and make a good living and do good work. My kids, and my older kids, and those stricken with muscular dystrophy or neuromuscular diseases, cannot go in the work place. There's nothing they can do . . . I'm trying to make the differential between those that can and those that cannot. Hire the disabled and hire the handicapped that can do the job. . . . But do this for me: Call your pledge in for my kids and my teenage kids and my older kids, who have been stricken by a vicious killer that will disrupt our future."

The Changing Telethon

As we have seen in earlier chapters, telethons were designed to frame children and adults as helpless, tragic burdens who needed to be cured. But increasingly some segments—and Lewis himself—contradicted that main message often during the same program. Late one night on the 1991 show, MDA had actor Danny Aiello declare: "Having a neuromuscular disease can mean people make assumptions about you, how you should live because you're in a wheelchair or a hospital bed. . . . MDA assists these people by providing equipment and care so they can hold down demanding jobs and raise families, do the things we all do, despite their life threatening disease."

The telethon made the same point by featuring retired United Airlines Vice President Robert Sampson and David Sheffield, an assistant district attorney from Texas. Both lived—and worked—with major neuromuscular conditions. Indeed, both men underscored the discrimination they had faced. As a young man, Sampson had won a college scholarship. "And the state took it away from me in 1942 because I was in a wheelchair. So I determined, if I ever got to be a lawyer, my first fight would be for school rights and equal treatment for disabled people." Yet Lewis followed this up by saying, "Bob Sampson, ladies and gentlemen, one of my oldest kids." David Sheffield had the experience of being close to the top of his class in law school and yet not being able to even get an interview at a major law firm. Sheffield continued: "I knew I was having an opportunity hardly any other of Jerry's Kids had. . .." It was the "opportunity . . . to go through law school and to prove something and to be something. And no matter how hard it seemed at times," even if he felt he "would like to give up, there's no way in the world I was going to," because he felt that as "one of Jerry's kids I had something to prove." In effect, he wanted to prove that he was an overcomer, not an invalid. Following this profile, Lewis read from cue cards that contradicted his remarks at the tele- thon's start: "Thanks to MDA many disabled people are now living produc- tive and happy lives."[31]

The contradictory segments in the telecast indicated that, as with other telethons in this new era of disability rights, MDA's was becoming a mélange of conflicting messages. At the same time, although as *U.S. News & World Report* explained, the "disorganized handful of demonstrators" got "just a smattering of attention," MDA saw them as a threat.[32] That danger seemed to grow following the 1991 telethon. In October "Jerry's Orphans" leader Mike Ervin wrote to MDA Executive Director Robert Ross, claiming that the pro- tests would grow until Lewis was removed, the telethon message was changed, and other demands were met, including putting disability rights advocates on MDA's board.[33] Meanwhile, Evan Kemp renewed his criticism of the telethon. Now chair of the US Equal Employment Opportunity Commission (EEOC) and the highest-ranking disabled person in the Bush administration, he drew media attention.[34]

MDA denied that it altered the content of the telethon in response to the protests, but observers noted changes in the 1992 and 1993 shows.[35] In fact, the differences were dramatic. In 1991 Lewis had said that people with neuro- muscular conditions "cannot go in the work place. There's nothing they can do." Yet segments on that and earlier telethons profiled some adults working productively. In 1992 and 1993, the telethon went much further, featuring doz- ens in many careers: a travel agent, a realtor, a sports reporter, a minister, an electronics engineer, a remedial reading teacher, a 911 operator, a coordinator at a temporary services agency, an accountant, a graphics designer, a couple of doctors, several lawyers, even some "disability advocates." Many said that MDA services made their careers possible. Local segments announced: "Every day MDA helps those with neuromuscular diseases maintain active and pro- ductive lifestyles."[36]

MDA awards were given to disabled professionals such as J. Steven Mikita, one of Utah's assistant attorneys general. Mikita said his father told him never to feel sorry for himself. "Don't be afraid, son. FDR did it, and so can you." Other adults were saluted for not letting "muscular dystrophy keep them on the sidelines." A college student trained in martial arts who aimed to become a lawyer and judge said he had been taught by his parents and doctor to "overcome" muscular dystrophy. A recent college graduate now working as a journalist talked about her motivation, positive outlook, and "never-say-die" attitude. The adults Lewis called "my older kids" who couldn't do anything "in the work place" were suddenly transformed from invalids into overcomers.

At the same time, some were presented and saw themselves simply as people with disabilities. Talk show host Sally Jessie Raphael described MDA's local and national Task Forces on Public Awareness as made up of "busy success- ful professional business people. They're parents, they're students, and they're community leaders." An accountant said they all were busy professionals and parents. Asked how neuromuscular disease affected his career, a middle-aged realtor said, "Well, it slows me down. It doesn't stop me." A number of adults said they hoped to be role models for children with disabilities.

Some telethons even added a disability rights message. Raphael inter- viewed several people about their experiences of prejudice and discrimina- tion and asked what difference the ADA would make. A disabled doctor said it would change attitudes and bring down barriers. David Sheffield, the assis- tant district attorney from Texas, said that people with disabilities would be able to join "our" able-bodied peers in places like restaurants from which "we" had been excluded and go to work because there would be reasonable accom- modations. J. Steven Mikita explained that the ADA guaranteed, not special rights, but equal rights. For the first time in its history, the MDA Telethon spoke of disability in terms of discrimination, accessibility, and civil rights rather than medical needs alone.

Also for the first time, the 1992 telethon informed its audience of the importance of PAS to support IL. In his *Parade* article, Lewis had called PAS an "additional indignity." Activists condemned his remarks and what they saw as MDA's failure to back IL.[37] In response, the 1993 telethon included segments declaring MDA's support of PAS, because it enabled people with neuromuscular diseases to go to school and work, to enjoy opportunity and productivity and social integration. But spokespersons stressed that most of MDA's "activities [were] not personal assistance services." In fact, "no one agency, including MDA, has the resources to provide personal assistance services" for the millions who needed them. They did not explain that the "agency" that funded PAS was the government. They did urge viewers to "act" regarding this issue, but did not ask them to call on Congress or their state legislature to fund PAS and IL. That request would have admitted that many MDA constituents had to rely on the Medicaid, Medicare, and social welfare programs discussed in chapter 2. Instead, this was the telethon in which Lewis proudly declared that MDA had never depended on the government. In future years, MDA provided its clients with information about IL resources, which were mostly governmental. MDA-connected advocates also joined disability rights lobbying to reform federal IL and PAS policies. Later telethons reported on some of that advocacy. The traditional telethon message depoliticized disability. Over time, the realities of its constituents' situation along with advocacy inside and outside MDA compelled it and its telethon to give attention to these policies.[38]

But one had to be paying careful attention to notice these changes. While the 1992 and 1993 shows presented new messages, they also repeated old ones steeped in traditional views of disability. For example, youngsters with neuromuscular disabilities remained "incomplete" children. In addition, spokespersons and clients reminded viewers that MDA's primary mission was medical, "to save lives" and "to find treatments and cures." Once again, viewers saw the Anheuser-Busch and Kellogg's spots that urged "Let's all help Jerry's kids just be kids." And the shows repeated the KinderCare Learning Centers films that segregated children with disabilities and made them objects of nondisabled children's charity. Together, such messages raised an important challenge to how activists were trying to frame the situation of people with disabilities.

The 1992 and 1993 telethons also rewrote disability rights history. Sandra Swift Parrino, the mother of three sons with disabilities, one with muscular dystrophy, had chaired the National Council on Disability as it drafted the ADA. "Largely through her efforts the Americans with Disabilities Act has become a reality," declared one host, while another asserted that she "took on the world of Washington politicians almost single-handedly and she created the ADA for every disabled American." Parrino did not say this about herself. By giving virtually sole credit for the ADA to a nondisabled person, MDA erased the central historical role of disabled activists, including many critics of telethons.

The telethon rewrote disability history in other ways. Announcer Ed McMahon claimed that the most gratifying thing about having done the telethon all these years was seeing ramps everywhere "for the wheelchair people. … [U]p until that time, no one thought about that. No one cared about that." In fact, those ramps had nothing to do with the telethon. Activists' lobbying put them in place. Other segments called Lewis a longtime champion of disability rights. "A lot of us believe," said one disabled man, "we have the Americans with Disabilities Act in part because for forty years Jerry Lewis and MDA promoted disability awareness by making the campaign against neuromuscular disease a national concern." Over the decades, Lewis and the telethon had indeed *heightened* public attention to neuromuscular diseases. (See chapters 1 and 2.) This was vital for people who relied on continuing advances in medical treatments to, as some of them put it, not only "survive but thrive." But attentive viewers noted that Lewis did not participate in the 1992 and 1993 segments portraying productively employed adults or supporting disability rights or PAS. Furthermore, until 1992 the telethon framed their situation primarily in terms of medical needs and the quest for cure, but completely overlooked their need for antidiscrimination protections, equal access, and reasonable accommodations.

Did activism affect the bottom line? Pledges on the 1992 and 1993 telethons topped previous totals. MDA and its supporters interpreted this as a rejection of the protests and a vindication of its traditional message. "With Record Telethon Tote, Critics Lose Sting," decided one headline. A news release from MDA put it even more bluntly: "Pledges to MDA Telethon Unaffected by Critics." The tallies allegedly proved that the activists "comprise a small minority out of touch with the general public."[39] And yet, the increased donations could have meant just the opposite: Not only the telethon's defenders but also its activist critics seemed to ignore the possibility that the public was responding favorably to the new framings about productive employment and civil rights.

Backlash

Alarmed by the mounting criticism, MDA took a "hard line," exaggerating the activists' impact and giving them "instant status," said *U.S. News*, by accusing them of causing "a $6 million shortfall" in collecting pledges from the 1991 telethon, "although the recession was a likelier suspect." At the same time, "citing budgetary problems," it closed a summer camp where Cris Matthews volunteered "and told unhappy campers to complain directly to [her], providing her address."[40] It also publicized that she was on a list to get a motorized wheelchair from the charity. Meanwhile, a law firm hired by MDA tried to intimidate her, warning that it would "monitor" her activities and that any actions that disrupted or damaged MDA's relations with its sponsors or affiliated stations would "provoke a swift and substantial reaction." "I don't know what they could do to us," said Matthews. "We have no money; we have nothing to lose."[41]

MDA also tried to neutralize Kemp. In December Lewis wrote him a "blistering letter" comparing his "tactics to David Duke's," the racist, anti-Semitic, former Ku Klux Klan leader.[42] In February 1992 Lewis called on President Bush to disavow "Mr. Kemp's assault on MDA" and accused Kemp of "misusing the power of his governmental office" by making statements that could hurt MDA fundraising.[43] Alluding to Bush's well-known exhortation to volunteerism that called for Americans to display "a thousand points of light," Lewis declared, "If ever there was a 'Point of Light'. . . I'm it!"[44] MDA's Task

Force on Disability Issues, composed of adults with disabilities, also wrote Bush criticizing Kemp.[45] At the time, he was up for reappointment as EEOC chair. When a rumor circulated among activists that MDA was trying to get him fired, MDA lawyers threatened action against an advocate who made that charge.[46] In April Bush reappointed Kemp. Meanwhile, the White House at first said it had no position on the telethon, then endorsed it, and asked Kemp to back off from his criticisms.[47] He did not. "Stereotyping, which the pity approach reinforces, leads to all kinds of discrimination," he said.[48] "For why should an employer hire someone who, admired public figures on the telethon tell them, is really helpless?"[49] Robert Ross complained that Kemp was flouting the president.[50]

In September 1992 when CNN's *Crier & Company* invited "Jerry's Orphans" cofounder Cris Matthews to explain her view of the MDA Telethon, it pitted her against both a disabled MDA spokeswoman and Nancy Mitchell, who was introduced as an economist with Citizens for a Sound Economy (CSE). CNN did not explain that CSE was a right-wing advocacy group fighting for less government, lower taxes, and less regulation. Mitchell's claims about private charities reflected that agenda. "[I]t's easy to forget about people with special needs," she said, using patronizing language activists scorned. She did not think the telethon promoted pity; it was "purely informative" about "special needs children" and "special needs individuals." Crier asked if the government had "to step in" with "things like the Americans with Disabilities Act" because "over the years" the telethon projected "the images that people can't work or can't participate in society." She apparently saw the ADA as a charitable boon of government rather than a civil rights law and the political achievement of the disability rights movement. Mitchell replied, "I would argue that it's a mistake to bring the government into the act, and that anything that encourages voluntary contributions is much better and will probably target your problems more effectively."[51]

Because Mitchell saw disabled people's needs and problems as exclusively medical, she ignored that only the government could enforce antidiscrimination protections and their legal rights of equal access and reasonable accommodations. But even regarding medical needs, she overlooked the government's major role. MDA was the largest nongovernmental funder of neuromuscular disease research, but the biggest overall was the federal government. As Mitchell tried to depoliticize disability by confining it to the realm of private charity, her ideological framing promoted the traditional line espoused on telethons.

Some in the broader culture scorned not only the telethon protests but disabled people's civil rights struggle in general. Denver's *Rocky Mountain News* typified that stance. Its editorials not only melodramatically denounced what they assumed would be the ADA's burdensome intrusion on business, they also took a local activist to task for criticizing the MDA Telethon. He and other protesters "seem to think their hard fortune in bearing with a neuromuscular disease entitles them to stipulate the very source of their assistance." In other words, as citizens, people with disabilities should have limited protections from discrimination and limited rights to access and accommodations; as objects of charity, they should have no say in how supports were provided and no right to complain about fundraising images of them.[52]

This political perspective was buttressed by the traditional casting of people with disabilities as charity recipients.[53] Critics condemned disabled protesters for violating the terms of that role. More offensive than their criticism of fundraising methods was their alleged ingratitude. They should call themselves "Jerry's Ingrates," fumed a columnist under a headline that infantilized them: "Ungrateful Child Sharp as Serpent's Tooth: Just Ask Jerry." "If no good deed goes unpunished," decried a Pennsylvania newspaper, "Jerry Lewis is getting exactly what he deserves. His good deeds are manifold, and he is punished annually by a loud minority of the disabled." *Time* magazine sympathetically said Lewis was "fend[ing] off attacks from the disabled folks he has tried to serve. . . ."[54] Lewis and people associated with MDA also accused the protesters of ingratitude. "You have to remember they're sitting in chairs I bought them," he charged.[55] In fact, many were not MDA clients, and those who were complained that they had few if any other options in the health insurance/health-care system to get the wheelchairs and other equipment they required.

Activists' "ingratitude" was said to signify emotional maladjustment and moral defect. A member of MDA's Task Force on Public Awareness accused telethon critic Laura Hershey of reinforcing "the false, age-old stereotype of disabled people as angry, deeply embittered, negative persons." MDA Executive Director Robert Ross called the activists an "embittered band of extremists." *Parade* magazine publisher Walter Anderson charged: "The assassin in his mind thinks: 'How do I become as big as the president? I shoot the president. How do I become as large as Jerry, per se? I criticize him.' Fortunately we live in a free society where criticism is encouraged and is part of our culture." Except that a disabled person who criticized a putative benefactor might be classified morally with Lee Harvey Oswald. Lewis himself said: "Because someone is in a wheelchair, that doesn't necessarily mean that they are devoid of being a malcontent. They can be not only a malcontent, but they could be a lousy rat! We have been taught that someone in a wheelchair should be given the kind of respect and the kind of sensitivity that we all give them, but I've got news for you. They could have been a neo-Nazi before they got in a wheelchair. And they haven't changed just because they're rolling their hands on a wheel."[56]

Conclusion

THE END OF TELETHONS AND CHALLENGES
FOR DISABILITY RIGHTS

The controversy over telethons left many matters unsettled. There was the evolving but conflicted status of people with disabilities in late-twentieth-century America. There were also the limitations and contradictions of disability rights advocacy and ideology. Both the telethons and the activism exemplified a distinctly American process that historian Peter Dobkin Hall describes in which private associations establish moral, perceptual, and political agendas.[1] As with voluntary associations throughout American history, the telethon-producing charities performed an unacknowledged social and political function by framing disease and disability as a public problem with certain appropriate solutions. In doing so, they also helped to define the social identities and roles assigned to people with disabilities as tragic victims of their flawed bodies. Through different voluntary associations disability rights activism offered a competing agenda that challenged the charity tradition and the medical model propagated on telethons and throughout American society. Claiming new identities and roles for people with disabilities, activists saw themselves as a minority group battling prejudice and discrimination. Both charity and activist framings reflected a number of ongoing American dilemmas.

The Struggle to Be Heard

The celebrities who hosted the telethons did not have visible disabilities. Neither did the guest stars nor the typical check presenters or many of the interviewees. The nondisabled presenters and participants addressed a viewing audience the charities obviously assumed was nondisabled, too. The producers authorized all of these nondisabled people to explain the experience of people with disabilities to the audiences. In 1994 UCP had its national MCs call the program a partnership between able-bodied and disabled people. However, if telethons reflected a partnership, people with disabilities were the silent partners. As we've seen, the nondisabled did almost all of the talking on telethons. They talked about disabled people. They talked about them endlessly.[2]

Within the telethon system of representing the world, people with disabilities and nondisabled people not only operated in different social spaces, at times they were presented in different physical spaces as well. For example, on the 1995 UCP Telethon, several Hearst newspaper executives noted that computer technology was revolutionizing their business. They then drew a parallel with the importance of technology to UCP clients. Their commentary was interspersed with videotapes of UCP clients, sometimes adults, but usually children. The executives did not mention disabled individuals as Hearst employees. At the conclusion of these segments, the head of each Hearst division would announce a corporate contribution and invite viewers to join the company in making a donation. The executives did all of the talking. And while they appeared in a TV studio, the inserts of the disabled people were taped at UCP centers. The two categories of persons were presented in separate spaces: the authoritative space of the Hearst executives-cum-charity donors who exercised the privilege and power to speak and thus to define the meaning of the moment, and the subordinated, distant space of the voiceless disabled persons.

By having nondisabled presenters do almost all of the talking, the charities reinforced the power of nondisabled people in general to define both the social meaning of disability and the social identities of people with disabilities. Telethons empowered nondisabled MCs to explain to nondisabled viewers disabled people's daily experience. "We hope to give you a little more understanding of what life is like for someone with a disability," announced a local Easter Seals host in 1990. But one of the frustrating things about hosting this show, admitted another MC in 1988, is that "we are often asked to describe what someone in a wheelchair is going through, and frankly we can only imagine what it is like." Nonetheless, undaunted by their own ignorance, authorized by the charities, and influenced by those fearsome imaginings, the nondisabled presenters talked on and on.

Sometimes the MCs and celebrities and other nondisabled participants got things right. Sometimes they got things wrong. Sometimes they got things right and wrong at the same time. Sometimes they were misinformed. Sometimes they were appalling. Sometimes they were hilarious. But whether right or wrong or lamentable or ludicrous, they got to do the talking. And often, adults and children with disabilities had to sit silently and listen while nondisabled people—"job coaches" and physical therapists, parents and benefactors, actors and comics and singers—talked about them. And in the ultimate act of silencing, some charity professionals even proposed new labels for them, such as during the Easter Seals program in 1998 when Pat Boone told viewers: "They are handicapable people, as we like to say around here."

They might like to say "handicapable" around there, but disability rights advocates found that term condescending and objectionable. "Handicapable sounds like a kitchen utensil," cracked one activist. Another disabled person called such euphemistic designations "too cute for words."[3] "Handicapable" was invented and mostly used by nondisabled people in the helping professions. Disabled people who rejected such terms not only scorned those words for their silliness, but also spurned the presumptuousness of nondisabled people who took it upon themselves to label and define disabled people. A disability rights activist put it this way: "We alone should decide on what we call ourselves. I've noticed terms like 'physically challenged,' 'People with Special Needs,' and other excuse-me terms being sold over the media as terms the disability community has agreed upon as the proper terminology to use. The first step in any struggle for basic human rights is what a people call themselves. . . . We need a cultural perspective of our own, as People with Disabilities. We need a vision of who we are, where we are going and where we have come from."[4]

Disability activists sought ways of talking back to telethons and to American society more broadly. But were they ready with a rigorous, comprehensive critique that spelled out a future in ways that made sense to disabled and nondisabled people alike? To be sure, they faced a nearly impossible task. Tapping into cherished, unquestioned American culture and values, the telethons' seemingly contradictory messages were easy to overlook and difficult to counter.

Simply bringing up the imbalance between the disabled and nondisabled was daunting. Telethon message-making reinforced a striking contradiction common in social attitudes about people with disabilities. The charities' framings affirmed the common humanity of people with and without disabilities, but they simultaneously asserted the radical differentness of disabled people. The 1994 Easter Seals broadcast had Kathie Lee Gifford repeat an avowal made on all of the shows: "People with disabilities are just like everyone else." The 1989 Easter Seals show cued national cohost Mary Frann, the sitcom actress, to say: "Mixed in with the music, you're also going to hear a message, the message that people with disabilities do belong." Yet at the same time, telethons ritualistically reiterated that people with disabilities were *not* "like everyone else," not like the *normal* people hosting the telethons or watching at home. The shows endlessly asserted that disabled people would not, indeed *could not*, "belong" unless their medical and consequent social pathologies were cured or corrected.[5]

Telethons constantly presented this radical separation between the nondisabled and disabled through a series of paired opposites with deep roots and far-reaching implications. In terms of medical pathology, the dichotomy contrasted the well and the sick, the whole and the unhealthy. That distinction supported a further differentiation based in alleged social pathology: It set apart the competent from the incompetent, the productive from the unproductive, the socially valid from the socially invalidated. Fit and attractive athletes, actors, and models literally embodied that fundamental dissimilarity. And they intensified the contrast by linking it to images of beauty versus deformity, strength versus weakness, helping versus helplessness. These were basic to the dichotomy at the heart of charitable solicitation: giver rather than receiver, donor rather than object of charity.

Perhaps no telethon image captured the disparity better than the one central to the disability-related agencies' general fundraising: a nondisabled adult holding or helping a child with a disability. The incommensurateness of these figures completed the radical differentiation by embodying notions of big versus little, whole versus crippled, strong versus weak, caring benefactor versus dependent ward, normal versus abnormal.

And yet, such dichotomies were complicated because the telethons also solicited charity by creating connections between potential donors and those they should benefit. Disability rights advocates sometimes likened the telethons to freak shows. But these programs did not portray people with disabilities as freakish or strange. To the contrary, telethons depicted them and their families as ordinary people, typical middle-class Americans, who had fallen victim to various "afflictions." As with the pictures of people with disabilities in Victorian sentimental literature, the very ordinariness of the disabled people and their families on telethons was one of the more important features of the image making. On one level, descriptions of them as "just like . . . your family, your neighbors" reflected the traditional aim of sentimental spectatorship to evoke a sense of common humanity. At the same time, the reminder that these people with disabilities and their families were not only "like you" or someone you know, but that, in fact, they "could be you" was an oblique way of beginning to address nondisabled people's fears and consequent ambivalence about people with disabilities. As Martha Stoddard Holmes observes, "The near normal is a more troubling cultural issue than the freak, and the one that we most resist unpacking."[6]

A big part of the problem was that the medical model and the charity tradition retained their hegemony. That hegemony, along with the complexity of the disability experience, posed an extraordinary challenge for activists in promoting the civil rights approach. The fundraising tactics of telethons drew viewers' attention away from ordinary experiences to focus on medical events that the fundraisers presented as socially de-legitimizing. In the process, telethons deliberately confirmed nondisabled viewers' stereotyped images of disabled people and told them that life with a disability was every bit as horrible as they feared. Not only that, but this hegemony privileged "cure" over all other responses to disability.

Within such framings, activists' protests against telethons in writing and on the streets often lacked a systematic critique or unified message. This was partly because the demonstrations were local uncoordinated actions. But more important was the absence of a rigorous comprehensive disability rights analysis and framework. Protesters' piecemeal criticisms expressed a cluster of ideas within a nascent ideology.

In activists' critique, both the charity and pathogenic framings reflected the prejudice that people with disabilities were not fully human. The MDA Telethon, they complained, reinforced the prejudice that people with disabilities were pitiful. That pathetic image, said an ADAPT member who had cerebral palsy, "puts us all down, not just muscular dystrophy people." In addition, the paternalistic "Jerry's Kids" imagery depicted disabled adults as helpless, eternal children.[7]

Activists also accused charity executives of profiting off of disabled people. When an MDA official claimed that the activist Laura Hershey's anti-telethon activities caused "a serious financial drop" that might force MDA "to curtail—or eliminate entirely—certain" programs, she responded sharply. "You seem very willing—even eager—to cut client programs. … Has the Association considered administrative salary cuts instead? Or is this part of the budget considered sacred?" Activists critically noted that Robert Ross, the founder and CEO of the MDA, was one of the highest-paid charity executives in the country.[8]

The telethon's medical-model message, said activists, also excused nondisabled donors and particularly corporate contributors from addressing other important issues. "To say a cure is the answer perpetuates the myth that we need cures more than decent housing or jobs," charged the disability rights advocate Yvonne Duffy. "The sad thing is that we still can't ride many public buses, work, shop or attend theaters and clubs others can enjoy. When [MDA] rakes in those big checks, it lets the [corporate] donors off the hook. They forget about installing ramps, widening aisles or lowering public telephones." Mike Ervin, better known as "Smart Ass Cripple"—his wry moniker of choice—highlighted this sharp discrepancy between the professed aims of the telethon and the reality in reference to his local store: "[It] has a coin canister for Jerry's Kids on the counter and steps at the front door. A local pizzeria took out the wheelchair ramp when it remodeled and put in stairs while its proprietor was giving the telethon big checks on camera." A further challenge came from the fact that not everyone appreciated the activists' goals. As a letter signed by one of "Jerry's Kids" declared, "It is not Jerry Lewis's or MDA's responsibility to fight for disabled rights."[9] Meanwhile, in 1993 and 1994, the number and size of the demonstrations criticizing the telethon grew smaller, while the media increasingly ignored them as "old news."[10] Worse still, they seemed to be fighting an uphill battle. No longer worried about the activists, MDA again revised its telethon's content. From 1994 on, it featured many fewer productively employed adults, and it reduced the Personal Achievement Award to a single national recipient. At the same time, it reverted to its traditional greater emphasis on doomed children and adults and the traditional talk about people with neuromuscular disabilities having to spend their lives "in wheelchairs." And Lewis perpetuated the old framings. He said that in the year 1994 he found it "inconceivable" that parents could "get through this life" after being told that their child would be "crippled in a wheelchair." In 1996 he asked rhetorically what a dad felt like "when he's told, 'Your child will be in a wheelchair.'" Perpetuating the old horrific dichotomy, he proclaimed that the dollars for research would protect healthy children "so that they never become a Jerry's kid." In 1997, standing next to a woman with ALS, he said that she allowed him "to use [her] as a prop on a telethon so that we can get the attention of people who will help us make that prop a human being again. . . ."

Also typical of much disability rights advocacy, telethon protesters had difficulty getting across their viewpoint. This was partly due to organization and logistics; most activists had limited experience in dealing with the media. In addition, leveling a multitude of criticisms of MDA and its telethon, they lacked a focused message. But the news media also had difficulty reporting their perspective on this as on other disability rights issues. The activists' reframing of the issues, interests, and needs of people with disabilities clashed with the entrenched ideologies of disability and charity, and seemed to many people not just inaccurate but irrational. Their views were not only deeply at odds with conventional thinking; they were more complicated than the oversimplified dominant framings. Their views could not be explained in a sound bite. At the same time, most activists presented their criticisms piecemeal rather than locating them within a broader critical analysis of the health insurance and health-care system or, more broadly still, the structural function of disability within the socioeconomic system as a whole.

Charity versus the Right to Health Care

The telethon controversy exposed the political function of charity. Conservative support of the telethon-producing charities reflected a late-twentieth-century shift of the American Right. For most of the century, explains Peter Hall, it "had been unremittingly hostile to philanthropy and philanthropically supported organizations." The Reagan Revolution reversed that stance by asserting that private groups could respond to community needs more efficiently and flexibly than "big government." Ronald Reagan's "rhetoric drew on traditional ideas about the intrinsic opposition of government and private action." Not just conservatives, says Hall, but also liberals and progressives all contributed in various ways to a process of devolution and privatization under way since the end of World War II.[11] The growth of the disability-related charities and the impact of their telethons during that era exemplified those developments. They also reflected historic American patterns of voluntarism and antistatism, even though those charities, like much of the nonprofit sector, were controlled by professionals and deeply involved with the government as contractors and lobbyists. This ideological and institutional situation was a key reason the United States failed to establish a comprehensive equitable system of national health insurance. That issue was also central to the telethon controversy.

The only problems some defenders of telethons recognized were medical and the only way they could see to pay for those medical needs was through private charities. The only method they could imagine to raise those funds was by promoting pity. While MDA insisted that it encouraged compassion not pity, some of its supporters saw "pity . . . everywhere in this show." Los Angeles Times columnist Robert A. Jones had no problem with stirring up pity. "As long as the emotional currency translates into the real currency of cash, who cares?" If Jerry Lewis was "drummed out of the telethon" and "emotional correctness" rather than "cashable pity" was enforced, who and what would "keep this cash machine going?" Another columnist wondered "if there isn't a better, less painful way to raise the money," but he could see no alternative. The bonds of ideology made other arrangements literally unthinkable.[12]

The vituperative response to disabled telethon protestors indicated that something more than a quarrel over fundraising methods was at stake. The enraged reactions reflected the view of disabled people at the core of the charity and pathogenic ideologies. They were morally worthy of charity as long as they were properly thankful. Complaints about charity methods evidenced bitterness about their conditions and, worse still, ingratitude toward their benefactors. The accusation that they were embittered malcontents also expressed the medical-model ascription of pervasive pathologizing. The ease with which these imputations were not just made but believed showed how readily the cheerfully grateful Tiny Tim could be recast as the vengefully discontented Richard the Third. Historian George Fredrickson's analysis of the counterpointed images of docile loyal "Sambo" and savage rebellious "Nat" in antebellum racist ideology suggests that this sort of dichotomous reversible imagery is a tool of all systems of domination, a means of suppressing resistance, or at least explaining it away. In the telethon controversy, the denunciations depoliticized activists' perspective by reframing their protest as individual psychopathology and moral monstrosity.[13]

The enormous entrenched power of the charity system was evidenced by activists' typical approach to it. From the early 1970s into the early 1990s, a handful of advocates called for abolishing all telethons, but most acquiesced to the charities as necessary to pay for needed services and equipment and only wanted telethons reformed. "Our goal," Mike Ervin of "Jerry's Orphans," had said "is not to put [MDA] out of business."[14] In 1992 the "Orphans" and ADAPT urged corporate sponsors to donate off the telethon until MDA changed the show's content. "This way," said an ADAPT leader, "the Telethon is neutralized while MDA's fundraising efforts are unharmed." ADAPT even helped TCI design its 1992 telethon spot. Activists accepted that in the current system people with many types of disabilities had to depend on private charities. But that pragmatic strategy left the premises of corporate almsgiving unchallenged. Cause-related marketing was a merchandising tool, not a call for health-care equity.

Because of the arrangements and inequities of the US health insurance/ health-care system, many people with disabilities did have to depend on private charities. They feared that the protests would reduce donations and cause cutbacks in the services they needed. Access to appropriate and affordable health care was always on the disability rights agenda. But that objective was often obscured in activists' refutations of the medical model and protests against depictions of disabled people as objects of charity. Their criticisms of telethons usually failed to offer a broader analysis of the deficiencies of the health insurance and health-care system or proposals for more equitable alternatives to the private charities. During their peak years (1992–1993), the protests mainly focused on negative telethon imagery while sometimes noting the system's inherent inequities. "We're not saying the services [from MDA] are not valuable," explained Cris Matthews, "but I shouldn't have to beg for this wheelchair. And others, without MD [muscular dystrophy], are not getting services."[15] Her complaint underscored that in America some people had to plead for what they needed, while others got no aid at all. There was no right to health care.

As time went on, a growing number of activists concluded that the entire system of telethons and charities was irremediably unjust.[16] In September 1993 Marta Russell, a leader of the Los Angeles protests, said charities and telethons should be replaced with a "sound universal health care plan that would allow all citizens to live independently, productively and with dignity."[17] The telethon "says that if people with disabilities need medical care or equipment, they should have to beg for it," complained Laura Hershey in 1994. "Those things, because we need them, should be a matter of civil rights."[18] The *Rocky Mountain News* dismissed the notion of "civil rights based on need" as "silly." But "it's the logical extension of today's appeal to 'special rights' for any beleaguered group or person who feels victimized by life."[19] In fact, Hershey and other activists were not demanding "special rights" for people with disabilities. They were calling for a universal, comprehensive national system that guaranteed adequate and appropriate health care as a basic right of all Americans.

This emergent agenda also marked a divide among disability rights advocates. One critic of the activists was Tedde Scharf, associate director of a university program for students with disabilities and a member of MDA's Task Force on Public Awareness. She was a quadriplegic ventilator user who employed personal assistants. Working hard for independence, dignity, and opportunity, she "confronted society's prejudices and doubts with self-confidence" and "dealt with paternalism and pity through awareness building," she said. Scharf also "survived a disease that could have threatened my independence and my life, because of technology and medical advances of the type MDA makes possible." Getting to her main point, she condemned disabled critics of the telethon who "insist[ed] that the government guarantee everything they need. We can't have it both ways. Either we accept the realities of 'independence'—including jobs with long hours, providing our own insurance and medical care, paying for our personal care needs, taking our place in line at the theater, paying for transportation—or we continue to accept government dole and charitable contribution. ... It's time to stop proclaiming we don't want 'to be taken care of' while demanding a national health care plan that will take care of us."[20]

This view of "independence" represented the conservative political side of "overcoming." It ignored that few people with major disabilities could earn enough to pay the high cost of health care, personal assistance, and other disability-related living and work expenses and that many could not get private insurance because of discrimination by insurers. Indeed, it didn't take into account the astronomically high unemployment rate among employable people with disabilities, much of it due to prejudice and inaccessible work environments. It scorned reliance on public aid as irresponsible dependency but relegated people with disabilities to dependence on private charities. It also overlooked that the charities never had the resources to fully meet their clients' needs and during downturns in donations had to cut services.

By 1994 many liberal activists were linking the telethon issue with the need for a complete overhaul of the health-care system. At protests there were "many more signs [that] condemned telethons in general." "No more telethons—Civil rights not pity," they demanded. Meanwhile, other placards proclaimed: "Health care is a right." "It is only because this country has never provided adequate health care for all its citizens that charity organizations can blackmail and embarrass us by reminding us that 'they gave us the chairs we're sitting on,'" declared Nadina LaSpina of Disabled in Action of Metropolitan New York. "If health care were a right, no one ever would have to beg in order to get needed services and equipment."[21]

This political position not only challenged existing health-care arrangements, it also exposed the limits of "civil rights" ideology. That American political and legal tradition pledged to protect individuals from discriminatory treatment by government, private institutions, and other individuals. It was an ideology of negative freedom; it sought to limit infringements on the liberty of individuals. Even when disability rights laws required material investment, for example, in architectural barrier removal, it justified those measures within the theoretical framework of eliminating restrictions on individuals' freedom. Policies mandating reasonable accommodations in employment and public services or guaranteeing children with disabilities appropriate education pushed the limits of that tradition by, in essence, calling for positive freedoms supported by state and private action. But when activists demanded health care as a right, they were implicitly invoking an alternative tradition in which the state promoted positive freedom by ensuring social and economic rights. That tradition, more associated with Western European social welfare states, was much less robust in the United States. Just as professional "sympathy entrepreneurs" sought to reframe social values and public sympathy through telethons, disability rights activists aimed to reframe values and feelings about what constituted justice and equity, not merely for people with disabilities but everyone. They sought to replace the charity tradition's normative system with a normative system that ensured social and economic rights.[22]

The Activist Conundrum

The charity tradition that shaped many Americans' perceptions posed a substantive and strategic problem for activists. But they did not develop an analysis of the material interests at stake that would be capable of supporting a transformative political agenda. Even when the disability rights movement and the academic field of disability studies put forth a bundle of ideas that critiqued dominant framings, they had yet to frame an adequately rigorous, empirical, and comprehensive explanation of the central role of disability in the socioeconomic and political structure.

The disability rights agenda needed to confront some basic realities. To be sure, it faced resistance from the charities and corporations that had a material stake in the existing system. But, less obviously, it also appeared to clash with the revered American tradition of voluntary neighborly assistance. Some editorialists accepted activists' demand for changes in charity messaging while reaffirming the necessity and virtue of the charity tradition. "At first glance," the telethon protests "appear to fall in the category of biting the hand that feeds," but in fact times and attitudes had changed, they said. So Lewis and MDA should revise their telethon message. It would be fine if " 'Jerry's Kids' and the 'poster child' mentality [became] an anachronism," but calls to cut government spending made individual and corporate charity more necessary than ever. Moreover, telethons tapped "an impulse in Americans that isn't pity—but a desire to help out. . . .." Disabled activists needed to understand that some well-meaning people felt overwhelmed by the tide of social change, "bewildered that what was once considered compassionate is now considered patronizing. Lewis is one of them."[23]

That observation was certainly correct. But it confronted activists with a major ideological and strategic challenge: What many nondisabled Americans considered compassionate was the product of an ideology that had schooled them to view disabled people as perpetual objects of charity. Though some people with disabilities embraced that framing as generously humane, others had always found it patronizing and socially discrediting. In the latter view, telethons both drew from and deliberately stoked an impulse that *was* pity. As we have seen, the origins of that impulse had strong ties with maintaining certain kinds of social distance. As sociologist David Wagner argues, "Charity is a *moral enterprise* with a clear social script. It produces heroes and model citizens who give, and deferential meek citizens who accept. It delineates society with a clear boundary between moral and immoral."[24] The telethons fit neatly within such a script that makes more sense to most Americans than alternatives such as European social welfare states or American liberal reform. If a more egalitarian society emerged, Wagner explains, it *might* have less room for individual moral heroics because need would be fulfilled more routinely and automatically, and with fewer clear rewards for both individuals and a private charitable industry.

Charity professionals shrewdly linked the revered American traits of neighborliness and volunteerism to a health-care financing and delivery system that made private charities a key component, mobilizing those hallowed values on behalf of an arrangement with enormous disparities. The charities provided vital health-care services, but they served narrowly defined populations, their fundraising capacities severely limited their services, and in times of economic constraint they had to curtail those services even more.

Meanwhile, many other Americans suffered without adequate health care because no celebrity-centered charity fundraising promoted their needs. Compassion was made "a substitute for justice." "Compassion," observed Hannah Arendt, "always already signifies inequality. The compassionate intend no justice, for justice might disrupt current power relationships."[25] In the case of American telethons, it would be more accurate to say that compassionate individual volunteers and donors intended no *in*justice, but the charities and their corporate sponsors channeled that compassion in ways that buttressed current inequalities and disparities in power. Telethon framings not only legitimated the inequitable health-care financing and delivery system, they also ritually reinforced disparate individual power relationships. Individuals' genuine desire to help was shaped by an institutionalized sympathy logic that not only propagated the radical dichotomy of normal versus disabled, but, as throughout the history of Western charity, also used disability and charity to reinforce other status hierarchies of class, gender, and ethnicity. Given the deeply entrenched power of the charity tradition, telethon defenders could easily and effectively accuse activists of attacking some of Americans' most cherished traditions and self-celebrated virtues: compassion and generosity, voluntarism and volunteerism.

The telethon controversy exemplified yet another major predicament of disability rights activism: Was it possible in late-twentieth-century American society to advocate for the vitally important health-care needs and rights of many people with disabilities without legitimating the pathologizing perspective? Could activists support disabled people's medical needs without endorsing the medical model? The charity and medical-model ideologies located the basic problem in the bodies of individuals. Physiological pathology was assumed to cause social invalidation. The hegemonic status of these ideologies made them seem simple statements of biological fact. They naturalized what were in significant measure socially constructed situations. In opposition to this thoroughgoing medicalization and pathologizing of disabled people's lives, activists framed a minority-group model that focused on prejudice and discrimination, inaccessibility and lack of accommodations, as the main causes of their marginalization. But the charity and medical-model ideologies were so deeply entrenched that activists found it extraordinarily hard to talk about the major medical needs of many people with disabilities without seeming to confirm the medical model. And so they often avoided the issue of medical needs or touched on them only obliquely as they struggled to shift public attention from obsessive preoccupation with illness and impairment to the pressing problem of injustice.

The difficulties with their reframing were most apparent in their criticism of telethons. In 1981 Reese Robrahn, executive director of the American Coalition of Citizens with Disabilities, complained that the MDA Telethon's "emphasis on finding cures creates the impression that disabled people are sick and that we cannot be happy unless we are cured."[26] Evan Kemp agreed: The "critical stress on the need to find cures supports the damaging and common prejudice that handicapped people are 'sick'. . . and should allow others to take care of all our needs until a cure is found."[27] A decade later, some telethon protesters chanted: "We are whole." "We are not sick."[28]

Kemp succinctly expressed activists' critique of telethons. "The real fight here is between the civil rights approach to disability and the medical model," he said.[29] In this instance, the phrase "medical model" was shorthand for two telethon framings activists opposed: the definition of disabled people's lives almost exclusively in terms of medical problems and the depiction of cure as their primary need and desire. They labored to replace that formulation with a minority-group model in which the central problem was prejudice and discrimination. This framing exposed not only distortions in telethon messages but also dilemmas in disability rights advocacy and ideology. Activists criticized the telethons and charities for distorting the lived experience of people with disabilities, yet the disability rights movement and disability studies lacked a complex complete account of that experience, an adequate explanation of disability. Ultimately, the issue need not have been a choice between treatment or cure on the one hand and civil rights on the other. As some activists came to recognize, the real issue was securing a right to health care as one key component of a comprehensive disability rights agenda.

Sickness/Illness versus Disability/Handicap

Further, activists faced the challenge that much of society conflated sickness/illness and disability/handicap while they needed to oversimplify the distinction in order to make a case. Both were seen as framing social identities and roles, the first caused by medical conditions, the second by social status. Sick people were viewed as dependent or likely to become so. They needed to be treated and even taken care of until they were cured. Handicapped/disabled people could be independent if they were assured of civil rights, equal opportunity, independent living, recognition of their capabilities, and social respect. The indignant chants "We are not sick" and "We are whole" implicitly accepted that insofar as one was ill or impaired one was incomplete. It unconsciously acquiesced to the bias that disease diminished one's humanity. In contrast, people with disabilities were whole, that is, socially valid.

MDA and its defenders accepted those distinctions, but they argued that people with neuromuscular diseases *were* sick. MDA declared that its primary mission was to help people who had life-threatening, life-shortening illnesses. On the telethon, parents said they desperately feared their children would die, while adults with neuromuscular diseases described themselves as seriously ill, not disabled. Some adults spoke favorably but also critically of disability rights activism. "I certainly support a lot of the things ADAPT has worked for," said an MDA volunteer who had ALS. "But I wish they'd be more concerned with what I want: a cure."[30] MDA's task force of adults with neuromuscular conditions more pointedly accused the activists of having "no regard for human suffering."[31] It was not just people with usually fatal conditions such as ALS who said they hoped for a cure. The majority of MDA constituents had serious but nonlethal neuromuscular diseases, and many of them, on and off the telethon, said they hoped someday to see a cure.

Activists repeatedly pointed out that the cure never came.[32] That criticism implied that if cure were, in fact, at hand, disability rights advocacy would be irrelevant. Still, they were trying to make a practical point about how one approached one's life. As in their criticism of actor Christopher Reeve's quest for a cure for spinal cord injuries, activists urged that individuals with any sort of illness, injury, or impairment should not wait around for an always elusive cure that supposedly would restore their predisability identities. They should instead not merely adjust to their situation, but affirm themselves in positive ways as people with disabilities, incorporating their disabilities into their identities and embracing disability community. Still, some people with major and progressive diseases regarded this exhortation as denying the seriousness of their medical conditions.

The differentiation between sickness/illness and handicap/disability made by both sides was problematic. First, it failed to note that research and treatments provided not only by MDA but any of the telethon-producing charities achieved, not cures, but improvements in health and functioning. On and off the telethon, people with neuromuscular diseases attested that MDA's services helped make it possible for them to have their families and homes and careers.[33] In 1993 a member of the Task Force on Public Awareness proclaimed: "It's through MDA that people with neuromuscular illnesses are able to live and indeed thrive with neuromuscular illness." From the mid-1990s on, living and thriving became a secondary theme of the telethon. As time went on, while many parents continued to talk only about their children's bleak future, a growing number on local segments spoke of their children living full lives with significant disabilities because of advances in medical treatments. And though the telethon continued to depict people with neuromuscular diseases as sick, MDA's informational materials often described them as having disabilities. The major telethon message remained the phantasmic quest for cure, but it overshadowed the most significant results of medical progress: Growing numbers of sick people were living—and thriving—as people with disabilities.[34]

At a deeper level, the dichotomization between sick and disabled people implicitly assumed that one could not simultaneously seek medical treatment (including cure) and demand civil rights. At the heart of the telethon controversy stood the false assumption that illness (or impairment) and injustice were mutually exclusive framings.[35] For some individuals, disability was mainly a different way of functioning, but for others, medical services and continued advances in medical research and treatments were essential. Contrary to some disability studies scholars' claims, they were not compelled by a cultural imperative to achieve an ideal of bodily perfection. They were laboring to maintain their health and enhance their functioning. Would it have been possible to affirm that people with disabilities did not need to be cured to have meaningful lives while acknowledging that health-care services were vital to many? The complex thinking of disabled writers such as philosopher Susan Wendell and psychologist Carol J. Gill laid the foundations for this more mature framing (see chapter 12).[36]

Some people with neuromuscular diseases and other conditions such as spinal cord injuries—Christopher Reeve became the prime example—did cling to the fantasy of cures. And parents of children with neuromuscular and other disabilities were urged to feed on those false hopes. While the MDA and Arthritis Foundation Telethons projected the chimera of cures through medical treatments, the Easter Seals and UCP Telethons propagated medical rehabilitation that enforced an ideology of overcoming and compulsory able-bodiedness. Both formulations pledged a medical restoration of some semblance of normality. But in fact, while many people might have wanted normalizing cures, they were relying on medical advances to support them in raising families and building careers and pursuing their daily lives. Those services were helping them deal with disease or injuries and live with disabilities. All of this indicated that at the turn of the century, personal and societal perceptions of what it meant to be sick or disabled were confused and in flux.

Insofar as activists avoided grappling with the bodily experiences of illness and impairment, they effectively surrendered those major areas of disabled people's lives to practitioners of the medical model. Sidestepping the daily experience of many people with disabilities, they unconsciously abdicated to the very ideologies and practices they condemned. Fearful of confirming the medical model, they failed to uphold fully the authority of people with disabilities over all aspects of their lives, including the physiological, medical, and functional. At the same time, these inadequacies of analysis and advocacy neglected to examine, let alone affirm, disabled people's distinctive complex embodiment.[37] The disability rights movement and disability studies need an explanation of disability experience in its totality.

This afterword must offer closing reflections not only on a book but also on a life. As Paul Longmore's close friend and colleague for almost thirty years, I feel a responsibility to address the fact that this book ends where he left it, without the carefully honed concluding statements we had come to expect from him.

As I have considered what to say about this, and have struggled with my own longing for more words from Paul, I recall the jarring image of his first book *The Invention of George Washington* melting into flames on a barbecue grill. As he chronicled in a later book, *Why I Burned My Book and Other Essays on Disability*, Paul regretfully but strategically decided to burn the hard-won product of his doctoral research in public protest of a Social Security policy that would cut funding for his ventilator and other disability-related needs if he accepted royalties from book sales. He burned the book to protest not only the specific policy that deemed book royalties unearned income for individuals receiving disability benefits but also its broader implication that people with disabilities are not likely to produce significant intellectual work. Crudely paraphrased, disabled people don't write books. Paul's use of street theater dramatized that demeaning pronouncement in extreme form. Its injustice and the power of his response to it are now both burned into our history. His protest sparked national collaborative activism leading to a policy revision, referred to as the Longmore Amendment, that allows individuals receiving Supplementary Security Income (SSI) to count royalties as earned income for their intellectual work. The image of the book in flames stays with me as an unforgettable symbol of scholarship and activism.

The scholarly part of Paul's identity is undeniable. When colleagues comment on his body of work, they are virtually unanimous in praising his rigor and noting both the painstaking depth and unexpected breadth of his research. They mention his persistent examination of details, his encyclopedic memory, his search for alternate explanations, his willingness to explore and then master knowledge from areas of history beyond his specializations, and his reach across disciplinary boundaries. One phrase that I have heard repeatedly from scholars who knew Paul's approach to research is, "He never settled." He refused to accept partial access to sources, he took nothing at face value, and he constantly challenged himself and others to think more deeply and to examine more evidence.

Paul worked on what we all knew as "the telethon book" during most of the years I knew him. I doubt that I will ever be able to relax on Labor Day, not because I associate it with the vexing MDA Labor Day Telethon but because of Paul's annual phone call to his friends across the country directing us to set up our videotape recorders at the beginning of our local telethon program, run them through the night, capture as many hours as possible until Lewis bawled out the closing theme song and our local hosts signed off, and then ship the multiple videocassettes to him as soon as we could. We never really knew how many individuals Paul conscripted into this project or how many hours of tape we contributed collectively to the cause. We were, after all, willing enablers, if not collateral victims, of his seemingly endless examination of the telethon and of the thoroughness of his methods.

He agreed with anti-telethon protesters that the images of disability exploited in charitable solicitation were damaging to disabled people, but he recognized something else that compelled him to study the phenomenon intensively and to excavate its roots: It was quintessentially American. As a dedicated US historian and disability studies scholar, he could not turn away. He felt driven to scrutinize telethon programs minute by minute, reflecting on recurrent themes, and processing ideas with colleagues from multiple disciplines and disability standpoints.

Although I had talked with Paul frequently about the book through the years, I could not imagine how he would convert all those recordings and related reading and discussions into a coherent analysis worthy of his own standards. I did know, though, that he was proud of the research and writing of this book—something that I found deeply comforting in the days after his death. Paul mentioned that he thought advocates expecting extensive discussion of how charities have oppressed Americans with disabilities might be surprised by the book. Although he meticulously documented the telethons' exploitation, exhibition, and invalidation of people with disabilities, Paul's primary focus was not specific charities or their promoters. Rather, he critically analyzed the American ideologies and systems that fostered the telethon as a social/cultural phenomenon of its time. In effect, his work suggests that protesters might need to reassess their target—that they have been up against much more than Jerry Lewis and demeaning stereotypes. They have been battling entrenched national beliefs and interests. Paul wondered how telethon protesters would respond to his analysis. Sadly, he did not get to engage in the dialogue with them that he believed might result.

As Paul had predicted but did not get to witness fully, disability telethons have receded from view in recent years, giving way to other forms of fundraising, such as benefit concerts and walk-a-thons, that emphasize life potential for adults and children with disabilities rather than tragic limitations. The Arthritis Foundation, United Cerebral Palsy, and National Easter Seal Society ended their national telethons in the mid-1990s, but a few affiliates still produce local televised fund drives referred to as "telethons." The Muscular Dystrophy Association (MDA) dropped Jerry Lewis as the host of its telethon in 2011, and in 2012 it shortened the program and titled it *MDA Show of Strength*. Although the word "telethon" was not used in 2012, it reappeared in 2013 and 2014 when the format changed to a two-hour special program airing only nationally on ABC.

Some observers attribute the decline of telethons to the impact of the post-ADA disability rights movement and anti-telethon activism. Others link it to general patterns of reduced donation, increased production costs, dwindling interest in telethon entertainment, and changes in public habits, such as the declining use of landline phones for pledge communications. As summed up by the manager of an Arthritis Foundation branch, "The event has simply run its course." In any case, efforts to increase awareness and to improve supports for living with a disability have substantially replaced appeals for pity in many disability-related fundraising campaigns.

Whether these developments signal the end of an era or a momentary pause to retool, the telethon remains a fascinating and revealing public phenomenon for scholars to examine. As Paul explained in this book's introduction, he was committed to employing disability as a useful and underacknowledged vantage point to illuminate American history. His research revealed that the telethon's ritualized invalidation of life with disability bolstered self-validation of "the able-bodied." In addition to selling beer and Harleys, telethons sold American ideals about superiority and inferiority, public and private, compassion and duty. Paul devoted much of his life to the study of this phenomenon not simply because Americans learned many of their dismal views of disability from watching telethons but because telethons helped define what it meant to qualify as worthy citizens.

The array of examples in the book and their scrupulous placement in his analysis aptly convey Paul's lifelong approach to research. Believing that evidence should carry the weight of an argument, he was known for using compelling examples, from the poignant to the absurd, to substantiate and enliven his points. He noticed the significance of snippets of conversations, written passages, actions, and interactions that might seem unremarkable to most of us, but when we revisited them in the context of his narrative, they would become fascinating.

To the list of Paul's strengths as a scholar, I would definitely add insight. He stood out as the person in the room who saw matters in a different light, revealing underlying connections and articulating them so clearly that they seemed suddenly self-evident. Because others respected his insight, he often found himself in the middle of debates with multiple parties vying for his support. Whether he was invited to contribute his viewpoint to a special journal issue on a controversial topic or to weigh in on the best plan for a conference program or campus initiative, Paul rarely threw his support behind any of the options presented. Instead, he characteristically presented an original position, pointing out issues and offering conclusions that were not on the table. It was common for his ideas to raise the dialogue to new levels of consensus. This was vintage Paul Longmore.

Personally and intellectually, Paul always remained down to earth, his penetrating thinking grounded in the life experiences of real people. This quality and his steadfast curiosity equipped him for a career in history and also positioned him to excel and lead in interdisciplinary disability studies where activism and scholarship are expected to synergize. Paul's commitment to activism was as passionate as his insistence on scrupulous scholarship. His capacity to pursue both without diminishing the strength of either stands as a formative model in disability studies. He embodied the principle that knowledge is power and lived by the proposition that power should be used for good. As the son of an evangelical minister, Paul had been taught to plan a life of important accomplishment and service to others. Even before he contracted polio at age 7, Paul's parents had urged him to engage in work with social impact. He had always been introspective and remembered spending hours "just thinking" since he was 5 years old. Acquiring a disability offered no dispensation regarding his mission. In the aftermath of polio, he continued to rely on his keen observation and deep reflection to understand the social world and his place in it. In many ways, his family's religious life had already placed him outside of mainstream America. As a young disabled man and nascent scholar, he conceptualized parallels between the social devaluation of "the handicapped" and prejudice toward people of color and other socially marginalized communities. His signature complex of values—moral commitment, sociopolitical activism, and intellectual integrity—coalesced in early adulthood and guided his work for the rest of his days.

It was in graduate school that he began to appreciate disability as a neglected lens for examining the nation's early struggles for liberty and justice. These ideas directed Paul on the path to excavating and advancing the new disability history—a history that acknowledged disability as complex, multiply determined, socially contingent, and informative, and that recognized disabled people as agents rather than simply patients or victims. He also became an influential voice in the field, disability studies. Although more than three decades old now, disability studies is still in dynamic growth, both in terms of the numbers of people and programs involved in it and in terms of its developing theory base. Early work in disability studies emphasized analysis at the level of societal systems, thereby consciously breaking with medicine's traditional focus on individuals and their bodies. Paul challenged that exclusive emphasis on systems rather than individuals in two significant ways that have helped shape disability studies scholarship.

First, although he produced incisive social and cultural analyses, he was also interested in studying society through its impact on individuals. That explains his frequent citation of work in psychology and his ongoing dialogue with colleagues in disability studies who work in the counseling fields. His own essays on the disabled leftist early-twentieth-century intellectual Randolph Bourne demonstrate how much social history Paul gleaned from the study of one life.

Second, Paul refused to downplay the importance of embodied difference and impairment-related difficulty in the experience of disability. He did not worry that frankness about such matters would undermine the social and cultural work of disability studies; he believed instead that it would lead to disability theorizing that encompassed and honored a fuller range of experiences of disabled people. He also felt that acknowledging the integrity of disability experiences—embodied as well as sociopolitical—supported the development of group identity, community, and alternative values as outgrowths of an evolving affirmative disability consciousness.

Although he had known few persons with disabilities until adulthood and had forged no connections with fellow disabled students in college, Paul's later struggles against employment barriers and restrictive health-care policies brought him into contact with others experiencing similar injustices. Individuals in the polio survivors' network, independent living advocates, and disability rights activists became his mentors, comrades, and trusted friends. He came to value his membership in the politically minded, active disability community of California and, later, his relationships with other disabled scholars from around the world. Despite health constraints, he rarely turned down an opportunity to address an audience of disabled people. He referred to such groups as his "brothers and sisters." Some of my favorite moments were watching Paul speak to a room full of disabled people about the meaning of their experience and the historical determinants of their societal problems. He framed facets of that experience in a way most had never heard before. You could almost feel air currents in the room from all the heads nodding in agreement. He spoke from his mind and heart, inspiring in his audience both ideas and action.

In addition to his role as scholar/activist, another image that I hold dear is Paul as mentor. I can picture him in the hallway at a conference or in a classroom or at a dinner. He is leaning forward attentively, asking questions in a soft voice, encouraging a young person to express views, concerns, or hopes that will become the critical first step to a clearer identity, a decision, or a sense of future possibilities. Despite his range of commitments, Paul seemed always to make time to teach and guide the next generation. As a historian, he was humble in his assessment of the lasting importance of any single individual's contribution to evolving knowledge and humanity. He expected ideas to change, and he enjoyed transmitting methods of discovery to younger scholars to launch them toward their development of new theories and expanded knowledge bases. I sometimes envied his capacity to be tenaciously committed to his ideas and yet able to accept their inevitable revision or replacement by thinkers to come. Paul's mentorship of scholars and activists fulfilled and energized him.

Incredibly, despite Paul's life of accomplishment and his decades of struggling against barriers to an academic career, to having his scholarship counted as work, and, before that, even to attending graduate school, he was in the midst of another battle for justice at the time of his death. He had just been awarded a fellowship to write a book on the disability rights movement, but a government policy interprets fellowship awards received by disabled people as fortuitous prizes rather than earned income. Again, he was facing a choice between funding for the disability-related services he needed to live and his life's work. His appeal of the fellowship policy was, like this book's conclusion, interrupted by his death. Significantly, as Paul documented in the book, the idea that individuals with extensive physical impairments cannot work or contribute to society was a damaging misconception broadcast by telethons.

The enduring images of Paul as scholar/activist and as mentor help to mitigate the sting of this book's abrupt ending, mostly because they inspire us to view it differently. As it stands, the book beckons us to make more connections and draw our own insights from the rigorous work it presents. It gives us space to build on its intellectual foundation and reminds us never to "settle" in our search for answers. Realistically believing that knowledge production moves forward by relay rather than static achievement, Paul, the scholar/activist and mentor, might have smiled at the irony yet elegance of this outcome. It is a strong nudge to carry on his work, another call from Paul alerting us to our tasks, this time charging us to dismantle constructed impediments that still limit the visible and full participation of people with disabilities in society and urging us to continue excavating, writing, and teaching the new disability history well past the time that it ceases to be new.

Carol J. Gill
Professor in the Department of Disability and Human Development
University of Illinois at Chicago

{ NOTES }

Introduction

1. "Telethon Will Seek Funds to Combat Blood Disease," *New York Times*, 1 July 1971; "400 to Aid Telethon for Mental Health," *New York Times*, 2 April 1959.

2. "Telethon for Quake Victims," *New York Times*, 14 February 1976; Larry Finley, "Telethon Raises Relief Funds for Puerto Rico," *Chicago Sun-Times*, 25 September 1989, http://www.highbeam.com/ (accessed 1 July 2009); "Nixon Calls Bob Hope, Lauds Drive," *Washington Post*, 25 August 1969; "$2-Million Is Pledged to Aid Flood Victims," *New York Times*, 24 July 1972; Thomas J. Tarpey, "River Grove Flood Telethon Hits $15,000," *Chicago Sun-Times*, 4 November 1986, http://www.highbeam.com (accessed 1 July 2009).

3. "Democrats End TV Fund Appeal; 19-Hour Telethon May Yield $5-Million Toward Debt," *New York Times*, 10 July 1972; Eileen Shanahan, "Democratic Show Earns Millions; Pledges in Telethon Likely to Halve Party's Debt $4-Million Last Year Pledges In State," *New York Times*, 17 September 1973; "Democratic Telethon Yields $4-Million Net," *New York Times*, 9 July 1974; Warren Weaver Jr., "Democrats' Telethon Is Short of Its Goal," *New York Times*, 28 July 1975.

4. "Telethon for College Fund," *Los Angeles Times*, 8 July 1980.

5. "5-Hour Dodgerthon: Notables Back Prop. B on TV," *Los Angeles Times*, 2 June 1958; "Telethon to Aid Blind: 16-Hour Show over WATV Will Feature Stars of Theatre," *New York Times*, 3 November 1953; Cecil Smith, "Telethon to Aid ACT in Its Hour of Crisis," *Los Angeles Times*, 29 July 1968; "A Telethon in Miami to Raise Funds to Help Cuban Refugees," *New York Times*, 1 December 1973; Frank Burgos, "N. Chicago Planning School-Aid Telethon," *Chicago Sun-Times*, 25 May 1993, http://www.highbeam.com (accessed 1 July 2009); "Pacers Reach Goal with Telethon," *New York Times*, 5 July 1977.

6. Paul Hoffmann, "Everybody Gets into Kingston Act: Telethon with a Variety of Talent Aids Ulster Fund," *New York Times*, 5 December 1966.

7. "Telethon Rings Up 'No Sale,'" *New York Times*, 27 November 1975.

8. Jack Gould, "Radio and Television: Hope and Crosby, Latter in His TV Debut, Receive $1,000,020 in Pledges on 'Telethon' for Olympics," *New York Times*, 23 June 1952; Thomas M. Pryor, "Crosby TV Debut Test for Movies; His Telethon with Bob Hope for Olympic Squad Seen as Hint of Things to Come," *New York Times*, 21 June 1952. Critically examining the power of the still-new medium, the theatrical motion picture *A Face in the Crowd* recounted the rise of a TV demagogue, Larry "Lonesome" Rhodes (Andy Griffith). In one scene that illustrates his growing power, he hosts a national telethon for "Crippled Children of America." *A Face in the Crowd*, directed by Elia Kazan, Newtown Productions, 1957.

9. Scott Simon, National Public Radio, 3 September 1989, weekend edition.

10. Mitchell Landsberg, "Comic Changed the Way America Gives," *Associated Press*, 1 September 1984.

11. Bob Greene, "Jerry Lewis: On Camera, on the Spot," *Los Angeles Times*, 7 September 1981.

12. I borrow this notion of the pedagogic function of a public space from Susan Schweik's important historical study of late-nineteenth and early-twentieth-century unsightly beggar ordinances, *The Ugly Laws: Disability in Public* (New York: New York University Press, 2009), 89.

13. This theoretical thinking is rooted in Karl Mannheim, *Ideology and Utopia: An Introduction to the Sociology of Knowledge* (1929; repr., New York: Harcourt and Brace, 1936); Karl Mannheim, *Essays on the Sociology of Knowledge,* ed. Paul Kecskemeti (1952; repr., London: Routledge and Kegan Paul, 1964); Erving Goffman, *Frame Analysis* (New York: Harper & Row, 1974), as well as recent work in cultural studies. See Paula Saukko, *Doing Research in Cultural Studies: An Introduction to Classical and New Methodological Approaches* (London: SAGE, 2003); Lawrence Grossberg, *Bringing It All Back Home: Essays on Cultural Studies* (Durham, N.C.: Duke University Press, 1997); Richard Johnson et al., *The Practice of Cultural Studies* (London: SAGE, 2004).

14. Longmore constantly struggled to define and bring greater nuance to these opposing views, to the point that this manuscript never spelled them out, even as he used the terms "medical model" and "minority model" in a number of places. For this reason, we opted to insert definitions from his *Why I Burned My Book*, 4, 205, knowing that his thinking had evolved since 2003 when these were initially drafted.—Ed.

15. I recount in detail the experience briefly summarized in the next three paragraphs in my essay "Why I Burned My Book" in *Why I Burned My Book and Other Essays on Disability* (Philadelphia: Temple University Press, 2003), 230–59.

16. My work in these areas includes: Early American history: "The Enigma of George Washington: How Did the Man Become the Myth," *Reviews in American History* 13, no. 2 (June 1985): 184–90; *The Invention of George Washington* (Berkeley: University of California Press, 1988); " 'All Matters and Things Relating to Religion and Morality': The Virginia Burgesses' Committee for Religion, 1769 to 1775," *Journal of Church and State* 38, no. 4 (Autumn 1996): 775–98; "From Supplicants to Constituents: Petitioning by Virginia Parishioners, 1701–1775," *Virginia Magazine of History and Biography* 103, no. 4 (October 1995): 407–42; " 'They . . . speak better English than the English do': Colonialism and the Origins of National Linguistic Standardization in America," *Early American Literature* 40, no. 2 (Summer 2005): 279–314; " 'Good English without idiom or tone': The Colonial Origins of American Speech," *Journal of Interdisciplinary History* 37, no. 4 (Spring 2007): 513–42. Disability history/disability studies: *The New Disability History: American Perspectives,* ed. Paul Longmore and Lauri Umansky (New York: New York University Press, 2001); *Why I Burned My Book and Other Essays on Disability* (Philadelphia: Temple University Press, 2003); Paul Longmore and Paul Steven Miller, " 'A Philosophy of Handicap': The Origins of Randolph Bourne's Radicalism," *Radical History Review* 94 (Winter 2006): 59–83; "Disability Rights Activism," in *Speaking Out: Activism and Protest in the 1960s and 1970s,* ed. Heather Thompson (Upper Saddle River, N.J.: Prentice-Hall, 2009), 115–24; " Making Disability an Essential Part of American History," *OAH Magazine of History* 23, no. 3 (July 2009): 11–15.

17. Longmore's *Why I Burned My Book and Other Essays on Disability* explores these intersections between scholarship and activism.—Ed.

18. Paul Longmore started teaching at San Francisco State in the fall of 1992.—Ed.

Chapter 1

1. Berle's manager Irving Gray was credited with the idea for the fundraising show. The second lasted nineteen-and-a-half hours. The third ran twenty-two hours and aired on forty-three NBC affiliates. The fourth and last Runyon Fund Telethon in 1952 saw a sharp drop-off in donations. "Radio and Television; WPIX to Show Eclipse of Moon Tomorrow, in Cooperation with Hayden Planetarium," *New York Times*, 11 April 1949; "Berle's Television Show Nets Million," *Washington Post*, 11 April 1949; Sonia Stein, "Berle Proves He's Real One-man Gang," *Washington Post*, 17 April 1949; Sidney Lohman, "News of TV and Radio: Only Six Video Stations Made Money in 1949," *New York Times*, 23 April 1950; "Berle to Do Better," *Washington Post*, 23 April 1950; Sonia Stein, "Milton Got 10,000 Phone Calls an Hour," *Washington Post*, 2 May 1950; "Berle Aids Cancer Fight; 22-Hour Non-Stop Television Program Under Way," *New York Times*, 10 June 1951; "Many Aid Cancer Fund; $1,127,211 in Pledges Received on 22-Hour TV Show," *New York Times*, 11 June 1951; "Berle Conducts Cancer Fund's Marathon TV," *Los Angeles Times*, 8 June 1952; "Television Highlights," *Washington Post*, 7 June 1952.

2. Sidney Lohman, "News and Notes from the Studios: End of the Telethons," *New York Times*, 1 February 1953.

3. Wayne Oliver, "Too Few Pay: Telethon Days Are Numbered," *Washington Post*, 20 July 1952; John Lester, "Radio and Television," *Chronicle-Telegram* (Elyria, Ohio), 9 November 1953.

4. The National Society for Crippled Children was founded in 1921, renamed itself the National Society for Crippled Children and Adults in 1944, and became the National Easter Seals Society in 1979, http://www.fundinguniverse.com/company-histories/Easter-Seals-Inc-Company-History.html (accessed 17 June 2009); "What Is the History of the Arthritis Foundation?," http://www.arthritis.org/history.php (accessed 20 August 2005); http://www.ucp.org/ucp_general.cfm/1/3/42/42-6587/216 (accessed 4 August 2003); Peter Romanofsky and Clarke A. Chambers, ed., *The Greenwood Encyclopedia of American Institutions: Social Service Organizations*, 2 vols. (Westport, Conn.: Greenwood Press, 1978), Vol. 1: 417–20; Vol. 2: 527–31, 698–700.

5. Among its guest stars were the comedy team of Dean Martin and Jerry Lewis. "Radio and Television; Stars of Entertainment World Take Part in Cerebral Palsy Fund Show Tonight," *New York Times*, 10 June 1950. One of the founders of UCP was Leonard Goldenson, who led the Paramount movie theater chain. His theaters had worked with the March of Dimes. In 1951 he became head of the new American Broadcasting Company (ABC). Leonard H. Goldenson with Marvin J. Wolf, *Beating the Odds* (New York: Charles Scribner Sons, 1991), 85–7.

6. United Cerebral Palsy, "Mission & History: The 1950's," http://www.ucp.org/ucp_generaldoc.cfm/1/3/42/42-6587/216 (accessed 18 June 2009).

7. "Broader Fight Set on Cerebral Palsy: $2,100,000 Obtained in U.S. Drive is 100% Above the Total of Last Year," *New York Times*, 24 October 1951.

8. Walter Ames, "Zsa Zsa Returns to Bachelor's Haven Tomorrow; Procession of Stars on KECA Telethon," *Los Angeles Times*, 24 May 1952; "Stars Give Talent on TV Palsy Benefit Marathon," *Los Angeles Times*, 25 May 1952; "Top Sports Figures Appear on Benefit Telethon Today," *Los Angeles Times*, 25 May 1952; Sidney Lohman, "News of TV and Radio: New Pre-School Age Show," *New York Times*, 16 November 1952; "All-Night Show Saturday to Benefit Cerebral Palsy," *Washington Post*, 14 June 1953; on San Francisco

and Los Angeles telethons, "$500,333 'Telethon' Pledges," *New York Times*, 29 June 1953; on a Philadelphia telethon, *New York Times*, 16 November 1953; on a New York City telethon, "Radio-TV Notes," *New York Times*, 26 November 1953; John Crosby, "Mostly It Takes Stamina to Handle a Telethon," *Washington Post*, 3 December 1953; "WRCA to Present a Review of Past: Events on Particular Days Will Be Summarized—Aide Leaves 'Tonight,' " *New York Times*, 5 October 1957; on a Jackson, Mississippi, telethon, "Eddie Hodges Has His Day Today," *New York Times*, 19 May 1958; UCP of Nebraska, "About UCP," http:// www.ucp.org/ucp_localsub.cfm/96/8535/13824 (accessed 17 June 2009); Paul Gardner, "Marathon '64—It's a Telethon," *New York Times*, 5 January 1964.

9. Crosby, "Mostly It Takes Stamina To Handle a Telethon"; "Dennis James Will Host CP Telethon," *Los Angeles Times*, 3 June 1974; "Cerebral Palsy Fund to Mark 25th Anniversary on Telethon," *Los Angeles Times*, 13 June 1975; "Dennis James: The 50 Million Dollar Man for Cerebral Palsy," *Los Angeles Times*, 16 September 1976; Myrna Oliver, "Dennis James Dies after Long TV Career," *Houston Chronicle*, 5 June 1997, http://www. chron.com (accessed 21 July 2009).

10. For example, see "Polio Dimes Drive Lags," *Abilene Reporter-News* (Abilene, Tex.), 19 January 1955; "Hirsch to Be on Telethon," *Wisconsin State Journal*, 8 January 1967; Amy S. Rosenberg, "Pinky Goes Gold; Pinky Kravitz, on and off the Air, Has Been Mr. Atlantic City for Half a Century," *Philadelphia Inquirer*, 2 August 2007, *Inquirer Daily Magazine*; "Bright & Brief," *Associated Press*, 22 June 1984; "Crippled Children's Society Gets New Program Challenge," *Mason City Globe-Gazette* (Mason City, Iowa), 18 May 1955; "TV Listings," *News Tribune* (Fort Pierce, Fla.), 15 April 1963; "Telethon Show Earns $66,700," *Southern Illinoisan* (Carbondale, Ill.), 25 November 1964; "Easter Seal Telethon Set," *Times Recorder* (Zanesville, Ohio), 26 March 1970.

11. See, for example, on the Virginia statewide arthritis telethon, "Arthritis Victim to Appear on TV," *Progress-Index* (Petersburg-Colonial Heights, Va.), 18 March 1958.

12. "Star-Studded Telethon to Aid Muscular Distrophy [*sic*] Research," *Washington Post*, 27 December 1952; "Muscular Dystrophy Fund Hits $52,000; Children Aid," *Washington Post*, 29 December 1952; *Washington Post*, 4 January 1953.

13. ABC fed it to 133 TV stations and 365 radio stations. Most sources incorrectly report that Lewis first hosted an MDA fundraiser in 1956. Romanofsky and Chambers, ed., *Greenwood Encyclopedia of American Institutions*, Vol. 1: 418; Lohman, "News and Notes from the Studios"; "On the Radio," *New York Times*, 25 November 1953; "On Television," *New York Times*, 25 November 1953. One source reported that movie industry executives pressured Martin and Lewis to reduce their muscular dystrophy fundraiser from a full-length telethon to a two-hour show because "box-office receipts take a nose-dive everytime" the charity shows aired. Hal Humphrey, "Film Czars Try to Pull Stars off Telethons," *Oakland Tribune*, 18 November 1953. In 1952 Martin and Lewis hosted a sixteen-and-a-half-hour local telethon in New York City for a cardiac hospital. "$1,148,419 Pledged to Heart Hospital: Martin and Lewis 16 1/2-Hour TV 'Telethon' Attracts Star Guests and Contributions," *New York Times*, 16 March 1952. In 1952 they also appeared on the Los Angeles cerebral palsy telethon. Ames, "Zsa Zsa Returns to Bachelor's Haven Tomorrow." Before it launched its first telethon, MDA, like the Arthritis and Rheumatism Foundation, used radio for fundraising. "Muscular Dystrophy Documentary: 'Johnny 100,000,' with Chester Morris-WOR," under "On the Radio," *New York Times*, 20 December 1952.

14. It was broadcast on WABD in New York City, the flagship station of the Dumont network, which disbanded the following year. Val Adams, "Musicals Slated by N.B.C. and C.B.S.: Song and Dance Shows Will Be Featured Next Season in Networks' 'Spectaculars,'" *New York Times*, 29 July 1955; Val Adams, "Ban on Pay Video Urged by C.B.S.; Network Seeks Dismissal by F.C.C. of Petitions for Box-Office Television," *New York Times*, 8 September 1955; "19-Hour Appeal on TV; $200,006 in Pledges Made for Muscular Dystrophy Fund," *New York Times*, 12 September 1955.

15. "On Television," *New York Times*, 29 June 1956; "On Television," *New York Times*, 30 June 1956.

16. "On Television," *New York Times*, 30 November 1957; "MD Drive Names Richard Rodgers," *Bridgeport Sunday Post* (Bridgeport, Conn.), 5 October 1958; "$575,208 Pledged on Telethon," *New York Times*, 23 November 1959; http://www.mdausa.org/telethon/2002_info.cfm?inc=faq (accessed 18 July 2003); two-hour MDA show called *Carnival of Stars* under "Television," *New York Times*, 18 September 1960 (accessed 12 June 2009); for a one-hour MDA program with guests that included Johnny Mathis, Connie Stevens, Richard Boone, George Raft, Donald O'Connor, and Paul Newman, see *High Hopes* under "Television," *New York Times*, 15 November 1961; "Lewis Tapes Show for Free Distribution," *Salt Lake Tribune*, 3 October 1961; a one-hour benefit show for MDA under "Television," *New York Times*, 24 November 1962. In 1964 MDA presented only a half-hour film entitled *Ten Pounds of Patience*. See "Television," *New York Times*, 8 August 1964. From the late 1950s through the late 1960s, Lewis appeared on and even MCed telethons for other causes, cohosting Los Angeles benefit shows for "Mental Health" and the Olympics. Jean McMurphy, "Telethon Draws Army of Stars," *Los Angeles Times*, 25 May 1958; "Olympic Fund Will Benefit from Show," *Los Angeles Times*, 20 May 1968. See, for example, "To Raise Funds Local Family on 'Telethon' at G. Rapids," *News-Palladium* (Benton Harbor, Mich.), 26 June 1953. The Berrien County Muscular Dystrophy committee produced a sixteen-hour local telethon in Grand Rapids; "Dystrophy Drive," *Kokomo Tribune* (Kokomo, Ind.), 24 May 1955. New Mexico held an eighteen-hour statewide telethon; "Dystrophy Support," *El Paso Herald-Post* (El Paso, Tex.), 11 September 1959; "Pledge Center to Support Telethon," *Wellington Leader* (Wellington, Tex.), 3 September 1961. See also "1979 Florida Arthritis Telethon," *St. Petersburg Independent* (St. Petersburg, Fla.), 27 January 1979, http://news.google.com/newspapers (accessed 10 June 2009).

17. "Television This Week," *New York Times*, 4 September 1966; "Television," *New York Times*, 4 September 1967; "Jerry Lewis Meets Goal of Telethon," *Los Angeles Times*, 3 September 1969; "Monday Highlights: Monday Programs," *Washington Post*, 31 August 1969; "Weekend TV: Telethon for Dystrophy," *Los Angeles Times*, 5 September 1970; "Marathon Benefit for Muscular Dystrophy," *Los Angeles Times*, 4 September 1971; Mitchell Landsberg, "Comic Changed the Way America Gives," *Associated Press*, 1 September 1984.

18. In addition to the news reports cited below, I obtained the number of TV markets and estimates on the size of the audiences directly from the charities in 1996. The number of hours each telethon was broadcast varied in different markets, depending on how much time local stations were willing to sell. The Arthritis Foundation Telethon was broadcast for up to eight hours, while the other three shows topped out at twenty-one to twenty-two hours for their national broadcasts. Some local broadcasts ran even longer. In 1998 WMAZ in Macon, Georgia, extended the MDA Telethon to twenty-four hours, going on the air one hour early and ending ninety minutes after the national broadcast. Joseph

Maar, "Network for a Day," *Television Broadcast* 21, no. 8 (August 1998): 18. In addition, one needs to distinguish between the number of households to which the programs were available and the number of households estimated to have actually tuned in. For example, in 1993, UCP overnight host Marvin Scott announced that some 22 million households watched that telethon at some point; the following year he put that figure at 21 million households. On the UCP Telethon, see "Weekend Telethon Raises More Than $20 Million for Cerebral Palsy," *Associated Press*, 23 January 1983. On the Easter Seals Telethon, see "Easter Seals Raises Record Contributions in Telethon," *Associated Press*, 9 March 1986; "Record $35.1 Million Raised for Handicapped in Easter Seal Telethon," *Associated Press*, 6 March 1988. On the MDA Telethon, see Landsberg, "Comic Changed the Way America Gives." On the Arthritis Telethon, see "People in the News," *Associated Press*, 28 April 1984: this broadcast went out to fifty stations; "People in the News," *Associated Press*, 26 April 1986: the broadcast reached seventy stations.

19. Jerry Buck, "Broadcaster Sees Trouble Ahead for Charity Telethons," *Associated Press*, 6 August 1987; Robert Macy, "Comic Upset by Rumors of Telethons' Demise," *Associated Press*, 8 August 1987; Robert Macy, "Entertainer Irate Over Telethon Flap," *Associated Press*, 9 May 1990; Kevin Brass, "Telethons Get a Busy Signal at the Networks Fund Raising: The Easter Seals Event Follows a Trend and Will Be Seen on Cable Tonight. Organizers Say That's Not So Bad—But the Revenue Tells a Different Story," *Los Angeles Times*, 7 March 1992, San Diego County edition. See also Steve Nidetz, "In the Late Hours, 'Rocky' to Beat Telethon to Punch," *Chicago Tribune*, 15 January 1995, Chicagoland final edition.

20. John Crosby, "Mostly It Takes Stamina to Handle a Telethon," *Washington Post*, 3 December 1953.

21. "Share-of-audience": the percentage of viewers watching a particular program out of the total audience tuned in to all television programs during a given time period. Kathleen Begley Brooks, "Dilemma for Dollars: Telethons Face a Battle as Jazzier Methods Raise Funds, and More Causes Seek Viewers' Donations," *Seattle Times*, 27 February 1986, third edition; "He's Hardly Mexican, But He'll Fake It," *St. Petersburg Times* (St. Petersburg, Fla.), 13 July 1987, metropolitan edition; Lisa Belkin, "Telethons Are Fading as Their Costs Increase," *New York Times*, 3 August 1987; Buck, "Broadcaster Sees Trouble Ahead for Charity Telethons"; Macy, "Comic Upset by Rumors of Telethons' Demise"; Brass, "Telethons Get a Busy Signal at the Networks Fund Raising"; Robert Epstein, "Telethons: More Than Pitches and Star Turns," *Los Angeles Times*, 16 January 1992, home edition; Raymond Roel, "The Future of Telethons: Cutting Through the Clutter," *Fundraising Management* 15, no. 2 (April 1984): 42–50.

22. "Names in the News," *Associated Press*, 3 September 1996; Paul Demko, "Shorter Telethon Raises Less Money for National Easter Seal Society," *Chronicle of Philanthropy* 9, no. 14 (1 May 1997): 28; Paul Demko, "Some Charities Pull the Plug on Telethons; Others Reduce Hours and Revise Formats," *Chronicle of Philanthropy* 9, no. 12 (3 April 1997): 30; David Robb, "Telethon Woes Squeeze Charity," *Hollywood Reporter* 351, no. 19 (20 February 1998): 1; James E. Williams, Jr., "Easter Seals Transforms the Telethon," *Fund Raising Management* 26, no. 7 (September 1995): 28–32; MDA reported the Nielsen ratings for its 2002 telethon as 60 million viewers. Muscular Dystrophy Association, http://www.mdausa.org/telethon/2002_info.cfm?inc=background (accessed 18 July 2003). In 2000 MDA fought the broadcast television networks' proposal to the Federal Communications

Commission "to lift the audience-reach cap from 35% of U.S. households." The deregula-
tory move would allow the networks to buy more local stations. *Broadcasting and Cable*,
an industry periodical, explained why MDA thought the plan would be "catastrophic" for
its telethon: "Virtually no O&Os [network owned-and-operated stations] air the telethon
because they don't want to preempt network programming and more stations will drop
the show if the nets are allowed to add more outlets, MDA says." "MDA Fights Dereg,"
Broadcasting and Cable 130, no. 48 (20 November 2000): 4.

Even after their full-length telethons stopped broadcasting, Easter Seals and UCP produced specials that were essentially truncated telethons, though they were not fundraisers. In 1997 the Easter Seals Society presented *Hollywood Salutes Easter Seals*. The program
celebrated the alleged integration of characters with disabilities in television series. A
Lifetime Achievement Award was presented posthumously to Gene Roddenberry, cre-
ator of *Star Trek* and its spinoffs. This segment praised the presence of the blind engineer
Geordi LaForge on *Star Trek: The Next Generation*, but failed to note that a sighted actor
played this blind man, a casting decision that would seem to have undercut Easter Seals
proclamation that anyone can do anything. Another segment lauded the incorporation
of other characters with disabilities in several TV series: Jake, a blind African American
vendor, on the sitcom *Becker*; Dr. Weaver, a physician who used a Canadian crutch, on *ER*;
a black wheelchair-riding convict on the HBO prison drama *Oz*; and "Lifeguard," a double amputee law-enforcement agent, on *Wiseguy*. Again, Easter Seals credited these programs for integrating the characters and making their disabilities incidental, but ignored
the casting of nondisabled actors in three of the four roles. Nor did Easter Seals recognize that the sighted characters on *Becker* constantly played pranks on Jake and made
stereotyped jokes about his blindness. The broadcast was characteristic of Hollywood's
penchant for self-congratulation. The stars who appeared continually praised television
and movies for the way they depicted people with disabilities. They seemed oblivious to
the stereotyping that had always been the most common feature of media portrayals.
The rest of the broadcast recycled all the elements of the old telethon: commercial spots
from Easter Seals' corporate sponsors linking product promotions to charitable donations; a segment on the current Easter Seals National Child Representatives; an update on
a former National Child Representative. The messages about people with disabilities were
identical to those on the Easter Seal telethons. The only thing missing was the pledges
from viewers. Michael Schneider, "Easter Seals Tries New 'Untelethon,'" *Electronic Media*
16, no. 46 (10 November 1997): 8, http://www.ebscohost.com (accessed 11 December 2008);
Cynthia Littleton, "Easter Seals Go Syndie: No More Telethon," *Variety*, 13 February 1998,
http://www.variety.com/index.asp?layout=upsell_article&articleID=VR1117467725&cs=1
(accessed 11 December 2008); Michael Schneider, "Easter Seals Will Hop to Pax for Fund-
Raiser, Bostwick to Host 'Swing,'" *Variety*, 16 February 2000, http://www.variety.com/
index.asp?layout=upsell_article&articleID=VR1117776503&cs=1(accessed 11 December
2008). Meanwhile, the Arthritis Foundation switched to an infomercial. Kim Cleland,
"Arthritis Foundation Turns to Infomercial," *Advertising Age* 68, no. 23 (9 June 1997): 14,
http://www.ebscohost.com (accessed 11 December 2008).

Early in the twenty-first century, some Easter Seals and UCP affiliates produced
local telethons, even combining forces to broadcast joint telethons. "Raising Funds,"
Pantagraph (Bloomington, Ill.), 1 April 1996; "WVBG Channels Make Slow Debut," *Times
Union* (Albany, N.Y.), 27 March 1998; Cathy Woodruff, "Cerebral Palsy Telethon Sets

$1.4M Record," *Times Union* (Albany, N.Y.), 25 January 1999; Kathleen Dooley, "'Annie' Star Chips In for CP Telethon," *Times Union* (Albany, N.Y.), 20 January 2000; Roma Khanna, "Telethon Tops $1.5M for a Record: The 41st Annual Cerebral Palsy Telethon Collected a Record $1,529,523 in Donations Sunday to Benefit the Center for the Disabled," *Times Union* (Albany, N.Y.), 8 January 2001; http://members.aol.com/msess1/dev.htm (accessed 4 August 2003); http://www.easterseals.org/whatwedo/events/telethon/default. asp?load=sponsorlevel3 (accessed 4 August 2003); http://www.confederationcentre.com/ eventdetail.asp?eventID=197 (accessed 4 August 2003); http://www.kyws.easterseals. org/new.htm (accessed 4 August 2003); http://www.timesleaderonline.com/community/ story/0331202003_com03_easterseals.asp (accessed 4 August 2003); http://www.eastersealsucp.org/index.php, (accessed 4 August 2003); "United Cerebral Palsy Telethon Scheduled Sunday," *State Journal-Register* (Springfield, Ill.), 10 January 2004; "United Cerebral Palsy Telethon This Sunday," *State Journal-Register* (Springfield, Ill.), 26 January 2008.

Twice in five years during the 1990s, MDA moved its telethon from Las Vegas to Los Angeles to save expenses. Nonetheless, it continued to see annual donations rise. "Jerry Lewis Telethon Moves to Los Angeles," *Chronicle of Philanthropy* 2, no. 8 (6 February 1990): 6; "Muscular Dystrophy Raises $44.2 Million," *Chronicle of Philanthropy* 2, no. 23 (18 September 1990): 7; "Muscular Dystrophy Moves Its Telethon," *Chronicle of Philanthropy* 7, no. 22 (27 July 1995): 25; "Muscular Dystrophy Raises $50.5 Million," *Chronicle of Philanthropy* 9, no. 23 (18 September 1997): 31.

The MDA Telethon was exported to other countries. MDA broadcast internationally on the World Wide Web. It also sought to develop foreign versions of its telethon. In addition, charities in Latin America and Western Europe produced their own telethons. Muscular Dystrophy Association News, "A Brief History," http://www. mdausa.org/news/030811telethonhistory.html (accessed 13 August 2003); "Worldwide Implications" under "Jerry's $53.1 Million Telethon Triumph! 'Let's Get Back to Work!,'" Muscular Dystrophy Association Publications, http://www.mda.org/publications/ Quest/q65telethon.html (accessed 13 January 2010); "Anne Murray on Lewis Telethon," *Globe and Mail*, 1 September 1978; Elaine Ganley, "France's Favorite American Comic Introduces the Telethon," *Associated Press*, 3 December 1987; "Jerry Lewis Telethon Raises More Than $35 Million in Pledged Donations," *Associated Press*, 6 December 1987; "Names in the News," *Associated Press*, 7 December 1987; Richard Boudreaux, "Chile's Telethon: A Touch of Melodrama Helps the Handicapped," *Associated Press*, 15 January 1986; United Press International, "French Pledge $33 Million to Jerry's Kids," *San Francisco Chronicle*, 7 December 1987, final edition; "1999 Jerry Lewis Telethon: World's First Live Multilingual Webcast," *PR Newswire*, 2 September 1999.

On health charity fundraising in the United Kingdom, see "Advertising by Medical Charities," *Lancet* 342, no. 8881 (13 November 1993): 1187–88, http://www.thelancet.com (accessed 13 January 2010).

23. Quoted in David Wagner, *What's Love Got to Do with It? A Critical Look at American Charity* (New York: New Press, 2000), 1–2. See also Michael D. Shear, "Bush, Obama Celebrate Volunteerism," *Washington Post*, 17 October 2009.

24. Arnaud C. Marts, *The Generosity of Americans: Its Source, Its Achievements* (Englewood Cliffs, N.J.: Prentice-Hall, 1966).

25. Richard Carter, *The Gentle Legions* (Garden City, N.Y.: Doubleday, 1961).

26. Appearing under various titles, this poem, whose author evidently remained anonymous, achieved enormous circulation throughout American culture.

27. Erma Bombeck, "Without Volunteers, A Lost Civilization," in *At Wit's End* (1965; repr., New York: Doubleday, 1967), reprinted in *America's Voluntary Spirit: A Book of Readings*, ed. Brian O'Connell (New York: Foundation Center, 1983), 27.

28. David L. Sills, *The Volunteers: Means and Ends in a National Organization* (1957; repr., New York: Arno Press, 1980), 18–19.

29. Robert H. Bremner, *American Philanthropy*, 2nd ed. (1960; repr., Chicago: University of Chicago Press, 1988), 1. Given Americans' self-perception of their generosity, it was perhaps significant that the United States ranked low in international giving. In 2007 it stood next to last among "rich" nations in the proportion of its gross national product that it devoted to aid for developing countries. Celia W. Dugger, "Norway Gives More to Fight Ills Overseas," *New York Times*, 30 September 2007, late edition.

30. Bremner, *American Philanthropy*, 1–2.

31. Carter, *The Gentle Legions*, 17–18. See, for example, Harold M. Schmeck Jr., "Polio Fund Plans Arthritis Drive: Expansion of Present Work Also Will Include Attack on Congenital Defects," *New York Times*, 23 July 1958; Philip Benjamin, "Charity Appeals Run into Revolts: Volunteers Set Up Combined Funds Over Opposition of Independent Agencies," *New York Times*, 16 June 1959.

32. Carter, *The Gentle Legions*, 26–7.

33. Carter, *The Gentle Legions*, 27–8.

34. Particularly pertinent here, people with disabilities figured frequently in his book as recipients of compassion. Robert Wuthnow, *Acts of Compassion: Caring for Others and Helping Ourselves* (Princeton, N.J.: Princeton University Press, 1991), 4–14, 18–46, 72–3, 196–7. See also Susan Jacoby, "Why Do We Donate? It's Personal," *New York Times*, 9 December 1997, late edition.

35. Jane and Michael Stern, *The Encyclopedia of Bad Taste* (New York: HarperCollins, 1990), 290–1. See also Harry Shearer, "Man Bites Town: 'Tis the (Telethon) Season[,] Don't Touch That Dial—It's Time Once Again for the Original Pay TV," *Los Angeles Times Magazine*, 2 September 1990, home edition; Walter Rosenthal, "Telethons: There's a Bottom-Line Value for Corporations," *Public Relations Journal* 37, no. 12 (December 1981): 22–3. See also John Lester, "Radio and Television," *Chronicle-Telegram* (Elyria, Ohio), 9 November 1953; Burt Prelutsky, "Nobody Loves a Critic," *Los Angeles Times*, 4 November 1973; Tom Shales, "Hamming It Up, But Good: Jerry Lewis and the Muscular Dystrophy Telethon: Jerry Lewis, Toting the Line for Love," *Washington Post*, 2 September 1980; Milton Rudich, "Tom Shales on the Telethon," *Washington Post*, 13 September 1980.

36. Carter, *Gentle Legions*, 242; Sterns, *Encyclopedia of Bad Taste*, 290–1. See also Tom Shales, "Hamming It Up, But Good"; Robert A. Jones, "On California: 'Jerry's Kids: It's a Pity but It Works,'" *Los Angeles Times*, 4 September 1991, home edition.

37. Bob Greene, "Jerry Lewis: On Camera, On the Spot," *Los Angeles Times*, 7 September 1981. See also Bill Barol, "I Stayed Up With Jerry," *Newsweek*, 21 September 1987; Tom Shales, "The Telethon's Touch: Jerry Lewis, With Sugar and Schmaltz," *Washington Post*, 7 September 1988.

38. Evan Kemp Jr., "Aiding the Disabled: No Pity, Please," *New York Times*, 3 September 1981, late edition.

39. Merle Curti, "Foreword," in Cutlip, *Fund Raising in the United States*, vii–viii, xii–xiii; Cutlip, *Fund Raising in the United States*, 3, 41, 45–8, 83–7, 157–202, 478–9, 488, 527, 529, 530–1, 538; F. Emerson Andrews, *Philanthropic Giving* (New York: Russell Sage Foundation, 1950), 136–8; Peter D. Hall, "The Welfare State and the Careers of Public and Private Institutions Since 1945," in *Charity, Philanthropy, and Civility in American History*, ed. Lawrence J. Friedman and Mark D. McGarvie (New York: Cambridge University Press, 2003), 373; Lawrence J. Friedman, "Philanthropy in America: Historicism and Its Discontents," in *Charity, Philanthropy, and Civility in American History*, 17; Charles A. Riley II, *Disability and the Media: Prescriptions for Change* (Hanover, N.H.: University Press of New England, 2005), 111.

40. Carter, *Gentle Legions*, 63–90; Cutlip, *Fund Raising in the United States*, 53–8, 83, 85, 87; Robert H. Bremner, *American Philanthropy*, 118–19, 133; Riley, *Disability and the Media*, 111.

41. Quotes from Cutlip, *Fund Raising in the United States*, 366, 368, 377–8. Other references, Cutlip, *Fund Raising in the United States*, 351–2, 359–61, 366–78, 388–90; Scott M. Cutlip, *The Unseen Power: Public Relations. A History* (Hillsdale, N.J.: Lawrence Erlbaum Associates, 1994), 560; Carter, *Gentle Legions*, 91–133, 242–3, especially 97, 106–10, and 242; Naomi Rogers, *Dirt and Disease: Polio Before FDR* (New Brunswick, N.J.: Rutgers University Press, 1992), 166–7, 170; Kathryn Black, *In the Shadow of Polio: A Personal and Social History* (Reading, Mass.: Addison-Wesley, 1996), 104–7; David Oshinsky, *Polio: An American Story* (New York, N.Y.: Oxford University Press, 2005), 47–52; Riley, *Disability and the Media*, 111–12; Fred Davis, *Passage Through Crisis: Polio Victims and Their Families* (1963; repr., with a new introduction by the author, New Brunswick, N.J.: Transaction Publishers, 1991), 6. On the historical development of corporate philanthropy, see Cutlip, *Fund Raising in the United States*, 318–19, 322, 329.

42. Carter, *Gentle Legions*, 111–12; Cutlip, *Fund Raising in the United States*, 365–6, 382–6; Goldenson and Wolf, *Beating the Odds*, 77–82, 85–7; Oshinsky, *Polio: An American Story*, 69; Rogers, *Dirt and Disease*, 170–1, 233; Riley, *Disability and the Media*, 111; Marc Shell, *Polio and Its Aftermath: The Paralysis of Culture* (Cambridge, Mass.: Harvard University Press, 2005), 140–3.

43. Cutlip, *Fund Raising in the United States*, 373, 85; Oshinsky, *Polio: An American Story*, 52–4, 68–9; Rogers, *Dirt and Disease*, 170; Goldenson and Wolf, *Beating the Odds*, 81–5; Jean-Noel Bassior, *Space Patrol: Missions of Daring in the Name of Early Television* (Jefferson, N.C.: McFarland, 2005), 85–7. On the function of celebrities in early-twentieth-century American culture, see Warren I. Susman, " 'Personality' and the Making of Twentieth-Century Culture," in *New Directions in American Intellectual History*, ed. John Higham and Paul K. Conkin (Baltimore: Johns Hopkins University Press, 1979), 223. On the deployment of nonentertainment "celebrities" in the late twentieth century, see Steve Mills, "Diana's Visit to Spin Fundraising Gold When Princess Talks, Philanthropies Benefit," *Chicago Tribune*, 30 May 1996, north sports final edition.

44. Other jurisdictions passing similar laws included San Francisco (1867); New Orleans (1879); Portland, Oregon, and Chicago (both 1881); Denver (1889); Omaha, Nebraska (1890); Columbus, Ohio (1894); and the State of Pennsylvania (1891). New York, in 1895, and Los Angeles, in 1913, considered instituting comparable ordinances but in the end did not adopt them. Susan Schweik has exhaustively and insightfully examined

these statutes in *The Ugly Laws: Disability in Public* (New York: New York University Press, 2009).

45. Schweik, *The Ugly Laws*.

46. Paul K. Longmore and David Goldberger, "The League of the Physically Handicapped and the Great Depression: A Case Study in the New Disability History," *Journal of American History* 87, no. 3 (December 2000): 904–5.

47. Some writers have asserted that FDR kept his "disability" hidden, but the evidence they present shows that, while he kept his wheelchair out of sight and minimized public knowledge of the extent of his physical condition, he appeared many times in public walking. His crutches, canes, and personal aides were, of course, visible, but he obscured sight of his leg braces by having them painted black. Hugh Gregory Gallagher inaccurately says that FDR sought to present himself as a "cured cripple." But Gallagher contradicts his own interpretation by recounting the many times FDR deliberately arranged for audiences and crowds to see him walk. He fashioned an image of himself, not as "cured," but as a man with a disability who was "overcoming" its presumed physical, psychological, and moral limitations. *FDR's Splendid Deception* (New York: Dodd Mead, 1985). Davis W. Houck and Amos Kiewe describe this as an attempt on his part to give the "appearance" of walking. That characterization reflects disability bias in its implicit assumption that walking with the aid of crutches, canes, orthoses, or assistants is not real walking. *FDR's Body Politics: The Rhetoric of Disability* (College Station: Texas A&M University Press, 2003). For FDR publicly talking about his physical handicap, see Franklin D. Roosevelt, *The Public Papers and Addresses of Franklin D. Roosevelt*, 13 vols., comp. Samuel Rosenman (New York: Random House, 1938), i, 334; Franklin D. Roosevelt, "Why Bother with the Crippled Child?," *Crippled Child* 5, no. 6 (1928): 140–3. Surely, the most important contemporary description of FDR making his disability publicly visible is the account by the widely read syndicated newspaper columnist Ernie Pyle, "A Tender Tribute to FDR's Courage," reprinted in *Ernie's America: The Best of Ernie Pyle's 1930s Travel Dispatches*, ed. David Nichols (New York: Random House, 1989), 102–3. (Longmore died prior to James Tobin making this same argument in *The Man He Became: How FDR Defied Polio to Win the Presidency* [New York: Simon & Schuster, 2013].—Ed.)

48. Cutlip, *Fund Raising in the United States*, 366, 376, 384; Oshinsky, *Polio: An American Story*, 32–3, 42, 45–7.

49. Carter, *Gentle Legions*, 139–72, especially 139, 140; Cutlip, *Fund Raising in the United States*, 432–3.

50. Carter, *Gentle Legions*, 207–8; Goldenson and Wolf, *Beating the Odds*, 75–93; Romanofsky and Chambers, ed., *Greenwood Encyclopedia of American Institutions*, Vol. 2: 698–700; Jennifer Bayot, "Isabelle Goldenson, 84, a Voice for People with Cerebral Palsy," 5 March 2005; Wolfgang Saxon, *New York Times*, "Obituary: Jack Hausman Raised Millions for Cerebral Palsy Fight," *Pittsburgh Post-Gazette*, 20 July 1998.

51. Carter, *Gentle Legions*, 221–42; Williams, "Easter Seals Transforms the Telethon"; Epstein, "Telethons: More than Pitches and Star Turns." See also "What Is the History of the Arthritis Foundation?" The 1950s and early 1960s were years of great progress for the Foundation, particularly in the area of communication. As Foundation-sponsored research efforts were well under way, initiatives directed toward educating and informing both the medical community and general public began. For the medical community, this marked the beginning of shared ideas concerning arthritis research and treatment at

conferences, highlighted by the first national conference held in Bethesda, Maryland, in 1953. Communicating to the public also became a priority in the 1950s and 1960s, which saw the establishment of the Russell L. Cecil Medical Journalism Awards in 1956. These awards recognize excellence in the news media by honoring reporters and editors who accurately convey information to the public about arthritis. At the same time, the success of the Arthritis Foundation's first telethon in Southern California charted the course for nationwide telethons. Over the years, these telethons have significantly increased both fundraising and awareness efforts. Communication efforts were also stepped up in 1960 with the publication of "Misrepresentation of Arthritis Drugs and Devices in the U.S.," a report designed to inform the public about widespread misinformation involving "miracle cures" for arthritis. The Foundation additionally continued to use celebrities to educate the public about arthritis and help raise money for research. Continuing the work Bob Hope had started in 1948 were national icons such as George Burns, Charlton Heston, and Lucille Ball. http://www.arthritis.org/history.php (accessed 19 January 2010).

52. Charles Rosenberg, editorial note for "The Illusion of Medical Certainty: Silicosis and the Politics of Industrial Disability, 1930–1960" by Gerald Markowitz and David Rossner, in Charles Rosenberg and Janet Golden, eds., *Framing Disease: Studies in Cultural History* (New Brunswick, N.J.: Rutgers University Press, 1992), 186; Cutlip, *Fund Raising in the United States*, 387–88, 428; Riley, *Disability and the Media*, 111. For examples of Australian health charities seeking to increase the visibility of particular medical conditions by preparing the public to fear them, see Ray Moynihan, "Claims by Charity Exaggerate Dangers of Osteoporosis," *BMJ: British Medical Journal* 327, no. 7411 (16 August 2003): 358, http://www.ebscohost.com/academic/academic-search-elite (accessed 1 June 2007).

Chapter 2

1. F. Emerson Andrews, *Philanthropic Giving* (New York: Russell Sage Foundation, 1950), 160–71; Richard Carter, *The Gentle Legions* (Garden City, N.Y.: Doubleday, 1961), 17–18; Scott M. Cutlip, *Fund Raising in the United States: Its Role in America's Philanthropy* (New Brunswick, N.J.: Rutgers University Press, 1965), 387, 217–18, 442–73, 533–6; Hank Bloomgarden, *Before We Sleep* (New York: G.P. Putnam's Sons, 1958), 107–8, 111; Peter D. Hall, "The Welfare State and the Careers of Public and Private Institutions Since 1945," in *Charity, Philanthropy, and Civility in American History*, ed. Lawrence J. Friedman and Mark D. McGarvie (New York: Cambridge University Press, 2003), 363–70.

2. Bloomgarden, *Before We Sleep*, 107–8; Cutlip, *Fund Raising in the United States*, 387, 499, see also 489.

3. "Los Angeles Gets a Telethon Curb," *New York Times*, 30 March 1954.

4. Jack Gould, "Television in Review: Telethons; $135,000 Pledged to Aid Work of Lighthouse on 16 1/2-Hour Program," *New York Times*, 16 November 1953.

5. "Lewis Distraught over Charge," *Globe and Mail* (Toronto), 6 September 1978; Michael Angeli, "God's Biggest Goof," *Esquire* 115, no. 2 (February 1991): 106.

6. Hall, "The Welfare State," 373–4; Mitchell Landsberg, "Comic Changed the Way America Gives," *Associated Press*, 1 September 1984; Joseph Bourque, "Fed Up With Charity," *Newsweek*, 4 September 1989, 10. See also Kristin Davis and Katie Young, "Where

Your Money Really Goes," *Kiplinger's Personal Finance Magazine* 47, no. 12 (December 1993): 104, http://www.ebscohost.com/ (accessed 11 December 2008).

7. On the 2006 MDA Telethon, a banner running across the bottom of the screen says that 77.25 percent of every dollar goes "directly to program services." The drawing power of the charities' iconic images sometimes led them to take legal action. Easter Seals took the American Lung Association to court over alleged trademark infringement, and MDA sued the Osmond Foundation on the same grounds. Both lawsuits were settled out of court. Grant Williams, "Charity Giants Wage Battle in Public over Appeals," *Chronicle of Philanthropy* 3, no. 17 (2 July 1991): 28–9; "Health Charities Settle Fund-Raising Battle," *Chronicle of Philanthropy* 14, no. 1 (22 October 1991): 24; Marianne Funk, "Osmonds, MDA Settle Spat over Telethons," *Deseret News*, 27 August 1995. Civil rights–oriented organizations of people with disabilities were also sometimes criticized for lack of accountability in fundraising. Jay Hancock, "A Warning to Charitable Donors and a Case for Tougher Disclosure Laws on Nonprofits," *Baltimore Sun*, 19 June 2005.

8. Marion K. Sanders, "Mutiny of the Bountiful," *Harper's Magazine* 217, no. 1303 (December 1958): 23.

9. Carter, *Gentle Legions*, 246–8; Cutlip, *Fund Raising in the United States*, 478–9, 488–9; Andrews, *Philanthropic Giving*, 122, 183; Bremner, *American Philanthropy*, 170, 184. A 1956 Sage Foundation–sponsored conference on the history of American philanthropy called for study of the rapidly expanding number of charities. Russell Sage Foundation, *Report of the Princeton Conference on the History of Philanthropy in the United States* (New York: Russell Sage Foundation, 1956), 27–8.

10. *Advertising Age*, 19 March 1951, 12, quoted in Andrews, *Philanthropic Giving*, 183.

11. Sanders, "Mutiny of the Bountiful," 23.

12. Bremner, *American Philanthropy*, 171; Sanders, "Mutiny of the Bountiful," 24.

13. Sanders, "Mutiny of the Bountiful," 26–7; Philip Benjamin, "Rival Health Camps Fight for Charity Dollars in U.S.: Independent and United Agencies Split on Methods as Soliciting Costs Soar—Tactics Stir Local Rebellions," *New York Times*, 15 June 1959; Philip Benjamin, "Charity Appeals Run into Revolts: Volunteers Set Up Combined Funds Over Opposition of Independent Agencies," *New York Times*, 16 June 1959; Philip Benjamin, "Charities Differ on United Funds; Some Shun Joint Drives-One Plan Asks Combining of Units in Allied Fields," *New York Times*, 17 June 1959; Carter, *Gentle Legions*, 249; Cutlip, *Fundraising in the United States*, 81, 216–18, 322, 409, 511, 519, 536–8; Peter Dobkin Hall, *"Inventing the Nonprofit Sector" and Other Essays on Philanthropy, Voluntarism, and Nonprofit Organizations* (Baltimore, Md.: Johns Hopkins University Press, 2001), 50, 58, 60.

14. Also at that gathering, the New York State Commissioner of Health urged voluntary organizations and official health agencies to survey jointly the problems of treating "crippled children" and coordinate their facilities and services. This would produce greater efficiency and economy, he said. "Efficiency Urged in Health Groups," *New York Times*, 5 November 1948.

15. Andrews, *Philanthropic Giving*, 122–3; Bloomgarden, *Before We Sleep*, 107, 223–4, 230–1; Sanders, "Mutiny of the Bountiful," 23; Bremner, *American Philanthropy*, 171; Cutlip, *Fund Raising in the United States*, 387, 489–91, 527, 531, 537–8; David L. Sills, *The Volunteers: Means and Ends in a National Organization* (1957; repr., New York: Arno Press, 1980), 117–30, 167–75; Benjamin, "Rival Health Camps Fight for Charity Dollars in U.S."

16. David M. Oshinsky, *Polio: An American Story* (New York: Oxford University Press, 2005), 69–72, 79–82, 128, 161–2; Naomi Rogers, *Dirt and Disease: Polio Before FDR* (New Brunswick, N.J.: Rutgers University Press, 1992), 178; Carter, *Gentle Legions*, 208–9; Kathryn Black, *In the Shadow of Polio: A Personal and Social History* (Reading, Mass.: Addison-Wesley, 1996), 27–31; Marc Shell, *Polio and Its Aftermath: The Paralysis of Culture* (Cambridge, Mass.: Harvard University Press, 2005), 16–17, 19, 29–30; Daniel J. Wilson, *Living with Polio: The Epidemic and Its Survivors* (Chicago: University of Chicago Press, 2005), 14–16.

17. Of course, MDA was able to serve only a fraction of that total. Still, its focus was far broader than in the late 1950s. MDA reported that 135,000 children had some sort of neuromuscular condition. On the early years of the MDA, see Carter, *Gentle Legions*, 208–9.

18. Easter Seals Telethons, 1991 and 1992.

19. Carter, *Gentle Legions*, 191–4; "Easter Seals Raises Record Contributions in Telethon," *Associated Press*, 9 March 1986; "Record $35.1 Million Raised for Handicapped in Easter Seals Telethon," *Associated Press*, 6 March 1988; Charlotte Snow, "Rehab Rival: Easter Seals Is a Healthcare Force to Be Reckoned With (National Easter Seals Society)," *Modern Healthcare* 27, no. 17 (28 April 1997): 18–19.

20. The Arthritis Foundation announced that between 100,000 and 200,000 children in the United States had a connective tissue disease. Arthritis-related conditions had a huge economic impact, accounting for billions of dollars annually in medical care and lost wages, plus millions of lost workdays. It was also a leading cause of disability-related insurance and welfare payments. Arthritis Telethons, 1991, 1992, and 1994. "What Services Does the Arthritis Foundation Provide?" and "What Is the History of the Arthritis Foundation? . . . Then . . . Now," http://www.arthritis.org/history.php (accessed 20 August 2005).

21. The Epilepsy Foundation reported that data from 1972 indicated that MDA recorded a total income of over $19 million to serve 250,000 clients, the March of Dimes more than $35 million for 9.5 million clients, the American Heart Association over $44 million for 27 million clients, and the American Cancer Society almost $79 million to support 1 million clients. Cited in Lawrence Joseph Londino, "A Descriptive Analysis of 'The Jerry Lewis Labor Day Telethon for Muscular Dystrophy,'" Ph.D. diss., University of Michigan, 1975, 164.

22. Cutlip, *Fund Raising in the United States*, 493; Sanders, "Mutiny of the Bountiful," 23, 26, 30; Donald Young quoted in Cutlip, *Fund Raising in the United States*, 493. "Heart disease is the king of killers in the United States, claiming more lives than all other causes combined. One in four Americans will be stricken by cardiovascular disease and nearly a million will die of it this year. The disease wreaks an economic drain of more than $94 billion in the United States annually. Despite those figures, the American Heart Association has long been the perennial and distant runner-up to the American Cancer Society in fund raising for health-care charities. Cancer kills half as many people as heart disease and affects about a tenth as many people. Still, the cancer society raised $333 million last year, nearly twice that of the heart association. . . . The inequities that exist in the world of charity, though, do not end with the heart disease and cancer contrast. Nor with alcoholism, mental retardation, arthritis or Jerry's kids with muscular dystrophy. There are several cases in which groups that work against diseases affecting the most people do not raise the most money. The mismatch between society's needs and the amount of money

raised is a problem that has persisted in the charity industry for decades, philanthropy experts say. The most money goes to the organizations with the greatest fund-raising skills," said Scott Cutlip, an author and scholar on charity for several decades. "Nobody is looking at the equity question. Morbidity and mortality rates have little to do with determining which health-care charities get the most public support. Instead, present and former charity officials say, fund-raising success depends primarily on how well a group 'emotionalizes' its cause and organizes its campaigns. . . . The inequity persists. For example, the nation's fourth-biggest killer, kidney disease, ranks close to the bottom in health fund-raising efforts. The National Kidney Foundation, the major agency in the field, raised $16 million last year from its New York headquarters and affiliates to battle a disease that afflicts 3.3 million Americans. Foundation executives touted the success of their record fund drive in the organization's annual report. Yet, the money totaled less than 20 percent of what was raised by the Muscular Dystrophy Association the same year. Muscular dystrophy, a degenerative muscle disease which primarily affects children, hits 250,000 people a year. Association officials acknowledge their success in fund raising for decades can be attributed to one man: Jerry Lewis, the group's national chairman." Phil Galewitz, "Emotionalized Causes Draw Funds. Mismatch Persists between Societal Needs, Dollars Raised Series: The Business of Charity," *Patriot News*, 12 December 1990.

23. Andrews, *Philanthropic Giving*, 151–9, 168, 183–4; Bloomgarden, *Before We Sleep*, 111; Sanders, "Mutiny of the Bountiful," 26–8; Cutlip, *Fund Raising in the United States*, 216–17, 497–8, 500, 536–8; "O'Connor Scores United Fund Plan," *New York Times*, 12 June 1959; Benjamin, "Rival Health Camps Fight for Charity Dollars in U.S."; Benjamin, "Charity Appeals Run into Revolts"; Benjamin, "Charities Differ on United Funds." The fullest defense of the private voluntary health charities was Carter's; see *The Gentle Legions*, 17–18, 27, 248–9, 250–312.

24. Sanders, "Mutiny of the Bountiful," 26–7. For figures on the numbers of volunteers participating in fundraising during the post–World War II era, see Cutlip, *Fund Raising in the United States*, 493. On the American mythology of voluntarism and an independent nonprofit sector, see Hall, *"Inventing the Nonprofit Sector,"* 85–7, 90; Bloomgarden, *Before We Sleep*, 107–8; Clarke A. Chambers, *Seedtime of Reform: American Social Service and Social Action 1918–1933* (Minneapolis: University of Minnesota Press, 1963), xiii–xiv. For late-twentieth-century American values about volunteerism and voluntarism, see Yankelovich, Skelly, and White, Inc., *The Charitable Behavior of Americans: A National Survey* (Washington, D.C.: Independent Sector, Commissioned by Rockefeller Brothers Fund, 1986), 25–7, 43, 47, 51, 54.

25. Cutlip, *Fund Raising in the United States*, 319, 322, 527, 530; Bloomgarden, *Before We Sleep*, 92, 93, 95, 106–7, 109–10; Carter, *Gentle Legions*, 221–42; Benjamin, "Rival Health Camps Fight for Charity Dollars in U.S."; Londino, "Descriptive Analysis of the Jerry Lewis MDA Telethon," 81–3, 91, 93, 119, 126–7, 131; Sanders, "Mutiny of the Bountiful," 27–9. Sanders reported on a protest that was, "in large part, against a form of philanthropy which downgrades the volunteer to a mere messenger and coin-collecting machine manipulated by professionals. The health agencies have not, of course, done this deliberately. If they could dream up worthy projects, most of them would likely keep their volunteers happily employed . . . ." On one level, according to Sanders, this struggle apparently pitted male charity professionals against female volunteers. "Resentment against their lonely role in the philanthropic scheme of things appears widespread among

women." Sanders, "Mutiny of the Bountiful," 29. See also Benjamin, "Charity Appeals Run into Revolts." Although volunteerism was most prevalent in the United States, it was a feature of other, modern anglophone capitalist cultures. Carol Boese, "Volunteerism Is Big Business," *Saskatchewan Business*, 1 April 1985.

26. This perspective is summarized by William F. May, "Introduction," in *The Ethics of Giving and Receiving: Am I My Foolish Brother's Keeper?* ed. William F. May and A. Lewis Soens Jr. (Dallas: Cary M. Maguire Center for Ethics and Public Responsibility and Southern Methodist University Press, 2000), xxi–xxv.

27. Bob Greene, "Jerry Lewis: On Camera, on the Spot," *Los Angeles Times*, 7 September 1981; Robert A. Jones, "On California: 'Jerry's Kids: It's a Pity but It Works,'" *Los Angeles Times*, 4 September 1991, home edition.

28. "Americans Give More If Asked in Person," *Associated Press*, 12 March 1986; Yankelovich, Skelly, and White, *The Charitable Behavior of Americans*, 9, 11, 21–2; Kevin Brass, "Telethons Get a Busy Signal at the Networks Fund Raising: The Easter Seals Event Follows a Trend and Will Be Seen on Cable Tonight. Organizers Say That's Not So Bad—But the Revenue Tells a Different Story," *Los Angeles Times*, 7 March 1992, San Diego County edition.

29. Rhoda Olkin, *What Psychotherapists Should Know About Disability* (New York: Guilford Press, 1999), 18, 29; Sonny Kleinfeld, *The Hidden Minority: A Profile of Handicapped Americans* (Boston: Little, Brown, 1979), 14, 62; Frank Bowe, *Handicapping America: Barriers to Disabled People* (New York: Harper and Row, 1978), 104–5; Frank Bowe, *Rehabilitating America: Toward Independence for Disabled and Elderly People* (New York: Harper and Row, 1980), 145–6; "News Briefs: Disability and Health Insurance," *Mainstream* 11, no. 8 (December 1986): 24; Susan Wendell, *The Rejected Body: Feminist Philosophical Reflections on Disability* (New York: Routledge, 1996), 48; Michael D. Goldhaber, "How Far Does the ADA Reach? 9th Circuit Weighs Law's Application to Insurance Rates," *National Law Journal*, 27 March 2000; Marta Russell, "'Rational' Discrimination in the Health Insurance Market," *ZNET Daily Commentaries*, 3 September 2001, http://www.zcommunications.org/zmag (accessed 31 May 2007); Peter G. Gosselin, "The New Deal: The Safety Net She Believed in Was Pulled Away When She Fell," *Los Angeles Times*, 21 August 2005; Joseph Pereira, "Left Behind-Casualties of a Changing Job Market-Parting Shot: To Save on Health-Care Costs, Firms Fire Disabled Workers," *Wall Street Journal*, 14 July 2003; On the Bazelon Center for Mental Health Law website, a search for "insurance discrimination" yielded 271 hits, http://www.googlesyndicatedsearch.com/u/bazelon?q=insurance+discrimin ation&sa=Search (accessed May 2009).

30. John Hockenberry, *Moving Violations: War Zones, Wheelchairs, and Declarations of Independence* (New York: Hyperion, 1995), 34–5.

31. "Woman Who Raised $3 Million for One Deadly Disease Stricken with Another," *Associated Press*, 27 August 1998; Douglas J. Rowe, "Scleroderma: Gets No Attention, But Thousands Suffer," *Associated Press*, 29 April 1991.

32. Rowe, "Scleroderma: Gets No Attention." See also Phil Galewitz, "Emotionalized Causes Draw Funds. Mismatch Persists between Societal Needs, Dollars Raised Series: The Business of Charity," *Patriot News*, 12 December 1990; Lola Sherman, "A Poster Child Offers Hope: Blind Girl, 5, and Comedian Share Telethon Stage," *San Diego Union-Tribune*, 24 October 1984.

33. Robert Macy, "Comic Upset by Rumors of Telethons' Demise," *Associated Press*, 8 August 1987.

34. Easter Seals Telethon, 1992.

35. Easter Seals Telethon, 1994 and 1992.

36. Easter Seals Telethon, 1994 and 1995.

37. Easter Seals Telethon, 1991.

38. MDA Telethon, 1993.

39. Easter Seals Telethon, 1995.

40. Quoted in Sills, *The Volunteers*, 169–71.

41. Fred Davis, *Passage through Crisis: Polio Victims and Their Families* (1963; repr., with a new introduction by the author, New Brunswick, N.J.: Transaction Publishers, 1991), 38 and 39n21. The NFIP provided financial aid to the families of more than 8 out of 10 of polio patients, but even with that assistance some families still faced significant financial burdens. Oshinsky, *Polio: An American Story*, 65; Wilson, *Living with Polio*, 64–5.

42. Davis, *Passage through Crisis*, 39n21.

43. Easter Seals Telethon, 1995.

44. UCP Telethon, 1989.

45. Easter Seals Telethon, 1993.

46. UCP Telethon, 1994.

47. MDA Telethon, 1993. See also Robert Macy, "Record $34 Million Raised in 21st Annual Telethon," *Associated Press*, 2 September 1986.

48. MDA Telethon, 1993.

49. MDA Telethon, 1994.

50. A newspaper account of a Southern California boy with juvenile rheumatoid arthritis reported the high financial cost to his parents. "'We'll never be wealthy,' said his father. 'There are expenses for doctors, hospitals and even for clothes we buy for Scott when we go to a fund-raiser,' he said. The cost of Scott's recent four-month stay in a hospital exceeded $100,000. He said insurance covered much of that, 'but our private policy has a $1-million limit, and we think half of that has already been used up.'" Herbert J. Vida, "Dana Point Boy Works Hard as Arthritis Foundation Poster Child," Los Angeles Times, 8 June 1986, Orange County edition.

51. Hockenberry, *Moving Violations*, 35. The National Foundation for Infantile Paralysis grappled with similar financial issues in the 1940s and 1950s. Black, *In the Shadow of Polio*, 107–10.

52. Christopher Quinn, "Muscular Dystrophy Association Cuts Programs, Donations Down," *Atlanta Journal-Constitution*, 25 January 2010. I thank Ingrid Tischer for calling this article to my attention.

53. On the MDA website under the heading "Eligibility & Payment," the subtitle "Payment for Authorized Medical Services" appears. It reads: "It is the policy of MDA to assist with payment only for those services authorized in its program that are not covered by private or public insurance plans or other community resources. Such payment is made directly to the institution in which the MDA clinic is located, or to authorized vendors. Association policy requires that only MDA may place orders and make payments. No services or durable medical equipment may be ordered directly by persons served or by their families if payment by MDA is desired. Only Association staff representatives may authorize vendors to provide equipment or services for which MDA will pay. Special

Note: Since MDA payment is limited to those services specified in its policy guidelines and clinic agreements, all participants in MDA clinic and related service activities are urged to familiarize themselves with the specific provisions of the Association's authorized program. Provisions described in this brochure may be changed at any time at the discretion of the Association." http://www.mdausa.org/publications/mdasvcs/eligpmt.html (accessed 25 July 2003). Under "Wheelchairs/Leg Braces," "When medically prescribed by the local MDA clinic physician, MDA assists with the purchase and reasonable repair of wheelchairs or leg braces. All those for whom a wheelchair or leg braces have been prescribed, regardless of age, education or employment status, are eligible for MDA assistance when the equipment is prescribed by an MDA clinic physician in relation to an individual's neuromuscular disease. In addition to utilizing whatever medical insurance may be applicable, the person for whom the equipment has been prescribed or that person's family may be asked to assist with its purchase through personal resources. The maximum allowable assistance toward the purchase of a wheelchair or leg braces is established by MDA annually." Under "Recycled Equipment," "MDA provides, to the extent feasible and when available, good-condition recycled wheelchairs and other durable medical equipment when medically prescribed in relation to an individual's neuromuscular disease. When the individual for whom it was prescribed no longer needs the equipment, families are encouraged to return it to MDA for use by others. Through its local chapters and field offices, MDA accepts for recycling durable medical equipment." Under "Repairs/Modifications," "The Association assists with payment toward the cost of repairs/modifications to the manual components of all wheelchairs routinely authorized for MDA payment. The amount allowable toward repairs/modifications is established by the Association annually." http://www.mdausa.org/publications/mdasvcs/progsvcs.html (accessed 25 July 2003). In one instance, MDA's policies refused to "replace the now-broken electric wheelchair it [had] helped" a former poster child buy. MDA had decided that it could pay for a chair only if the person was going to school or a job. That left this young man "imprisoned" in the mobile home of his parents, who could not "afford an electric wheelchair." He was trying to get Medi-Cal, California's version of federal Medicaid, to purchase an electric wheelchair for him. Keith Stone, "Muscle Disease Group Faced with Funding Dilemma," *Los Angeles Daily News*, 5 August 1990.

54. On the Easter Seals website: "How Is Easter Seals Supported Financially?," http://www.easter-Seals.org/site/PageServer?pagename=ntl_faq (accessed 25 July 2003); "Paying for Medical Rehabilitation Services: How Do I Pay for Therapy," http://www.easterseals.com/site/PageServer?pagename=ntl_MedRehab_Services_Cost (accessed 24 December 2011); "How Do I Pay for Job Training and Employment Services?," http://www.easter-Seals.org/site/PageServer?pagename=ntl_pay_job_training (accessed 25 July 2003); "Patient Accounts," http://www.easterSeals-ucp.org/index.php?option=displaypage&Itemid=57&op= page&SubMenu=57 (accessed 4 August 2003). The United Cerebral Palsy Association provided referrals to funding sources and on occasion financial help to individuals. http://www.ucpa.org/ucp_channeldoc.cfm/1/14/86/86-86/2936 and http://www.ucpa.org/ucp_channeldoc.cfm/1/12/70/70-70/2006 (accessed 26 July 2003). The Arthritis Foundation did not provide financial aid to individuals. "Frequently Asked Questions," http://www.arthritis.org/Resources/faq.asp#Financial Aid (accessed 26 July 2003).

55. Easter Seals offered to help families learn about government benefits programs. Easter Seals Disability Services, "Easter Seals Resources: Providing Support," http://www.

easter-Seals.org/site/PageServer?pagename=ntl_resources_support (accessed 25 July 2003). For historical examples of the humiliating eligibility processes for public assistance, see Jacobus tenBroek and Floyd W. Matson, "The Disabled and the Law of Welfare," *California Law Review* 54 (1966): 811–12, reprinted in *Changing Patterns of Law: The Courts and the Handicapped*, ed. William R. F. Philips and Janet Rosenberg (New York: Arno Press, 1980), 830–3; Jacobus tenBroek and Floyd Matson, *Hope Deferred: Public Welfare and the Blind* (Berkeley: University of California Press, 1959), 131–5, 149–50; Paul K. Longmore and David Goldberger, "The League of the Physically Handicapped and the Great Depression," and Paul K. Longmore, "Why I Burned My Book," both in *Why I Burned My Book and Other Essays on Disability*, ed. Paul K. Longmore (Philadelphia: Temple University Press, 2003), 53–102, 230–59; Steve Blow, "Let's Raise a Buck Instead of Passing It," *Dallas Morning News*, 23 October 1992.

Chapter 3

1. Peter Dobkin Hall, "Private Philanthropy and Public Policy: A Historical Appraisal," in *Philanthropy: Four Views*, ed. Robert Payton, Michael Novak, Brian O'Connell, and Peter Dobkin Hall (New Brunswick, N.J.: Transaction Books, 1988), 39–72.

2. From the beginning of the telethon era, some opinion leaders praised the telecasts for demonstrating that private voluntary efforts provided an effective alternative to federal government funding. A syndicated opinion piece about telethons made that argument in 1952. It appeared in many local and regional newspapers including the *Logansport Press* (Logansport, Ind.), 26 June 1952; *Daily Inter Lake* (Kalispell, Mont.), 26 June 1952; *Daily Capital News* (Jefferson City, Mo.), 27 June 1952.

3. A full examination of the telethon-hosting organizations' political activities is beyond the scope of this study, but it should be noted that lobbying became an increasingly important function of the agencies: They educated members of Congress and executive branch administrators about their clients' needs and mustered those clients to contact leaders in Washington, as the example of the Arthritis Foundation makes clear: "Arthritis, Rheumatism Telethon Nets $100,000: 16-Hour KTTV Program Pledges Seen Exceeding Last Year's Total Figure," *Los Angeles Times*, 16 February 1959. The 1988 Arthritis Telethon introduced actress Victoria Principal as the Arthritis Foundation's new Ambassador to Government. Among other issues, she would address the Medicaid program's withdrawal of coverage of some anti-inflammatory drugs. Still later, the Arthritis Foundation website reported: "In recent years, the Arthritis Foundation has continued to speak for the millions of Americans with arthritis. Two key examples of these successful efforts were the revision of Social Security Administration rules on children's disability benefits and the support of the Health Insurance Portability Act. In addition, over a recent five-year period, the Arthritis Foundation helped triple funding for NIAMS." Arthritis Foundation History, http://www.arthritis.org/history.php (accessed 7 July 2010). For a brief overview of the legislative efforts of the UCP during its first three decades, see Peter Romanofsky and Clarke A. Chambers, ed., *The Greenwood Encyclopedia of American Institutions: Social Service Organizations*, 2 vols. (Westport, Conn.: Greenwood Press, 1978), Vol. 2: 700–1.

4. F. Emerson Andrews, *Philanthropic Giving* (New York: Russell Sage Foundation, 1950), 180–1; Scott M. Cutlip, *Fund Raising in the United States: Its Role in America's*

Philanthropy (New Brunswick, N.J.: Rutgers University Press, 1965), 538; Peter Dobkin Hall, *Inventing the Nonprofit Sector and Other Essays on Philanthropy, Voluntarism, and Nonprofit Organizations* (Baltimore: Johns Hopkins University Press, 1992), 51–4; Peter D. Hall, "The Welfare State and the Careers of Public and Private Institutions Since 1945," in *Charity, Philanthropy, and Civility in American History*, ed. Lawrence J. Friedman and Mark D. McGarvie (New York: Cambridge University Press, 2003), 382; Lawrence J. Friedman, "Philanthropy in America: Historicism and Its Discontents," in *Charity, Philanthropy, and Civility in American History*, 18–20, 260–1; David Wagner, *What's Love Got to Do with It? A Critical Look at American Charity* (New York: New Press, 2000), 116, 194n4.

5. FDR dropped universal coverage in order to ensure passage of the Social Security Act. Robert H. Bremner, *American Philanthropy*, 2nd ed. (Chicago: University of Chicago Press, 1960, 1988), 136–55; Lizabeth Cohen, *Making a New Deal: Industrial Workers in Chicago, 1919–1939* (New York: Cambridge University Press, 1990), 1–10, 251–89, 361–8; David C. Hammack, "Failure and Resilience: Pushing the Limits in Depression and Wartime," in *Charity, Philanthropy, and Civility in American History*, 263–8; Frank Emerson Andrews, *Corporation Giving* (New York: Russell Sage Foundation, 1952), 173–6; Richard Carter, *The Gentle Legions* (Garden City, N.Y.: Doubleday, 1961), 20–1; Cutlip, *Fund Raising in the United States*, 297–9, 301, 303–6, 309, 317, 489, 529; Hall, *Inventing the Nonprofit Sector*, 58–9.

6. Bremner, *American Philanthropy*, 144; Hall, *Inventing the Nonprofit Sector*, 59–61; Hammack, "Failure and Resilience," 269–70; Marc Shell, *Polio and Its Aftermath: The Paralysis of Culture* (Cambridge, Mass.: Harvard University Press, 2005), 181–6. James T. Patterson explains that FDR favored decentralization and states' rights and left the states to decide what, if any, financial assistance they would provide to blind, physically disabled, or other residents regarded as "dependent." This approach contributed to "wide fluctuations in the quality and quantity of public services." "American Politics: The Bursts of Reform, 1930s to 1970s," in *Paths to the Present: Interpretive Essays on American History Since 1930*, ed. James T. Patterson (Minneapolis, Minn.: Burgess, 1975), 61.

7. Hank Bloomgarden, *Before We Sleep* (New York: G.P. Putnam's Sons, 1958), 98–100, 110–12.

8. In later years, the national disability charities engaged in such lobbying on a large and influential scale. Regarding the advocacy efforts of the Arthritis Foundation, see "AF History," http://www.arthritis.org/history.php (accessed 20 August 2005); "Advocacy," http://www.arthritis.org/advocacy.php (accessed 12 July 2010); "About the Arthritis Foundation," http://www.arthritis.org/about-us.php (accessed 12 July 2010). Regarding the advocacy efforts of Easter Seals and UCP, see Easter Seals Disability Services, "Legislative Advocacy Center," http://www.easterseals.com/site/PageServer?pagename=OPA_public_affairs (accessed 12 July 2010); United Cerebral Palsy, "Advocacy Tools: Media Advocacy," http://www.ucp.org/ucp_generalsub.cfm/1/8/6602/6602-6630 and "Advocacy Tools: Legislative Advocacy," http://www.ucp.org/ucp_generalsub.cfm/1/8/6602/6602-6629 (accessed 12 July 2010).

9. Bremner, *American Philanthropy*, 143, 184–6, 201–4; Friedman, "Philanthropy in America," 13–15, 18–20, 261; Hall, *Inventing the Nonprofit Sector*, 7–8, 57, 61–5, 89, 101, 103; Hall, "The Welfare State," 363, 370–2; Hammack, "Failure and Resilience,"

270; Julian Wolpert, *Patterns of Generosity in America: Who's Holding the Safety Net?* (New York: Twentieth Century Fund Press, 1993), 6, 11–12, 19.

10. Glen Johnson, "Bush's Compassion Gets Public Test," *Associated Press*, 17 February 2000. For a critical historical perspective on the Bush administration's approach, see Friedman, "Philanthropy in America," 19.

11. Hall, *Inventing the Nonprofit Sector*, 101–3.

12. Bremner, *American Philanthropy*, 178, 180, 206–8; William B. Cohen, "Epilogue: The European Comparison," in *Charity, Philanthropy, and Civility in American History*, 411–12; "Americans Give More If Asked in Person," *Associated Press*, 12 March 1986; Yankelovich, Skelly and White, Inc., *The Charitable Behavior of Americans: A National Survey* (Washington, D.C.: Independent Sector, Commissioned by Rockefeller Brothers Fund, 1986), 25–7, 43, 47, 51, 54; Hall, "The Welfare State," 378–81; James T. Patterson, *Restless Giant: The United States from Watergate to Bush v. Gore* (New York: Oxford University Press, 2005), 8, 78, 121.

13. Ralph Blumenthal, "At Snowmobile 'Ranches,' Dudes from the City Take a Spin," *New York Times*, 12 March 1972; Andrew H. Malcolm, "Snowmobile Transforms Once Quiet Rural Winter," *New York Times*, 11 February 1972; "Deere to Expand Plant," *New York Times*, 8 June 1972; Berkeley Rice, "The Snowmobile Is an American Dream Machine," *New York Times*, 13 February 1972; Jean Christensen, "U.S. Business Round-Up: Snowmobiles Out in the Cold," *New York Times*, 3 March 1974.

14. Rice, "Snowmobile Is an American Dream Machine"; for letters commenting on Rice's article, see "American Bad-Dream Machine," *New York Times*, 12 March 1972; Nelson Bryant, "Wood, Field and Stream: Early Close of Grouse Season Sought to Balk Hunters Using Snowmobiles," *New York Times*, 17 December 1970; Editorial, "Snowmobile Menace," *New York Times*, 4 February 1971; "Nuisance on Runners," letter to the editor, *New York Times*, 30 January 1971; "The Noisemakers," letter to the editor, *New York Times*, 20 February 1971; "Letters: Critics Slam the Brakes on 'Growling, Smelly' Snowmobiles," *New York Times*, 31 January 1971; Robert Claiborne, "Outlaw the Snowmobile," letter to the editor, *New York Times*, 21 February 1971; Robert Claiborne, "Outlaw the Snowmobile," letter to the editor, *New York Times*, 13 February 1972; Nelson Bryant, "Wood, Field and Stream: An Impossible Wish That Snowmobiles Would Be Put in Their Place," *New York Times*, 2 January 1972; Harold Faber, "Preserving the Catskills an Author's Main Goal," *New York Times*, 25 November 1972; Nelson Bryant, "Wood, Field and Stream: Need for More Restrictions on Hunting of Game by Snowmobile Is Endorsed," *New York Times*, 15 December 1972; Nelson Bryant, "Wood, Field and Stream: Regulating the Snowmobile," *New York Times*, 25 October 1973. For a defense of snowmobiles, see James Tuite, "Wood, Field and Stream: New View Sees Snowmobile as Vehicle for Doing a Vast Amount of Good," *New York Times*, 28 December 1972.

15. "Travel Notes: Snowmobile Safety," *New York Times*, 25 November 1973; Blumenthal, "Snowmobile 'Ranches'"; Rice, "Snowmobile Is an American Dream Machine"; "Pediatrics Academy Reports on Dangers of Snowmobiles," *New York Times*, 26 December 1974; Bayard Webster, "Eskimos Harmed by Snowmobiles: Canadians' Hearing Loss Linked to Noise Level," *New York Times*, 26 October 1975; David Dempsey, "Noise," *New York Times*, 23 November 1975.

16. E. W. Kenworthy, "Nixon to Seek Tax on Sulphur Oxides Emitted by Industry," *New York Times*, 9 February 1972; Associated Press, "Snowmobile Regulation on U.S. Land Ordered," *New York Times*, 13 February 1972; John D. Morris, "Safety Board Presses for Rules on Vehicles Used in Recreation," *New York Times*, 8 September 1972; "Metropolitan Briefs: Noise Check Bans Snowmobiles," *New York Times*, 30 September 1972; "Snowmobile Safety Pushed," *New York Times*, 15 November 1973; Robert J. Dunphy, "Note: A Moveable Feast of Passports," *New York Times*, 3 November 1974.

17. "Governor of Maine Calls for Reduction in Snowmobile Use," *New York Times*, 9 December 1973; ". . . And at Home," *New York Times*, 21 April 1975; "Snowmobiles Out in the Cold," *New York Times*; "Outboard Marine to End Production of Its Snowmobiles," *Wall Street Journal*, 14 March 1975; JoAnn S. Lublin, "What Do You Do When Snowmobiles Go on a Steep Slide?," *Wall Street Journal*, 8 March 1978.

18. Rice, "Snowmobile Is an American Dream Machine"; C. W. Griffin, "Capital Cowardice," letter to the editor, *New York Times*, 25 March 1976; Philip Shabecoff, "Outcry Greets Carter Plan to Curb Off-Road Vehicles on Public Lands," *New York Times*, 29 March 1977; Editorial, "The Taming of the Snowmobile," *New York Times*, 31 March 1977.

19. Easter Seals Disability Services, "Corporate Sponsors—National Snowmobile Foundation," http://www.easterseals.com/site/PageServer?pagename=ntl_nsf (accessed 2 June 2007).

20. The literature on institutional abuse of persons with disabilities is vast. See, for example, Burton Blatt, *Christmas in Purgatory* (1967; repr., Syracuse, N.Y.: Syracuse University Center on Human Policy, 1974); Burton Blatt, *Exodus from Pandemonium: Human Abuse and a Reformation of Public Policy* (Boston: Allyn & Bacon, 1970); Geertje Boschma, "High Ideals versus Harsh Reality: A Historical Analysis of Mental Health Nursing in Dutch Asylums, 1890–1920," *Nursing History Review* 7 (1999): 127–51; T. J. Brown, *Dorothea Dix: New England Reformer* (London: Harvard University Press, 1998); Maureen Crossmaker, "Behind Locked Doors—Institutional Sexual Abuse," *Sexuality and Disability* 9, no. 3 (Fall 1991): 201–19; Harriet McBryde Johnson, "The Disability Gulag," *New York Times Magazine*, 23 November 2003, 58–62, 64; Steven Kaye, *Status Report on Disability in the United States* (Oakland: Disability Rights Advocates, and Disability Statistics Center, University of California, San Francisco, 1998), 39–40; Samuel X. Radbill, "Reared in Adversity: Institutional Care of Children in the 18th Century," *American Journal of Diseases of Children* 130 (July 1976): 751–61; Geoffrey Reaume, *Remembrance of Patients Past: Patient Life at the Toronto Hospital for the Insane, 1870–1940* (Don Mills, Ont.: Oxford University Press, 2000); David J. Rothman and Shelia M. Rothman, *The Willowbrook Wars* (New York: Harper, 1984); Andrew T. Scull, "A Convenient Place to Get Rid of Inconvenient People: The Victorian Lunatic Asylum," in *Buildings and Society: Essays on the Social Development of the Built Environment*, ed. Anthony D. King (Boston: Routledge & Kegan Paul, 1980), 37–60; James W. Trent Jr. *Inventing the Feeble Mind, A History of Mental Retardation in the United States* (Berkeley: University of California Press, 1994); Wolf Wolfensberger, *The Origin and Nature of Our Institutional Models* (Syracuse, N.Y.: Human Policy Press, 1975).

21. John Hurst and Claire Spiegel, "Beverly Enterprises: For Nursing Homes, Big Isn't Best," *Los Angeles Times*, 7 April 1988.

22. Barry Meier, "Big Nursing Home Company Is Accused of Mistreatment," *New York Times*, 13 January 1995.

23. Ibid.; Hurst and Spiegel, "Beverly Enterprises"; Laura Katz Olson and Frank L. Davis, "Mass-Membership Senior Interest Groups and the Politics of Aging," in *Teamsters and Turtles? U.S. Progressive Political Movements in the 21st Century*, ed. John C. Berg (Lanham, Md.: Rowman & Littlefield, 2003), 74–5. The for-profit nursing home industry had a tremendous political impact on Medicaid and Medicare policies. The Balanced Budget Act of 1997 aimed to fight fraud and save on Medicare expenditures by cutting payments to hospitals, home-health-care agencies, and nursing homes. Responding to this threat to its profits, nursing home industry associations lobbied Congress members intensely in 1999, mounting a media blitz and mobilizing mass mailings. The Alliance for Quality Nursing Home Care, a political coalition of eleven nursing home corporations, spent around $15 million on this campaign. It and the American Health Care Association pressed for restoration of the cuts to industry facilities. As a result, Congress boosted payments to Medicare providers by $30 billion over five years. It did not, however, pass either a nursing home patient rights bill or legislation to safeguard HMO beneficiaries. Nor did it mandate that a proportion of Medicaid funds support independent and community-based living, as ADAPT had demanded.

24. Arthritis Telethon, 1991.

25. Arthritis Telethon, 1990.

26. ADAPT claimed that most funding, private as well as public, went "for nursing homes and other institutions" rather than "independent living." In 1991 ADAPT charged that during the quarter century since the Johnson administration began federal aid to nursing homes, those facilities had grown into "mega-businesses, supporting skilled and expensive lobbyists who keep the 'patients' and Medicaid/Medicare dollars flooding in. . . ." As a result, federal policies required states receiving Medicaid funds to pay for nursing home care. Alternatives, namely personal assistance at home, were either not offered at all or funded in small pilot programs that served only "a fraction of the people needing them." ADAPT flyer, 1991; ADAPT newsletter, *Access* (April 1991), in author's possession. The acronym ADAPT represented American Disabled for Attendant Programs Today. It originally stood for American Disabled for Accessible Public Transit, which signified the group's first focus. Following passage of the Americans with Disabilities Act, although ADAPT continued to advocate regarding that issue, it directed its main efforts to promoting public policies and funding that supported independent living. The organization changed the meaning of the acronym to reflect that shift in objectives.

27. The World Institute on Disability in Oakland, California, estimated that only about 1 out of 4 disabled persons living in the community and needing personal-assistance services got them. The Health Care Financing Administration feared that government funding would prompt enormous numbers who had been struggling on their own to apply for financial help. Policy analysts nicknamed this sort of response "the woodwork effect." That contemptuous metaphor pictured millions of disabled people as cockroaches scurrying out of the shadows and onto the layer cake of public aid. Mary Johnson, "The Nursing Home Rip-Off," *New York Times*, 2 June 1991. Federal financial aid for personal assistance provided services for over 2 million individuals through some 250 programs, but the World Institute on Disability estimated that these recipients represented only 26 percent of all those living in the community who needed PAS for personal needs and

housekeeping. Simi Litvak, "State and Federal Funding Sources for PAS," *Empowerment Strategies for Development of a Personal Assistance Service as a System: Resource Book* (Oakland, Calif.: World Institute on Disability, 1991).

28. The remaining $1.46 billion in nursing home revenues came from such sources as private insurance. Hurst and Spiegel, "Beverly Enterprises"; ADAPT flyer, 1991, in author's possession; Johnson, "The Nursing Home Rip-Off"; Olson and Davis, "Mass-Membership Senior Interest Groups and the Politics of Aging," 74.

29. ADAPT Flyer, 1991; *Access* (April 1991).

30. Andrews, *Philanthropic Giving*, 66–8; Cutlip, *Fund Raising in the United States*, 318–19, 322, 329; Hall, *Inventing the Nonprofit Sector*, 44, 49–50, 58. Nineteenth-century European benevolence was spurred by similar motives to protect the capitalist system from state intervention in the private sector in order to relieve poor people's distress. Cohen, "Epilogue: The European Comparison," 403.

31. UCP Telethon, 1993.

32. Michael J. Major, "Turning Good Deeds into Good Business, Faced with Dwindling Corporate Donations, Charities Are Creating Promotion Programs That Deliver Positive PR and Increased Sales," *Promo: The International Magazine for Promotion, Marketing* (February 1992), http://www.psaresearch.com/bib4307.html (accessed 2 June 2007).

33. Cutlip, *Fund Raising in the United States*, 409, 519; Wagner, *What's Love Got to Do with It?*, 101–3.

34. Safeway Stores made Easter Seals its primary charity, becoming the Society's number one corporate sponsor. Each regional division came up with creative ways to build its share of Safeway's "contribution" by raising money from customers. Some held golf tournaments, wine auctions, or Monte Carlo nights. Others sold hot dogs or root-beer floats or ice-cream sundaes. In 1991 the Arizona division organized a volleyball challenge. Seventy teams played thirty-five volleyball games simultaneously. To enter the challenge, each team had to raise $200. Safeway sold refreshments. One of Safeway's Denver stores held a haircut-a-thon at which it sold donated barbecued foods. Employees in one Oregon town baked a huge cake; their theme was "A Slice for Life." Safeway Eastern Division stores held cookouts in their parking lots in 1994, even as they conducted root-beer float sales, golf tournaments, and bake sales. See also Major, "Turning Good Deeds into Good Business." The March of Dimes hosted bowling tournaments in the post–World War II era. Cutlip, *Fund Raising in the United States*, 390.

35. Easter Seals Telethon, 1994: San Francisco segment.

36. Sue Adkins, *Cause Related Marketing: Who Cares Wins* (Oxford: Butterworth Heinemann, 1999), 96–9. For an examination and critique of other advantages to businesses in controlling their employees through charitable activities, see Wagner, *What's Love Got to Do with It?*, 101–2.

37. MDA Telethon, 1994. See also "CITGO Contributes Record-Breaking $7 Million to MDA," *PR Newswire*, 1 September 2003.

38. The percentages of workers obtaining health insurance through employment went down from 66 percent to 54 percent. James L. Medoff, Howard D. Shapiro, Michael Calabrese, and Andrew D. Harless, *How the New Labor Market Is Squeezing Workforce Health Benefits* (New York: Center for National Policy for the Commonwealth Fund,

2001), 1–3, 9. From 1993 through the end of the century, that trend appeared to level off. The seeming stabilization resulted largely from high employment rates and the ongoing shift toward two-worker families. In fact, a growing percentage of private-sector workers no longer had job-related health insurance. Between 1979 and 1998, the proportion of US workers under the age of 65 obtaining health insurance through their own employer dropped from two-thirds to a little over half. This trend appeared across the board in most industries in both manufacturing and the service economy. Medoff et al., *How the New Labor Market Is Squeezing Workforce Health Benefits*, 6–7, 9.

39. The proportion shrank from 45.5 percent to 26.6 percent. Medoff et al., *How the New Labor Market Is Squeezing Workforce Health Benefits*, 7.

40. For the argument that business philanthropy was an instrument of social control, see Wagner, *What's Love Got to Do with It?*, 100–21.

Chapter 4

1. Ronald Alsop, "More Firms Push Promotions Aimed at Consumers' Hearts," *Wall Street Journal*, 29 August 1985, eastern edition; Sue Adkins, *Cause Related Marketing: Who Cares Wins* (Oxford: Butterworth Heinemann, 1999), 14–15. According to Adkins, American Express "credit card use rose by 28 percent in the first month of the promotion, compared with the previous year, and new card applications increased by 45 percent." John R. Garrison (President, National Easter Seal Society), "A New Twist to Cause Marketing, Social Responsibility Marketing Takes Cause Marketing to a New Dimension of Shared Personal Commitment to Help People with Disabilities," *Fund Raising Management* (1 February 1990), http://www.psaresearch.com/index.html (accessed 6 June 2007). Sue Adkins, "The Wider Benefits of Backing a Good Cause," *Marketing* (2 September 1999): 20–1, http://www.psaresearch.com/index.html (accessed 4 August 2010).

2. In a 1982 personal interview, Horst Petzell, the charity's former fundraising director, credited the MDA Telethon with pioneering the efforts to attract corporate telethon sponsors. Indeed, scholarship on marketing gives little attention to those organizations and their pathbreaking telethons, an omission that is part of the long history of disabled people's social invisibility. See, for instance, Minette E. Drumwright and Patrick E. Murphy, "Corporate Societal Marketing," in *Handbook of Marketing and Society*, ed. Paul N. Bloom and Gregory T. Gundlach (Thousand Oaks, Calif.: SAGE, 2001), 169; Philip Kotler and Gary Armstrong, *Principles of Marketing*, 9th ed. (Upper Saddle River, N.J.: Prentice Hall, 2001), 34–5, 114–15, 298–9. The earliest examples of marketing linked to a philanthropic cause come from the United States and England in the 1890s. Adkins, *Cause Related Marketing*, 9. In addition to the citations in the previous note, publications on marketing that credit American Express with pioneering cause-related marketing include: Drumwright and Murphy, "Corporate Societal Marketing," 168; L. Lawrence Embley, *Doing Well While Doing Good: The Marketing Link Between Business & Nonprofit Causes* (Englewood Cliffs, N.J.: Prentice Hall, 1993), 26; Bill Goodwill, "Cause Marketing Pros and Cons: How Issues Are Handled Can Raise Concerns for Broadcasters and Non-Profits," *Broadcast Café Newsletter* (October 1999), http://www.psaresearch.com/index.html (accessed 6 June 2007); Kotler and Armstrong, *Principles of Marketing*, 34–5, 298–9; Zachary Schiller, "Social Issues, Philanthropy: Doing Well by Doing Good," *Business Week* 3082 (5 December 1988): 53; Richard Steckel and Robin Simons, *Doing Best by Doing*

Good: How to Use Public Purpose Partnerships to Boost Corporate Profits and Benefit Your Community (New York: Dutton/Penguin, 1992), 78.

3. In June 1952 the pharmaceutical industry campaign in support of "the muscular dystrophy appeal" enlisted radio commentator Maxine Keith as a radio and television consultant. About 55,000 drugstores participated in the effort. "Advertising & Marketing," *New York Times*, 21 June 1952. MDA Telethon, 2005; Lawrence Joseph Londino, "A Descriptive Analysis of 'The Jerry Lewis Labor Day Telethon for Muscular Dystrophy,'" Ph.D. diss., University of Michigan, 1975, 78–80, 119, 120, 187–9.

4. Walter Rosenthal, "A Study of the Factors Which Influence Corporate Use of National Charity Telethons as a Marketing Tool," Ph.D. diss., New York University, 1985, 45.

5. "The promotion started with an introductory meeting to all Schick regional, divisional and district managers. The meeting explained the MDA tie-in, the value of the program period (comfortably situated between an All-Star game and a World Series promotion) and the added value of being associated with a drive that did some good for some kids badly in need of all the help they could get. Jerry Lewis spoke to the men on film and they each received other special-for-Schick Lewis film clips to carry back to their sales people and wholesaler–retailer customers. At Schick's urging, Lewis pulled no punches and said, 'Look, together we can do a job for these kids and at the same time you can get the extra sales opportunities that make corporate sense.'" Morton B. Elliot, "Promotion in Depth: Schick Makes Sales While Helping a Good Cause," *Advertising Age* 49, no. 51 (18 December 1978): 52.

6. Harry Shearer, "Mid-Section: Telethon," *Film Comment* 15 (May–June 1976): 40.

7. Rosenthal, "A Study of the Factors," 9–10.

8. Ibid., 46–7.

9. Ibid., 8.

10. Louis J. Haugh, "Promotion Trends: Coupons, Charities Team Up," *Advertising Age* 52, no. 36 (31 August 1981): 32. In 1984 Coca-Cola planned a tie-in campaign called "Share the Love" linked to the March of Dimes. K. Brown, "Soft Drinks Put Fizz in Promotions," *Advertising Age* 55, no. 25 (October 1984): 37.

11. Garrison, "A New Twist to Cause Marketing."

12. Walter Rosenthal, "There's a Bottom Line Value for Corporations," *The Public Relations Journal* 37, no. 12 (December 1981): 22–3.

13. Ibid.

14. Natasha Zaretsky, *No Direction Home: The American Family and the Fear of National Decline, 1968–1980* (Chapel Hill: University of North Carolina Press, 2007), 109.

15. "What Americans Think of Business Leaders," *U.S. News and World Report* 92 (6 September 1982): 29; Stanley J. Goodman, "The Fallen Image of Business Is Dangerous," *U.S. News and World Report* 76 (28 January 1974): 78–80, excerpts from a speech by the chairman of May Department Stores Company; Howard Flieger, "Friend or Foe?," *U.S. News and World Report* 79 (8 September 1975): 72; "National Survey: Why Business Has a Black Eye," *U.S. News and World Report* 81 (6 September 1976): 22–5; "Why People Gripe About Business," *U.S. News and World Report* 84 (20 February 1978): 16–18; George Gallup Jr., *Gallup Report*, no. 192 (September 1981): 21; George Gallup Jr., *Gallup Report*, no. 279 (December 1988): 19.

16. Goodman, "Fallen Image of Business," 79; "Why People Gripe About Business," 16–18; Flieger, "Friend or Foe?," 72.

17. Zaretsky, *No Direction Home*, 123–4, see also 98–103.

18. "Why People Gripe About Business," 18.

19. F. Emerson Andrews, *Philanthropic Giving* (New York: Russell Sage Foundation, 1950), 64–144, 180–1; Scott M. Cutlip, *Fund Raising in the United States: Its Role in America's Philanthropy* (New Brunswick, N.J.: Rutgers University Press, 1965), 30, 318, 510–13, 515–17, 519–20.

20. Andrews, *Philanthropic Giving*, 66–8, 185–7; Cutlip, *Fund Raising in the United States*, 512.

21. Andrews, *Philanthropic Giving*, 66–8; Michael J. Major, "Turning Good Deeds into Good Business: Faced with Dwindling Corporate Donations, Charities Are Creating Promotion Programs That Deliver Positive PR and Increased Sales," *Promo* (February 1992), http://www.psaresearch.com/index.html (accessed 6 June 2007); Mark Stevenson, "What's in It for Me?," *Canadian Business* 66, no. 12 (December 1993): 5460; Noreen Brubeck, "Cause and Effect, Charities Are Wooing Marketers with Turnkey Programs That Make Them Look Good and Move Products, Too," *Promo* (February 1991), http://www.psaresearch.com/index.html (accessed 6 June 2007).

22. UCP Telethon, 1992. See also Major, "Turning Good Deeds into Good Business."

23. Easter Seals Telethon, 1992.

24. Hilary Abramson, "Sell a Case, Save a Kid? Activists Knock Health Charities for Taking Alcohol $," *Marin Institute for the Prevention of Alcohol and Other Drug Problems* 7 (Winter 1993): 3.

25. A Friendly's Restaurants' spokesperson told the Easter Seals audience: "Friendly's is a neighborhood organization that is dedicated to its local communities and strives to make a difference for its friends with disabilities." Easter Seals Telethon, 1993. "For the last nine years," said Circle K's representative, "Circle K has followed through on its commitment to community service by promoting UCP fundraising activities to its employees." UCP Telethon, 1992.

26. UCP Telethon, 1995.

27. MDA Telethon, 1994.

28. Easter Seals Telethon, 1982.

29. Anheuser-Busch's executive vice president of corporate marketing and communications reminded Lewis that "twelve years ago . . . you told August [Busch, the company's CEO,] and I (sic) about your kids. Ever since then, he has been deeply involved, and as a consequence, so are all of us." Anheuser-Busch's Sea World in San Antonio "had the kids over, and August came by, and he did a delightful video telling people why they should contribute to this wonderful cause." MDA Telethon, 1991.

30. MDA Telethon, 1994.

31. Paul Longmore's original manuscript contained long passages of notes from the hours and hours of telethons he watched, but a specific reference was not included for this telethon.—Ed.

32. Shearer, "Midsection: Telethons," 48. See also Mark Crispin Miller, "Mark Crispin Miller on Television: Sickness on TV," *The New Republic* 185, no. 14, issue 3482 (7 October 1981): 28–9.

33. "Why Business Has a Black Eye," 22; *Gallup Report*, no. 192 (September 1981): 21; *Gallup Report*, no. 279 (December 1988): 19; *Gallup Report*, no. 253 (October 1986): 12; Floris W. Wood, ed., *An American Profile: Opinions and Behavior, 1972–1989* (Farmington Hills, Mich.: Gale Group, 1990), 644; *Gallup Poll* (1994): 58–9. On the 1992 San Francisco Bay Area Easter Seals broadcast, a cohost reported that 75 percent of the people who called in that day would be women. Two former charity executives who had helped produce two of the telethons told the author in confidential interviews that the typical viewer was a grandmother.

34. A forerunner of this image appeared in a 1954 magazine article, George Koether, "Charity on the Assembly Line," *Look* 18, no. 21 (19 October 1954): 87. It included a photo of a child with a disability, "surrounded by powerful white male executives, including the presidents of Chrysler and General Motors, the general managers of Ford and Cadillac, and the leaders of the AFL and the CIO." Ellen L. Barton, "Textual Practices of Erasure: Representations of Disability and the Founding of the United Way," in *Embodied Rhetorics: Disability in Language and Culture*, ed. James C. Wilson and Cynthia Lewiecki-Wilson (Carbondale: Southern Illinois University Press, 2001), 193.

35. UCP Telethon, 1991.

36. MDA Telethon, 1991; Easter Seals Telethon, 1992.

37. UCP Telethon, 1993.

38. Easter Seals Telethon, 1992.

39. Public opinion surveys suggested that PR campaigns such as those connected with the telethons had some impact. Public confidence in business leaders never returned to the high levels of earlier years, but in the late 1980s and early 1990s, it did rebound slightly. *Gallup Report*, no. 253 (October 1986): 12; Dennis Gilbert, *Compendium of American Public Opinion* (New York, N.Y.: Facts on File, 1988), 20–2; Wood, *An American Profile*, 644; *Gallup Poll* (1994): 58–9, 153.

40. Steckel and Simons, *Doing Best by Doing Good*, 66.

41. "Parties, be they business, charities or causes, enter a Cause Related Marketing relationship in order to meet their objectives and to receive a return on their investment, whether that investment may be in cash, time or other resource or combination of all three. . . ." Adkins, *Cause Related Marketing*, 11.

42. The price of stardom or angelhood or VIP-ness varied in local markets over time. In Los Angeles in the early 1990s, MDA required $500 for gold and $250 for silver, while up in San Jose the prices were $250 and $125, respectively. By the mid-1990s, telethon inflation had boosted the MDA prices in San Jose to the LA levels. In Chicago in 1994, gold stars went for $350, but in Denver gold cost $500 and silver $250.

43. Easter Seals Telethon, 1989.

44. Easter Seals Telethon, 1991; MDA Telethon, 1992.

45. Arthritis Telethon, 1990.

46. See also "Medicine Shoppe to Help 'Jerry's Kids,'" *Drug Store News* 18, no. 13 (19 August 1996): 25, http://www.proquest.com (accessed 4 August 2010); Major, "Turning Good Deeds into Good Business."

47. MDA Telethon, 1993: Los Angeles segment.

48. Heritage Cablevision (a TCI Company) advertisement, *San Jose Mercury News*, 25 September 1991.

49. Haugh, "Promotions Trend," 32; American Marketing Association Dictionary, s.v. "freestanding insert," http://www.marketingpower.com/_layouts/Dictionary.aspx?dLetter=F (accessed 6 June 2007); Brubeck, "Cause and Effect, Charities Are Wooing Marketers with Turnkey Programs"; Easter Seals Disability Services, "Corporate Sponsors News America Marketing," http://www.easterseals.com/site/PageServer?pagename=ntl_newsamerica (accessed 6 June 2007); "ValPak to Help Promote MDA Telethon," *Direct Marketing Magazine* 59, no. 4 (9 August 1996).

50. Although corporate sponsors tended to prefer visible linkages with particular telethons, some supported more than one. Budweiser brewing company associated itself at a national level with the MDA Telethon, but on the 1992 Easter Seals San Francisco Bay Area cutaway, a local Budweiser distributor backed a three-minute "Matching Minutes." In 1991 another MDA corporate sponsor, United Airlines, made a donation on the Arthritis Telethon. In the early 1990s, PayLess Drug Stores was a corporate sponsor of both the Arthritis Foundation and UCP, while A&W, the root-beer franchise, supported both the Arthritis Foundation and Easter Seals.

51. "By redeeming the high-value coupon for Kellogg's new Heartwise cereal in today's newspapers, everyone can help Kellogg's help Easter Seals. Cilium, a natural grain with more than eight times the soluble fiber of oat bran, is what makes Kellogg's Heartwise so special. … Based on what we believe will be an exceptional response, we at the Kellogg's Company are proud to present Easter Seals our check for $75,000." Easter Seals Telethon, 1990.

52. As a result, the company pledged to increase its "total commitment from $63,000 last year to $185,000." CIBA stated that Eucalyptamint's "success as one of the major topical analgesics can largely be traced to its three-year commitment to the Arthritis Foundation. Due to this success, Dulcolax, the number one, doctor-recommended laxative, will also be in this year's program." (No broadcast date provided.—Ed.)

53. Arthritis Foundation Telethon, 1994. A $1-off coupon on Motrin I-B appeared in the May–June 1991 issue of *Arthritis Today*. For every coupon redeemed, the Upjohn Company would donate 50 cents to the Arthritis Foundation, "up to $100,000." In 1994 the coupons were available in both *Modern Maturity* and *Arthritis Today*. Brubeck, "Cause and Effect, Charities Are Wooing Marketers with Turnkey Programs"; Major, "Turning Good Deeds into Good Business."

54. Arthritis Telethons, 1990 and 1989.

55. Anheuser-Busch proclaimed that from 1980 to 1993, it donated $50 million to MDA. In fact, $47 million, 94 percent of the donation, had come from the St. Patrick's Day "Shamrocks" promotion. Moreover, the putative gift represented only a share of the brewer's bigger profits. Abramson, "Sell a Case, Save a Kid?," 1, 3. Miller and Anheuser-Busch also recruited their distributors to contribute through "case commitment programs." For each case of 12-ounce cans sold during a specified period, distributors passed along a few cents to UCP or MDA. But since these promotions boosted sales, the distributor donations, like the paper wreath and shamrock sales, were really customer contributions.

56. Abramson, "Sell a Case, Save a Kid?," 3, 4. See also "Miller Home for Holidays," *Supermarket News* 46, no. 49 (2 December 1996): 14; "Miller Brewing Co. Offers 3 Promotions for Holiday Season That Will Encourage Customers to Donate to United Cerebral Palsy," *Drug Store News* 19, no. 15 (22 September 1997): 112; "Miller Brewing Co. will Run Holiday Promotions Intended to Help Consumers Celebrate Holidays While Raising Funds for United Cerebral Palsy," *Supermarket News* 47, no. 44 (3 November 1997): 12;

"Marketing Beverages with (Jingle) Bells on ... Budweiser Will Introduce 'Clydesdale Christmas' Commercials in 11/00, Along with Gift Sets, Point of Sale Items: Miller Will Donate Proceeds from Its 'Spread The Holiday Cheer' Promotion to United Cerebral Palsy," *Drug Store News* 22, no. 17 (13 November 2000): 47; "Move Over, eBay ... Miller Lite Conducting the Get the Goods Summer Promotion," *Beverage Aisle* 10, no. 4 (April 2001): 26; Catherine Robinson, "'Tis the Season to Be Jolly!: Beverage Alcohol Companies Are Reeling Twinkling Bait," *Beverage Aisle* 10, no. 10 (15 October 2001): 42–3; "Miller Offers 'Warm Wishes' (Marketing)," *Beverage Industry* 93, no. 9 (September 2002): 70; Lisa M. Rant, "'Tis the Season: We're Fast Approaching the Holiday Season, and, as Ever, the Beverage Alcohol Category Is Full of Gift Giving Possibilities for Every Taste and Budget (Beverage Watch—Holiday Roundup)," *Beverage Aisle* 11, no. 10 (15 October 2002), 38–41.

57. Jeff Smyth, "Non-Profits Get Market-Savvy," *Advertising Age*, 29 May 1995, http://www.psaresearch.com/index.html (accessed 6 June 2007); Jennifer Moore, "Pills to Carry Name, Hopes of Arthritis Fund," *Chronicle of Philanthropy* (26 July 1994): 28; Jennifer Moore, "Drug Manufacturer Kills Controversial 'Arthritis Foundation' Pain Relievers," *Chronicle of Philanthropy* 9, no. 2 (31 October 1996): 64; Adkins, *Cause Related Marketing*, 214–19; Adkins, "Wider Benefits of Backing a Good Cause." For other examples of financial relationships between health charities and pharmaceutical companies criticized by consumer watchdogs, see Thomas Ginsberg, "Donations Tie Drug Firms and Nonprofits: Many Patient Groups Reveal Few, If Any, Details on Relationships with Pharmaceutical Donors," *Philadelphia Inquirer*, 28 May 2006. The charities reported on were the American Diabetes Association (ADA); the National Alliance on Mental Illness (NAMI); the National Gaucher Foundation; Children & Adults with Attention Deficit/Hyperactivity Disorder (CHADD); the Arthritis Foundation (AF); and the National Organization on Rare Diseases (NORD).

When the Arthritis Foundation discontinued its telethon because of the changing economics of broadcasting, it tried to replace it with a half-hour syndicated program hosted by John Davidson. Like other infomercials, it would air on cable outlets, "including the Learning Channel and Nostalgia Channel, as well as local stations across the country." Though most of the telethon's corporate sponsors did not back the new broadcast, Johnson & Johnson did buy commercial time to advertise Tylenol. The show's other two sponsors were MCI Communications and HealthSouth, a national chain of outpatient rehabilitation centers. HealthSouth's CEO Richard Scrushy would appear in a sixty-second spot to deliver a message from his company. Scrushy, a shrewd exploiter of telethons, appeared many times on UCP's charity fundraiser. Meanwhile, Mike Gault, a vice president for campaign development at the Arthritis Foundation, explained, "We wanted to come up with something that would appeal to our sponsors, who are ... willing to take risks with us." John Ebert, an executive at the production company that created the show, elaborated. "It's a natural affiliation for a nonprofit like the Arthritis Foundation to partner effectively with marketers who have an interest in people with arthritis." Kim Cleland, "Arthritis Foundation Turns to Infomercial," *Advertising Age* 68, no. 23 (9 June 1997): 14, http://www.ebscohost.com (accessed 6 June 2007).

58. Abramson, "Sell a Case, Save a Kid?," 1–7.

59. Ibid., 2.

60. Ibid., 1; UCP Telethon, 1993.

61. Abramson, "Sell a Case, Save a Kid?," 2; Rhoda Olkin, *What Psychotherapists Should Know About Disability* (New York: Guilford Press, 1999), 257–63.

62. Abramson, "Sell a Case, Save a Kid?," 2; Olkin, *What Psychotherapists Should Know About Disability,* 258.

63. Abramson, "Sell a Case, Save a Kid?," 2.

64. Ibid.

65. Ibid., 5, 4.

66. Ibid., 6

67. Ibid., 2.

68. Ibid., 6.

69. Ibid., 5, 7.

70. Ibid., 5–7. Despite their explanations and defenses, some charity executives and workers seemed troubled by their relationship with the alcohol industry. "Once every year or two, a discussion at our highest policy-making level takes place about the appropriateness of taking money from Miller," said the head of UCP. "A certain amount of concern is raised. I'd say that today, given the nature of our relationship, it is acceptable and well-managed."

71. Ibid., 2–3, 6.

72. Ibid., 2–3; Irving K. Zola and Anthony Tusler, "Commentary: Help That Hurts," *Marin Institute for the Prevention of Alcohol and Other Drug Problems* 7 (Winter 1993): 12.

73. Zola and Tusler, "Commentary: Help That Hurts," 12; Abramson, "Sell a Case, Save a Kid?," 3.

74. Sean Mehegan, "Sweet Charity," *Restaurant Business* 94, no. 12 (August 1995): 32–4. See also Walter M. Rogers, "Charities, Marketers Find Common Cause," *Dallas Morning News*, 5 September 1988.

75. Adkins, "Wider Benefits of Backing a Good Cause"; Adkins, *Cause Related Marketing*, 4, 43–51, 81–3; Goodwill, "Cause Marketing Pros and Cons"; Mehegan, "Sweet Charity," 34.

76. John R. Graham, "Corporate Giving: Is It Good for Business?," *USA Today Magazine* 123, no. 2596 (January 1995): 61.

77. "Charitable marketing is a way to change a company's image. The powerful, predatory corporate image of the 1980s is out of place in the 1990s. ... Image may not be everything, but being held in high regard by the public can be a big plus to companies seeking to influence customers, prospects, stockholders, and government regulators. ... A shrinking, precarious economy burdened with intense and unrelenting competition increases the importance of image. In other words, a dollar designation can be placed upon how a business is perceived. Any edge—even the slightest one—can turn loss into profit or mediocre performance into success. ... Affiliation with causes that convey a positive message to appropriate audiences is viewed in a favorable light. If the results of charitable support are covered by the media, the value is inestimable since the effort has achieved the ultimate goal—third-party endorsement." Graham, "Corporate Giving," 61.

78. Schiller, "Doing Well by Doing Good," 53; Graham, "Corporate Giving," 61. For later criticism of cause-related marketing, see Stephanie Strom, "Charity's Share from Shopping Raises Concern," *New York Times*, 13 December 2007, http://topics.nytimes.com/top/reference/timestopics/people/s/stephanie_strom/index.html?inline=nyt-per (accessed 13 December 2007).

79. Shearer, "Mid-Section: Telethon," 40.

80. Robert Macy, "Comic Upset by Rumors of Telethons' Demise," *Associated Press,* 8 August 1987; Kevin Brass, "Telethons Get a Busy Signal," *Los Angeles Times* (7 March 1992).

81. Personal interviews conducted by the author with former high-ranking executives who helped produce telethons at two of the disability-related charities.

82. Laura Miller, "Tough Issues, Tough World," *PR Watch* 8, no. 1 (2001), http://www. prwatch.org/prwissues/2001Q1/prsa.html (accessed 21 July 2001). See also Reynold Levy, *Give and Take: A Candid Account of Corporate Philanthropy* (Boston: Harvard Business School Press, 1999).

83. Macy, "Comic Upset by Rumors."

84. MDA Telethon, 1989. On its website, the National Easter Seals Society explained: "Companies and organizations partner with Easter Seals to: 'strengthen their ties in local communities, provide meaningful volunteer opportunities for their employees, build a positive image with their customers, their employees and their communities, increase marketing reach and visibility of their brands, and make a positive difference in the lives of children and adults with disabilities.'" Easter Seals Disability Services, "Easter Seals National Corporate Sponsors," http://www.easterseals.com/site/ PageServer?pagename=ntl_corporate_sponsors (accessed 21 January 2005).

Chapter 5

1. MDA Telethon, 1989.

2. Gordon Wood, *The Radicalism of the American Revolution* (New York: Vintage, 1992); J. R. Pole, *The Pursuit of Equality in American History* (Berkeley: University of California Press, 1978); Jack P. Greene, "The Limits of the American Revolution," in *The American Revolution: Its Character and Limits,* ed. Jack P. Greene (New York: New York University Press, 1987), 6–12.

3. Adam Smith provided the philosophical and ideological link between benevolence and capitalism in his companion works *The Theory of Moral Sentiments* (1759) and *The Wealth of Nations* (1776). Robert A. Gross, "Giving in America: From Charity to Philanthropy," in *Charity, Philanthropy, and Civility in American History,* ed. Lawrence J. Friedman and Mark D. McGarvie (New York: Cambridge University Press, 2003), 7.

4. Robert N. Bellah, Richard Madsen, William M. Sullivan, Ann Swidler, and Steven M. Tipton, *Habits of the Heart: Individualism and Commitment in American Life* (Berkeley: University of California Press, 1985), 27–35, 37–8.

5. Alexis de Tocqueville, *Democracy in America,* ed. J. P. Mayer (New York: Doubleday Anchor Books, 1969), 508, quoted and discussed in Bellah et al., *Habits of the Heart,* 37–8.

6. Gross, "Giving in America," 46.

7. Robert Wuthnow, *Acts of Compassion: Caring for Others and Helping Ourselves* (Princeton, N.J.: Princeton University Press, 1991), 19–20, 72, 73, see also 11–14, 18–19.

8. Joel Kovel, *History and Spirit: An Inquiry into the Philosophy of Liberation* (Boston: Beacon Press, 1992), 92.

9. "To live for the moment is the prevailing passion—to live for yourself, not for your predecessors or posterity. We are fast losing the sense of historical continuity, the sense of belonging to a succession of generations originating in the past and stretching into the

future. It is the waning of the sense of historical time—in particular, the erosion of any strong concern for posterity—that distinguishes the spiritual crisis of the seventies from earlier outbreaks of millenarian religion, to which it bears a superficial resemblance." Christopher Lasch, *The Culture of Narcissism: American Life in an Age of Diminishing Expectations* (1991; repr., New York: W.W. Norton, 1979), 5.

10. Bellah et al., *Habits of the Heart*, 82–3.

11. Ibid., 72–4, 82, 84, 251.

12. Ibid., 50–1, 251. "The contemporary climate is therapeutic, not religious. People today hunger not for personal salvation, let alone for the restoration of an earlier golden age, but for the feeling, the momentary illusion, of personal well-being, health, and psychic security." Lasch, *The Culture of Narcissism*, 7.

13. James T. Patterson, *Restless Giant: The United States from Watergate to* Bush v. Gore (New York: Oxford University Press, 2005), 254–9.

14. Bellah et al., *Habits of the Heart*, 50.

15. "The production is presented more as coverage of a news event, than a variety program. No effort is made to avoid shooting the other studio cameras or production floor personnel. As indicated earlier, the director talks directly over the studio intercom to talent on the studio floor while the program is on the air. It is this informal casual atmosphere, this feeling of immediacy which makes the viewer feel part of the production, and therefore a part of the entire MDA campaign. The members of the viewing audience are made aware of the physical dimensions of the set, lighting limitations, microphone difficulties, and they relate to these problems as they relate to problems in their own lives. The viewer is not watching a television program, but rather taking part in an important nationwide community event." Lawrence Joseph Londino, "A Descriptive Analysis of 'The Jerry Lewis Labor Day Telethon for Muscular Dystrophy,'" Ph.D. diss., University of Michigan, 1975, 149–50.

16. William B. Cohen, "Epilogue: The European Comparison," in *Charity, Philanthropy, and Civility in American History*, ed. Lawrence J. Friedman and Mark D. McGarvie (New York: Cambridge University Press, 2003), 411–12. In the 1970s and beyond, Americans harbored "an often profound ambivalence . . . about the proper role of the state: Again and again, people damned the federal government as bloated and bumbling, but they rarely stopped demanding that it act to help them and to expand their rights and entitlements." "The reluctance of Americans to sacrifice exposed an equally durable aspect of popular attitudes in the 1970s and thereafter. While Americans regularly denounced their government, they expected it to assure and to expand their rights and comforts. Nothing must be allowed to dampen their expectations about living standards that had ascended during the heady, upbeat years in the 1950s and 1960s." Patterson, *Restless Giant*, 8, 121, see also 78.

17. Easter Seals Telethon, 1994.

18. MDA Telethon, 1992.

19. Arthritis Telethon, 1988. Marie Anne Bach, "Building the French Muscular Dystrophy Association: The Role of the Doctor-Patient Interaction," *Social History of Medicine* 11, no. 2 (1988): 233–53. Wikipedia provides a lengthy list of telethons that have been held worldwide beginning in the late 1980s.

20. Scott M. Cutlip, *Fund Raising in the United States: Its Role in America's Philanthropy* (New Brunswick, N.J.: Rutgers University Press, 1965), 120–1.

21. For examples from the polio crusade of the 1930s and the United Fund drive in post–World War II Detroit, see Scott M. Cutlip, *The Unseen Power: Public Relations. A History* (Hillsdale, N.J.: Lawrence Erlbaum Associates, 1994), 558, and George Koether, "Charity on the Assembly Line," *Look* 18, no. 21 (19 October 1954): 87–8, 90, 93.

22. "March of Dimes Hopes to Raise $13 Million in Telethon," *Associated Press*, 29 June 1986.

23. For a discussion of the religious origins and symbolism in modern secular charity fundraising and the ideology of voluntarism and personal service, see David Wagner, *What's Love Got To Do With It? A Critical Look at American Charity* (New York: New Press, 2000), 74–6. Charity donation could serve as a symbolic means of redemption for every sort of American. In 1983, for the second year in a row, an inmate at the Nebraska State Penitentiary organized a show to "put everybody into the spirit for the Jerry Lewis Muscular Dystrophy Labor Day Telethon." The event honored that year's Nebraska state MDA poster child and raised money for the charity. The inmate who planned the fundraiser explained: "This project not only is a tremendous help to the children and adults of [*sic*] muscular dystrophy but also shows the citizens of Nebraska that, 'Hey, we prisoners and employees at the Nebraska State Penitentiary do care and love our fellow man.'" MDA's Nebraska coordinator "said he thought Nebraska's prison fund drive was the only one in the country. 'This is unique. It shows that even though these guys are inmates, they care about other human beings.'" Steven Stingley, "Poster Boy, Livewire Band Open Dystrophy Drive at Penitentiary," *Omaha World-Herald*, 23 August 1983.

24. MDA Telethon, 1988.

25. Easter Seals Telethons, 1989 and 1990.

26. UCP Telethon, 1991.

27. Profile and interview of Jerry Lewis by Scott Simon, *National Public Radio*, 2 September 1989, weekend edition.

28. Robert Macy, "Comedian Readies for Telethon After Brush with Death," *Associated Press*, 1 September 1983; Robert Macy, "Annual Jerry Lewis Special Raises $30.7 Million," *Associated Press*, 5 September 1983; Larry Bonko, "A Labor of Love: Lewis, McMahon Return to MDA Telethon," *Virginian-Pilot and Ledger-Star* (Norfolk, Va.), 3 September 1999.

29. Robert Macy, "Reagan, Mondale Call; Lewis Takes Aims to Raise $30.6 Million," *Associated Press*, 3 September 1984.

30. Robert Macy, "Annual MDA Telethon Begins Sunday," *Associated Press*, 3 September 1988.

31. "People in the News," *Associated Press*, 19 April 1984.

32. A 2003 report from Reuters news service details that Lewis's "weight had ballooned to as much as 242 pounds as a side effect from the [medication] prednisone, which he began taking in the spring of 2001 for treatment of pulmonary fibrosis, an inflammatory lung disease" according to his then-publicist: http://www.cnn.com/2003/SHOWBIZ/Movies/11/18/ple.lewis.reut/. Michael Fleeman, "Lewis Telethon Moves from Las Vegas to Hollywood," *Associated Press*, 1 September 1990; Robert Macy, "Entertainer Irate Over Telethon Flap," *Associated Press*, 9 May 1990; Rob Owens and Wire Reports, "TV Notes: Recovering Jerry Lewis Remains Telethon's Center," *Pittsburgh Post-Gazette*, 6 September 1999; "Lewis Leads Telethon to New Record despite Recent Health Problems,"

Associated Press, 6 September 1999; Bonko, "A Labor of Love"; "Lewis Telethon Posts New Record," *Associated Press*, 2 September 2002; "Medication Affects Jerry Lewis," *Associated Press*, 14 November 2002; Michael A. Lipton and David A. Keeps, "Coping: Jerry's Encore Enduring a Wave of Illnesses, Jerry Lewis Survives a Near-Suicidal Bout with the Effects of a Prescribed Drug," *People* 58, no. 24 (9 December 2002): 191; Tom Shales, "Jerry Lewis's Labor Day Labor of Love," *Washington Post*, 3 September 2003, http://www.washingtonpost.com (accessed 3 September 2003).

33. Sometimes less famous and less noticed individuals offered themselves in similar sacrificial acts. For instance, the 1990 MDA Telethon featured a segment about a disc jockey in the high desert at Victorville, California, who spent six days living on top of a building in 120-degree heat. "I thought it was time maybe somebody ought to suffer a little bit to raise money for Jerry's Kids," he explained.

34. Arthritis Telethon, 1989.

35. Easter Seals Telethon, 1989: Los Angeles Segment; Easter Seals Telethon, 1993: Chicago Segment.

36. Easter Seals Telethon, 1989. Fervent exhortation sometimes broke out on national telecasts, too. At the Easter Seals rally, Eugene Freedman, president of the Enesco Corporation, ardently announced that for the next three minutes Enesco would match "every pledge you make . . . dollar for dollar, up to a hundred-and-fifty thousand dollars!" Co-host Robb Weller cheered and yelled into the camera: "Get on your phone right now!" The show immediately switched to the local stations, where the MCs enthusiastically urged viewers to call. Back on the national telethon, Weller jumped up and down, yelling out the names and pledges of donors from around the country. Weller and Freedman victoriously exchanged high fives. Easter Seals Telethon, 1993.

37. UCP Telethon, 1993.

38. Fred Rothenberg, "Waking up Telethon's Wee Hours," *Toronto Globe and Mail*, 3 September 1982, early edition.

39. UCP Telethon, 1995.

40. MDA Telethon, 1989. In the competitive marketplace of telecast charity fundraising, "the system of putting numbers on the tote board [was] a secret that MDA guarded closely." Harry Shearer, "Mid-Section: Telethon," *Film Comment*, 15 (May–June 1976), 38.

41. UCP Telethon, 1993.

42. UCP Telethon, 1994.

43. The critics caricatured the lineup of entertainers, which, in fact, included many currently popular performers. Rothenberg, "Waking up Telethon's Wee Hours"; Bill Barol, "I Stayed Up with Jerry," *Newsweek* 110, no. 12 (21 September 1987): 66; Tom Shales, "The Telethon's Touch: Jerry Lewis, With Sugar and Schmaltz," *Washington Post*, 7 September 1998; "Critics' Choice Television: Jerry's Kids," *Los Angeles Daily News*, 1 September 1989, Valley edition; Rod Dreher, "Jerry, Please, Take Telethon Back to Vegas," *Baton Rouge Morning Advocate*, 5 September 1990; Joe Williams, "You'll Never Walk Alone; Love It or Hate It, the Telethon Is a Tough Act to Miss," *St. Louis Post-Dispatch*, 28 August 1997; "CUE & JUMP: Jerry and His 'Kids' Carry on a Tradition," *Milwaukee Journal Sentinel*, 30 August 2002; Scott Feschuk, "Jerry Is the Telethon: Without His Manic Energy, the Show Is Just Not the Same," *National Post*, 4 September 2002; Peter Carlson, "The Shtick Shift; Watching Jerry Lewis's

Tears-and-Laughter Marathon Means Miles to Go Before We Sleep," *Washington Post*, 5 September 2006.

44. Shales, "Jerry Lewis's Labor Day Labor of Love."

45. Ibid. See also Rothenberg, "Waking up Telethon's Wee Hours."

46. This statement is often incorrectly attributed to the historian Sidney Mead. Mead borrowed the phrase from G. K. Chesterton and elaborated the insight into an important interpretation of the role of religion in the American experience. G. K. Chesterton, *What I Saw in America: The Collected Works of G. K. Chesterton*, Vol. 21 (San Francisco: Ignatius, 1990), 41–5; Sidney E. Mead, "The 'Nation with the Soul of a Church,'" *Church History* 36, no. 3 (September 1967): 262–83.

Chapter 6

1. Quoted in Lawrence Joseph Londino, "A Descriptive Analysis of 'The Jerry Lewis Labor Day Telethon for Muscular Dystrophy,'" Ph.D. diss., University of Michigan, 1975, 99.

2. Easter Seals Telethon, 1990 and 1991.

3. Easter Seals Telethon, 1993 and 1994.

4. Easter Seals Telethon, 1991.

5. Debra E. Blum, "For Many Charities, Sweepstakes Fall Out of Favor as a Fund-Raising Idea," *Chronicle of Philanthropy* 11, no. 15 (20 May 1999): 25–6.

6. Easter Seals Telethon, 1992, 1994, and 1995; Arthritis Foundation Telethon, 1992; UCP Telethon, 1992.

7. The March of Dimes had a comparable program, one function of which was to enlist young schoolchildren in fundraising activities: to socialize them into volunteerism that not only drew donations but also offered them both social status and material rewards while teaching them the contrast between themselves and other children who had disabilities. "Young Children Raise Money for March of Dimes," *Chronicle of Philanthropy* 6, no. 4 (30 November 1993): 36.

8. Easter Seals Telethon, 1991: San Francisco Bay Area.

9. David Hevey, *Creatures That Time Forgot* (London: Routledge, 1992), 35.

10. Holy Bible, *Matthew* 6:2, 6:4 (Revised Standard Version).

11. James B. Simpson, *Simpson's Contemporary Quotations* (Boston: Houghton Mifflin, 1988), 243, quoting from *Washington Post*, 15 November 1979.

12. MDA Telethon, 1994. Over time, the prices of MDA Stars went up. On the San Francisco Bay Area MDA Telethons in the early years of the twenty-first century, individual and small business donors had three Star Board options: $250 bought a Silver Star, $500 a Gold Star, and $1,000 a Platinum Star.

13. On the 1994 Arthritis Telethon, cohosts Crystal Gayle and Sarah Purcell read from pledge cards the names, geographical locations, and amounts promised by phone-in pledge makers, while Fred Travalena read from a huge video screen the names, the amounts donated by individuals, organizations, and small businesses, and their locations. UCP had a series of revolving national announcers sitting in a "sky booth" who read the same information from pledge cards. On UCP's New York segments, labor leaders read the names of various donors and contributing union locals. On the 1993 MDA show, Jerry Lewis read the names and hometowns of people from all over

the country who had been phoning in pledges. "The amounts are of no consequence," Lewis declared. "It demeans the program," evidently meaning that to announce how much individual callers had pledged would undercut the moral validity of the telethon. Immediately afterward, the broadcast cut away to the local stations where segment hosts read callers' names *and* the amounts of their pledges. If Lewis, in fact, disagreed with this practice of his own telethon, he certainly endorsed the principle of conspicuous contribution. "If you around this country want your name mentioned," he promised, "call up."

14. MDA Telethon, 1991.

15. Easter Seals Telethon, 1993.

16. MDA Telethon, 1991.

17. Throughout the 2006 San Francisco Bay Area MDA Telethon, a banner was run across the bottom of the screen giving the names of local donors, the towns they lived in, and the amounts they pledged.

18. John Lear, "The Business of Giving," *Saturday Review* 44 (2 December 1961): 63; quoted in Scott M. Cutlip, *Fund Raising in the United States: Its Role in America's Philanthropy* (New Brunswick, N.J.: Rutgers University Press, 1965), 202.

19. Cutlip, *Fund Raising in the United States*, 202.

20. John R. Seeley et al., *Community Chest: A Case Study in Philanthropy* (Toronto: University of Toronto Press, 1957), 396; quoted in Cutlip, *Fund Raising in the United States*, 530.

21. Jack Gould, "Television in Review: Telethons; $135,000 Pledged to Aid Work of Lighthouse on 16 1/2-Hour Program," *New York Times*, 16 November 1953. Others praised the practice. John Crosby, "Mostly It Takes Stamina to Handle a Telethon," *Washington Post*, 3 December 1953.

22. Quoted in Lizabeth Cohen, *Making a New Deal: Industrial Workers in Chicago, 1919-1939* (New York: Cambridge University Press, 1990), 59–60. For a fictional illustration of *tzdokoh*, see I. L. Peretz's short story "If Not Higher," in *Short Shorts: An Anthology of the Shortest Stories,* ed. Irving Howe and Ilana Wiener Howe (New York: Bantam Books, 1982, 1983), 63–6.

23. Easter Seals Telethon, 1990.

24. Robert H. Bremner, *American Philanthropy*, 2nd ed. (Chicago: University of Chicago Press, 1960, 1988), 1.

25. David Brion Davis, "The American Dilemma," *New York Review of Books* 39, no. 13 (16 June 1992): 3.

26. William Roth, "Handicap as a Social Construct," *Society* 20, no. 3 (March/April 1983): 56–61.

27. W. David Lewis, "The Reformer as Conservative: Protestant Counter-Subversion in the Early Republic," in *The Development of an American Culture*, 2nd ed., ed. Stanley Coben and Lorman Ratner (New York: Saint Martin's Press, 1983), 99; Ruth Crocker, "From Gift to Foundation: The Philanthropic Lives of Mrs. Russell Sage," in *Charity, Philanthropy, and Civility in American History*, ed. Lawrence J. Friedman and Mark D. McGarvie (New York: Cambridge University Press, 2003), 199–215.

28. Ann Gerber, "Seasoned VIPs Flavor Benefits," *Chicago Sun-Times*, 19 March 1989, five star sports final edition, http://www.newslibrary@newsbank.com (accessed 1 July 2009).

29. See also Patti Doten, "Cookin' Up the Ritz," *Boston Globe*, 14 May 1990, third edition; Shelby Hodge, "Galleria Jewelry Store Hosts Glittery Benefit," *Houston Chronicle*, 8 October 1996.

30. Easter Seals Telethon, 1993.

31. Later on, MDA renamed the lockups "Stars behind Bars." MDA Telethon, 2006.

32. On the ways in which philanthropy and charity bolstered the status and power of elites, see David Wagner, *What's Love Got to Do with It? A Critical Look at American Charity* (New York: New Press, 2000), 83–5.

33. William B. Cohen, "Epilogue: The European Comparison," in *Charity, Philanthropy, and Civility in American History*, 401–3.

34. Easter Seals Telethon, 1992.

35. Edward D. Berkowitz, *America's Welfare State: From Roosevelt to Reagan* (Baltimore: Johns Hopkins University Press, 1991), 91–3, 169; Theda Skocpol, *Protecting Soldiers and Mothers: The Political Origins of Social Policy in the United States* (Cambridge, Mass.: Harvard University Press, 1992), 118–20, 141–3, 148–51, 155–7, 467–8.

36. James Baldwin, "The Discovery of What It Means to Be an American," in *The Price of the Ticket: Collected Nonfiction, 1948–1985* (New York: St. Martin's/Marek, 1985), 175.

37. Quoted in Gordon S. Wood, *The Radicalism of the American Revolution* (New York: Vintage, 1992), 135.

38. Baldwin, "Down at the Cross, Letter from a Region in My Mind," reprinted in *The Fire Next Time* (New York: Dial Press, 1963) and in *The Price of the Ticket*, 371.

39. Baldwin, "Down at the Cross," *The Price of the Ticket*, 371; Baldwin, "In Search of a Majority," reprinted in *Nobody Knows My Name: More Notes of a Native Son* (New York: Dial Press, 1961) and in *The Price of the Ticket*, 231.

40. Robert N. Bellah, Richard Madsen, William M. Sullivan, Ann Swidler, and Steven M. Tipton, *Habits of the Heart: Individualism and Commitment in American Life* (Berkeley: University of California Press, 1985), 148–50.

41. Baldwin, "In Search of a Majority," 231.

42. Bellah et al., *Habits of the Heart*, 149.

43. Crocker, "From Gift to Foundation," 213.

44. Easter Seals Telethon, 1990, 1989, and 1993.

45. Robert Wuthnow, *Acts of Compassion: Caring for Others and Helping Ourselves* (Princeton, N.J.: Princeton University Press, 1991), 52–6, 86–8.

46. Wuthnow, *Acts of Compassion*, 95–7, 116–17, quoting Bellah and Bell.

47. Henri-Jacques Stiker, *A History of Disability*, trans. William Sayers (1982, 1997; repr., Ann Arbor: University of Michigan Press, 1999), 66–8, 84–6.

48. Boniface Ramsey, "Almsgiving in the Latin Church: The Late Fourth and Early Fifth Centuries," *Theological Studies* 43 (1982): 241–52.

49. Cohen, "Epilogue: The European Comparison," 386–7, 393.

50. Ramsey, "Almsgiving in the Latin Church," 239–40; Peter Brown, "Late Antiquity," in *A History of Private Life*, Vol. 1: *From Pagan Rome to Byzantium*, ed. Phillippe Aries and Georges Duby (Cambridge, Mass.: Belknap Press of Harvard University Press, 1987), 277–9.

51. Robert A. Gross, "Giving in America: From Charity to Philanthropy," in *Charity, Philanthropy, and Civility in American History*, 34; Cohen, "Epilogue: The European Comparison," 394.

52. Susan M. Ryan, *The Grammar of Good Intentions: Race and the Antebellum Culture of Benevolence* (Ithaca, N.Y.: Cornell University Press, 2005), 10.

53. Andrew Carnegie, "Wealth," *North American Review* 148, no. 391 (June 1889): 653–65, republished as "The Gospel of Wealth" in *The Gospel of Wealth and Other Timely Essays* (New York: Century, 1901), 1–46.

54. Cohen, "Epilogue: The European Comparison," 387, 389, 393, 401–2. For an early-twentieth-century American example, see Crocker, "From Gift to Foundation."

55. For example, preaching on the parable of the rich man's encounter with the sickly beggar Lazarus (Luke 16:19–31), Peter Chrysologus interpreted Lazarus's poverty as intended by God to provide the rich man with "a didactic experience." God even prolonged Lazarus's suffering, covering his body with sores and sending dogs to lick them, in order "to open the rich man's heart." Ramsey, "Almsgiving in the Latin Church," 226–38, 252–6.

56. Ramsey, "Almsgiving in the Latin Church," 248–9, 252, 256.

57. Ibid., 248; Cohen, "Epilogue: The European Comparison," 386; Gross, "Giving in America," 45.

58. Leon R. Kass, "Am I My Foolish Brother's Keeper? Justice, Compassion, and the Mission of Philanthropy," in *The Ethics of Giving and Receiving: Am I My Foolish Brother's Keeper?*, ed. William F. May and A. Lewis Soens Jr. (Dallas: Cary M. Maguire Center for Ethics and Public Responsibility and Southern Methodist University Press, 2000), 1, 3.

59. For a thoughtful critique of the underlying philosophical premises of charity, their influences on modern social welfare policies, and their impact on people with disabilities, see Jerome E. Bickenbach, *Physical Disability and Social Policy* (Toronto: University of Toronto Press, 1993), 192–7.

60. Cheryl Heppner, "You Decide: Donations," *Disability Rag* 8, no. 1 (January/February 1987): 2.

61. Joseph P. Shapiro, *No Pity: People with Disabilities Forging a New Civil Rights Movement* (New York: Times Books, 1993), 19.

62. Heppner, "You Decide: Donations." See also Jim Belshaw, "Cry for Help? No, Thanks," *Albuquerque Journal* (2004); Chris Hewitt, "Sticks and Stones," in *Queer Crips: Disabled Gay Men and Their Stories,* ed. Bob Guter and John R. Killacky (New York: Harrington Park Press/Haworth Press, 2004), 13–16.

63. Paul Longmore's original manuscript contained long passages of notes from the hours and hours of telethons he watched, but a specific reference was not included for this telethon.—Ed.

64. Ed Hooper, "The Dignity Thief," *Disability Rag* 9, no. 1 (January/February 1988): 18–19.

65. Ibid., 19.

Chapter 7

1. "King of Comedy; Comedian Jerry Lewis," *CBS Sunday Morning*, 20 May 2001.

2. Lewis expressed his admiration for the "courage, cheerfulness, energy, enthusiasm, dreams, hope" of children with neuromuscular disabilities, which he said was God's compensation for the bad thing that has happened to them. "Seeing That Light in a Child's Eyes," *Parade* (1 September 1991), 4.

3. "[S]entimentalism might be defined as the political sense obfuscated or gone rancid. Sentimentalism . . . never exists except in tandem with failed political consciousness." Ann Douglas, *The Feminization of American Culture* (1977; repr., New York: Noonday Press/Farrar, Straus, and Giroux, 1998), 254.

4. Candace Clark, *Misery and Company: Sympathy in Everyday Life* (Chicago: University of Chicago Press, 1997), 3–6, see also 16–17, 30–2.

5. Ibid., 84–5, 93. See also Robert Wuthnow, *Acts of Compassion: Caring for Others and Helping Ourselves* (Princeton, N.J.: Princeton University Press, 1991), 196–7, 200.

6. This archetype was most explicitly exemplified by the protagonist of Henry Mackenzie's 1771 novel *The Man of Feeling*.

7. For full examinations of the "culture of sensibility," see G. J. Barker-Benfield, "The Origins of Anglo-American Sensibility," in *Charity, Philanthropy, and Civility in American History*, ed. Lawrence J. Friedman and Mark D. McGarvie (New York: Cambridge University Press, 2003), 71–89; Karen Halttunen, "Humanitarianism and the Pornography of Pain in Anglo-American Culture," *American Historical Review* 100 (April 1995), 303–34; Mary Klages, *Woeful Afflictions: Disability and Sentimentality in Victorian America* (Philadelphia: University of Pennsylvania Press, 1999), 11–13.

8. Halttunen, "Humanitarianism and the Pornography of Pain," 306–7. Although some scholars treat sensibility and sentimentalism as virtually synonymous, others describe an evolution from the one to the other during the Victorian era. If sensibility involved heightened emotional, moral, and aesthetic responsiveness especially to suffering but also to beauty, sentimentalism, according to this distinction, carried sensitivity to the point of overindulgence in emotional excess. Barker-Benfield, "Origins of Anglo-American Sensibility," 73; Fred Kaplan, *Sacred Tears: Sentimentality in Victorian Literature* (Princeton, N.J.: Princeton University Press, 1987), 12–38.

9. Martha Stoddard Holmes, *Fictions of Affliction: Physical Disability in Victorian Culture* (Ann Arbor: University of Michigan Press, 2004), 14–15.

10. Martha Stoddard Holmes, "Working (With) the Rhetoric of Affliction: Autobiographic Narratives of Victorians with Physical Disabilities," in *Embodied Rhetorics: Disability in Language and Culture*, ed. James C. Wilson and Cynthia Lewiecki-Wilson (Carbondale: Southern Illinois University Press, 2001), 27–44; Klages, *Woeful Afflictions*, 16–17, 18, 20–1, 60–1, 88.

11. Stoddard Holmes, *Fictions of Affliction*, 2–3, 16–22. Rosemarie Garland-Thomson reports that in America, sentimental Victorian portrayals did other cultural work by activating humanitarian reform sensibilities while at the same time setting limits to them, offering up marginalized characters such as slaves and factory girls with disabilities both to signify their marginalization and to mobilize middle-class women readers' sympathies. Rosemarie Garland-Thomson, *Extraordinary Bodies: Figuring Physical Disability in American Culture and Literature* (New York: Columbia University Press, 1997), 81–102.

12. Klages, *Woeful Afflictions*, 62–4. In *Cricket on the Hearth* (1852), Dickens goes on at great length depicting the highly emotional, mostly miserable experience of the "Blind Girl" Bertha Plummer. Stoddard Holmes, "Working (With) the Rhetoric of Affliction," 28. Dickens and other writers believed that sympathy could counteract the harshness of capitalist marketplace relations and that sentimental fiction had the power to generate such sympathy. Literary historian and critic Michael Bell observes that for Dickens,

"the larger order is changed for the better through the moral growth and emotional education of individuals." Michael Bell, *Sentimentalism: Ethics and the Culture of Feeling* (New York: Palgrave/St. Martin's, 2000), 127.

13. MDA Telethon, 1988.

14. Easter Seals Telethon, 1990: Los Angeles segment.

15. Easter Seals Telethon, 1990.

16. Winfried Herget, "Towards a Rhetoric of Sentimentality," in *Sentimentality in Modern Literature and Popular Culture*, ed. Winfried Herget (Tübingen, Germany: Narr, 1991), 4.

17. Halttunen, "Humanitarianism and the Pornography of Pain," 307; Klages, *Woeful Afflictions*, 62–4, Stoddard Holmes, *Fictions of Affliction*, 1–2, 16–22. See also Stoddard Holmes, "Working (With) the Rhetoric of Affliction," 30–1.

18. *Disability Rag* 7, no. 2 (March/April 1986), 22; David Zinman, "Critics Say Drives Foster Stereotyping of Disabled," *Los Angeles Times*, 16 December 1984.

19. Ellen L. Barton, "Textual Practices of Erasure: Representations of Disability and the Founding of the United Way," in *Embodied Rhetorics*, 187.

20. Arthritis Telethons, 1989 and 1990; Easter Seals Telethons, 1990 and 1988: Los Angeles segments.

21. Herget, "Towards a Rhetoric of Sentimentality," 5–6; Jane Tompkins, "Sentimental Power: *Uncle Tom's Cabin* and the Politics of Literary History," in *Sensational Designs: The Cultural Work of American Fiction 1790–1860* (New York: Oxford University Press, 1985), 125.

22. Arthritis Telethons, 1989 and 1990.

23. UCP Telethon, 1989.

24. Easter Seals Telethon, 1988.

25. Arthritis Telethon, 1991.

26. Easter Seals Telethon, 1988.

27. UCP Telethons, 1992 and 1993; Easter Seals Telethon, 1991.

28. MDA Telethons, 1988, 1990, and 1991.

29. UCP Telethons, 1994 and 1995.

30. Easter Seals Telethons, 1988, 1991, and 1992.

31. Arthritis Telethon, 1989.

32. Herget, "Towards a Rhetoric of Sentimentality," 7; Bjorn Tysdahl, "Sentimentality in Modern TV-Series? (With Special Reference to *Dynasty* and *Falcon Crest*)," in *Sentimentality in Modern Literature and Popular Culture*, 82–3.

33. MDA Telethon, 1989.

34. Arlie Russell Hochschild, *The Managed Heart: The Commercialization of Human Feeling* (Berkeley: University of California Press, 1983).

35. Ibid., 19.

36. Ibid., 189.

37. Jonathan Lamb, *The Evolution of Sympathy in the Long Eighteenth Century* (London: Pickering & Chatto, 2009).

38. Adam Smith, *The Theory of Moral Sentiments* (1759), http://www.econlib.org/library/Smith/smMS1.html (accessed 30 June 2014).

39. Ann Douglas observes, "Sentimentalism provides a way to protest the power to which one has already in part capitulated." It "was an inevitable part of the self-evasion

of a society both committed to laissez-faire industrial expansion and disturbed by its consequences." *Feminization of American Culture*, 12, 13, 254.

40. For an examination of the comparable Victorian British ambivalence about poor people with disabilities and efforts to detect who was authentically disabled and therefore legitimately deserved social aid, see Stoddard Holmes, *Fictions of Affliction*, 33, 100–1, 108–22.

41. Clark, *Misery and Company*, 46–9, 84, 100–2; Edward E. Jones et al., *Social Stigma: The Psychology of Marked Relationships* (New York: W.H. Freeman, 1984), 59–60.

42. Irving Kenneth Zola, "Medicine as an Institution of Social Control," *Sociological Review* (November 1972): 491–2; Jones et al., *Social Stigma*, 37–8, 56–7, 59–60, 61–2; Harold Yuker, "Variables That Influence Attitudes Towards Persons with Disabilities: Conclusions from the Data," *Journal of Social Behavior and Personality* 9, no. 5 (1994): 10.

43. Gary L. Albrecht, "Disability Values, Representation and Realities," in *Rethinking Disability: The Emergence of New Definitions, Concepts, and Communities*, ed. Patrick Devlieger, Frank Rusch, and David Pfeiffer (Antwerp, Belgium: Gavant, 2003), 27–44. For examples of late modern American grappling with these issues, see Gregory S. Kavka, "Disability and the Right to Work," *Social Philosophy & Policy* 9, no. 1 (1992): 262–90; William F. May and A. Lewis Soens Jr., ed., *The Ethics of Giving and Receiving: Am I My Foolish Brother's Keeper?* (Dallas: Southern Methodist University Press, 2000).

44. In his classic study of polio patients and their families, sociologist Fred Davis observed that in the mid-twentieth century, many Americans attributed illness or injury to individual willfulness or carelessness. The causes lay not so much in impersonal disease processes or accidental occurrences as in "moral or behavioral deviation." Parents often accused themselves or blamed their children. Even when they did not see illness as retribution, "they sought to reassure themselves that nothing within their control had been responsible for the child's contracting the disease." Davis linked this to an American assumption that "misfortune rarely touches those who take the proper precautionary measures." Here again was the need to believe that individuals largely control their destinies. But these parents' concern was more than "the practical, insurance-minded American attitude toward misfortune." It also reflected "guilt feelings of a theological or metaphysical kind." Some held traditional religious beliefs that God sent afflictions. Others took a more secular view. But in either case, they often believed that their families had "pursued a faulty scheme of life that in unknown but predetermined ways resulted in misfortune to the child." These Americans interpreted their lives according to the just world hypothesis mediated through a modern capitalist economic and cultural system. The same framings underlay community determinations of worthiness to receive sympathy and social aid. The March of Dimes' focus on innocent children tried to combat those beliefs when it came to polio. But Davis's and other studies found that many people still ascribed moral causes and meanings to illness and disability. Fred Davis, *Passage through Crisis: Polio Victims and Their Families* (1963; repr., New Brunswick, N.J.: Transaction Publishers, 1991), 22, 36–7. See also Daniel J. Wilson, *Living with Polio: The Epidemic and Its Survivors* (Chicago: University of Chicago Press, 2005), 143–4. In her study of the portrayal of disability in safety and injury prevention advertising campaigns, Caroline Wang found that it was often depicted "as the tragic penalty for a failure to take action." Caroline C. Wang, "Portraying Stigmatized Conditions: Disabling Images in Public Health," *Journal of Health Communication* 3 (1998), 149–59.

45. The *New York Times'* holiday season "Neediest Cases Appeal" reflects similar criteria to those presented on telethons. Candace Clark and her associates sampled these articles from their first appearance in 1912 into the 1980s. Disability frequently figured in them. The early vignettes recounted the stories of one hundred families or individuals the editor deemed most needy and most worthy of charity. Over the decades, the tone changed little. Packing heartbreaking details in fifty or so words per story, the articles were so formulaic that they might have been "following a rule book of 'routine procedures' for eliciting sympathy." They also drew on "an implicit set of criteria for defining legitimate plights." Four traits signified deservingness. Most frequent was devotion to family. Next was industriousness, followed by a determination to overcome one's problems (those meriting sympathy were "undaunted," "indomitable," "brave," "a fighter"). Last, particularly in the early decades, was lack of sin. Clark, *Misery and Company*, 8, 87–92, 105–6.

46. Leonard H. Goldenson and Marvin J. Wolf, *Beating the Odds* (New York: Charles Scribner's Sons, 1991), 76–7, 84, 86–7; Alison Carey, *On the Margins of Citizenship: Intellectual Disability and Civil Rights in Twentieth-Century America* (Philadelphia: Temple University Press, 2009), 107. See MDA Telethon, 1989, for other examples. A cursory search on Proquest using terms such as "locked in basement and disability" yields a depressingly large number of contemporary examples.

47. On the distinction between disease and illness or sickness, see Bryan S. Turner, *The Body and Society: Explorations in Social Theory*, 2nd ed. (Thousand Oaks, Calif.: SAGE, 1984, 1996), 39, 82, 178–9, 198, 200.

48. Mary Klages analyzed Maria Susanna Cummins's novel *The Lamplighter* (1854), in which a blind woman is both a role model of true womanhood for an orphan girl and an object of that girl's sympathy. Klages also examines Samuel Gridley Howe's fundraising strategies to draw support for the Perkins School for the Blind in Boston. Klages, *Woeful Afflictions*, 89–96, 105–6, 124–5.

49. Mark Twain, for one, "hungered for proof that sentimental values still existed and had power" in the world. He found that proof in Helen; Klages, *Woeful Afflictions*, 176–96. See also Ernest Freeberg, "The Meanings of Blindness in Nineteenth-Century America," *Proceedings of the American Antiquarian Society* 110, no. 1 (April 2000): 119–52; Elisabeth Gitter, *The Imprisoned Guest: Samuel Howe and Laura Bridgman, the Original Deaf-Blind Girl* (New York: Farrar, Straus, and Giroux, 2001); Gitter, "The Blind Daughter in Charles Dickens's *Cricket on the Hearth*," *Studies in English Literature, 1500–1900* 39, no. 4 (1999): 675–89.

50. Arthritis Telethons, 1989 and 1990. Antebellum reformers "also resorted to romantic racialism, idealizing the 'childlike, affectionate, docile, and patient' traits that allegedly characterized the African race and that were needed to humanize an overly competitive and rationalistic white society." David Brion Davis, "The American Dilemma," *New York Review of Books* 39, no. 13 (16 June 1992): 14.

51. Clark, *Misery and Company*, 6; Herget, "Towards a Rhetoric of Sentimentality," 4.

52. Joseph Addison, *Spectator* 418 (30 June 1712), in *Spectator: New Edition Reproducing the Original Text Both as First Issued and as Corrected by Its Authors*, Vol. 3, ed. Henry Morley (London: George Routledge and Sons, Ltd., 1891), reproduced online by Project Gutenberg, http://www.gutenberg.org/files/12030/12030-8.txt (accessed 13 August 2007).

53. G. J. Barker-Benfield, "Origins of Anglo-American Sensibility," 82–7. On eighteenth-century British and American prosperity, see Neil McKendrick and John Brewer, *The Birth of Consumer Society: The Commercialization of Eighteenth-Century England* (Bloomington: Indiana University Press, 1982); T. H. Breen, "'Baubles of Britain': The American Consumer Revolution of the Eighteenth Century," *Past and Present* 119 (May 1988): 73–104; T. H. Breen, "An Empire of Goods: The Anglicization of Colonial America," *Journal of British Studies* 25 (1986): 467–99; Richard L. Bushman, *The Refinement of America: Persons, Houses, Cities* (New York: Random House, 1993); John J. McCusker and Russell R. Menard, *The Economy of British America, 1607–1789* (Chapel Hill: University of North Carolina Press for the Institute of Early American History and Culture, 1985).

54. MDA Telethon, 1989.

55. MDA Telethon, 1990. Jerry Lewis himself gave the same rationale for donations on the MDA Telethon in 1999.

56. UCP Telethon, 1989.

57. Addison, *The Spectator* 418.

58. Ibid.

59. Edmund Burke, *A Philosophical Enquiry Into the Origin of Our Ideas of the Sublime and Beautiful*, 2nd ed., ed. and intro. Adam Phillips (1759; repr., Oxford: Oxford University Press, 1990), 36–7. See also 41–4, 47–8.

60. Halttunen, "Humanitarianism and the Pornography of Pain in Anglo-American Culture," 309.

61. Joseph Addison, *Spectator* 397 (5 June 1712).

62. The phrases the "sweet emotion of pity" and "the luxury of grief" are quoted by Brian Vickers, "Introduction," in Henry Mackenzie, *The Man of Feeling*, ed. and intro. Brian Vickers (1771; repr., London: Oxford University Press, 1967), xi; Halttunen, "Humanitarianism and the Pornography of Pain," 304, 308–9.

63. As Herget explains, "A rhetoric of sentimentality cannot take stock of the actual reader's responses. It can only account for the constituent features of a text meant to generate feelings. It provides the basis for an analysis of individual works so that common strategies and characteristic differences become recognizable. . . . Such analyses need not be limited to the printed text, but could also account for the incessant flood of TV series and films which employ the rhetoric of sentimentality effectively and with undiminished commercial success." Herget, "Towards a Rhetoric of Sentimentality," 10.

64. Mark Crispin Miller, "Mark Crispin Miller on Television: Sickness on TV," *New Republic* 185, no. 14, issue 3482 (7 October 1981): 29.

65. Charles Mee, *A Nearly Normal Life* (Boston: Little, Brown, 1999), quoted in Marc Shell, *Polio and Its Aftermath, The Paralysis of Culture* (Cambridge, Mass.: Harvard University Press, 2005), 139.

66. Carol E. Walters, "The Complete Jerry Lewis Telethon Party Guide," *Village Voice* 32, no. 35 (1 September 1987): 47–8. "Here are ten gifts for those people for whom you have a sweet but secret detestation. . . . Explain to your target that you wanted to donate to a charity in his or her name, but couldn't decide which worthy cause to give to, so you gave to 40–25 cents each. Make sure the organizations you choose are the most aggressive, annoying solicitation groups around: the NRA, Save the Whales, Jerry's Kids, etc. Soon that person will be on every mailing list in the country." Eric Kaplan, "Holiday

Shopping Fever: Presents for People You Hate," *Long Island Monthly* (1 November 1988); Ray Richmond, "Television Labor Day Telethon Is Year's High Point in Schmaltz," *Los Angeles Daily News* (6 September 1993). See also Harry Shearer, "Man Bites Town: 'Tis the (Telethon) Season[,] Don't Touch That Dial—It's Time Once Again for the Original Pay TV," *Los Angeles Times Magazine* (2 September 1990).

67. Bell, *Sentimentalism: Ethics and the Culture of Feeling*, 2. For a critical discussion of sentimentalism, see Philip Fisher, "Making a Thing Into a Man: The Sentimental Novel and Slavery," *Hard Facts: Setting and Form in the American Novel* (New York: Oxford University Press, 1985), 87–127; Jane Tompkins, "Sentimental Power: *Uncle Tom's Cabin* and the Politics of Literary History," *Sensational Designs: The Cultural Work of American Fiction 1790–1860* (New York: Oxford University Press, 1985), 122–46; Herget, "Towards a Rhetoric of Sentimentality"; Douglas, *Feminization of American Culture*.

68. Halttunen, "Humanitarianism and the Pornography of Pain," 304, 308–9.

69. Bell, *Sentimentalism: Ethics and the Culture of Feeling*, 2.

70. Tom Shales, "The Telethon's Touch: Jerry Lewis, With Sugar and Schmaltz," *Washington Post* (7 September 1988).

71. Social psychology research found that majority-group attitudes toward marginalized groups, such as racial minorities, older persons, and people with disabilities, were typically neither positive, negative, or neutral, but ambivalent and contradictory. Majority-group members tended to view socially marginalized people "as deviant ... possessing certain disqualifying attributes of mind or body. . . .." But minorities were also seen "as disadvantaged—either by the attribute itself . . . or by the social and economic discrimination that having it entails." Perception of both deviance and disadvantage generated contradictory feelings, sympathy and compassion accompanied by aversion and even hostility. Irwin Katz, R. Glen Hass, and Joan Bailey, "Attitudinal Ambivalence and Behavior Toward People with Disabilities," in *Attitudes Toward Persons with Disabilities*, ed. Harold A. Yuker (New York: Springer, 1988), 47–55.

72. Douglas, *Feminization of American Culture*, 12. Twentieth-century condemnation of sentimentality aligned what literary scholar Victor Strandberg describes as "two particular transgressions against the modern sensibility: emotional excess and falsification of reality." Victor Strandberg, "Sentimentality and Social Pluralism in American Literature," in *Sentimentality in Modern Literature and Popular Culture*, 59. That scorn expressed not rejection of feeling but critically self-conscious criteria for discriminating true or authentic emotions from insincere self-indulgent ones. Philosopher Joseph Kupfer charged sentimentality with reducing thought and emotion "into routine, automatic channels" that yielded "a quick and easy affective resolution, leading us on the emotional surface of things." Reflecting modern repugnance to emotionally extravagant falsification, he accused its "trite phrases, clichés, and stock metaphors" of oversimplifying complex realities or substituting illusions. Its pleasures partly came from this comforting lack of complexity. Its "one-dimensional emotional response" confirmed familiar reactions and allowed individuals to avoid ambivalent feelings about people or practices. In contrast, realistic portrayals elicited rich, even conflicting feelings. They prompted questioning of "our social world and our habitual feelings toward it," as well as consideration of new perspectives on "what we usually take for granted." Joseph Kupfer, "The Sentimental Self," *Canadian Journal of Philosophy* 26, no. 4 (December 1996): 543–60.

73. In examining Henry Mayhew's *London Labour and the London Poor*, Stoddard Holmes concludes that, despite his attempts to control the life narratives of poor people with disabilities, it becomes clear that his informants were, for their part, seeking to frame their stories within the "rhetoric of affliction" in order to generate charitable support from nondisabled people while at the same time retaining as much control as they could over their own lives and the definition of their identities. Stoddard Holmes, "Working (With) the Rhetoric of Affliction," 2, 17, 30, 32, 37–42, 133–90.

74. Nancy Weinberg, "Another Perspective: Attitudes of People with Disabilities," in *Attitudes Toward Persons with Disabilities*, 141–53.

75. Ibid., 141–2. Other research compared people with and without disabilities regarding life satisfaction. The first major study in 1973 asked a group of physically disabled individuals and a similar number of nondisabled individuals of comparable age, sex, and status to rate their levels of life satisfaction, happiness, frustration with life, and difficulties in life. While disabled subjects saw their lives as more difficult than nondisabled informants did, there were no differences in life satisfaction, happiness, and frustration. A 1978 survey involving more than 9500 interviews and over 90,000 mail-in questionnaires found only a weak link between health and happiness, with that link mostly occurring in instances of critical illness. People with chronic conditions did not minimize their difficulties, yet they "not only seemed to be quite happy, but even seemed to derive some happiness from their ability to cope with their difficulty."

76. One survey of 1,266 "adults with physical, sensory, psychiatric, and cognitive disabilities found that self-esteem and perceived support from family and friends were more important for positive adjustment to disability than were a variety of demographic characteristics, disability conditions, or other psychosocial factors." Kristi L Kirschner, Kelly E Ormond, and Carol J. Gill, "The Impact of Genetic Technologies on Perceptions of Disability," *Quality Management in Health Care* 8, no. 3 (Spring 2000): 21–2.

77. This played out in other stigmatized identities such as race. Wright cited one investigator who showed "that interracial contact in cooperatively oriented work settings favorably affects the attitudes of extremely prejudiced white adults." Beatrice Wright, "Attitudes and the Fundamental Negative Bias: Conditions and Corrections," in *Attitudes Towards Persons with Disabilities*, 6–7. The more positive the context, the more favorable the attitudes. In one study, feelings toward a person identified as either a former mental patient or an amputee were more positive if that individual "was described as functioning adequately than when the negative label stood alone." When a different experiment characterized both a nondisabled person and a physically disabled person as "having undesirable personality traits," subjects' attitudes toward the person with the disability were more negative. Yet if nondisabled people encountered people with disabilities in situations that revealed positive aspects of their experience, the context could lessen negative perceptions and bias. Public health researcher Caroline Wang reported that research on the effectiveness of "fear-arousing approaches" in health communication safety and prevention advertising failed to consider how persuasion through fear might reinforce stigma by widening the social distance between people with and without disabilities. Wang, "Portraying Stigmatized Conditions," 153.

78. Wright reported that the research findings were consistent. And they held not just for people with disabilities but even those with potentially fatal diseases. For her

discussion of research on insider versus outsider perspectives and the importance of such studies, see "Attitudes and the Fundamental Negative Bias," 8–12.

79. Wright, "Attitudes and the Fundamental Negative Bias," 89. "To my knowledge," she noted, "all research on insider versus outsider perspectives shows not only that the meaning of the experience differs, but also that the insider is generally more inclined than the outsider to take into account positives in the situation." See also Wang, "Portraying Stigmatized Conditions," 152–3.

80. Wright called this distorting perspective "a powerful source of prejudice." Wright, "Attitudes and the Fundamental Negative Bias," 3–5.

81. Kirschner et al., "Impact of Genetic Technologies on Perceptions of Disability," 22.

82. A survey of emergency-care professionals reported that while more than 8 out of 10 believed they would have a poor quality of life if they were spinal cord–injured quadriplegics, more than 9 out of 10 quadriplegics rated their quality of life average or better than average. Fewer than 2 in 10 emergency-care staffers thought they would be glad to be alive with that disability, but well over 8 out of 10 quadriplegics were, in fact, glad they were alive. Another survey of emergency personnel corroborated the first: 82 percent said they would prefer death to quadriplegia. Fourteen percent of the quadriplegics in the first study of emergency-care professionals rated their quality of life as poor. The significance of that figure was that other studies found that an identical percentage of the general population also graded their quality of life as poor. Carol J. Gill, "Health Professionals, Disability, and Assisted Suicide: An Examination of Relevant Empirical Evidence and Reply to Batavia," *Psychology, Public Policy, & Law* 6, no. 2 (March 2000): 526–45. "Studies consistently demonstrate that quality of life assessments are generally lower than the actual assessments made by people with disabilities." Kirschner et al., "Impact of Genetic Technologies on Perceptions of Disability," 22.

83. Several studies documented professionals' tendency to overestimate depression in people with spinal cord injuries. Another found that primary-care physicians underestimated "the global quality of life" of elderly patients with chronic conditions. Doctors in one survey significantly overestimated laryngectomy patients' "willingness ... to die rather than lose their ability to use their voice." Other research determined that physicians tended to overstate "the negative effect on families of having a child with spina bifida" and underrate "the future capabilities of children with developmental disabilities." Gill concluded that while disabled people met with "a great deal of devaluation from the general public," health-care professionals' attitudes were as negative and sometimes more so. They also generally took a far more negative view of living with a disability than did people with disabilities themselves.

84. MDA Telethon, 1988.

85. Consider the case of Tom Mecke. An electrical engineer, he worked for Southwestern Bell, and when he retired, he started his own website design and computer customization company. Bill Norman, "Texas Achiever with DMD Turns 50," *Quest*, 12 May 2010, http://quest.mda.org/news/texas-achiever-dmd-turns-50 (accessed 18 June 2010).

86. For scholarly analysis of this phenomenon, see Stoddard Holmes, *Fictions of Affliction*, and Klages, *Woeful Afflictions*.

Chapter 8

1. Naomi Rogers, *Dirt and Disease: Polio Before FDR* (New Brunswick, N.J.: Rutgers University Press, 1992), 172, 233n33. Dr. Michael Hoke, the Warm Springs rehabilitation center's chief surgeon, was horrified by these misleading messages. Other researchers and doctors also felt uneasy about the propaganda.

2. Scott M. Cutlip, *Fund Raising in the United States: Its Role in America's Philanthropy* (New Brunswick, N.J.: Rutgers University Press, 1965), 378; Rogers, *Dirt and Disease*, 172.

3. Arthritis Telethon, 1994: San Jose, Calif., segment.

4. Robert Macy, "Jerry Lewis Telethon Raises $28 Million for Muscular Dystrophy," *Associated Press*, 6 September 1982; Robert Macy, "Parade of Celebrities, Victims in MDA Appeal," *Associated Press*, 5 September 1988; Robert Macy, "Muscular Dystrophy's 26th Annual Telethon Begins Sunday," *Associated Press*, 31 August 1991; Robert Macy, "Stars Sign Up for MDA's 26th Annual Telethon," *Associated Press*, 1 September 1991; Robert Macy, "28th Annual Jerry Lewis Telethon Begins," *Associated Press*, 5 September 1993.

5. Laura Hershey, "How to Deal with the Telethon?," *Crip Commentary* (1 September 1998), http://www.cripcommentary.com/prev98.html#9/1/98 (accessed 21 August 2009).

6. UCP Telethons, 1989 and 1996. In 1994 New York overnight cohost Julie Budd said that "there are degrees of how ill someone is with cerebral palsy."

7. Peter Romanofsky and Clarke A. Chambers, ed., *The Greenwood Encyclopedia of American Institutions: Social Service Organizations*, Vol. 2 (Westport, Conn.: Greenwood Press, 1978), s.v. "United Cerebral Palsy Associations, Inc. (UCPA)," 699.

8. MDA described itself as "the leading voluntary health agency in the world in genetic research." MDA Telethon, 1994. The US National Institutes of Health was the largest funder of genetic research.

9. Hershey, "How to Deal with the Telethon?"

10. MDA Telethon, 1990. See also Muscular Dystrophy Association, "Research," http://www.mda.org/research/ (accessed 22 July 2009); Fred Shuster, "Telethon Man Jerry Lewis and Friends Hit the Stage for the 36th MDA Fund-Raiser," *Los Angeles Daily News*, 3 September 2001.

11. Romanofsky and Chambers, *Greenwood Encyclopedia of American Institutions*, s.v. "United Cerebral Palsy Associations, Inc. (UCPA)," 699.

12. Arthritis Foundation, "AF History," http://www.arthritis.org/history.php (accessed 1 July 2004); Arthritis Telethon, 1990.

13. "Directs Campaign Unit of Arthritis Foundation," *New York Times*, 11 November 1954; Arthritis Foundation, "AF History," http://www.arthritis.org/history.php (accessed 1 July 2004).

14. Arthritis Telethons, 1991 and 1992.

15. Laura Hershey, "From Poster Child to Protestor," *Spectacle* (Spring/Summer 1997), http://www.cripcommentary.com/frompost.html (accessed 22 August 2009). The MDA had a multifaceted agenda that included the following purposes:

(a) To foster and promote the cure and alleviation of the condition of persons suffering from the disease known as muscular dystrophy or any similar or allied disease;

(b) To promote research into causes and cure of such diseases and development of remedies therefor;

(c) To promote the training of competent personnel to aid in the cure, care, education, adjustment and rehabilitation of suffers from such diseases;

(d) To promote the training, vocational guidance and occupational placement of sufferers from such diseases;

(e) To promote adjustment to normal living of sufferers of such diseases;

(f) To disseminate information with respect to such diseases, and programs for the benefit of sufferers from such diseases.

National Information Bureau, "Report on Muscular Dystrophy Association, Inc." (21 April 1977), 3; in Lawrence Joseph Londino, "A Descriptive Analysis of 'The Jerry Lewis Labor Day Telethon for Muscular Dystrophy,'" Ph.D. diss., University of Michigan, 1975, 53.

16. Laura Hershey, "From Poster Child to Protestor."

17. In the 1990s, following a horseback riding accident in which he sustained a high-level spinal cord injury, movie star Christopher Reeve became a major advocate and focus of these arguments. He served as the spokesman and icon of not only spinal cord injury cure research but also research to cure virtually every other chronic medical condition. But while medical research produced major advances in enhancing the health of people with spinal cord injuries, it did not lead to the promised cure. At times, Reeve contrasted this medical crusade with the civil rights approach. In one interview, he indicated that he was not interested in advocating for "lower sidewalks," by which he apparently meant curb cuts for wheelchair access, but said that a cure would eliminate the enormous costs of long-term care. Roger Rosenblatt, "New Hopes, New Dreams," *Time* 148, no. 10 (26 August 1996): 40–53. For both political and medical criticisms of Reeve's crusade, see Steven E. Brown, "Super Duper? The (Unfortunate) Ascendancy of Christopher Reeve," *Mainstream: Magazine of the Able-Disabled* (October 1996), http://www.independentliving.org/docs3/brown96c.html (accessed 11 September 2009), and my contribution to this forum; Maura Lerner, "Christopher Reeve's Award Drawing Fire," *Minneapolis-St. Paul Star-Tribune*, 16 October 1996, http://www.startribune.com (accessed 11 September 2009); Charles Krauthammer, "Restoration, Reality and Christopher Reeve," *Time* 155, no. 6 (14 February 2000): 100, http://www.ebscohost.com/academic/academic-search-premier (accessed 11 September 2009).

18. Hershey, "From Poster Child to Protestor."

19. See Susan Sontag, *Illness as Metaphor* (New York: Farrar, Straus, and Giroux, 1978).

20. Hershey, "How to Deal with the Telethon?"

21. Arthritis Telethon, 1989.

22. MDA Telethon, 1991. Laura Hershey, "Necessity Is the Mother of Activism," *Denver Post*, 25 June 1994.

23. Arthritis Telethon, 1988.

24. Easter Seals Telethon, 1989.

25. Hershey, "From Poster Child to Protestor."

26. MDA Telethons, 1991 and 1993.

27. Arthritis Telethon, 1989.

28. "And forget any notion that people with MD can be sexual. The [MDA] telethon presents even spouses as caretakers, not lovers." Hershey, "From Poster Child to Protestor."

29. Easter Seals Telethon, 1989.

30. Arthritis Telethon, 1989: Los Angeles segment.

31. Arthritis Telethons, 1990 and 1994.

32. Arthritis Telethons, 1990 and 1994.

33. Arthritis Telethon, 1990.

34. MDA Telethons, 1988 and 1993.

35. Arthritis Telethon, 1989.

36. Arthritis Telethon, 1990.

37. The film was based on real-life incidents that led Wade Blank to found the disability-rights organization ADAPT.

38. MDA Telethon, 1990.

39. Arthritis Telethon, 1991.

40. UCP Telethon, 1994.

41. Arthritis Telethons, 1988, 1991, and 1996.

42. Figure reported on MDA Telethon, 1991. A fraction of the 135,000 youngsters with neuromuscular disabilities had DMD, but most of MDA's "good-will ambassadors" were boys with DMD. The disproportionate number was reported by cohost Jann Karl on the Los Angeles segment of the 1993 MDA Telethon. (Note that DMD almost exclusively affects males.)

43. Of the forty-odd conditions MDA addressed, only a few could be called terminal. Most were, with appropriate medical care, long-term. The MDA show also propagated an image of doom by annually displaying photos of individuals who had died during the year since the last telethon. For example, the Denver cutaway in 1994 listed the names and ages of recently deceased clients. Most had ALS. Some teenage boys had DMD. Several infants had one type of spinal muscular atrophy. Other adults had a variety of conditions. Significant but unmentioned by the MCs, most of those who had died were older adults in their sixties and seventies. And the scroll did not report how long any of them had lived with their conditions.

44. Arthritis Telethon, 1991: San Jose, Calif., segment.

45. Cutlip, *Fund Raising in the United States*, 428.

46. Easter Seals Telethons: Los Angeles, 1990, and Chicago, 1993.

47. Arthritis Telethon, 1988.

48. UCP Telethon, 1992.

49. MDA Telethon, 1988.

50. John Gliedman and William Roth, *The Unexpected Minority: Handicapped Children in America* (New York: Harcourt, Brace, Jovanovich, 1980), 23–4.

51. Easter Seals Telethon, 1990.

52. See David M. Oshinsky, *Polio: An American Story* (New York: Oxford University Press, 2005), 32–3, 42, 45–7, 61–4, 69–72, 79–81, 282–5; Daniel J. Wilson, "Covenants of Work and Grace: Themes of Recovery and Redemption in Polio Narratives, "*Literature and Medicine* 13 (1994): 22–41; Daniel J. Wilson, "Fighting Polio Like a Man: Intersections of Masculinity, Disability, and Aging," in *Gendering Disability*, ed. Bonnie G. Smith and Beth Hutchison (New Brunswick, N.J.: Rutgers University Press, 2004), 119–32; Daniel J. Wilson, *Living with Polio: The Epidemic and Its Survivors* (Chicago: University of Chicago Press, 2005), 17, 71–2, 81–2, 84–5, 95–6, 136–7, 149–50, 154, 171–2, 177–8, 236–8; Marc Shell, *Polio and Its Aftermath: The Paralysis of Culture* (Cambridge, Mass.: Harvard University Press, 2005), 70; Kathryn Black, *In the*

Shadow of Polio: A Personal and Social History (Reading, Mass.: Addison-Wesley, 1996), 167, 169–70, 181–2; Hugh Gregory Gallagher, *FDR's Splendid Deception* (New York: Dodd, Mead, 1985).

53. For an early example of the application of the overcoming ideology to people with neuromuscular disabilities, see Morris Kaplan, "Dystrophic Child Accepts His Fate; Rehabilitation Group Gives Care and Therapy to Those Who Are Chairbound," *New York Times*, 16 November 1958. The 1999 MDA Telethon reported on a traveling exhibit of artistic works by both amateur and professional artists with neuromuscular disabilities. The narrator of the segment described it as "a triumph of the human spirit." Two phrases framed the segment: "Creativity Transcends Disability" and "Ability not Disability."

54. Robert McRuer, *Crip Theory: Cultural Signs of Queerness and Ability* (New York: New York University Press, 2006), 1–2, 8, 36–7. "Disciplinary techniques and practices that produce 'disability' generate the compulsion towards an ableist heteronormativity," in Fiona A. Campbell, "'Refleshingly Disabled': Interrogations Into the Corporeality of 'Disablised' Bodies," *The Australian Feminist Law Journal* 12 (March 1999): 58.

55. UCP Telethons, 1993 and 1994.

56. UCP Telethons, 1993, 1995, and 1994. An Easter Seals host echoed James: "The children are not able-bodied, but we're going to change that." Usually though, Easter Seals did not equate overcoming with cure. But it did make overcoming the path to social integration. Easter Seals Telethon, 1988: Los Angeles.

57. Londino completely misunderstands the criticism. "Descriptive Analysis of the Jerry Lewis MDA Telethon," 48. By the 1990s, the telethon would drop this song in response, as we shall see, to disability rights activists' criticisms.

58. Easter Seals Telethon, 1988.

59. UCP Telethon, 1993.

60. Arthritis Telethon, 1988.

61. Easter Seals Telethons, 1991, 1992, 1993, and 1994: San Francisco and national segments.

62. Easter Seals Telethons, 1992 and 1993.

63. Neil Jacobson describes a particularly potent example of the stigma associated with his mobility impairment. He spent hours a day doing physical therapy in a vain effort to get himself to walk. "I never had a wheelchair until I was in high school. . . . My father built a dog house for the wheelchair, because he didn't want the wheelchair in the house. To him, the wheelchair was a symbol of disability. A symbol of pity." See oral history conducted by Sharon Bonney, appearing in Neil Jacobson and Scott Luebking, *The Computer Training Project in Berkeley, Accessible Technology, and Employment for People with Disabilities* (Berkeley: Regional Oral History Office, Bancroft Library, University of California, 1997), 10.

64. Easter Seals Telethon, 1993.

65. Easter Seals Telethons, 1992 and 1993. See also Anne B. Isaacs, "Md. Girl Speaks to Ability to Achieve: 11-Year-Old with Cerebral Palsy Represents Easter Seal across U.S.," *Washington Post*, 2 March 1989.

66. On the Easter Seals Telethon, a young man whose parents "pushed" him "to overcome the limitations of his disability" disclosed that this way of living caused him medical and physical problems. "I was pushing myself a little bit too hard. I kind of didn't

acknowledge the limits that I do have. 'Cause I do have them, you know. But I've kind of gotten to the point where I know what they are now, and I'm kinda sticking to 'em." MC Robb Weller said: "You're behaving yourself." "I'm behaving myself," replied the young man with a slight edge in his voice at this patronizing remark. Easter Seals Telethon, 1993.

67. Easter Seals Telethon, 1992.

68. Easter Seals Telethons, 1991, 1992, and 1993.

69. Robert Wuthnow, *Acts of Compassion: Caring for Others and Helping Ourselves* (Princeton, N.J.: Princeton University Press, 1991), 14.

70. Easter Seals Telethon, 1993.

71. Edward D. Berkowitz, *Disabled Policy: America's Programs for the Handicapped* (Cambridge, U.K.: Cambridge University Press, 1987); Douglas Biklen, "The Culture of Policy Disability Images and Their Analogues in Public Policy," *Policy Studies Journal* 15 (March 1987): 515–36; Frank Bowe, *Handicapping America: Barriers to Disabled People* (New York: Harper & Row, 1978); Frank Bowe, *Rehabilitating America: Toward Independence for Disabled and Elderly People* (New York: Harper & Row, 1980); Matthew Diller, "Dissonant Disability Policies: The Tensions Between the Americans with Disabilities Act and Federal Disability Benefit Programs," *Texas Law Review* 76, no. 5 (1998): 1003–1082; Matthew Diller, "Entitlement and Exclusion: The Role of Disability in the Social Welfare System," *UCLA Law Review* 44, no. 2 (1996): 361–464; Jonathan Drimmer, "Cripples, Overcomers, and Civil Rights: Tracing the Evolution of Federal Legislation and Social Policy for People with Disabilities," *UCLA Law Review* 40 (June 1993): 1341–410; Howard S. Erlanger and William Roth, "Disability Policy: The Parts and the Whole," *American Behavioral Scientist* 28 (1985): 319–45; Ruth O'Brien, *Crippled Justice: The History of Modern Disability Policy in the Workplace* (Chicago: University of Chicago Press, 2002); Richard K. Scotch, "Conceptions of Disability Policy in Twentieth Century America," in *The New Disability History: American Perspectives*, ed. Paul K. Longmore and Lauri Umansky (New York: New York University Press, 2001), 80–9.

72. Sharon N. Barnartt, Katherine D. Seelman, and Bonnie Gracer, "Policy Issues in Communications Accessibility," *Journal of Disability Policy Studies* 1, no. 2 (Summer 1990): 47–63; Michael J. Bednar, ed., *Barrier-Free Environments* (Stroudsburg, U.K.: Dowden, Hutchinson & Ross, 1977); Virginia Cassiano, "Participation in Cultural Activities," in *White House Conference on Handicapped Individuals*, Vol. 1: *Awareness Papers* (Washington, D.C.: US Government Printing Office, 1977), 133–45; Cheryl Davis, "Disability and the Experience of Architecture," in *Rethinking Architecture: Design Students and Physically Disabled People*, ed. Raymond Lifchez (Berkeley: University of California Press, 1987), 19–33; Rob Imrie, *Disability and the City, International Perspectives* (New York: St. Martin's Press, 1996); Rob Imrie, "Oppression, Disability and Access in the Built Environment," in *Disability Reader: Social Science Perspectives*, ed. Tom Shakespeare (New York: Cassel, 1998), 129–46; Mary Johnson, "Disabled Americans Push for Access," *The Progressive* 55, no. 8 (August 1991): 21–3; Steven Kaye, "Disability Rights Advocates, and Disability Statistics Center, University of California, San Francisco," in *Status Report on Disability in the United States* (Oakland: Disability Rights Advocates/ San Francisco: Disability Statistics Center, University of California, San Francisco, 1998); Raymond Lifchez, *Rethinking Architecture: Design Students and Physically Disabled People* (Berkeley: University of California Press, 1987); Raymond Lifchez and Barbara

Winslow, *Design for Independent Living: The Environment and Physically Disabled People* (New York: Whitney Library of Design, 1979); Raymond Lifchez and Cheryl Davis, "What Every Architect Should Know," in *Disabled People Are Second-Class Citizens*, ed. Myron G. Eisenberg, Cynthia Griggins, and Richard Duval (New York: Springer, 1982), 88–102; Ronald L. Mace, "Architectural Accessibility," in *White House Conference on Handicapped Individuals*, 147–65; Marcia J. Scherer, *Living in the State of Stuck: How Technology Impacts the Lives of People with Disabilities*, 2nd ed. (Cambridge, Mass.: Brookline Books, 1996).

73. Paul K. Longmore, "Screening Stereotypes: Images of Disabled People in Television and Motion Pictures," *Social Policy* 16, no. 1 (Summer 1985): 317, reprinted in Paul K. Longmore, *Why I Burned My Book and Other Essays on Disability* (Philadelphia: Temple University Press, 2003), 131–46; George Anders, "Winning Metaphors: At Office Retreats, Tales of Adversity Fire Up the Staff," *Wall Street Journal*, 13 October 2006, eastern edition.

74. William G. Johnson and James Lambrinos, "The Effect of Prejudice on the Wages of Disabled Workers," *Policy Studies Journal* 15, no. 3 (1987): 571–90; Paul K. Longmore, "Why I Burned My Book," in *Why I Burned My Book and Other Essays on Disability*, 230–60; O'Brien, *Crippled Justice*; Gary L. Albrecht, *The Disability Business: Rehabilitation in America* (Newbury Park, Calif.: SAGE, 1992); Jacobus tenBroek and Floyd W. Matson, *Hope Deferred: Public Welfare and the Blind* (Berkeley: University of California, 1959).

75. Gliedman and Roth, *Unexpected Minority*, 24.

76. Harriet McBryde Johnson, *Too Late to Die Young: Nearly True Tales from a Life* (New York: Henry Holt, 2005), 2–3.

77. Dai R. Thompson, "Anger," in *With the Power of Each Breath: A Disabled Women's Anthology*, ed. Susan E. Browne, Debra Connors, and Nanci Stern (Pittsburgh: Cleis Press, 1985), 78.

78. Hershey, "How to Deal with the Telethon?"; Hershey, "From Poster Child to Protestor."

79. Susan Wendell, *The Rejected Body: Feminist Philosophical Reflections on Disability* (New York: Routledge, 1996), 83–4.

80. Irving Kenneth Zola, *Missing Pieces: A Chronicle of Living with a Disability* (Philadelphia: Temple University Press, 1982), 52, see also 70–1, 138.

81. Carol J. Gill, "Overcoming Overcoming," in *Managing Post Polio: A Guide to Living Well with Post-Polio Syndrome*, ed. Lauro S. Halstead (St. Petersburg, Fla.: ABI Professional Publications, 1998), 207–10.

82. Ibid., 209–10.

83. Louis Harris and Associates, *The ICD Survey of Disabled Americans: Bringing Disabled Americans into the Mainstream* (New York: International Center for the Disabled, 1986).

Chapter 9

1. Longmore here seems to be drawing on the work of Norbert Elias, *The Civilizing Process*, 2 vols. (New York: Pantheon Books, 1982).—Ed.

2. Chris Shilling, *The Body and Social Theory*, 2nd ed. (1993; repr., London: SAGE, 2003), 2; Peter E. S. Freund, with the assistance of Miriam Fisher, *The Civilized Body: Social Domination, Control, and Health* (Philadelphia: Temple University Press, 1982), 69–73; Bryan S. Turner, "Recent Developments in the Theory of the Body," in *The Body: Social*

Process and Cultural Theory, ed. Mike Featherstone, Mike Hepworth, and Bryan S. Turner (London: SAGE, 1991), 14–15; Michel Foucault, *Discipline and Punish: The Birth of the Prison*, trans. Alan Sheridan (1977; repr., New York: Vintage, 1995), 135–69.

3. Shilling, *The Body and Social Theory*, 2; Bryan S. Turner, *The Body and Society: Explorations in Social Theory*, 2nd ed. (Thousand Oaks, Calif.: SAGE, 1984, 1996), 1–4. See also Freund, *The Civilized Body*, 73–4; Turner, "Recent Developments in the Theory of the Body," 19. The phrase "high modernity" was coined by the British sociologist Anthony Giddens, *Modernity and Self-Identity: Self and Society* (Stanford, Calif.: Stanford University Press, 1991).

4. Shilling, *The Body and Social Theory*, 2–3, 4–6, 32, 111–12, 115, 157–9; Turner, *The Body and Society*, 4–5, 20–1, 23–4, 195; Susan Bordo, "'Material Girl': The Effacements of Post Modern Culture," in *Unbearable Weight: Feminism, Western Culture, and the Body* (Berkeley: University of California Press, 1993), reprinted in *The American Body in Context: An Anthology*, ed. Jessica R. Johnston (Lanham, Md.: Rowman & Littlefield, 2001), 124. See also Freund, *The Civilized Body*, 74; Brian Caldwell, "Muscling in the Movies: Excess and the Representation of the Male Body in Films of the 1980s and 1990s," in *American Bodies: Cultural Histories of the Physique*, ed. Tim Armstrong (New York: New York University Press, 1996), 139.

5. Shilling, *The Body and Social Theory*, 1; Turner, *The Body and Society*, 3, 6–7.

6. Shilling, *The Body and Social Theory*, 1; Bryan S. Turner, "Disability and the Sociology of the Body," in *Handbook of Disability Studies*, ed. Gary L. Albrecht, Katherine D. Seelman, and Michael Bury (Thousand Oaks, Calif.: SAGE, 2001), 252.

7. Shilling, *The Body and Social Theory*, 126.

8. Despite the importance of disability to the high modern body regime, sociologists of the body and scholars in body studies largely ignored it. They scrutinized values, attitudes, and practices regarding fitness and illness, aging and death but in general stayed away from disability. Sociologists who did take up disability often conflated it with illness and viewed it as a matter of coping with tragic loss and lack. The actual life experiences of people with disabilities were unexamined and unknown or misinterpreted, which is to say, invisible. Arthur W. Frank, "For a Sociology of the Body: An Analytical Review," in *The Body: Social Process and Cultural Theory*, 85–9. Frank's brief and problematic discussion appeared in this important anthology collected from the influential journal *Theory, Culture & Society*. None of the other pieces examined disability. In their "Preface" to *The Body*, editors Featherstone, Hepworth, and Turner announced that they chose the essays to illustrate "theoretical perspectives . . . [that] illuminate representations of the body in a (wide) range of contexts." They did not list disability among those sociologically significant "representations" (p. viii). In the sociological literature on the body, two studies did consider disability: Turner, "Disability and the Sociology of the Body," in *Handbook of Disability Studies*, Chap. 10 and Wendy Seymour, *Remaking the Body: Rehabilitation and Change* (New York: Routledge, 1998).

9. Ann Dils and Ann Cooper Albright, *Moving History/Dancing Cultures: A Dance History Reader* (Middletown, Conn.: Wesleyan University Press, 2001), 62.

10. Quoted in Ann Cooper Albright, *Choreographing Difference: The Body and Identity in Contemporary Dance* (Hanover, N.H.: University Press of New England/Wesleyan University Press, 1997), 73–4.

11. *San Jose Mercury News*, 9 March 1992.

12. UCP Telethon, 1994; MDA Telethon, 1993. See also Melanie Mangum, "Teams, Twirlers Walk to Fund MDA," *Telegram & Gazette* (Worcester, Mass.), 23 May 2005, final edition.

13. Lena Williams, "New Fund-Raising Strategy for Charities: Get Up and Go," *New York Times*, 7 May 1995. See also Patrick Keating, "Greg Gumbel to Host March of Dimes Event," *Michigan Chronicle* 58, no. 20 (1 February 1995); "Runners Step Out to Help a Good Cause," *Sarasota Herald-Tribune* (Sarosta, Fla.), 5 September 2005; "Healthy Steps," *Evansville Courier* (Evansville, Ind.), 29 May 2006; Scott Rabalais, "Charities Can Benefit from Special Sporting Events," *Baton Rouge State Times*, 31 January 1990.

14. Scott M. Cutlip, *Fund Raising in the United States: Its Role in America's Philanthropy* (New Brunswick, N.J.: Rutgers University Press, 1965), 361, 365–6.

15. MDA Telethon, 1988; Arthritis Telethon, 1994. In 1977 Youth for Muscular Dystrophy staged "marathon dance contests, bike-a-thons, a basketball marathon, a ski-a-thon, and a horse-a-thon," in all "184 marathons during 1977" that raised over $1.2 million. Lawrence Joseph Londino, "A Descriptive Analysis of 'The Jerry Lewis Labor Day Telethon for Muscular Dystrophy,'" Ph.D. diss., University of Michigan, 1975, 77. See also "High School Dance at the Citadel to Help 'Jerry's Kids,'" *Colorado Springs Gazette Telegraph*, 1 December 1988.

16. Leslie Sowers, "Each Mile They Walk Helps Little Ones to Live," *Houston Chronicle*, 11 April 1990, 2 star edition; Tara Gruzen, "Taking Steps to Good Health," *Chicago Tribune*, 29 April 1990, final edition; "Young Children Raise Money for March of Dimes," *Chronicle of Philanthropy* 6, no. 4 (30 November 1993): 36.

17. MDA Telethon, 1988.

18. Ibid.

19. Easter Seals Telethons, 1990, 1991, and 1994 (Longmore's original chapter listed these three programs.—Ed.).

20. Ibid.

21. MDA Telethon, 1991.

22. For example, in 1838 Samuel Gridley Howe described the "dreary isolation" and lack of human connection of deaf-blind Laura Bridgman. She was "a human soul, shut up in a dark and silent cell." Charles Dickens also framed Bridgman's disability as a "marble cell" that blocked her from connecting with other people, and portrayed himself as one of her rescuers. Mary Klages, *Woeful Afflictions: Disability and Sentimentality in Victorian America* (Philadelphia: University of Pennsylvania Press, 1999), 122–5, 128.

23. UCP Telethon, 1995.

24. Arthritis Telethons, 1990 and 1991.

25. Easter Seals Telethon, 1988; Steve Lipsher, "New Multiple Sclerosis Society Ads to Reach Out to Public," *Denver Post*, 12 November 1993.

26. Arthritis Telethon, 1988.

27. Robert Dawidoff, "Physical Disability and Cultural Representation," comment made at the American Studies Association Annual Meeting Session, Boston, 7 November 1992, 2–3; document in author's possession.

28. Easter Seals Telethon, 1995.

29. Arthritis Telethons, 1989, 1992, and 1994; MDA Telethon, 1989.

30. Quoted in François Furstenberg, *In The Name of the Father: Washington's Legacy, Slavery, and the Making of a Nation* (New York: Penguin Books, 2006), 199–200. See also

Jack P. Greene, *The Intellectual Construction of America: Exceptionalism and Identity from 1492 to 1800* (Chapel Hill: University of North Carolina Press, 1993), 201.

31. Wendy Gamber, "Antebellum Reform: Salvation, Self-Control, and Social Transformation," in *Charity, Philanthropy, and Civility in American History*, ed. Lawrence J. Friedman and Mark D. McGarvie (New York: Cambridge University Press, 2003), 129–53.

32. Literary critic T. Walter Herbert quoted in Michael Kimmel, *Manhood in America: A Cultural History* (New York: Free Press, 1996), 28.

33. Susan M. Ryan, *The Grammar of Good Intentions: Race and the Antebellum Culture of Benevolence* (Ithaca, N.Y.: Cornell University Press, 2005), 7–8.

34. Ronald G. Walters, *American Reformers 1815–1860* (New York: Hill and Wang, 1978), 145; Robert H. Wiebe, *The Opening of American Society: From the Adoption of the Constitution to the Eve of Disunion* (New York: Knopf, 1984), 160–3; Kimmel, *Manhood in America*, 3–9, 47, 111–12.

35. Irving Kenneth Zola, "Medicine as an Institution of Social Control," *Sociological Review* (November 1972): 491–2; Gregory S. Kavka, "Disability and the Right to Work," *Social Philosophy & Policy* 9, no. 1 (1992): 282–3.

36. See, for example, Kathryn Black, *In the Shadow of Polio: A Personal and Social History* (Reading, Mass.: Addison-Wesley, 1996), 47.

37. Tom Shales, "The Telethon's Touch: Jerry Lewis, With Sugar and Schmaltz," *Washington Post*, 7 September 1998.

38. UCP Telethon, 1995: Chicago segment.

39. Laura Hershey, "From Poster Child to Protestor," *Spectacle* (Spring/Summer 1997), http://www.cripcommentary.com/frompost.html (accessed 22 August 2009).

40. Karen Peltz Strauss, *A New Civil Right: Telecommunications Equality for Deaf and Hard of Hearing Americans* (Washington, D.C.: Gallaudet University Press, 2006); Sonny Kleinfeld, *The Hidden Minority: A Profile of Handicapped Americans* (Boston: Little, Brown, 1979), 158–71.

41. Kleinfeld, *The Hidden Minority*, 54–6; Nick Watson and Brian Woods, "The Origin and Early Developments of Special/Adaptive Wheelchair Seating," *Social History of Medicine* 18, no. 3 (December 2005): 459–74; Brian Woods and Nick Watson, "No Wheelchairs Beyond this Point: A Historical Examination of Wheelchair Access in the Twentieth Century in Britain and America," *Social Policy and Society* 4, no. 1 (2005): 97–105; Brian Woods and Nick Watson, "A Short History of Powered Wheelchairs," *Assistive Technology* 15, no. 2 (2003): 164–80; "How to Choose a Wheelchair," *Disability Articles*, http://www.disabilityarticles.com/Article/How-To-Choose-A-Wheelchair/4394 (accessed 9 December 2007). Some of the advertising provoked controversy. A series of highly eroticized print ads for Colours wheelchairs elicited both praise for affirming disabled people's sexuality and sharp criticism for objectifying women. Sharon Waxman, "One Company's Surprising Spin; Firm's Ads Sell Sexuality Along With Wheelchairs," *Washington Post*, 29 November 1996.

42. Katherine Ott, "The Sum of Its Parts: An Introduction to Modern Histories of Prosthetics," in *Artificial Parts, Practical Lives: Modern Histories of Prosthetics*, ed. Katherine Ott, David Serlin, and Stephen Mihm (New York: New York University Press, 2002), 21–2. Often the term "adaptive" or "assistive" slapped onto a common item such as a timer or a pen tripled or even quadrupled the price.

43. UCP Telethons, 1992 and 1993.

44. Easter Seals Telethons, 1989 and 1993.

45. Frank Bowe, *Handicapping America: Barriers to Disabled People* (New York: Harper and Row, 1978), 89. On the 1991 MDA Telethon, the San Jose, California, poster child, a seventh-grade boy who drove an electric wheelchair, said that his chair cost $8000. MDA paid $5000 of that price tag. He did not explain where the other $3000 came from.

46. Ott, "The Sum of Its Parts," 22.

47. Karen Campbell, "Wheelchair Performers Widen the Sweep of Dance Moves, International Festival Focuses on Cutting Edge Art Form," *Christian Science Monitor* (17 June 1997), 15. "Mixed-ability" dance companies operating in the United States in the 1990s included: Axis Dance Company of Oakland; Buen Vaije Dancers of Santa Fe; Dance Force of Atlanta; Dance Umbrella in Boston; Dancing Wheels and Theatrical Expressions of Cleveland; Gallaudet Dance Company, composed of deaf or hard-of-hearing dancers; Infinity Dance Theatre of New York City; Joint Forces Dance Company of Eugene, Ore.; Karen Peterson & Dancers of Miami; Light Motion Dance Company of Seattle; Sun Dance Non-Traditional Dance Theatre of Hastings-on-Hudson, N.Y. I thank Tari Hartmann Squire for providing me with this information.

48. MDA Telethons, 1988, 1990, 1991, and 1992. Contradicting the imagery on the telethon, MDA's *Quest* magazine reported on a device for disabled bowlers. See Tara Wood, "Ikan Puts Bowlers in a New League," *Quest* 12, no. 3 (May–June 2005), http://www.mdausa.org/Publications/Quest/q123power_soccer.html (accessed 24 February 2008).

49. UCP Telethons, 1993 and 1989.

50. Parasport, "About Us," http://www.parasport.org.uk/page.asp?section=0001000 10001&itemTitle=About+us (accessed 13 December 2007); Karen P. DePauw and Susan J. Gavron, *Disability Sport*, 2nd ed. (Champaign, Ill.: Human Kinetics, 1995), 8, 38–9, 43, 45–7, 57, 73–4, 76–82, 83, 86–8, 90–1, 96, 147, 151, 277–883, 286, 311–19, 324–9.

51. Jeré Longman, "Embracing the Quality of Opportunity," *New York Times*, 18 August 2008; DePauw and Gavron, *Disability Sport*, 4, 13, 58, 263, 277–8, 280–2, 286–7; Texas Woman's University, "Project INSPIRE: A History and Background of Disability Sport," https://www.twu.edu/inspire/history-and-background.asp (accessed 15 January 2008).

52. DePauw and Gavron, *Disability Sport*, 16, 18, 47–9, 116, 161–80, 207–8, 210, 212, 227–32, 280, 283, 287.

53. Tara Wood, "Get in the Game! Wheelers Kicking It Up in Power Soccer," *Quest* 12, no. 3 (May–June 2005), http://www.mdausa.org/Publications/Quest/q123power_soccer.html (accessed 23 February 2008).

54. The game became popular among youth and adults with cerebral palsy, high-level spinal cord injuries, and neuromuscular disabilities such as spinal muscular atrophy (SMA) and Duchenne muscular dystrophy (DMD). SMA and DMD were progressive, often significantly impairing, and even life-shortening. None of that stopped people with SMA and DMD from playing power soccer full tilt. Aficionados said that if you could drive a power wheelchair, you could play power soccer. Founder of a team known as The Thunder, a software developer who himself had SMA, proclaimed, "We have kids on ventilators. We have people that can't even move their arms. But they're playing a team sport, and they're playing the number one sport in the world—soccer." Many of the players with neuromuscular disabilities learned to play the game at the MDA summer camps where it became especially popular. On its telethon, MDA traditionally

presented SMA and DMD as terminal illnesses. In a remarkable shift—or, more accurately, a complicating addition—MDA's *Quest* magazine began to promote power soccer and report on international competitions. See http://www.ncpad.org/videos/fact_sheet. php?sheet=323&section=1977 (accessed 23 February 2008); Wood, "Get in the Game!"; Bill Norman, "Team USA," *Quest* 14, no. 5 (September–October 2007), http://www.mda.org/ publications/Quest/extra/qe14-5_soccer_players.html (accessed 23 February 2008); Bill Norman, "Stars & Stripes Grab World Cup in Overtime," *Quest* 15, no. 1 (January–February 2008), http://www.mda.org/publications/Quest/q151worldcup.html (accessed 23 February 2008). See also the United States Power Soccer Association (UPSA) website at http://www. powersoccerusa.net/, which includes links to online videos.

55. Diane E. Taub, Elaine M. Blinde, and Kimberly R. Greer, "Stigma Management through Participation in Sport and Physical Activity: Experiences of Male College Students with Physical Disabilities," *Human Relations* 52, no. 11 (November 1999): 1469–84. Some disability studies scholars criticized disability sport as complying with dominant nondisabled values. Harlan Hahn, "Sports and the Political Movement of Disabled Persons: Examining Non-Disabled Social Values," *Arena Review* 8 (1984): 115; Marie Hardin, "Marketing the Acceptably Athletic Image: Wheelchair Athletes, Sports-Related Advertising and Capitalist Hegemony," *Disability Studies Quarterly* 23, no. 1 (Winter 2003): 108, www.cds.hawaii.edu; Seymour, *Remaking the Body*, 93–9, 107–27.

Chapter 10

1. On the historical usage of charity and philanthropy to redefine the gendered roles available to American women, see Lawrence J. Friedman, "Philanthropy in America: Historicism and Its Discontents," in *Charity, Philanthropy, and Civility in American History*, ed. Lawrence J. Friedman and Mark D. McGarvie (New York: Cambridge University Press, 2003), 12; David Wagner, *What's Love Got to Do with It? A Critical Look at American Charity* (New York: New Press, 2000), 2. On disability and "hegemonic masculinity" and "emphasized femininity," see Wendy Seymour, *Remaking the Body: Rehabilitation and Change* (London: Routledge, 1998), especially 32–3.

2. Monica Davey, "Harley at 100: Mainstream Meets Mystique," *New York Times*, 1 September 2003.

3. Ibid.

4. Ibid.

5. Harley Davidson and its customers retooled the image of motorcycling by also getting involved with other charities. Paul Demko, "Doing Good Turns for Charity," *Chronicle of Philanthropy* 10, no. 1 (16 October 1997): 31–2.

6. I am grateful to Rosemarie Garland-Thomson for calling my attention to this connection.

7. *Today*, 25 March 1994; Davey, "Harley at 100."

8. *San Jose Mercury News*, 30 March 1992.

9. The commercial ran on San Francisco Bay Area television stations in September 1991 and again in February–March 1992. The print advertisement appeared in the *San Jose Mercury News*, 11 September 1991 and 2 March 1992.

10. Easter Seals Telethon, 1992.

11. Ibid.

12. Scott M. Cutlip, *Fund Raising in the United States: Its Role in America's Philanthropy* (New Brunswick, N.J.: Rutgers University Press, 1965), 390; Arthritis Telethon, 1989.

13. On Easter Seals' 1993 Chicago cutaway, four beauty pageant winners took calls as "VIP" phone operators: "Junior Pre-Teen Princess," Miss Illinois Teen, Miss Illinois, and Mrs. Illinois U.S.A.

14. UCP Telethon, 1993.

15. Rosemarie Garland-Thomson, *Extraordinary Bodies: Figuring Physical Disability in American Culture and Literature* (New York: Columbia University Press, 1997), 28–9.

16. Personal communication with author.

17. MDA Telethon, 1988.

18. Arthritis Telethon, 1992; MDA Telethon, 1993.

19. Arthritis Telethon, 1989; Easter Seals Telethons, 1991–1994.

20. Daniel J. Wilson, "Crippled Manhood: Infantile Paralysis and the Construction of Masculinity," *Medical Humanities Review* 12, no. 2 (Fall 1998): 10–13, 15, 18–21; Daniel J. Wilson, "Fighting Polio Like a Man: Intersections of Masculinity, Disability, and Aging," in *Gendering Disability*, ed. Bonnie G. Smith and Beth Hutchison (New Brunswick, N.J.: Rutgers University Press, 2004), 120, 128. See also David Serlin, "Engineering Masculinity: Veterans and Prosthetics after World War Two," in *Artificial Parts, Practical Lives: Modern Histories of Prosthetics*, ed. Katherine Ott, David Serlin, and Stephen Mihm (New York: New York University Press, 2002), 56–8. On the inadequacies of research regarding the sexuality of people with disabilities and prejudicial stereotypes, see Rhoda Olkin, *What Psychotherapists Should Know about Disability* (New York: Guilford Press, 1999), 226–8.

21. MDA Telethons, 1991 and 1993.

22. Michelle Fine and Adrienne Asch, "Introduction: Beyond Pedestals," in *Women with Disabilities: Essays in Psychology, Culture, and Politics*, ed. Michelle Fine and Adrienne Asch (Philadelphia: Temple University Press, 1988), 12–15. For the survey p. 34 cites an unpublished paper from 1986 by W. J. Hanna and B. Rogovsky, "Women and Disability: Stigma and 'the Third Factor.'"

23. Marian Blackwell-Stratton, Mary Lou Breslin, Arlene Byrnne Mayerson, and Susan Bailey, "Smashing Icons: Disabled Women and the Disability and Women's Movements," in *Women with Disabilities*, 306–7. See also Roberta Galler, "The Myth of the Perfect Body," in *Pleasure and Danger: Exploring Female Sexuality*, ed. Carole S. Vance (1984; repr., London: Pandora Press/HarperCollins, 1989), 165–72. Women with disabilities continued to have lower marriage rates and higher divorce rates than either nondisabled women or men with disabilities. Steven Kaye, *Status Report on Disability in the United States* (Oakland: Disability Rights Advocates/ San Francisco: Disability Statistics Center, University of California, San Francisco, 1998), 35.

24. The Easter Seals Telethon featured two women with families and jobs, a Safeway store clerk in 1991 and 1992 and a court reporter in 1994 and 1995. The MDA Telethon in 1988 and 1993 included segments about three married women with neuromuscular conditions: One had just gotten married, a second had just had a baby, and the third had three children and had been a schoolteacher for thirty years. MDA Telethons, 1988 and 1993; Robert Macy, "Jerry Lewis Pushes the Positive at 28th Telethon," *Associated Press*, 6 September 1993.

25. Irving Kenneth Zola, *Missing Pieces: A Chronicle of Living with a Disability* (Philadelphia: Temple University Press, 1982), 147.

26. See Kristin Lindgren, "Bodies in Trouble: Identity, Embodiment, and Disability," in *Gendering Disability*, 147.

27. MDA Telethon, 1992.

28. MDA Telethons, 1993 and 1994.

29. "Administration Helps to Kill Plan to Help Disabled Marry, Work," *Item* (24 July 1994), 6A. See also D. A. Martin, R. W. Conley, and J. H. Noble Jr., "The ADA and Disability Benefits Policy: Some Research Topics and Issues," *Journal of Disability Policy Studies* 6, no. 2 (July 1995): 1–15.

30. "[F]orget any notion that people with MD can be sexual. The telethon presents even spouses as caretakers, not lovers. The denigration of our potential for relationships is perhaps one of the most dehumanizing and negative aspects of the telethon." Laura Hershey, "From Poster Child to Protestor," *Spectacle* (Spring/Summer 1997), http://www.cripcommentary.com/frompost.html (accessed 22 August 2009).

31. MDA Telethon, 1988.

32. Barbara Mandell Altman, "Disabled Women in the Social Structure," in Susan E. Browne, Debra Connors, and Nanci Stern, ed., *With the Power of Each Breath: A Disabled Women's Anthology* (Pittsburgh and San Francisco: Cleis Press, 1985), 69–76. Also Stephen Mihm, "'A Limb Which Shall Be Presentable in Polite Society': Prosthetic Technologies in the Nineteenth Century"; Elspeth Brown, "The Prosthetics of Management: Motion Study, Photography, and the Industrialized Body in World War I America"; Serlin, "Engineering Masculinity"—all in *Artificial Parts, Practical Lives: Modern Histories of Prosthetics*, ed. Katherine Ott, David Serlin, and Stephen Mihm (New York: New York University Press, 2002), 45–74, 249–81, 287–99; Wilson, "Crippled Manhood"; Wilson, "Fighting Polio Like a Man"; Asch and Fine, "Introduction: Beyond Pedestals," in *Women with Disabilities*, 12; Nancy Felipe Russo and Mary A. Jansen, "Women, Work, and Disability: Opportunities and Challenges," in *Women with Disabilities*, 240–1; Lisa Schur, "Is There Still a 'Double Handicap'? Economic, Social, and Political Disparities Experienced by Women with Disabilities," in *Gendering Disability*, 257–60, 265–6.

33. From the beginning, the Arthritis Foundation aimed to return people to work through rehabilitation. "Directs Campaign Unit of Arthritis Foundation," *New York Times*, 11 November 1954; "Arthritis Appeal on TV; 17-Hour Drive Saturday Offers Eisenhower Portrait as Prize," *New York Times*, 8 December 1954; "On Television," *New York Times*, 11 December 1954.

34. Deborah Kent, "In Search of a Heroine: Images of Women with Disabilities in Fiction and Drama," in *Women with Disabilities*, 90–110. See also Asch and Fine, "Introduction: Beyond Pedestals," in *Women with Disabilities*, 16–18.

35. Ibid., 19. See also Carrie Sandahl, "Queering the Crip or Cripping the Queer? Intersections of Queer and Crip Identities in Solo Autobiographical Performance," *GLQ: A Journal of Lesbian and Gay Studies* 9, nos. 1–2 (2003): 34–6.

36. Russell P. Shuttleworth, "Disabled Masculinity: Expanding the Masculine Repertoire," in *Gendering Disability*, 166–78; Kenny Fries, *Body Remember* (New York: Dutton, 1997); Bob Guter and John R. Killacky, ed., *Queer Crips: Disabled Gay Men and Their Stories* (New York: Harrington Park Press/Haworth Press, 2004).

37. Fine and Asch, "Introduction: Beyond Pedestals," in *Women with Disabilities*, 14–15. See also Galler, "Myth of the Perfect Body," 167; Harilyn Rousso, "Daughters with Disabilities: Defective Women or Minority Women?" in *Women with Disabilities*, 139–71.

38. Fine and Asch, "Introduction: Beyond Pedestals," in *Women with Disabilities*, 21–2; Frank Bowe, *Handicapping America: Barriers to Disabled People* (New York: Harper and Row, 1978), 185. Also Donna Hyler, "To Choose a Child"; Jo Ann le Maistre, "Parenting"; Anne Finger, "Claiming All of Our Bodies: Reproductive Rights and Disability"—all in *With the Power of Each Breath*, 280–307; Anne Finger, *Past Due: A Story of Disability, Pregnancy, and Birth* (Seattle: Seal Press, 1990); Galler, "Myth of the Perfect Body," 167–8; Catherine Kudlick, "Modernity's Miss-Fits: Blind Girls and Marriage in France and America, 1820–1920" in *Women on Their Own: Interdisciplinary Perspectives on Being Single*, ed. Rudolph Bell and Virginia Yans (New Brunswick, N.J.: Rutgers University Press, 2008), 201–18.

39. Fine and Asch, "Introduction: Beyond Pedestals," in *Women with Disabilities*, 8, 15, 23; Galler, "Myth of the Perfect Body," 168–70.

40. Diane E. Taub, Elaine M. Blinde, and Kimberly R. Greer, "Stigma Management through Participation in Sport and Physical Activity: Experiences of Male College Students with Physical Disabilities," *Human Relations* 52, no. 11 (November 1999): 1469–84; Sharon R. Guthrie and Shirley Castelnuovo, "Disability Management Among Women with Physical Impairments: The Contribution of Physical Activity," *Sociology of Sport Journal* 18 (2001): 6–7, 12, 17. See also Daniel J. Wilson, *Living with Polio: The Epidemic and Its Survivors* (Chicago: University of Chicago Press, 2005), 149–50, 154–5.

41. Fine and Asch, "Introduction: Beyond Pedestals," in *Women with Disabilities*, 24; Galler, "Myth of the Perfect Body," 165–6. Note that concrete data are unusually difficult to access, yet another consequence of the marginalization of women with disabilities.

42. Fine and Asch, "Introduction: Beyond Pedestals," in *Women with Disabilities*, 22–5; Rebecca S. Grothaus, "Abuse of Women with Disabilities," in *With the Power of Each Breath*, 124–8.

43. Shuttleworth, "Disabled Masculinity."

44. Fine and Asch, "Introduction: Beyond Pedestals," in *Women with Disabilities*, 25.

45. Ibid., 25–6. See also Deborah S. Abbott, "This Body I Love," in *With the Power of Each Breath*, 271–3.

46. Fine and Asch, "Introduction: Beyond Pedestals," in *Women with Disabilities*, 25–6; Susan E. Browne, Debra Connors, and Nanci Stern, "Introduction," in *With the Power of Each Breath*, 10–11. Disabled feminists criticized nondisabled feminists for distancing themselves from women with disabilities in developing community among women, political organizing, and feminist research and theorizing. Fine and Asch, "Introduction: Beyond Pedestals," in *Women with Disabilities*, 3–4; Dai R. Thompson, "Anger," and Anne Finger, "Claiming All of Our Bodies: Reproductive Rights and Disability," in *With the Power of Each Breath*, 80, 292–3, 297–8; Galler, "Myth of the Perfect Body," 166; Jenny Morris, *Pride Against Prejudice, Transforming Attitudes to Disability* (1991; repr., North Pomfret: Trafalgar Square, 1998), 7–8. Other important publications by disabled American feminists during the 1980s and 1990s include: Ann Cupolo Carrillo, Katherine Corbett, and Victoria Lewis, *No More Stares* (Berkeley: Disability Rights Education and Defense Fund, 1982); Marsha Saxton and Florence Howe, ed., *With Wings: An Anthology of Literature by and About Women with Disabilities* (New York: Feminist Press at the City University of

New York, 1987); Georgina Kleege, *Sight Unseen* (New Haven, Conn.: Yale University Press, 1999); Nancy Mairs, *Plaintext: Deciphering a Woman's Life* (New York: Perennial/ Harper & Row, 1986), repr. as *Plaintext: Essays* (Tucson: University of Arizona Press, 1997); Nancy Mairs, *Waist-high in the World: A Life Among the Nondisabled* (Boston: Beacon Press, 1996). For a critical review of disabled feminist writings in the 1980s, see Rosemarie Garland-Thomson, "Feminist Disability Studies," *Signs: Journal of Women in Culture and Society* 30, no. 2 (2005): 1557–87. For a recent examination of feminist disability studies, see Rosemarie Garland-Thomson, "Integrating Disability, Transforming Feminist Theory," in *Gendering Disability*, 73–104.

47. Emily Rapp, *Poster Child: A Memoir* (New York: Bloomsbury, 2007), 179. On disabled feminists supporting disabled women, see Galler, "Myth of the Perfect Body," 166.

48. *Prenatal Testing and Disability Rights*, Hastings Center Studies in Ethics series, (Washington, D.C.: Georgetown University Press, 2000); Edwin Black, *War Against the Weak: Eugenics and America's Campaign to Create a Master Race* (New York: Four Walls Eight Windows 1ST Edition, 2003).

49. On the 1989 Arthritis Telethon, a young woman with arthritis explained how she had persuaded her local chapter to establish support groups to deal with lifestyle issues, including dating and sexuality.

50. Emphasis added. UCP Telethons, 1992, 1993, and 1994. For two accounts of disabled motherhood, see Denise Sherer Jacobson, *The Question of David* (Oakland, Calif.: Creative Arts, 1999), an eloquent memoir by a woman with cerebral palsy; Pam Adams, "Special Day for Noah's Parents: Quadriplegic Mom Celebrates Her Day," *Peoria Journal Star* (Peoria, Ill.), 13 May 2001, a news feature story about a former MDA poster child. In contrast, here is how long-time UCP host Dennis James reacted to a mother and son, Native Americans, both of whom had cerebral palsy. "Now, what have we got here? We've got. . . . Here is a very unusual case. . . . Now this is one of the most unusual cases I have heard of in forty-three years of being connected with United Cerebral Palsy. Mother with cerebral palsy. Child with cerebral palsy. Extremely unusual, because it is not hereditary. We are going to make that point very very emphatic. It's an injury. Yet this was a full-term baby, wasn't it?" *Mother:* "Yes, it was." James mentions that "they" think maybe it was "genetic." The mother acknowledges this. *James:* "Well, you're the first case I've ever heard of, so we just hope that they're wrong and we're right. Okay? Does he walk?" *Mother:* "Yes, he does, with a walker." James has the walker brought onstage and asks the boy to walk with it. The audience and the studio applaud. *James:* "Now, he is thrilled to be doing that. Now, do you realize that mommy and the volunteers work just hours and hours at a time to get this boy to take those steps?" James then instructs the boy to turn around and pause and "look at the camera and give us a big smile, and everybody'll run in there. There he goes!" The boy flashes a big smile. UCP Telethon, 1993.

51. During the 1990s, the Easter Seals Telethon featured as National Adult Representatives several married women. Profiles and interviews of them focused on those marital relationships, though not their sexuality.

Chapter 11

1. The names of many of the actors who played Scrooge are included with each entry. Live-action motion pictures and television programs: *A Christmas Carol* (1901); *A*

Christmas Carol (Essanay, 1908); *A Christmas Carol* (Edison, 1910), Mark McDermott; *A Christmas Carol* (1912); *A Christmas Carol* (dir. Leedham Bantock, Zenith Film Company, 1913), Seymour Hicks; *A Christmas Carol* (dir. Harold M. Shaw, Fenning London Film Company, 1914); Charles Rock; *The Right to Be Happy* aka *A Christmas Carol* (dir. Rupert Julian, Universal, 1916); *Scrooge* (dir. George Wynn, 1922), H. V. Esmond; *Tense Moments with Great Authors: "#7 Scrooge"* (dir. H. B. Parkinson, W. Courtney Rowden, 1922), H. V. Esmond; *Scrooge* (dir. Edwin Greenwood, 1923), Russell Thorndike; *Scrooge* (dir. Hugh Croise, 1928), Bransby Williams; *Scrooge* (dir. Henry Edwards, Julius Hagen-Twickenham, 1935), Seymour Hicks; *A Christmas Carol* (dir. Edwin L. Marin, MGM, 1938), Reginald Owen; *A Christmas Carol* (dir. George Lowther, 1943), William Podmore, this version was 60 minutes and, at the time, was the longest US TV program yet broadcast; *A Christmas Carol* (dir. James Caddigan, 1947), John Carradine; *The Philco Television Playhouse: "A Christmas Carol"* (dir. Fred Coe, 1948), Dennis King; *The Christmas Carol* (dir. Arthur Pierson, 1949), a US TV film narrated by Vincent Price with Taylor Holmes as Scrooge; *A Christmas Carol* (BBC, 1950), Bransby Williams; *Fireside Theatre: "A Christmas Carol"* (dir. Gordon Duff, 1951), Ralph Richardson; *Scrooge*, aka *A Christmas Carol* (dir. Brian Desmond Hurst, Showcorporation/George Minter/Renown, 1951), Alistair Sim; *Kraft Television Theatre: "A Christmas Carol"* (1952), Malcolm Keen; *Shower of Stars: "A Christmas Carol"* (dir. Ralph Levy, 1954), Fredric March; *The Alcoa Hour: "The Stingiest Man in Town"* (dir. Daniel Petrie, 1955), Basil Rathbone; *Story of the Christmas Carol* (dir. David Barnheizer, 1955), Norman Gottschalk; *General Electric Theater: "The Trail to Christmas"* (dir. James Stewart, 1957), a cowboy tells a boy the Dickens tale with John McIntire as Scrooge; *Tales from Dickens: A Dickens Christmas: "A Christmas Carol"* (dir. Neil McGuire, 1958), TV series hosted by Fredric March with Basil Rathbone as Scrooge; *Mr. Scrooge* (dir. Bob Jarvis, 1964), Cyril Ritchard; *Carry on Christmas* (dir. Ronnie Baxter, 1969), comedy with Sid James; *Scrooge* (dir. Ronald Neame, Cinema Center, 1970), musical version with Albert Finney; *A Christmas Carol* (dir. Richard Williams, 1971), British TV movie with Alistair Sim; *A Christmas Carol* (dir. Moira Armstrong, BBC, 1976), Michael Hordern; *Scrooge* (dir. John Blanchard, Canadian TV movie, 1978); *An American Christmas Carol* (Scherick-Chase-Slan/Scrooge Productions/Smith-Hemion, 1979), Henry Winkler as a New England "Scrooge" during the Great Depression, who is redeemed by helping the family of a boy (Chris Crabb) who needs rehabilitation from polio; *A Christmas Carol at Ford's Theatre* (1979); *Skinflint: A Country Christmas Carol* (1979), a country music version with Hoyt Axton as Cyrus Flint; *A Christmas Carol* (dir. Laird Williamson, 1981), William Paterson, a US TV movie; *The Guthrie Theatre Presents a Christmas Carol* (The Entertainment Channel, 1982), film of stage production, narrated by John Gielgud; *The Gospel According to Scrooge* (dir. Mark S. Vegh, 1983); *A Christmas Carol* (dir. Clive Donner, CBS, 1984), George C. Scott; *A Christmas Carol* (1994), US ballet; *Ebbie* (dir. George Kazcender, Victor Television Productions/Maverick Crescent Entertainment Limited, 1994), Susan Lucci as a hard-driving department store owner Elizabeth "Ebbie" Scrooge, whose widowed assistant Roberta Cratchit has a son named Timmy who needs medical treatment; Ebbie decides to provide adequate health insurance for all her employees; *John Grin's Christmas* (1986), features an African American Scrooge, Robert Guillaume, and no Tiny Tim, but does feature a generous and insightful blind woman; *Scrooged* (dir. Richard Donner, 1988), Bill Murray as a heartless executive producing a telecast of *A Christmas Carol* with Buddy Hackett as Scrooge; *Bah! Humbug!: The Story of Charles Dickens' "A*

Christmas Carol" (dir. Derek Bailey, PBS, 1994), a reading by actors James Earl Jones and Martin Sheen; *Ebenezer* (dir. Ken Jubenvill, 1997), a Wild West version with Jack Palance as a ruthless cattle baron; *Ms Scrooge* (Wilshire Court/Power Pictures, 1997), Cicely Tyson as Ebenita Scrooge who, like "Ebbie," decides to pay for medical treatment for Tim (who this time has a slow-growing congenital tumor in his leg) and health insurance for her employees; *A Christmas Carol* (dir. David Hugh Jones, Flying Freehold, 1999), Patrick Stewart; *A Christmas Carol* (dir. Catherine Morshead, 2000), British TV movie, Ross Kemp as Eddie Scrooge; *A Diva's Christmas Carol* (dir. Richard Shankman, 2000), a TV movie made for VH1 with Vanessa L. Williams as pop singing star Ebony Scrooge; *Scrooge and Marley* (dir. Fred Holmes, 2001), an evangelical Christian version with Dean Jones; *A Carol Christmas* (dir. Matthew Imas, Hallmark, 2003), Tori Spelling as Carol Cartman, a selfish TV talk show host; *A Christmas Carol: The Musical* (dir. Arthur Alan Seidelman, 2004), Kelsey Grammer; *A Carol of Christmas* (dir. Roland Black, 2005); *Chasing Christmas* (dir. Ron Oliver, 2005), a time-traveling version with Tom Arnold as a Scrooge-like single dad; *The Carol Project* (dir. Tim Folkmann, 2006), musical; *The Nutcracker: A Christmas Story* (2007), a ballet combining the E. T. A. Hoffman story with the Dickens tale. Animated productions: *Mister Magoo's Christmas Carol* (dir. Abe Levitow, UPA, 1962); *Bah, Humduck! A Looney Tunes Christmas* (dir. Charles Visser, Warner, 2006), Daffy Duck; *A Christmas Carol* (dir. Zoran Janjic, Australia, Air Programs International, 1969), screened on US TV 1970; *The Stingiest Man in Town* (dirs. Jules Bass, Arthur Rankin Jr., Rankin-Bass, 1978), Walter Matthau as the voice of Scrooge and Robert Morse as the voice of Young Scrooge; *A Christmas Carol* (Australia, 1982); *A Christmas Carol* (Burbank Productions, 1982), narrated by Michael Redgrave; *Mickey's Christmas Carol* (dir. Burny Mattinson, Disney, 1983), Alan Young as the voice of Scrooge McDuck; *The Muppet Christmas Carol* (dir. Brian Henson, 1992), Michael Caine as the voice of Scrooge; *A Christmas Carol* (dirs. Toshiyuki Hiruma, Takashi Masunaga, Jetlag, 1994); *A Flintstones Christmas Carol* (dir. Joanna Romersa, 1994); *A Christmas Carol* (dir. Stan Phillips, DIC Entertainment, 1997), narrated by Tim Curry; *Christmas Carol: The Movie* (dir. Jimmy T. Murakami, 2001), Simon Callow as the voice of Scrooge; *A Sesame Street Christmas Carol* (dirs. Ken Diego, Victor DiNapoli, Emily Squires, Jon Stone, 2006); *Barbie in A Christmas Carol* (Australia, 2008); *A Christmas Carol* (dir. Robert Zemeckis, Disney, 2009), Jim Carrey as the voice of Scrooge. Internet Movie Database, http://www.imdb.com (accessed 20–22 November 2009); Martin F. Norden, *The Cinema of Isolation, A History of Physical Disability in the Movies* (New Brunswick, N.J.: Rutgers University Press, 1994), 33; Patricia King Harrison and Alan Gevinson, ed., *American Film Institute Catalog 1931–1940* (Berkeley: University of California Press, 1993), 347.

2. In June 1999 *Books in Print* listed sixty-six different editions of the story, including adaptations based on Dickens's basic plot.

3. In the late 1930s, the WPA Federal Theater Project in Los Angeles and other places made a theatrical version part of every Christmas Season program. William F. McDonald, *Federal Relief Administration and the Arts* (Columbus: Ohio State University Press, 1969), 554. That customary programming continued decades later. A sampling of the myriad stage productions from 1998 alone included not only major theaters such as Radio City Music Hall in New York City, the San Diego Repertory Theater, and the Geary Theater in San Francisco, but also the Totempole Playhouse in Chambersberg, Pennsylvania; the Bardavon Opera House in Poughkeepsie, New York; Triangle Church in Chapel Hill,

North Carolina; Hale Center Theater in Orem, Utah; the Hippodrome State Theater in Gainesville, Florida; the Alley Theater in Houston; and *Scrooge: The Ballet!* at the Hawaii Theater Center in Honolulu. In 1999 comedian and composer Steve Allen was reportedly writing songs for a stage musical adaptation. Reed Johnson, "Steve Allen Writes Songs for 'Christmas Carol' Musical," *San Francisco Chronicle,* 24 November 1999. In 2007 playwright Christopher Durang satirized the Dickens' tale. Robert Hurwitt, " 'Christmas Carol' Meets 'Wonderful Life' in 'Wild Binge,' " *San Francisco Chronicle,* 4 December 2007, http://www.sfgate.com (accessed 4 December 2007).

4. "Adopt-a-Child" donors received a statuette of a disabled child leaning on crutches behind a small dog. Easter Seals Telethon, 1990.

5. UCP Telethon, 1993.

6. William B. Cohen, "Epilogue: The European Comparison," in *Charity, Philanthropy, and Civility in American History,* ed. Lawrence J. Friedman and Mark D. McGarvie (New York: Cambridge University Press, 2003), 393.

7. Linda Colley, *Britons: Forging the Nation 1707–1837* (New Haven, Conn.: Yale University Press, 1992), 59. The London Foundling Hospital cared for children with many kinds of disabilities, medically and vocationally rehabilitating some and providing lifelong maintenance for others. Alysa Levene, *Childcare-Health and Mortality at the London Foundling Hospital 1741–1800: "Left to the Mercy of the World"* (Manchester, U.K.: Manchester University Press, 2007), 165–8.

8. The organization officially adopted the name National Easter Seals Society in 1979. Charles A. Riley II, *Disability and the Media: Prescriptions for Change* (Lebanon, N.H.: University Press of New England, 2005), 110–11; Easter Seals Telethon, 1991; James E. Williams Jr., "Easter Seals Transforms the Telethon," *Fund Raising Management* 26, no. 7 (September 1995): 28–32; Charlotte Snow, "Rehab Rival: Easter Seals Is a Healthcare Force to Be Reckoned With," *Modern Healthcare* 27, no. 17 (28 April 1997): 18–19.

9. Scott M. Cutlip, *The Unseen Power: Public Relations. A History* (Hillsdale, N.J.: Lawrence Erlbaum Associates, 1994), 558–60, 561; Riley, *Disability and the Media,* 111–12. Christy's illustrations for the 1936, 1937, and 1938 Birthday Balls program covers are reproduced online at http://www.disabilitymuseum.org (accessed 7 July 2007).

10. Scott M. Cutlip, *Fund Raising in the United States: Its Role in America's Philanthropy* (New Brunswick, N.J.: Rutgers University Press, 1965), 361, 365–71.

11. Ibid., 376, 383–7, quotes from 384 and 387; Richard Carter, *The Gentle Legions* (Garden City, N.Y.: Doubleday, 1961), 112; David L. Sills, *The Volunteers: Means and Ends in a National Organization* (1957; repr., New York: Arno Press, 1980), 126–7, 169–70.

12. David Zinman, "Many Former Poster Kids Lead Normal Lives Today," *Los Angeles Times,* 16 December 1984; David M. Oshinsky, *Polio: An American Story* (New York: Oxford University Press, 2005), 83.

13. Tony Gould, *A Summer Plague: Polio and Its Survivors* (New Haven, Conn.: Yale University Press, 1995), xi; Oshinsky, *Polio: An American Story,* 68, 81–3. In 1974 MDA presented a video monologue entitled "I Hate People, Especially Children," in which an actor personified muscular dystrophy and, like "The Crippler," "ominously hovers over the figure of a healthy child." The vignette was written by Budd Schulberg and directed by Jerry Lewis. Lawrence Joseph Londino, "A Descriptive Analysis of 'The Jerry Lewis Labor Day Telethon for Muscular Dystrophy,' " Ph.D. diss., University of Michigan, 1975, 127–8.

14. See chapters 7–8. Cutlip, *Fund Raising in the United States*, 51; Riley, *Disability and the Media*, 111–12; Zinman, "Many Former Poster Kids Lead Normal Lives Today"; Ellen L. Barton, "Textual Practices of Erasure: Representations of Disability and the Founding of the United Way," in *Embodied Rhetorics: Disability in Language and Culture*, ed. James C. Wilson and Cynthia Lewiecki-Wilson (Carbondale: Southern Illinois University Press, 2001), 178–9, 184, 187, 193.

15. See, for instance, Shawn Hubler, "After Initial Anguish, Family of Cerebral Palsy Poster Child Is Picture of Happiness," *Los Angeles Times*, 21 January 1990, South Bay edition.

16. The 1988 Arthritis Telethon paraded photos of kids with arthritis while a singer urged: "Share your love with all the children of the world." See also Herbert J. Vida, "Dana Point Boy Works Hard as Arthritis Foundation Poster Child," *Los Angeles Times*, 8 June 1986, Orange County edition.

17. *Disability Rag* 7, no. 2 (March/April 1986): 22; Dennis Hall and Susan G. Hall, *American Icons: An Encyclopedia of the People, Places, and Things That Have Shaped Our Culture*, Vol. 1 (Westport, Conn.: Greenwood Publishing Group, 2006), 574.

18. For a summary of disability prevalence rates in the 1990s' US population among African Americans, Asian Americans/Pacific Islanders, Hispanic Americans, and Native Americans as compared to European Americans, see Rhoda Olkin, *What Psychotherapists Should Know about Disability* (New York: Guilford Press, 1999), 19–20.

19. Naomi Rogers, "Race and the Politics of Polio: Warm Springs, Tuskegee, and the March of Dimes," *American Journal of Public Health* 97, no. 5 (May 2007), 784–95; Oshinsky, *Polio: An American Story*, 65–7.

20. MDA Telethon, 1996; "Benjamin Gives Hope to Others—Again," *Parade* (31 August 1997). In 1986 the MDA poster child for the District of Columbia was an African American lad. Anne Simpson, "People: MDA Poster Child," *Washington Post*, 8 May 1986. Service organizations in the black community supplied volunteers for the disability charities that may have, over the years, won them greater attention from those agencies. "First Year of Service Noted by AKA Chapter," *Los Angeles Sentinel*, 23 August 1979. The Chicago UCP's 1991 poster child was a 10-year-old Latino boy. "Mutual Admiration," *Chicago Sun-Times*, 8 January 1991.

21. Scott Kraft, "Poster Child Quest: Cute Isn't Enough," *Los Angeles Times*, 7 April 1986. See also Laura Kavesh, "It Takes a Tough Kid to Be a Poster Child," *Chicago Tribune*, 29 March 1985, c edition. On the March of Dimes selecting poster children for both medical and cosmetic reasons, see Zinman, "Many Former Poster Kids Lead Normal Lives Today."

22. Kraft, "Poster Child Quest"; David Zinman, "Critics Say Drives Foster Stereotyping of Disabled," *Los Angeles Times*, 16 December 1984; Kavesh, "It Takes a Tough Kid to Be a Poster Child"; Fred Rothenberg, "Waking up Telethon's Wee Hours," *Toronto Globe and Mail*, 3 September 1982, early edition. In a TV commercial publicizing "Aisles of Smiles," he appeared with his "friend," that year's National Poster Child. The boy sat on a wheelchair, not a power chair he could have operated on his own, but a manual chair pushed by his paternal benefactor Lewis. The spot created an image of helplessness and dependency. Likewise, the 1993 MDA extravaganza opened with a musical number and then showed Lewis approaching and bending to embrace the National Poster Child who was sitting on a wheelchair.

23. Easter Seals Telethon, 1993; Kavesh, "It Takes a Tough Kid to Be a Poster Child."

24. Kraft, "Poster Child Quest." See also Kavesh, "It Takes a Tough Kid to Be a Poster Child."

25. Kavesh, "It Takes a Tough Kid to Be a Poster Child."

26. Easter Seals Telethons, 1991 and 1992.

27. Zinman, "Many Former Poster Kids Lead Normal Lives Today."

28. MDA Telethon, 1989; Jerry Lewis, "Seeing That Light in a Child's Eyes," *Parade* (1 September 1991). Some individuals defended the term "Jerry's Kids." It was not meant to make adults with neuromuscular disabilities seem childlike, they asserted. It instead expressed "a sense of family." But they ignored that this image framed these adults as children within this metaphorical family and sidestepped the common infantilization of people with diseases and disabilities within both charity and medical-model practices. Bill Thompson, "Ungrateful Child Sharp as Serpent's Tooth Just Ask Jerry," *Fort Worth Star-Telegram*, 6 September 1992, final AM edition.

29. Easter Seals Telethon, 1989.

30. Robert Dawidoff, "Physical Disability and Cultural Representation," comment made at American Studies Association Annual Meeting Session, Boston, 7 November 1992; document in author's possession.

31. Easter Seals Telethon, 1993; UCP Telethon, 1994.

32. Easter Seals Telethon, 1992.

33. MDA Telethons, 1993 and 1991.

34. Kathryn Black reports examples of this sort of treatment and these attitudes without understanding that the infantilization was enforced on these disabled patients rather than being their psychological response to disability. *In the Shadow of Polio: A Personal and Social History* (Reading, Mass.: Addison-Wesley, 1996), 171–2. For other examples, see Daniel J. Wilson, *Living with Polio: The Epidemic and Its Survivors* (Chicago: University of Chicago Press, 2005), 50–1.

35. Erving Goffman, *Stigma: Notes on the Management of Spoiled Identity* (Englewood Cliffs, N.J.: Prentice-Hall, 1963).

36. Laura Hershey, "A Skeptic's Guide to the Jerry Lewis Telethon," http://laurahershey.omeka.net/items/show/27 , accessed July 9, 2014

37. Ben Mattlin, "Personal Perspective: An Open Letter to Jerry Lewis: The Disabled Need Dignity, Not Pity," *Los Angeles Times*, 1 September 1991.

38. UCP Telethon, 1989.

39. The Rice Krispies commercial aired in 1991. A 1987 Anheuser-Busch prime-time commercial conveyed the standard message: A child with a disability could not be a real child. Opening shot: A pony gambols across a meadow. Cut to a boy's face. "Youth," says the announcer, "a time to race with the wind, to run free. That's only a dream for some kids." The next shot reveals that the boy is seated on a wheelchair. Leaning forward, he reaches toward the pony, wanting to touch it and, the imagery suggests, longing to ride it, but he is *confined* to that wheelchair. "You can help them fight to make that dream come true," explains the announcer. "Every time you buy Budweiser and Bud Lite this August [shot of the boy smiling], we make a contribution to the Muscular Dystrophy Association." The pony walks slowly toward the boy. The boy holds out his hand. Cut to a Budweiser display with a picture of the MDA poster child and the slogan: "Help us fight muscular dystrophy." Cut back to the pony approaching the boy, then the boy stroking its nose. In

1992 Anheuser-Busch produced a prime-time spot called "Sand Castles." Six boys run along a beach. They come upon another boy sitting on a pier. The camera starts on his legs to emphasize that he wears braces. It pans up to his lap to show that he is petting a puppy. "At Anheuser-Busch, we believe a child should experience it all," says the announcer. "That's why we support the Muscular Dystrophy Association." Fundamentally inferior to other boys, a lad with a disability could not experience real boyhood. To make him real, beer drinkers should buy Bud and "help Jerry's Kids just be kids."

40. MDA Telethon, 1994.

41. UCP Telethon, 1993.

42. UCP Telethon, 1995.

43. UCP Telethons, 1992, 1993, 1994; MDA Telethon, 1991.

44. MDA Telethon, 1994.

45. Michael Angeli, "God's Biggest Goof," *Esquire* 115, no. 2 (February 1991): 101.

46. MDA Telethon, 1991.

47. Quoted in Mary Klages, *Woeful Afflictions: Disability and Sentimentality in Victorian America* (Philadelphia: University of Pennsylvania Press, 1999), 136–7.

48. Hannah Joyner, *From Pity to Pride: Growing Up Deaf in the Old South* (Washington, D.C.: Gallaudet University Press, 2004), 13–14, 40–1, 169–70n15. In its promotional materials, one Victorian British educational institution asserted that "the uninstructed Deaf and Dumb must be causes of unceasing sorrow to their afflicted parents and friends, and in most cases useless and burdensome, often dangerous and injurious, members of Society." *An Historical Sketch of the Asylum for Indigent Deaf and Dumb Children, Surrey* (London: Edward Brewster, 1841), iv, quoted in Martha Stoddard Holmes, "Working (With) the Rhetoric of Affliction: Autobiographic Narratives of Victorians with Physical Disabilities," in *Embodied Rhetorics*, 31. For similar views of blind children in nineteenth-century Scotland, see John Oliphant, "'Touching the Light': The Invention of Literacy for the Blind," *Paedagogica Historica* 44, nos. 1–2 (February–April 2008): 76. For an analysis of the melodramatic uses of children with disabilities in fundraising by British Victorian institutions, see Martha Stoddard Holmes, *Fictions of Affliction: Physical Disability in Victorian Culture* (Ann Arbor: University of Michigan Press, 2004), 103–8.

49. Brad Byrom, "A Pupil and a Patient: Hospital-Schools in Progressive America," in *The New Disability History: American Perspectives*, ed. Paul K. Longmore and Lauri Umansky (New York: New York University Press, 2001), 133–56; R. C. Elmslie, "The Care of Invalid and Crippled Children in School," quoted in Hugh Gregory Gallagher, *FDR's Splendid Deception* (New York: Dodd, Mead, 1985), 30. See also Janice Brockley, "Rearing the Child Who Never Grew," in *Mental Retardation in America: A Historical Reader*, ed. Steven Noll and James Trent (New York: New York University Press, 2004), 139–40, 144–6, 147; Edward E. Jones et al., *Social Stigma: The Psychology of Marked Relationships* (New York: W.H. Freeman, 1984), 63.

50. The rehabilitation center that restricted parents' visiting of their children to four hours a week was Rancho Los Amigos in Downey, California, where the author was a patient as a child. Marc Shell, *Polio and Its Aftermath: The Paralysis of Culture* (Cambridge, Mass.: Harvard University Press, 2005), 68–9; Wilson, *Living With Polio*, 60–1, 81–2, 124–5.

51. Kraft, "Poster Child Quest."

52. UCP Telethon, 1993.

53. Easter Seals Telethon, 1989.

54. "For several years," Valerie Brew-Parish explained, "I was employed at a large university that sponsored an annual 'Disability Awareness Day.' Despite protests from students and staff with disabilities, the nondisabled sponsors of the event continued the spectacle." Valerie Brew-Parrish, "The Wrong Message," *Ragged Edge* (March/April 1997), http://www.raggededgemag.com/archive/aware.htm. See also Sally French, "Simulation Exercises in Disability Awareness Training: A Critique," *Disability & Society* 7, no. 3 (1992): 257–66, reprinted in *Beyond Disability*, ed. Gerald Hales (London: SAGE, 1996), 114–23; David Pfeiffer, "Disability Simulation Using a Wheelchair Exercise," *Journal of Postsecondary Education and Disability* 7, no. 2 (Spring 1989): 53–60; Philip A. Scullion, "'Quasidisability' Experiences Using Simulation," *British Journal of Therapy and Rehabilitation* 3, no. 9 (1996): 498–502.

55. "Disability 'Awareness Days,'" *Ragged Edge Online* (5 September 2006), http://www. raggededgemagazine.com/departments/spotlight/002843.html (accessed 7 July 2007).

56. Catherine S. Fichten summarized studies done in the 1970s and 1980s in "Students with Physical Disabilities in Higher Education: Attitudes and Beliefs That Affect Integration," in *Attitudes Toward Persons with Disabilities*, ed. Harold E. Yuker (New York: Springer, 1988), 184.

57. "Universal design is a worldwide movement based on the concept that all products, environments, and communications should be designed to consider the needs of the widest possible array of users; if a design works well for people with disabilities, it works better for everyone." Institute for Human Centered Design, "Universal Design: What Is Universal Design?," http://www.adaptiveenvironments.org/index.php?option=Content&Itemid=3 (accessed 7 July 2007). On accessibility and the basic principles of universal design, see "The Barrier-Free City," *Urban Studies* 38, no. 2 (February 2001); Michael Bednar, ed., *Barrier-Free Environments* (Stroudsburg, Penn.: Dowden, Hutchinson & Ross, 1977); Frank G. Bowe, *Universal Design in Education: Teaching Non-traditional Students* (Westport, Conn.: Bergin & Garvey, 2000); Center for Universal Design, IDeA Center, Global Universal Design Educator's Network, "Universal Design Education," National Institute on Disability and Rehabilitation Research (8 July 2004), http://www.udeducation.org/; "Designing for the 21st Century: An International Conference on Universal Design," http://www.adaptiveenvironments.org/index.php?option=Project&Itemid=142 and http://www.designfor21st. com; Rob Imrie, *Disability and the City, International Perspectives* (New York: St. Martin's Press, 1996); Rob Imrie and Peter Hall, *Inclusive Design* (New York: Spon Press/Taylor and Francis, 2001); Mary Johnson, "Disabled Americans Push for Access," *The Progressive* 55, no. 8 (August 1991): 21–3; Raymond Lifchez and Barbara Winslow, *Design for Independent Living: The Environment and Physically Disabled People* (New York: Whitney Library of Design, 1979); Raymond Lifchez, *Rethinking Architecture: Design Students and Physically Disabled People* (Berkeley: University of California Press, 1987); Wolfgang Preiser and Elaine Ostroff, ed., *Universal Design Handbook* (New York: McGraw Hill, 2001).

58. For psychological research on prejudice reduction and disability published from the 1960s through the 1990s, see Olkin, *What Psychotherapists Should Know About Disability*, 63–5; Fichten, "Integration in Higher Education," 183–4; Marcia D. Horne, "Modifying Peer Attitudes Toward the Handicapped: Procedures and Research Issues" and Harold E. Yuker, "The Effects of Contact on Attitudes Toward Disabled Persons: Some Empirical Generalizations," both in *Attitudes Toward Persons with*

Disabilities, 205, 262–74; Harold Yuker, "Variables That Influence Attitudes Towards Persons with Disabilities: Conclusions from the Data," *Journal of Social Behavior and Personality* 9, no. 5 (1994): 6–7, 16–17. The research indicated that some types of role-playing were effective in reducing prejudice. In one instance, architecture students role-played having various sensory disabilities in order to learn how to design more user-friendly environments. Another study involved "assertive role-play concerning how people with a disability could attain rights denied them. . . ." A third role-play study of "helping situations" designed "a problem-solving set, where the task [was] to discover how the giving and receiving of help could be improved." Fichten, "Students with Physical Disabilities in Higher Education," 184. John Gliedman and William Roth reached similar conclusions about social interactions between disabled and nondisabled children in integrated school settings. Because existing research on this subject was "deplorably poor," they recommended that investigators look at the social-psychological studies of racism. "Perhaps the most important lesson to be learned from the race relations literature is that the *quality* of the interactions between able-bodied and handicapped children is likely to be crucial." John Gliedman and William Roth, *The Unexpected Minority: Handicapped Children in America* (New York: Harcourt, Brace, Jovanovich, 1980), 230–1.

59. MDA Telethon, 1989.

60. MDA Telethons, 1988, 1992, and 1993.

61. In the settlements, the chains agreed that centers' owners and staff could not simply assume that a child's disability would justify excluding that child from their program. They must assess each child individually to see if the center could meet his or her needs without fundamentally altering their programs. And they must take input from professionals and parents. Between 1 and 3 percent of school-age children nationwide had severe allergies requiring regular treatment. They had been shut out of private day care by corporate policies prohibiting staff from administering medications. Hence, staff would "administer epinephrine, a form of adrenaline, to children with allergies if authorized by parents and physicians." In addition, more than 100,000 school-age children had diabetes. The centers would "implement a policy to provide finger prick tests to measure the blood glucose levels of children with diabetes." Other provisions of the agreement promised that staff at some centers would "assist children with motor disabilities to use the toilet" and make architectural accessibility improvements at other locations. "Child Care Chain Settles with DOJ" and "Facts about ADA and Child Care Centers," *Washington Watch* 3, no. 19 (4 November 1997).

62. MDA Telethon, 2003.

63. Easter Seals Telethon, 1990: Los Angeles segment.

64. MDA Telethon, 1994: Denver local cohost.

65. Easter Seals Telethon, 1991.

66. Easter Seals Telethon, 1988.

67. MDA Telethon, 1993.

68. Easter Seals Telethon, 1991: San Francisco segment.

69. Longmore's original contains local Bay Area MDA Telethons for 2007 and 2008 that use almost identical phrases so they have been conflated here.—Ed.

70. MDA Telethon, 1989: Los Angeles segment.

71. *Disability Rag* 7, no. 3 (May–June 1986): 9–10; *Disability Rag* 7, no. 5 (September–October 1986): 345. For a letter from a nondisabled counselor defending Camp Greentop, see *Disability Rag* 7, no. 4 (July–August 1986): 2.

72. Easter Seals Telethon, 1989: Los Angeles segment.

73. MDA Telethons, 2006 and 2007: San Francisco Bay Area segment.

74. MDA Telethon, 1992.

75. Ibid.

76. Easter Seals Telethon, 1991.

77. MDA Telethon, 1984; Easter Seals Telethon, 1990.

78. Easter Seals Telethon, 1990.

79. Laura Hershey, "From Poster Child to Protestor," *Spectacle* (Spring/Summer 1997), http://www.cripcommentary.com/frompost.html (accessed 22 August 2009).

80. *Disability Rag* 7, no. 3 (May–June 1986): 9–10.

81. MDA Telethon, 2007: San Francisco Bay Area segment.

82. Easter Seals Massachusetts, "Youth Leadership Forum," http://ma.easterseals.com/site/PageServer?pagename= MADR_youthleadership (accessed 12 February 2010).

83. Linda Rowley, "Accessible Playgrounds," *Disability Research*, 8 July 1996.

84. Easter Seals Telethon, 1995.

85. "Why are there so many disabled persons waiting to get into a camp like this one?," asked Robert Ardinger. He attributed it to their "lack of economic power," as well as "the prevalent inaccessibility of vacation and other recreation facilities." *Disability Rag* 7, no. 5 (September/October 1986): 35.

86. In September 2002, the federal Architectural and Transportation Barriers Compliance Board issued new accessibility guidelines for recreation facilities under the Americans with Disabilities Act and applied them to facilities covered by the Architectural Barriers Act, which requires federally funded facilities to be accessible. "ADA Accessibility Guidelines for Recreation Facilities" (Washington, D.C.: Federal Register, 3 September 2002), http://www.accessboard.gov/recreation/final.htm (accessed 12 February 2010).

Chapter 12

1. John Gliedman and William Roth, *The Unexpected Minority: Handicapped Children in America* (New York: Harcourt, Brace, Jovanovich, 1980), 55.

2. Michel Foucault, *"Society Must Be Defended": Lectures at the College de France, 1975–76*, ed. Mauro Bertani and Alessandro Fontana, trans. David Macey (New York: Picador, 1997, 2003), 7–9; Gliedman and Roth, *Unexpected Minority*, 56, 302–3, 141–5, see also 136–7, 198–9, 219–20.

3. They and other scholars criticized most disability research as theoretically barren and methodologically weak. Particularly problematic, investigators applied "able-bodied norms of behavior" without questioning their relevance to the experience of handicapped children. As an inevitable result, researchers discovered deviance and social pathology. Gliedman and Roth, *Unexpected Minority*, 57–8, 136–8. This deficiency partly stemmed from the underrepresentation or absence of people with disabilities in groups used to validate standardized assessment instruments.

Researchers then compounded the problem by applying those tests in ways inappropriate for children with particular disabilities. Rhoda Olkin, *What Psychotherapists Should Know About Disability* (New York: Guilford Press, 1999), 29, 104. Proposing an alternative approach, Gliedman and Roth drew on developmental psychologists' finding that children actively participate in their own growth and that all but the most seriously cognitively or emotionally disabled could develop in emotionally and socially healthy ways. Researchers mistakenly took for granted that theories based on nondisabled children's experience could "correctly interpret the developmental significance of the handicapped child's behavior." That crucial oversight risked "perpetuating the traditional deviance analysis of disability in a more subtle and more socially acceptable form." Gliedman and Roth called for studies grounded in disabled children's actual lives. "Because of stigma and misunderstanding," they often operated in "a social world radically different from the one inhabited by their able-bodied peers. . . ." Developmentalists recognized the need to get away from ethnocentric, culture-bound theories based on the experience of white, middle-class American children. Some studied minority children, others children in non-Western societies. Likewise, studying handicapped children on their own terms could provide more accurate understanding of *their* development. It might also help "sort out the degree to which today's theories of personality, social behavior, and intellectual growth are culture-bound or culturally unbiased." Laying the basis for a developmental psychology of childhood with a disability, they urged investigation of the complex interplay of "social class, ethnic group, gender, the nature of the handicap, and its sociological significance in the child's milieu." Their proposal recognized both the diversities and commonalities in the experiences of children with a variety of disabilities. They also urged that rather than simply correcting disabled children's presumed deficiencies, parents and professionals should foster their growth in positive ways. Gliedman and Roth, *Unexpected Minority*, 58–9, 62–4, 68–95, see also 137, 199–200. They note that one of the few longitudinal studies of handicapped children validated this new approach. Its subjects were Canadian children with disabilities resulting from thalidomide. Contrary to the researchers' expectations, the extent of these children's physical disabilities was "of only secondary importance" in their "overall emotional and intellectual development." The growth of their sense of self "was first and foremost a social problem." The investigators concluded that "personality theories developed for able-bodied children simply don't seem to fit the facts of [these] children's lives." For one thing, the categories so often used in studies of handicapped children and their parents—"acceptance, rejection, over-protection, guilt feelings, etc."—appeared neither adequate to explain their experience nor useful in supporting their growth. Moreover, their lives were "so tightly intertwined with sociological context" that the analytical methods of social psychology, "especially those used to treat the problems of minorities," seemed "far better able to do justice to the reality. . . ." Gliedman and Roth, *Unexpected Minority*, 59–60.

4. Olkin critically summarized the premises shaping that perspective: "Having and caring for a child with a disability is a burden"; "this burden will tax and strain the family's resources in every respect"; "[w]e need to understand more about how families cope with this burden." Olkin, *What Psychotherapists Should Know About Disability*, 93. In 1994 disabled psychologist Harold Yuker, the leading authority on attitudes toward people with

disabilities, criticized much of the research on attitudes as flawed and urged colleagues to "stop studying the presumably horrible negative effects of a child with a disability on parents and siblings." Harold Yuker, "Variables That Influence Attitudes Towards Persons with Disabilities: Conclusions from the Data," *Journal of Social Behavior and Personality* 9, no. 5 (1994): 12. See also Eva Feder Kittay, *Love's Labor: Essays on Women, Equality, and Dependency* (New York: Routledge, 1999), 178. Despite his injunction, Olkin found that approach persisting throughout the 1990s. Alexandra L. Quittner, Lisa C. Opipari, Mary Jean Regoli, Jessica Jacobsen, and Howard Eign, "The Impact of Caregiving and Role Strain on Family Life: Comparisons between Mothers of Children with Cystic Fibrosis and Matched Controls," *Rehabilitation Psychology* 37, no. 4 (1992): 275–90.

5. Olkin, *What Psychotherapists Should Know About Disability*, 44–7, 92, 95. See also Yuker, "Variables That Influence Attitudes Towards Persons with Disabilities," 9, 11; Richard J. Duval, "Psychological Theories of Physical Disability: New Perspectives," in *Disabled People as Second-Class Citizens*, ed. Myron G. Eisenberg, Cynthia Griggins, and Richard J. Duval (New York: Springer, 1982), 182–3.

6. Gliedman and Roth, *Unexpected Minority*, 57, 137–8, see also 198 and Olkin, *What Psychotherapists Should Know About Disability*, 30. Olkin characterized some of the research as a form of "mother bashing" (p. 316). Other research indicated "that, on average, people with disabilities report a quality of life comparable to those without disabilities, that families with disabled children do not inevitably report more stress than families without disabled children, and that parents frequently find unexpected rewards in raising a disabled child, such as increased family unity, new social relationships, and a revised sense of what is most valuable in life. . . . This kind of empirical information is often overlooked in medical settings but can be important in decision-making." One study "found that the perceived absence of rewards associated with raising a disabled child was a critical determinant of motivation to pursue prenatal screening," while another reported that in genetic counseling parental decisions are focused on the social meaning and expected social consequences of having a child with a disability. Kelly M. Munger, Carol J. Gill, Kelly E. Ormond, and Kristi L. Kirschner, "The Next Exclusion Debate: Assessing Technology, Ethics, and Intellectual Disability after the Human Genome Project," *Mental Retardation and Developmental Disabilities Research Reviews* 13 (2007): 126.

7. Gliedman and Roth, *Unexpected Minority*, 89–95.

8. Ibid., 71.

9. Ibid., 71–2.

10. Olkin, *What Psychotherapists Should Know About Disability*, 13, 107; Carol J. Gill, "A Bicultural Framework for Understanding Disability," *Family Psychologist: Bulletin of the Division of Family Psychology* 10, no. 4 (1994): 14–15. "Children with disabilities are often raised to deny their disabilities, to look and behave as able-bodied as possible. . . . They are loved *in spite of*, not *with*, their disabilities." Olkin, *What Psychotherapists Should Know About Disability*, 13.

11. "When parents are distressed by the mere idea that their children might enjoy the company of others with disabilities, it raises the concern that those parents have not made peace with the fact of their child's differentness. This form of denial not only prevents disabled children from forming chosen friendships with disabled peers, but it introduces the pressure of adult sanction into the relationships they form with nondisabled children. As a result, the latter relationships may have an artificial quality or may center on

the nondisabled child's commitment to 'being nice' to the disabled child. Ironically, the parents' investment in such friendships can actually interfere with their children's ability to work out relationships with nondisabled children spontaneously on their own terms. Adults with disabilities who recall being discouraged as children from associating with other disabled children say they experienced this as a confusing and hurtful double message. It was hard for them to trust their parents' approval and acceptance of them in view of their parents' simultaneous devaluation of others with disabilities." Gill, "Bicultural Framework," 14.

12. Olkin, *What Psychotherapists Should Know About Disability*, 13–14.

13. Gill, "Bicultural Framework," 13–15.

14. Ibid., 14; Olkin, *What Psychotherapists Should Know About Disability*, 13–14, 102, 108.

15. Ibid., 101–2, 107–8, 105, 320–1. See also Kittay, *Love's Labor*, 150–2, 154–5, 162–81.

16. Gill, "Bicultural Framework," 15.

17. Olkin, *What Psychotherapists Should Know About Disability*, 14, 100–5.

18. Gliedman and Roth, *Unexpected Minority*, 79.

19. UCP Telethon, 1989.

20. MDA Telethon, 1994.

21. See chapters 2 and 3; Olkin urged that research focus on how services and public policies could maximize family functioning. Olkin, *What Psychotherapists Should Know About Disability*, 320–1. See also Kittay, *Love's Labor*, 169, 176–7.

22. UCP Telethon, 1989.

23. Scott Kraft, "Poster Child Quest: Cute Isn't Enough," *Los Angeles Times*, 7 April 1986.

24. Yuker, "Variables That Influence Attitudes Towards Persons with Disabilities," 11; Olkin, *What Psychotherapists Should Know About Disability*, 95. On how families variously dealt with members who contracted polio, see Daniel J. Wilson, *Living with Polio: The Epidemic and Its Survivors* (Chicago: University of Chicago Press, 2005), 142–5.

25. "All the families are described as 'courageous'; and they all seem to bear total responsibility for the care and support of the person with MD. Spouses and parents alike are shown carrying the person with MD up and down stairs, pushing their wheelchair, and so on. Rarely if ever is the disabled family member shown making any positive contribution. In these stories, the disabled person's status is clearly (even if the word was never used) that of 'burden.'" Laura Hershey, "From Poster Child to Protestor," *Spectacle* (Spring/Summer 1997), http://www.cripcommentary.com/frompost.html (accessed 22 August 2009).

26. UCP Telethon, 1993.

27. MDA Telethon, 1989.

28. MDA Telethon, 1993. "There was another vignette about a family with two sons, one of whom has MD," said Laura Hershey. "In focusing on the younger, non-disabled son, the narrator made a statement to the effect that he doesn't have a big brother who can take him places and teach him things—he has a brother he has to take care of." "This statement implies that people with disabilities are incapable of giving to *any* kind of relationship, that we are undesirable even as siblings. . . ." "The next day, a different family appeared on the local segment of the telethon. Like the first family, there were two teenage boys, one, named Paul, with MD. The brothers were obviously very close. Again, the host made a major point of talking about how the non-disabled boy 'takes care of' and

assists his brother Paul. At this statement, the father leaned over to the microphone and said pointedly, 'Paul helps him a lot too.'" "The host ignored this attempt to set the record straight, but I was very moved by it. I feel real compassion for people like that family, who participate in the telethon, yet try (usually in vain) to preserve their own dignity and truth." Laura Hershey, "From Poster Child to Protestor."

29. Olkin, *What Psychotherapists Should Know About Disability*, 108–10. See also Yuker, "Variables That Influence Attitudes Towards Persons with Disabilities," 11, 12.

30. "Last summer, I had the pleasure of addressing an audience of disabled college students on the subject of identity. I proposed to them that they could rightly view themselves as bicultural (or multicultural if they had membership in other cultural communities), pointing out that as Americans with disabilities, they were entitled to identify both as disabled and as American in every way. I recommended that they enjoy the benefits of the majority culture and the love of their original families while cultivating pride in their honorable disability heritage." Gill, "Bicultural Framework," 14–16. Children with disabilities did, of course, become adults with disabilities and many became parents, but scholarship focused overwhelmingly on children while typically ignoring adults. "It is as if these children will never grow up," remarked Olkin. And so the families parented by disabled adults became invisible. When the research did consider those families and those parents, it often pathologized them. Olkin, *What Psychotherapists Should Know About Disability*, 110, 125–34. For historical examples of this "new breed of parent" among parents of children with mental retardation in the post–World War II era, see Kathleen W. Jones, "Education for Children with Mental Retardation: Parent Activism, Public Policy, and Family Ideology in the 1950s"; Katherine Castles, "'Nice, Average Americans': Postwar Parents' Groups and the Defense of the Normal Family"; Elizabeth F. Shores, "A Pivotal Place in Special Education Policy: The First Arkansas Children's Colony"—all in *Mental Retardation in America: A Historical Reader*, ed. Steven Noll and James W. Trent Jr. (New York: New York University Press, 2004), 322–70, 384–409.

31. Kraft, "Poster Child Quest."

32. Easter Seals Telethon, 1990. At the same time, some parents on the Easter Seals Telethon talked about how professionals discouraged them, telling them that their child would not be able to do many things. But at Easter Seals, they said, the emphasis was on what the child could do, not what the child could not do. Easter Seals staff stressed abilities, not disabilities. They also encouraged parents to "celebrate" their children's capacities and accomplishments. These moments on the telethon contrasted health-care professionals' pessimism with the hope instilled at Easter Seals. On one level, this encouragement by Easter Seals' staffers was a very positive contrast. At the same time, coming alongside the telethon's other scenes of parental despair, these expressions of hope reflected a theme that recurred throughout the modern history of rehabilitation and special education: Professionals redeemed disabled people's lives from the tragedy of disability. Easter Seals Telethon, 1994.

33. For an excellent study of Canadian activist mothers of children with disabilities, see Melanie Panitch, *Disability, Mothers, and Organization: Accidental Activists* (New York: Routledge, 2008).

34. Laura Hershey, "From Poster Child to Protestor."

35. Natasha Zaretsky, *No Direction Home: The American Family and the Fear of National Decline, 1968–1980* (Chapel Hill: University of North Carolina Press, 2007).

36. See chapter 3.

37. Bureau of Labor Statistics, http://www.bls.gov/opub/mlr/2007/02/art2full.pdf.

38. Joseph E. Illick, *American Childhoods* (Philadelphia: University of Pennsylvania Press, 2002), 126–7; Zaretsky, *No Direction Home.*

39. Illick, *American Childhoods*, 125–6.

40. The report was followed by four other Council publications, all issued by Harcourt Brace Jovanovich or its subsidiary, Academic Press: *Child Care in the Family: A Review of Research and Some Propositions for Policy* (1977) by Alison Clarke-Stewart; *Minority Education and Caste: The American System in Cross-Cultural Perspective* (1978) by John U. Ogbu; *Small Futures: Children, Inequality, and the Limits of Liberal Reform* (1979) by Richard de Lone—with Gliedman and Roth's *Unexpected Minority* coming out last in 1980. The Carnegie studies focused on the pressures of family life, "including changes in family structure, the increase in one-parent households, the growing number of working wives, the lack of adequate income, and the encroachments of television and other forms of modern technology." Part 2, "What Is to Be Done," outlined the Council's policy recommendations, in particular, provisions for income support available to all, flexible work schedules, improved health care, and legal protection to safeguard the personal integrity of the child. *Guide to the Carnegie Council on Children Records 1972–1980*, University of Chicago Library, http://www.lib.uchicago.edu/e/scrc/findingaids/view.php?eadid=ICU.SPCL.CCCR (accessed 8 July 2014).

41. Zaretsky, *No Direction Home*, 10–11; Edward D. Berkowitz, *Something Happened: A Political and Cultural Overview of the Seventies* (New York: Columbia University Press, 2006), 111.

42. Zaretsky, *No Direction Home*, in particular, 18–20. For another general discussion of the cultural crisis of the last decades of the twentieth century, see James T. Patterson, *Restless Giant: The United States from Watergate to Bush v. Gore* (New York: Oxford University Press, 2005), 8–11.

43. Zaretsky, *No Direction Home*, 90, 94–5, 138, 159–60, 163–4; Daniel Moynihan, *The Politics of a Guaranteed Income: The Nixon Administration and the Family Assistance Plan* (New York: Vintage Books, 1973), quoted in Zaretsky, *No Direction Home*, 94.

44. Easter Seals Telethon,1990.

45. Easter Seals Telethons, 1990 and 1992: Los Angeles. On the 1988 Arthritis Telethon, celebrities often noted that they did not have arthritis and neither did any members of their families, for which they were very thankful. To which an MC might respond: "Thank God."

46. MDA Telethon, 1989.

47. Fred Davis, *Passage Through Crisis: Polio Victims and Their Families* (New Brunswick, N.J.: Transaction Publishers, 1990), 39–41.

48. Fred Davis, *Passage Through Crisis: Polio Victims and Their Families*, rev. ed. (New Brunswick, N.J.: Transaction publishers, 1991), 41.

49. Marc Shell, *Polio and Its Aftermath: The Paralysis of Culture* (Cambridge: Harvard University Press, 2005), 68.

50. Davis, *Passage Through Crisis*, 40–1; Kathryn Black, *In the Shadow of Polio: A Personal and Social History* (Reading, Mass.: Addison-Wesley, 1996), 47–8. On varying parental and familial responses, see Wilson, *Living With Polio*, 17, 171–2, 177.

51. Shell, *Polio and Its Aftermath*, 53, 57–62, 84–90.

52. MDA Telethon, 1991.

53. In the early 1990s, the author attended a conference of disability rights leaders. Several reported that their relatives had recently bought inaccessible homes. Those purchases puzzled them.

54. Olkin, *What Psychotherapists Should Know About Disability*, 29, 31–2. See also Dai R. Thompson, "Anger," in *With the Power of Each Breath: A Disabled Women's Anthology*, ed. Susan E. Browne, Debra Connors, and Nanci Stern (Pittsburg: Cleis Press, 1985), 78–9.

55. Easter Seals Telethon, 1992. On people with cognitive/developmental disabilities complying with a stereotype of "cheeriness" in order to pacify "a potentially aggressive external world," see Deborah Marks, *Disability: Controversial Debates and Psychosocial Perspectives* (London: Routledge, 1999), 48.

Chapter 13

1. Most of them had belonged to MDA's Queens Chapter, but the national office had revoked its charter the previous April. The chapter's former Vice President Alan Gornitz said it was because the members refused to "be a rubber stamp to the association." An MDA spokesman replied that they had violated MDA's bylaws, "including obtaining an 'appliance' for a patient after the national office had turned down the client application." Associated Press, "Lewis Telethon Protested by Disabled in Wheelchairs," *Des Moines Register*, 5 September 1972.

2. In the mid-1970s, New York Congressman Edward Koch surveyed nine voluntary health organizations. Five responded. Koch reported that out of a total of 382 employees, only 23 had a disability. "There is no excuse for the discriminatory hiring practices of the voluntary agencies, which have been created to serve the handicapped," declared Koch. "The handicapped individual should be the usual employee of these agencies and the non-handicapped should be the exception." James Haskins and J. M. Stifle, *The Quiet Revolution: The Struggle for the Rights of Disabled Americans* (New York: Thomas Y. Crowell, 1979), 78.

3. "Cerebral Palsy Telethon Gets $2.5 Million Pledges," *New York Times*, 2 February 1976; Associated Press, "Handicapped Protest Telethon," *Journal Times* (Racine, Wis.), 2 February 1976.

4. One of the protesters, a woman with cerebral palsy, explained to a reporter, "They portray us as helpless cripples. But people with C.P. grow up, and a lot of us work, keep house and make love." Mark Rattner and Terri Shultz, "Thousands Are Picketing, Filing Suits and Lobbying for Promised Equal Protection of the Law; The Handicapped, a Minority Demanding Its Rights," *New York Times*, 13 February 1977.

5. Ibid.; Bruce P. Hillam, "Charity Telethons Raise Money, Not Self-Esteem, for the Handicapped," *Los Angeles Times*, 9 September 1977; Sonny Kleinfeld, *The Hidden Minority: A Profile of Handicapped Americans* (Boston: Little, Brown, 1979), 184.

6. Frank Bowe, *Handicapping America: Barriers to Disabled People* (New York: Harper and Row, 1978), 110, 111, 211, see also ix.

7. Kleinfeld, *Hidden Minority*, 147. See also Diane Lattin, "Telethons—A Remnant of America's Past," *Disabled USA* 1, no. 4 (1977): 18–19.

8. The conference came out of the Rehabilitation Act Amendments in 1974 to address the "unmet needs of handicapped individuals." See *The White House Conference on Handicapped Individuals, Special Concerns, State White House Conference Workbook* (1977), https://archive.org/details/whitehousespecoowhit (accessed 2 October 2014).

9. "Summary," *Final Report: The White House Conference on Handicapped Individuals* (HEW 1978), 35.

10. The conference proceedings state, "Observers were invited from national organizations serving the disabled, business and labor, Federal and State Service delivery programs and Congress to fill the 900 observer positions." There is a list of some attendees, but it did not list affiliations, though some names appeared from National Society for Crippled Children and Adults (Easter Seals), Congress of the Physically Handicapped (COPH), and Disabled In Action, but it's likely that those critical of telethons were in the minority. Thanks to Lindsey Patterson for information related to the conference.

11. Hillam, "Charity Telethons Raise Money, Not Self-Esteem, for the Handicapped"; *The White House Conference on Handicapped Individuals Held in Washington, DC, May 23–27, 1977*, Vol. 3: *Implementation Plan* (Washington, D.C.: Government Printing Office, 1978), 39, see also 53. For criticism of stigmatizing print advertising in this era, see the Center for Independent Living, http://www.cilberkeley.org/, and Editorial, "At Whose Expense?," *Independent* 3, no. 2 (Spring 1976).

12. Berkeley, California, disability rights leader Ed Roberts recalled: "We had a vision we could take over the charities and we resented and disliked telethons." Interview with Ed Roberts, *Disability Rag* 6, no. 9 (September 1985), 28.

13. Kemp quoted Kaplan in his letter to Ross. Evan J. Kemp Jr. to Robert Ross, 19 June 1980, Regional Oral History Office, Bancroft Library, University of California at Berkeley. I thank Bess Williamson for providing me with this document. On the private investigator, see Brian T, McMahon and Linda R. Shaw, ed., *Enabling Lives: Biographies of Six Prominent Americans with Disabilities* (Boca Raton, Fla.: CRC Press, 2000), 54.

14. Kemp to Robert Ross; *ABC News: World News Tonight with Peter Jennings*, "Person of the Week," 24 July 1992; *Report on Muscular Dystrophy Association, Inc.* (New York: National Information Bureau, Inc., 21 April 1977), 3, quoted in Lawrence Joseph Londino, "A Descriptive Analysis of 'The Jerry Lewis Labor Day Telethon for Muscular Dystrophy,'" Ph.D. diss., University of Michigan, 1975, 53.

15. Jim Trombetta, "Jerry and the 'Pity Approach,'" *Los Angeles Times*, 6 September 1981.

16. Mike Feinsilber, "Lewis MD Telethon Does More Harm than Good, Groups Claim," *Associated Press*, 1 September 1981.

17. Both Kemp and Robrahn detailed the concerns about disabled people being seen as eternal children. In addition, claimed Kemp, the telethon reinforced "the public's tendency to equate handicap with total 'hopelessness,'" thereby intensifying "the awkward embarrassment" of interpersonal interactions, as well as strengthening public fears and buttressing social barriers.

18. Reese Robrahn, "It's the Telethon That Hurts," *Washington Post*, 22 August 1981; Evan Kemp Jr., "Aiding the Disabled: No Pity, Please," *New York Times*, 3 September 1981, late edition; "New England Briefs; Telethon Protest Planned," *Boston Globe*, 4 September 1981, 6th edition.

19. Marjorie Pritchard, "Advocate for Handicapped Raps Jerry Lewis Telethon," *Boston Globe*, 5 September 1981, 1st edition.

20. Quoted by a member of the board of directors of the Muscular Dystrophy Association, Robert G. Sampson, letter to the editor, "Unconscionable Exploitation of Telethons," *New York Times*, 5 October 1983; Mary Johnson, "A Test of Wills: Jerry Lewis, Jerry's Orphans, and the Telethon," *Disability Rag* (September 1992), http://www.ragged-edgemagazine.com/archive/jerry92.htm (accessed 28 February 2010). See also Frank E. James, "Why a Magazine for Disabled Ignores Handicapped Heroes—Controversial 'Disability Rag' Says Lionizing 'Supercrips' Is No Help for Majority," *Wall Street Journal*, 11 January 1985. For the first time in seventeen years, the 1982 telethon's final figure was lower than the year before. MDA attributed the drop to the sluggish economy. The editors of the *Encyclopedia of Bad Taste* incorrectly linked the shortfall to Kemp's appearance. Robert Macy, "Jerry Lewis Telethon Raises $28 Million for Muscular Dystrophy," *Associated Press*, 6 September 1982; Jane and Michael Stern, "Telethons," in the *Encyclopedia of Bad Taste* (New York: HarperCollins, 1990), 292.

21. Lilly Bruck, "Consumer Activists: Promoting Equal Access to the Marketplace," in *Disabled People as Second-Class Citizens*, ed. Myron G. Eisenberg, Cynthia Griggins, and Richard J. Duval (New York: Springer, 1982), 265; Steven Brown, "The Truth about Telethons," *Oklahoma Coalition of Citizens with Disabilities Newsletter* 7 (Summer/Fall 1985): 45, reprinted in *Institute on Disability Culture Manifesto* 6 (August 1999), http://www.dimenet.com/disculture/archive.php?mode=N&id=17 (accessed March 2010); Anne Peters, "Telethons," *Disability Rag* (May 1982; repr., Fall 1985), Jubilee edition, 1618; William Roth, "The Politics of Disability: Future Trends as Shaped by Current Realities," in *Social Influences in Rehabilitation Planning: Blueprint for the 21st Century. A Report of the Ninth Mary E. Switzer Memorial Seminar*, ed. Leonard G. Perlman and Gary F. Austin (Alexandria, Va.: National Rehabilitation Association, 1985), 41–2; Dai R. Thompson, "Anger," in *With the Power of Each Breath: A Disabled Women's Anthology*, ed. Susan E. Browne, Debra Connors, and Nanci Stern (Pittsburgh: Cleis Press, 1985), 78; Anne Finger, "Claiming All of Our Bodies: Reproductive Rights and Disability," in Browne, Connors, and Stern, *With the Power of Each Breath*, 302. For criticism of the Ontario March of Dimes advertisement that won an award for public service ads at the 1985 Marketing Awards Gala, see "We Wish We Wouldn't See . . . ," *Disability Rag* 6, no. 7 (July 1985), 31; quoting the *Staten Island Advance*, "Polio Victim Forced to Quit When Her Car Dies," in "We Wish We Wouldn't See . . . ," *Disability Rag* 6, no. 8 (August 1985), 23. For criticism of an ad for the Canton, Ohio, United Way, see "We Wish We Wouldn't See," *Disability Rag* 7, no. 1 (January/February 1986), 30; *Disability Rag* 7, no. 5 (September/October 1986), 1821, for several articles on telethons, see also 29; *Disability Rag* 7, no. 6 (November/December 1986), 15; "A Form of Pornography," *Disability Rag* 7, no. 6 (November/December 1986), 19. For criticism of ads for the MS society and the National Society to Prevent Blindness, see *Disability Rag* 7, no. 6 (November/December 1986), 39; *Disability Rag* 8, no. 1 (January/February 1987), 29; *Disability Rag* 8, no. 2 (March/April 1987), 12, 32–3; *Disability Rag* 8, no. 3 (May/June 1987), 37; Anne Finger, ". . . And the Greatest of These Is Charity," *Disability Rag* 8, no. 5 (September/October 1987), 6; "Troubling Questions about Special Olympics," *Disability Rag* 8, no. 5 (September/October 1987), 32; Mary Johnson, "Do the Disabled Like Telethons?," *Fund Raising Management* 18, no. 9 (November 1987); Shirley Frederick, letter to the editor, *Disability Rag* 9, no. 1, (January/February 1988), 2; "We Wish We Wouldn't See . . . ," *Disability Rag* 9, no. 1 (January/February 1988), 37; Lisa Blumberg, "The Revolt

of the Easter Seal Kids," *Disability Rag* 10, no. 2 (March/April 1989) 1, 45. For criticism of an Amway "Salutes" ad about the National Easter Seals Society, see *Disability Rag* 10, no. 4 (July/August 1989), 31; Mary Johnson, "Tin Cups and Tiny Tim," *Disability Rag* 10, no. 5 (September/October 1989), 18. "Of all embattled evangelical couple Jim and Tammy Bakker's fundraising scams, none pulled in the dollars more than gimmicks to 'help the handicapped.' Last year, Bakker raised over $1 million dollars for a 'home for handicapped children' on the grounds of his Heritage U.S.A. resort. Last July the blue, gingerbread-style house with ramps intended to house 8 disabled kids, and dubbed 'Kevin's House' after a 17-year-old the Bakker's had used in their maudlin appeal was ready for occupancy. ... But today the house has only two occupants—Bakker's cousins. Bakker's aides say they reviewed 'scores of applications' looking for children that met their standards—'poor, handicapped but ambulatory' and 'mentally alert'—but couldn't find any who met the criteria." "Where are those kids when you need 'em?" *Disability Rag* 8, no. 4 (July/August 1987), 18. An opinion piece criticizing the MDA Telethon and using the same arguments as the 1981 campaign appeared in September 1983, provoking a sharp response from MDA. Robert Allen Bernstein, "Do-Good Pitythons," *New York Times*, 6 September 1983; Sampson, "Unconscionable Exploitation of Telethons."

22. "MDA Hails Signing of Disabilities Act," *Business Wire*, 26 July 1990.

23. Jerry Lewis, "If I Had Muscular Dystrophy," *Parade* (2 September 1990), 46.

24. Adam Smith, *The Theory of Moral Sentiments, Glasgow Edition of the Works and Correspondence of Adam Smith*, Vol. 1, rev. ed., ed. D. D. Raphael and A. L. MacFie (Oxford: Clarendon Press, 1976), 9, 10; Karen Halttunen, "Humanitarianism and the Pornography of Pain in Anglo-American Culture," *American Historical Review* 100 (April 1995), 305, 307.

25. Lattin, "Telethons—A Remnant of America's Past," 19.

26. Carole Ashkinaze, Editorial, "Jerry Lewis Defends Himself against Critics," *Chicago Sun-Times*, 11 September 1990; Carole Ashkinaze, Editorial, "Jerry Lewis—Saint or Jerk? Readers Reply," *Chicago Sun-Times*, 23 September 1990; Dianne B. Piastro, "Jerry Demeans 'His Kids,'" *Long Beach (California) Press-Telegram*, 25 September 1990; Noel Holston, "Jerry Lewis Gives Them 'Everything,'" *Minneapolis Star Tribune*, 19 October 1990, metro edition; Dianne B. Piastro, "Jerry Lewis, Disability Columns Draw Letters," *Minneapolis Star Tribune*, 4 November 1990, metro edition.

27. *Businessweek*, 13 September 1992. http://www.businessweek.com/stories/1992-09-13/some-of-jerrys-kids-are-mad-at-the-old-man (accessed 9 July 2014).

28. Johnson, "Test of Wills"; Dianne B. Piastro, "'Jerry's Orphans' Oppose Telethon," *St. Louis Post-Dispatch, Everyday Magazine*, 3 August 1991; Dianne B. Piastro, "MDA Telethon Takes Emotional Toll," *St. Louis Post-Dispatch, Everyday Magazine*, 17 August 1991; Bonnie Malleck, "Entertainment: Cease the Pity Philosophy, MD 'Orphans' Tell Jerry Lewis," *Kitchener-Waterloo Record*, 17 August 1991; Dianne B. Piastro, "Do 'Jerry's Kids' Get Your Dollars?" *St. Louis Post-Dispatch, Everyday Magazine*, 24 August 1991; Bob Dyer, "Former Poster Child Battles Jerry Lewis/Portrayal of 'Cripples' Provokes Wrath," *Houston Chronicle*, 1 September 1991; Ken White, "Television: Trouble at the Telethon," *Las Vegas Review-Journal*, 1 September 1991. See also Ben Mattlin, "Personal Perspective: An Open Letter to Jerry Lewis: The Disabled Need Dignity, Not Pity," *Los Angeles Times*, 1 September 1991, home edition; Christina Del Valle, "Some of Jerry's Kids Are Mad at the

Old Man—Disabled Activists Want the Comedian Off the Labor Day Telethon," *Business Week* 3283 (14 September 1992): 36.

29. Edmund S. Tijerina, "Protesters Call Jerry Lewis Telethon Exploitive," *Chicago Tribune*, 2 September 1991; Jim Kirksey, "Telethon Protested as 'Degrading,' " *Denver Post*, 2 September 1991; Associated Press, "Disabled Activists Blast Telethon/Protesters Say Lewis' Pitch Evokes Only Pity," *Colorado Springs Gazette Telegraph*, 3 September 1991.

30. For the varying estimates, see Robert Macy, "Criticism Loses Sting with Record Tote," *Associated Press*, 7 September 1993, http://www.lexisnexis.com (accessed 5 April 2010); Alexandra M. Biesada, "Protesters Object to 'Jerry's Kid' Image," *Austin American Statesman* (Austin, Tex.), 7 September 1993, final edition; Laura Hershey, "A Skeptical Viewer's Guide to the Perennial Jerry Lewis Telethon," *Denver Post*, 28 August 1993.

31. This profile of Sheffield was presented for the first time on the 1990 telethon, a year before the protests. At one point on the 1991 telethon, Lewis had some difficulty reading the current total on the tote board. Making a joke out of it, announcer Ed McMahon carefully explains to him the difference between a six and a nine. Jerry Lewis says to McMahon, "Why do I always feel like you think I'm a retarded person or something?" McMahon and the audience laugh.

32. Joseph P. Shapiro, "Disabling 'Jerry's Kids,' " *U.S. News & World Report* 113, no. 10 (14 September 1992): 39–40.

33. In his letter, Ervin listed five demands: First, Jerry Lewis had to go. That was not negotiable. Second, MDA must negotiate "with a group of consumers with disabilities of our choosing to determine how or if the Telethon can be restructured so that it does not continue to sabotage the hard work of those in disability rights." Third, MDA must stop using "the archaic and degrading word 'patient' to describe those it serves" and use instead "something more dignified, like 'client' or 'consumer.' " This demand was a version of the distinction between "sick people and "disabled" people. Fourth, MDA would have to provide services for its clients' "more immediate needs, including advocating for their rights." Fifth, MDA must place people with disabilities in "meaningful positions of power" within its organization, including adding disability rights advocates onto its board. Some MDA board members were people with neuromuscular conditions, but Ervin and other activists found them deficient as advocates. "We are not necessarily out to put the Telethon—or MDA—out of business," said Ervin, "but we are definitely out to put Jerry Lewis out of the disability business." Whether that would be the downfall of either the telethon or MDA "is totally up to MDA. We wish to avoid it as much as you do, but we will do our battle on whatever field you choose. As long as you cling to Jerry and your charity-laden fashion of depicting the disability struggle, the fight will continue. . . . We will challenge you in greater numbers; we will protest in your local offices. We will pressure your corporate sponsors to pressure you. We will make Jerry Lewis and the pity pitch as much a liability for you as he is for the rest of the community of disability. You can choose to doubt our ability to win this fight," Ervin continued, "but we have been in bigger fights than this." Quoted in Johnson, "Test of Wills."

34. Shapiro, "Disabling 'Jerry's Kids.' "

35. Robert Macy, "Jerry Lewis 'Bummed Out,' Keeps Low Profile As He Prepares for Telethon," *Associated Press*, 4 September 1993; Joe Dirck, "Jerry Deserves Credit, Maybe

Some Updating," *Plain Dealer* (Cleveland, Ohio), 8 September 1992; Raymond C. Cheever, "MDA Telethon Turns Around," *Accent on Living* 38, no. 3 (Winter 1993): 26.

36. The "advocates" included several directors of IL centers and offices for services to college students with disabilities along with the founder of a state coalition for disability rights. MDA Telethon, 1992: Los Angeles segment.

37. In Colorado in 1992, an MDA official sent Laura Hershey a newspaper clipping about a 38-year-old man in a Colorado nursing home. MDA had given him a wheelchair. The executive wondered "how much longer MDA" would be able "to provide [this] kind of help" if the antitelethon protests continued. Hershey shot back, "MDA has condoned, and even participated in, the widespread institutionalization of people with disabilities . . . with its medical-model approach," but done little to support independent living. If this man "were living independently . . . he would most likely be eligible for Medicaid" and could obtain not only that wheelchair, but also the in-home services and other equipment "he required to stay independent and healthy." Johnson, "Test of Wills."

38. In later years, MDA's *Quest* online magazine carried many stories about employment, PAS, and IL. See Carol Sowell, "Work Incentives Improve: New Bill May Knock Down Major Employment Barrier," *Quest* 7, no. 1 (February 2000), http://www.mdausa.us/publications/quest/q71workinc.html (accessed 18 June 2010); Tara Wood, "Unlocking Independence: Centers Nationwide Have Resources, Experience, and Inspiration Ready to Help," *Quest* 8, no. 5 (October 2001), http://www.mda.org/Publications/Quest/q85independence.html (accessed 18 June 2010); "Independence Resources," *Quest* 11, no. 6 (1 November 2004), http://quest.mda.org/series/journey-independence-road-map/independence-resources (accessed 18 June 2010); "Caregivers," *Quest*, http://quest.mda.org/categories/caregivers (accessed 18 June 2010); "Housing," *Quest*, http://quest.mda.org/categories/daily-living/housing (accessed 18 June 2010); "Independence," *Quest*, http://quest.mda.org/categories/daily-living/independence (accessed 18 June 2010). In July 1996 MDA's National Task Force on Public Awareness wrote to congressional leaders advocating for a national "Community-Based Personal Assistance Policy." Muscular Dystrophy Association, "MDA Advocacy," http://www.mda.org/advocacy/taskforce/letter4.html (accessed 18 June 2010). See also Muscular Dystrophy Association, "Re: Expression of Strong Support for Public Policy Initiatives That Expand for People with Disabilities the Provision of Long-Term Care at Home and Support of Family Caregivers," 23 June 1999, http://www.mda.org/advocacy/taskforce/letter10.html (accessed 18 June 2010). On the 2002, 2006, and 2008 MDA Telethons, the work of the Task Force on Public Awareness was explained. Over time, that work seemed to expand. It promoted awareness and enforcement of the ADA. Later it educated the public about important issues such as national health care. In 2008 Jerry Lewis reported that MDA's advocacy office in Washington, DC, had recently joined with other advocacy groups to outlaw genetic discrimination, protect Medicare benefits, and advance and accelerate research and treatments for neuromuscular diseases on an international scale. He described MDA's ongoing quest "to lessen and ultimately eliminate the harmful effects of neuromuscular diseases." This last segment aired in the morning hours of the telethon.

39. "With Record Telethon Tote, Critics Lose Sting," *Boston Globe*, 8 September 1993; "Opinion: Let the People Speak Another Record for Jerry," *Las Vegas Review-Journal*, 9 September 1992; MDA Press Release, "Pledges to MDA Telethon Unaffected by Critics," *PR Newswire*, 8 September 1993.

40. Joseph P. Shapiro, "Jerry's Biz," *U.S. News & World Report* 111, no. 24 (9 December 1991): 22.

41. Johnson, "Test of Wills."

42. Shapiro, "Jerry's Biz"; Shapiro, "Disabling 'Jerry's Kids.'"

43. "Jerry Lewis Asks Bush to Stop MDA Bashing by EEOC Chairman," *Associated Press*, 14 February 1992.

44. N. Zeman and L. Howard, "Jerry Lewis: Points of Spite," *Newsweek* 119, no. 12 (23 March 1992): 6.

45. "Jerry Lewis Asks Bush to Stop MDA Bashing by EEOC Chairman."

46. Robert Macy, "Lewis Promises Best Telethon Despite Controversy," *Associated Press*, 6 September 1992.

47. Susan Harrigan, "Controversy Hits Lewis Telethon; Comic Stereotypes the Disabled, Critics Say," *Washington Post*, 1 September 1992.

48. "Jerry Lewis Telethon Sparks Dissent from Disabled; Critics Say Lewis Telethon Promotes Pity," *Newsday* (5 September 1992).

49. Harrigan, "Controversy Hits Lewis Telethon."

50. MDA's Task Force on Disability Issues renamed itself the MDA Task Force on Public Awareness. In 1987 President Ronald Reagan appointed Kemp to the US Equal Employment Opportunities Commission; in 1990 President George H. W. Bush named him to chair the EEOC. Lewis charged that Kemp had started attacking MDA a decade earlier because the charity had rejected a grant application from Kemp's Disability Rights Center. *U.S. News* also reported that MDA urged its chapters to contact local dealers that sold products made by Invacare, the nation's number one wheelchair maker and a company in which Kemp was an important stockholder. MDA wanted the dealers "to tell Invacare to tell Kemp to stop attacking MDA. That set off a round of lawyerly letters over whether the charity was pressuring its chapters—big buyers of wheelchairs—to stop purchasing Invacare products." Shapiro, "Jerry's Biz"; Shapiro, "Disabling 'Jerry's Kids'"; Zeman and Howard, "Jerry Lewis: Points of Spite"; "MDA Advisory Group Assails Kemp, Other Critics," *Business Wire*, 5 February 1992; "Jerry Lewis Criticized over Telethon's Approach," *New York Times*, 6 September 1992, late edition; Rebecca Yerak, "Invacare Dragged into MDA Dispute," *Plain Dealer* (Cleveland, Ohio), 19 September 1992.

51. Among CSE's supporters were the Scaife Foundations, the Enron Corporation, and Archer Daniels Midland. Catherine Crier, "Crier & Company," *CNN*: 'Jerry's Kids' Fight for Respect," *Cable News Network*, 4 September 1992.

52. The *Rocky Mountains News* was a Scripps Howard newspaper. These two anti-ADA editorials appeared in other papers in the syndicate. Editorial, "Feel-Good Statute Bound to Keep the Courts Busy," *Rocky Mountain News*, 24 May 1990; Editorial, "Handicapping Businesses," *Rocky Mountain News*, 5 March 1991; Editorial, "MDA and the 'Pity Bucks,'" *Rocky Mountain News*, 8 September 1994. Deborah Saunders, a conservative columnist in the *San Francisco Chronicle*, accused the activists of attacking their biggest supporter while she repeatedly criticized and distorted the provisions of the ADA. Deborah J. Saunders, "Biting the Hand That Feeds You," *San Francisco Chronicle*, 11 September 1995, final edition; Deborah J. Saunders, "American Businesses' Disability: Congress," *San Francisco Chronicle*, 11 January 1993; Deborah J. Saunders, "ADA—Paving the Road to Mexico," *San Francisco Chronicle*, 22 January 1993; Deborah J. Saunders, "Equality and Need Come to a Head," *San Francisco Chronicle*, 19 May 1993. In one later instance, Saunders began to

show a limited understanding of disability discrimination although she still opposed a legal assertion of disability rights. Deborah J. Saunders, "To Dream, To Dance, To Sue," *San Francisco Chronicle*, 31 January 1996. See also Editorial, "We're All Disabled Now," *Washington Times*, 23 May 1990, final edition; Editorial, "In Defense of Jerry Lewis," *Washington Times*, 5 September 2001, final edition.

53. In the words of playwright and disability activist Victoria Ann Lewis, "Contesting one's status as a tragic-but-brave object of charity would most likely only result in being labeled as its opposite, the only other role available, that of the bitter cripple, eager to attack and revenge him/herself upon the more fortunate, nondisabled world. The typecasting of the person with a disability has been set for centuries—either 'victim' or 'villain.'" Victoria Ann Lewis, "Introduction," in *Beyond Victims and Villains: Contemporary Plays by Disabled Playwrights*, ed. Victoria Ann Lewis (New York: Theatre Communications Group, 2006), xiii, xiv.

54. Bill Thompson, "Ungrateful Child Sharp as Serpent's Tooth: Just Ask Jerry," *Fort Worth Star-Telegram*, 6 September 1992, final AM edition, http://www.star-telegram.com (accessed 5 April 2010); Editorial, "Critics of Lewis Telethon Miss the Point of Charity," *Lancaster New Era* (Lancaster, Penn.), 11 September 1993; "Revenge of the 'Orphans,'" *Time* 140, no. 12 (21 September 1992): 20, http://ebscohost.com (accessed 11 December 2008). Interviewing Lewis, *ABC's PrimeTime Live* correspondent Chris Wallace asked, "You've devoted most of your life to this. Now you have former poster children, kids that you hugged, and they are turning on you and calling themselves 'Jerry's Orphans.' Forget the issues; personally, what does this do to you?" Harold Schindler, "Jerry Lewis Defends Telethon against Critics," *Salt Lake Tribune*, 3 September 1992. In response to Ben Mattlin's *Los Angeles Times* op-ed piece, "An Open Letter to Jerry Lewis: The Disabled Need Dignity, Not Pity," one letter writer declared, "Regardless of Mattlin's physical problems, his real handicap is an ungrateful heart." Ellen Clark, "Letters Desk," *Los Angeles Times*, 12 September 1991.

55. "Turned off by the Telethon," *Palm Beach Post*, 6 September 1993. See also "Revenge of the 'Orphans,'" *Time*.

56. Johnson, "Test of Wills"; Robert Ross quoted in Edmund S. Tijerina, "Protesters Call Jerry Lewis Telethon Exploitive," *Chicago Tribune*, 2 September 1991; *Parade* magazine publisher on MDA Telethon 1992; transcript of Jerry Lewis on CNN, *Larry King Live*, "Jerry Lewis—27 Years for His Kids," 4 September 1992.

Conclusion

1. See chapters 1, 2, and 3, and Peter Dobkin Hall, "Private Philanthropy and Public Policy: A Historical Appraisal," in *Philanthropy: Four Views*, ed. Robert Payton, Michael Novak, Brian O'Connell, and Peter Dobkin Hall (New Brunswick, N.J.: Transaction Books, 1988), 39–72.

2. I have found only one telethon host with a disability. In 1988 Easter Seals' overnight MC was Nancy Becker Kennedy, a disabled actress. On rare occasions, check presenters or telephone operators or other volunteers or contributors were people with disabilities. I have been able to find a total of only nineteen such instances, between 1988 and 1995, among the four telethons studied: the Arthritis Foundation, Easter Seals, MDA, and UCP.

3. Sharon Snyder, *Report on the Disability Media Action and Awareness Project of the University of Illinois, Chicago, Disability Studies Program,* "Media Crip/Crib Sheet," Disability Studies in the Humanities, University of Maryland, 28 March 2003; *Guidelines for Reporting and Writing about People with Disabilities,* 5th ed. (Lawrence: University of Kansas, 1996); "Identity Politics and Words," 13 July 1998; See also the writings of W. Carol Cleigh in *Disability Rag.*

4. Letter from William J. Pavuk, *Disability Rag* 10, no. 6 (November/December 1989), 2, 26.

5. As Erving Goffman explained, "The special situation of the stigmatized is that society tells him he is a member of the wider group, which means he is a normal human being but at the same time that he is also 'different,'" which was to say that he has been set apart socially. *Sigma: Notes on the Management of Spoiled Identity* (Englewood Cliffs, N.J.: Prentice-Hall, 1963), 123.

6. Martha Stoddard Holmes, *Fictions of Affliction: Physical Disability in Victorian Culture* (Corporealities: Discourses of Disability) (Ann Arbor: University of Michigan Press, 2004), 14–15.

7. Debbie Hiott, "Fight Pits Protesters against Jerry, Disabled People Challenge Labor Day Telethon's Image of Muscular Dystrophy," *Austin American Statesman* (Austin, Tex.), 8 September 1992, final edition; Alexandra M. Biesada, "Protesters Object to 'Jerry's Kid' Image," *Austin American Statesman* (Austin, Tex.), 7 September 1993, final edition; "Protesters Decry Labor Day Telethon," *Chicago Tribune,* 4 September 1993, lake sports final edition; "Turned Off by the Telethon," *Palm Beach Post,* 6 September 1993, http://www.newslibrary.com (accessed 6 April 2010).

8. Mary Johnson, "A Test of Wills: Jerry Lewis, Jerry's Orphans, and the Telethon," *Disability Rag* (September 1992), http://www.raggededgemagazine.com/archive/jerry92.htm (accessed 28 February 2010). Syndicated columnist Dianne Piastro also questioned MDA's financial management. Cynthia Todd, "MDA Telethon: Realistic or Condescending?," *St. Louis Post-Dispatch,* 5 September 1992. For MDA's response to Piastro's charges, see "Jerry's Backers Are Stung by Activists' Attack on MDA," *Plain Dealer* (Cleveland, Ohio), 8 April 1992, http://www.newslibrary.com (accessed 6 April 2010); Robert A. Sills, "Columns, Headline on "Jerry's Kids' Unfair to MDA's Efforts," *Patriot-News* (Mechanicsburg, Penn.), 1 September 1991, final edition.

9. Johnson, "A Test of Wills."

10. Robert Macy, "Criticism Loses Sting with Record Tote," *Associated Press,* 7 September 1993; Nadina LaSpina, "Anti-Telethon Protest '94," *DIA Activist,* http://www.disabilityculture.org/nadina/Articles/telethon.htm (accessed 4 April 2010).

11. Peter D. Hall, "The Welfare State and the Careers of Public and Private Institutions Since 1945," in *Charity, Philanthropy, and Civility in American History,* ed. Lawrence J. Friedman and Mark D. McGarvie (New York: Cambridge University Press, 2003), 378–81.

12. Robert Macy, "Jerry Lewis 'Bummed Out,' Keeps Low Profile as He Prepares for Telethon," *Associated Press,* 4 September 1993; Robert A. Jones, "Jerry's Kids: It's a Pity but It Works," *Los Angeles Times,* 4 September 1991; "Lewis Walks a Sad but Necessary Path," *Rocky Mountain News,* 2 September 1993, http://www.newslibrary.com (accessed 6 April 2010). "[T]he telethon's appeal is undeniably cornball," said the *Tulsa World,* "overly dramatic and emotionally overwrought, right down to the traditional tear-stained singing of 'You'll Never Walk Alone' at the show's closing. In a word, sappy. But that approach appears

to have worked. Lewis' telethon has raised more than $600 million over the years, more than $1 billion when corporate contributions are counted. The sappy stuff plays well on TV. It's doubtful a more dry-eyed telethon would have lasted as long or raised as much money. It's understandable that some of "Jerry's Kids" might feel demeaned by the approach Lewis takes. But by appealing to Americans' instinctive sympathy for victims of a terrible disease, the comedian has done undeniable good." Staff Reports, "Jerry's Kids," *Tulsa World*, 4 September 1991, final home edition, http://www.tulsaworld.com/news/article.aspx?no=sub j&articleid=250533&archive=yes (accessed 29 May 2010). See also Deborah Sardone, letter to the editor, "Respect for Jerry Lewis," *Newsday*, 5 October 1987; Editorial, "Speaking for 'Jerry's Kids,'" *Salt Lake Tribune*, 11 September 1992. Some people with disabilities agreed with the pragmatic justification for the telethon. *Accent on Living*, a periodical on the conservative end of the disability community spectrum, surveyed its readers about Jerry Lewis and the MDA Telethon. Of the respondents, 8 out of 10 thought he should not be removed, seeing him as "sincere in his efforts and that he is very dedicated—not to mention the millions of dollars raised over the past 26 years he has hosted the telethon." "While I do feel that too much sympathy is displayed," said one letter writer, "this 'method' seems to work. I only wish our UCP Telethon (I'm a CP adult) were as successful as MDA's." Said another, "It matters not how he performs as long as the results are working." "MD Telethon Is not a Pity Party," *Accent on Living* 36, no. 3 (Winter 1991): 54–7.

13. See Fredrickson on the contrapuntal racist, slave system stereotypes of Sambo, "the happy negro," docile and childlike, and Nat, the ungrateful, disloyal, rebellious, and violent savage. George Fredrickson, "White Images of Black Slaves in the Old South," in *The Arrogance of Race: Historical Perspectives on Slavery, Racism, and Social Inequality* (Hanover, N.H.: Wesleyan University Press, 1988), 206–15.

14. Evan Kemp said Lewis could continue as host if he dropped his stigmatizing descriptions. "Jerry's Orphans" said the telethon could stay "but Lewis must go." In an interview on *ABC's Prime Time*, Kemp finally concluded that Lewis probably would have to leave the telethon. But he never called for abolishing the telethon. Joseph P. Shapiro, "Disabling 'Jerry's Kids,'" *U.S. News & World Report* 113, no. 10 (14 September 1992): 39–40; Judy McDermott, "Telethon Raises Pros and Cons," *Oregonian*, 5 September 1992, http://www.oregonlive.com/search/oregonian (accessed 27 May 2010); William G. Stothers, Editorial, "People with Disabilities Need Jobs, Not Pity of People Like Jerry Lewis," *Atlanta Journal and Constitution*, 4 September 1992; Lynda Richardson, "In Wheelchairs and on Crutches, Some Disabled Protest a Telethon," *New York Times*, 7 September 1993, late edition; Bill Thompson, "Ungrateful Child Sharp as Serpent's Tooth: Just Ask Jerry," *Fort Worth Star-Telegram*, 6 September 1992, final AM edition, http://www.star-telegram.com (accessed 5 April 2010).

15. Gary Wisby, "We Don't Want Pity, Jerry's Orphans Say," *Chicago Sun-Times*, 7 September 1992.

16. "Turned Off by the Telethon."

17. "Disabled Protest Lewis's Telethon," *United Press International*, 6 September 1993.

18. Natalie Soto, "Telethon Protesters: We're Not Jerry's Kids: Activists Call Tradition 'Pity for a Buck' Show," *Rocky Mountain News*, 5 September 1994.

19. Editorial, "MDA and the 'Pity Bucks,'" *Rocky Mountain News*, 8 September 1994.

20. Tedde Scharf, "Telethon's Critics Ignore Contributions," *Austin American Statesman* (Austin, Tex.), 21 October 1994, final edition.

21. LaSpina, "Anti-Telethon Protest '94." For criticism of telethons in general, see Yvonne Duffy, "Skip Sympathy, Treat the Problems of Jerry's Kids," *Newsday* (Melville, N.Y.), 23 August 1993, http://www.newslibrary.com (accessed 6 April 2010).

22. Some activists grounded disability rights advocacy in an economic analysis. Laura Hershey, "Economic Literacy and Disability Rights," *Disability Studies Quarterly* 16, no. 4 (Fall 1996): 15–18; Marta Russell, *Beyond Ramps: Disability at the End of the Social Contract* (Monroe, Maine: Common Courage Press, 1998); Marta Russell, "Disablement, Oppression, and the Political Economy," *Journal of Disability Policy Studies* 12, no. 2 (Fall 2001): 87–95; Marta Russell, "The New Reserve Army of Labor?," *Review of Radical Political Economics* 33, no. 2 (2001): 224–34; Marta Russell, "What Disability Civil Rights Cannot Do: Employment and Political Economy," *Disability and Society* 17, no. 2 (March 2002), 117–35; Marta Russell, "Backlash, the Political Economy, and Structural Exclusion," in *Backlash Against the ADA: Reinterpreting Disability Rights*, ed. Linda Hamilton Krieger (Ann Arbor: University of Michigan Press, 2003), 254–96.

23. Editorial, "Dealing with Disabilities, Protests Signal Time for Change in Commendable Annual Telethon," *San Antonio Express-News*, 9 September 1992; "Muscular Dystrophy Telethon/Timeless Generosity," *Press of Atlantic City*, 10 September 1993, http://www.newslibrary.com (accessed 6 April 2010). See also Joe Dirck, "Jerry Deserves Credit, Maybe Some Updating," *Plain Dealer* (Cleveland, Ohio), 8 September 1992.

24. David Wagner, *What's Love Got to Do with It? A Critical Look at American Charity* (New York: New Press, 2001), 73.

25. Hannah Arendt, *On Revolution* (Penguin Classics, 2006), 74–5.

26. Reese Robrahn, "It's the Telethon That Hurts," *Washington Post*, 22 August 1981.

27. Evan Kemp Jr., "Aiding the Disabled: No Pity, Please," *New York Times*, 3 September 1981.

28. Debbie Hiott, "Fight Pits Protesters against Jerry."

29. Quoted in Mary Johnson, "Jerry's Kids," *Nation* 255, no. 7 (14 September 1992), 233.

30. Biesada, "Protesters Object to 'Jerry's Kid' Image."

31. "MDA Advisory Group Assails Kemp, Other Critics," *Business Wire*, 5 February 1992.

32. Robrahn, "It's the Telethon That Hurts."

33. Letter to the editor, *Lyon County Reporter* (Rock Rapids, Iowa), 26 August 1992; Letters to the editor, "People with MD Talk Back," *Post-Standard* (Syracuse, N.Y.), 29 August 1992.

34. "Quality of life" became a theme on the 2004, 2005, and 2006 MDA Telethons. In viewing hundreds of hours of MDA Telethons from more than two decades, I have found only one instance of what seems to have been a cure. MDA Telethon, 1993; Macy, "Criticism Loses Sting with Record Tote."

35. This same contradiction has been a major flaw in the insistence of some British social model theorists that "impairment" is not the business of the disability rights movement.

36. Susan Wendell, *The Rejected Body: Feminist Philosophical Reflections on Disability* (New York: Routledge, 1996), 83–4; Carol J. Gill, "Overcoming Overcoming," in *Managing Post Polio: A Guide to Living Well with Post-Polio Syndrome*, ed. Lauro S. Halstead (St. Petersburg, Fla.: ABI Professional Publications, 1998), 207–10.

37. Tobin Siebers, *Disability Theory* (Ann Arbor: University of Michigan Press, 2008), 3–5, 14–15, 25–7, 53–69.

{ INDEX }